Both Eastern

MW01132523

Since the Iranian revolution of 1979, many observers of Iran have seen the country caught between its "Eastern" or Islamic history and "Western" modernity, between religion and secularity. As a result, intellectual histories of modern Iran have become subsumed by this narrative. Here, Afshin Matin-Asgari proposes a revisionist work of intellectual history, challenging many of the dominant paradigms in Iranian and Middle Eastern historiography and offering a new narration. In charting the intellectual construction of Iranian modernity during the twentieth century, Matin-Asgari focuses on broad patterns of influential ideas and their relation to each other. More than all previous studies, he analyses these intellectual trends in their global context, showing how Iranian modernity has been shaped by at least a century of intense interaction with global ideologies. Turning many prevailing narratives on their heads, the author concludes that modern Iran can be seen, culturally and intellectually, as both Eastern and Western.

AFSHIN MATIN-ASGARI is Outstanding Professor of Middle East history at California State University, Los Angeles. He was born in Iran and completed his Ph.D. in Middle East history at University of California, Los Angeles. He was active in the international movement of Iranian students during the 1970s and took part in the 1978–1979 Iranian Revolution. He is the author of *Iranian Student Opposition to the Shah* (2002), which has been translated into Persian and published in Iran. Matin-Asgari has authored more than twenty articles and book chapters on twentieth-century Iranian political and intellectual history.

Both Eastern and Western

An Intellectual History of Iranian Modernity

AFSHIN MATIN-ASGARI
California State University, Los Angeles

CAMBRIDGE
UNIVERSITY PRESS

CAMBRIDGE
UNIVERSITY PRESS

University Printing House, Cambridge CB2 8BS, United Kingdom

One Liberty Plaza, 20th Floor, New York, NY 10006, USA

477 Williamstown Road, Port Melbourne, VIC 3207, Australia

314–321, 3rd Floor, Plot 3, Splendor Forum, Jasola District Centre, New Delhi – 110025, India

79 Anson Road, #06–04/06, Singapore 079906

Cambridge University Press is part of the University of Cambridge.

It furthers the University's mission by disseminating knowledge in the pursuit of education, learning, and research at the highest international levels of excellence.

www.cambridge.org
Information on this title: www.cambridge.org/9781108428538
DOI: 10.1017/9781108552844

First published 2018

Printed in the United States of America by Sheridan Books, Inc.

A catalog record for this publication is available from the British Library.

Library of Congress Cataloging in Publication Data
Names: Matin-Asgari, Afshin, 1955– author.
Title: Both Eastern and Western : an intellectual history of Iranian modernity / Afshin Matin-Asgari.
Description: Cambridge, United Kingdom : Cambridge University Press, 2018. | Includes bibliographical references and index.
Identifiers: LCCN 2017061803 | ISBN 9781108428538 (alk. paper)
Subjects: LCSH: Iran – Intellectual life – 20th century. | Iran – Intellectual life – 21st century. | Political science – Iran – Philosophy. | Islam and politics – Iran. | Iran – History – 1979–1997. | Iran – History – 1997– | Iran – History – Historiography. | East and West.
Classification: LCC DS266 .M378 2018 | DDC 955.05/4–dc23
LC record available at https://lccn.loc.gov/2017061803

ISBN 978-1-108-42853-8 Hardback
ISBN 978-1-108-44997-7 Paperback

To Jasi and Sofi

Contents

Acknowledgments

My acknowledgments must begin with remembering the book's inspiration, twentieth-century Iranian intellectuals, particularly those dedicated or "committed" to social justice and the public good. The book's cover image thus remembers one such individual, Bizhan Jazani. Titled "Siahkal," it is the most famous of his prison paintings, depicting the launch of Marxist guerrilla armed struggle in the Siahkal forests of northern Iran. While the painting shows cubist and surrealist influences, the right arm and its glaring eye obviously nod to the traditional imagery of Shi'i Islam. Jazani's painting thus captures the book's theme of modernist intellectual eclecticism in artistic production.

This book took many years to finish, mostly because I work at a public university with heavy teaching responsibilities and little support for research and writing. Its genesis is owed to Hamid Dabashi, who first encouraged me to expand a paper on the intellectual impact of French Orientalist Henry Corbin on Iran into a short book. Writing that small book turned into a long and laborious project leading to a larger and very different manuscript, which was eventually submitted to Cambridge University Press at the suggestion of its Middle East and Africa editor, Maria Marsh. My second debt of gratitude therefore is owed to Maria, whose unassuming professionalism and keen understanding of global intellectual history guided this book to completion. I am also indebted to the Cambridge University Press production team, particularly Julie Hrischeva, Abigail Walkington and Allan Alphonse, as well as to the anonymous readers whose comments and criticism improved my manuscript significantly. My good friends and academic colleagues, Mehrdad Amanat, Maziar Behrooz, Houri Berberian, Shahrokh Haghighi, Mojtaba Mahdavi, Rudi Matthee and Peyman Vahabzadeh, read and commented on different chapters. I thank them all, as well as the following colleagues, friends and family members with whom I discussed my book's topics and/or who helped me find and collect source material in Los Angeles, Toronto and Tehran: Choi Chatterjee, Sasan Fayazmanesh, Afsaneh Matin, Kamran Matin, Mani Matin-Asgari, Jasamin Rostam-Kolayi, Mehrdad Samadzadeh, Vida Samian and Scott Wells. Last but not least, Shahrouz Khalifian also belongs to the above list, but I owe him special thanks for his painstaking indexing of the book.

I dedicate this book to Jasi and Sofi, whose invaluable support made its writing possible, with the regretful acknowledgment of how much it took away from our time together.

Note on Translation and Transliteration

Unless a translator is cited, all translations from Persian sources are mine. My text mostly follows a modified version of Persian transliteration systems in *Iranian Studies* and the *International Journal of Middle East Studies*. However, I have simplified their common rules, while striving for closer proximity of actual Persian pronunciations using the English alphabet. As much as possible, I have dropped diacritical marks and rendered the Persian *ezafeh* as *e* or *ye* sound attached at the end of words. For example, I use Al-Ahmad, rather than Al-e Ahmad, and Shariati, rather than Shari'ati.

Introduction
Intellectual Constructions of Iranian Modernity

This book is about the intellectual construction of Iranian modernity during the twentieth century, up to the end of the 1970s. As a work of intellectual history, it focuses on broad patterns of influential ideas, and their relation to each other, in a historical context. In a sense, this is what historians often do, as they "rethink past thoughts," to quote R. G. Collingwood's succinct definition of our profession. Traditionally, intellectual history, as well as historiography in general, has been the study of recognizably "influential ideas," traceable in written or printed texts, thus implicitly biased toward elite or high culture. Historians admit, however, that "influential ideas" are defined as such via the consensus of their profession, primarily because, appearing in printed texts, they are the most accessible type of historical record. Given this definition, intellectual history focuses neither on the most objectively important ideas of a given age, nor necessarily on its "ruling ideas," in the sense of Marx's famous dictum. At the same time, despite focusing mainly on individual thinkers, intellectual history can be "the social history of ideas" by locating intellectual discourses and movements within broader social, political and cultural contexts. This kind of intellectual history, for example, links the ideas of nationalist, religious or revolutionary thinkers to state policies, popular culture and social movements.

Recently, intellectual history seems to have been demoted to the margins of mainstream historiography. This is a curious development since, during the past few decades, the dominant trend in American historiography has been cultural history, which, like intellectual history, is concerned ultimately with patterns of meaning, deciphered within broad clusters of ideas.[1] The marginality of intellectual history is more pronounced when it comes to Middle Eastern, including Iranian, historiography. According to a fairly recent study:

A deep and unjustified divide remains between the modes of thought which intellectual history is developing in the study of Western (and non-Western, mainly South-Asian) societies and cultures and the study of the intellectual history of the Middle East, which seems to lag behind and remains ghettoized.[2]

English-language intellectual histories of the Middle East have largely dealt with Arab nationalist thought, while Iranian intellectual history is a new scholarly field, emerging in the aftermath of Iran's 1978–1979 Revolution. Counting no more than a dozen major English-language works, the field of Iranian intellectual history emerged mainly in response to the paradox of a late twentieth-century popular revolution leading to a theocratic regime, dominated by Shi'i clerics. The Iranian Revolution's deviation from the expected trajectory of modernity, primarily the demise of religion, made it a harbinger of the arrival of a global "post-modern condition." In particular, the revolution's triumphant "Islamic ideology" was widely perceived as a challenge to modernity's "meta-narratives" of Marxism, liberal democracy, modernization and secularization. Michel Foucault, for example, welcomed the fall of the Shah as a "revolution against Modernity," calling Ayatollah Khomeini's ideas a new kind of "spiritual politics" that could come only from outside Europe.[3]

While hasty generalizations, such as Foucault's, were gradually tempered by more sober reflections, the paradox of the Iranian Revolution endured as the Islamic Republic consolidated and survived into the twenty-first century. Though never repeated elsewhere, Iran's "Islamic Revolution" initiated a burgeoning literature on topics such as Islamic fundamentalism, political Islam and Islamism, as well as on comparable global trends of religious revivalism. During the 1980s, this literature focused on particular doctrinal and/or historical features that presumably made Iranian Shi'ism a potentially revolutionary ideology. The most influential works of this genre were by sociologist Said Amir Arjomand, who recognized that the Iranian Revolution was not generically Islamic or Shi'i, but instead "an ideological revolution in Shi'ism."[4] Nevertheless, as with similar 1980s studies, Arjomand's analysis remained preoccupied with the minutiae of Shi'i doctrine and the vicissitudes of its history, paying less attention to the revolution's embeddedness in modern Iran's intellectual and ideological landscape.[5]

At the same time, pioneering studies by Ervand Abrahamian showed Iran's revolutionary "Islamic Ideology" was a species of modern political ideology, deeply indebted to Marxism. A similar understanding of

"Islamic Ideology" meanwhile had emerged in Iran, where the post-revolutionary regime was purging its leftist factions, consciously removing Marxist "contaminations."[6] The first major scholarly work devoted entirely to the study of "Islamic Ideology" was Hamid Dabashi's *Theology of Discontent: The Ideological Foundations of the Islamic Revolution in Iran* (1993). Building on Arjomand's and Abrahamian's focus on "Islamic Ideology," Dabashi traced its geneal-ogy in works by eight twentieth-century thinkers. Making a new thought-world available to non-Persian readers, *Theology of Discontent* also launched the genre of modern Iranian intellectual history, setting standards and opening pathways for studies that fol-lowed. Among these were Dabashi's attention to the intertwining of secular and religious aspects of revolutionary ideology, and his focus on the textual authority of intellectuals in conferring, denying and challenging political legitimacy. Dabashi had diagnosed "Islamic Ideology" as Iran's intellectual response to a painful encounter with Western modernity. Still, his emphasis remained on the religious side of "Islamic Ideology," leading him to conclude: "The theological lan-guage of discontent was inevitable, perhaps because theology is the ultimate language of truth."[7] Related to Dabashi's (over)estimation of theology/religion as "truth language" was his choice only of Muslim thinkers as authoritative pre-revolutionary intellectuals. In 1996, poli-tical scientist Mehrzad Boroujerdi's *Iranian Intellectuals and the West: The Tormented Triumph of Nativism* added a number of important secular thinkers to Dabashi's roster, provided more social and political context, and showed the continuity of pre- and postrevolutionary intellectual production along "the central concepts of *other-ness, orientalism, orientalism in reverse, and nativism.*"[8] Boroujedri's focus on "nativism," i.e. the project of constructing an "authentic" indigen-ous national identity, moved the analysis of Iranian intellectual dis-course in a more secular direction. Moreover, Boroujerdi was the first scholar to note the influence, on both pre- and postrevolutionary Iranian intellectuals, of German Counter-modernist thought, and spe-cifically the philosopher Martin Heidegger.

The contributions of Abrahamian, Dabashi and Boroujerdi were followed by only a few notable works in the specific genre of intellectual history. Ali Gheissari's *Iranian Intellectuals in the 20th Century* (1998) was a succinct but meticulous survey beyond "mas-ter thinkers" to consider less familiar authors and texts, collectively engaged in the intellectual labor of crafting a modern Iranian national identity. Like Dabashi, he mainly covered the prerevolutionary period, noting, but not analyzing, the mid-century hegemony of Marxist intellectuals. The latter topic was eventually addressed in Negin Nabavi's *Intellectuals and the State in Iran: Political, Discourse and the Dilemma of Authenticity* (2003). Focusing on the intellectual production of the 1950s to the 1970s via books and periodicals, Nabavi showed the prerevolutionary discourse of nativism and cultural authenticity was articulated mainly by secular leftist and Third Worldist intellectuals.[9] Dabashi's prolific output often returned to Iranian intellectuals, while remaining more concerned with postcolonial theory, literary criticism, and the politics and aesthetics of cinema.[10] Postmodern and postcolonial theory informed also Mohammad Tavakoli-Targhi's *Refashioning Iran* (2001), an important work moving the historiography of Iranian modernity from a national to a global context, postulating a "Persianate modernity," coeval with its European counterpart, emerging in Mughal India's Persian-language texts (see Chapter 1). More recently, the study of Iranian intellectuals has been avidly pursued by sociologist Ali Mirsepassi, who has published four books on the subject within about a decade. Reflecting a pervasive intellectual trend, Mirsepassi's intervention is a critique of both Marxist and right-wing intellectuals from a liberal and presumably "non-ideological" perspective. His *Intellectual Discourse and the Politics of Modernization: Negotiating Modernity in Iran* (2000) expanded on Boroujerdi's work to directly trace prerevolutionary Iran's "authenticity" discourse to Nietzsche and Heidegger. In *Democracy in Modern Iran: Islam, Culture, and Political Change* (2010), he urged Iranian intellectuals to follow American philosopher Richard Rorty's blueprint for building democracy pragmatically and without recourse to "philosophical systems." His *Political Islam, Iran, and the Enlightenment: Philosophies of Hope and Despair* (2011) argued passionately, if not persuasively, that Heidegger's influence on leading pre-revolutionary intellectuals "helped enormously to articulate the Islamist ideology that paved the way to the 1979s revolution"[11] (see Chapters 5–6). Similarly, *Transnationalism in Iranian Political Thought: The Life and Times of Ahmad Fardid* (2017) exaggerates Fardid's political and intellectual significance.[12]

Taking stock of the above-mentioned body of academic work on Iranian intellectual history, as well as outstanding similar works in Persian, one could make a number of observations about this field's accomplishments and remaining challenges. First, the field is dominated by sociologists and political scientists, hence showing a propensity for theorization, lacking adequate attention to the complex interplay of intellectual history and historical narration. In other words, existing scholarship does not sufficiently address intellectual history's problematic entanglement with historical meta-narratives that it implicitly presupposes and potentially also subverts. Second, and partly due to the field's disciplinary divergence, individually notable contributions remain largely unengaged with each other, thus producing little debate or cumulative consensus. On the positive side, existing scholarship already has moved the question of Iran's engagement with modernity beyond the dichotomies of Iranian/foreign, clergy/state, religious/secular, traditional/modern, authentic/derivational and singular/universal. More specifically, this scholarship shows the discourses of Iranian nationalism, official Pahlavi state ideology, Iranian cultural authenticity and "Islamic Ideology" are interconnected, as well as intertwined with Orientalist, Marxist and counter-modernist discourses. In other words, without having done so itself, existing scholarship suggests Iranian intellectual history makes sense only when framed within a broad global context.

This book therefore aims to complement as well as critique existing scholarship by approaching modern Iranian intellectual history within the perspective of global and comparative history. The book's first and overarching argument is that Iranian modernity, or the ideational project for crafting a modern Iran, has been sustained by at least a century of intense intellectual interaction with global ideologies. Iran is "Neither Eastern, Nor Western." This was a defiant declaration of national and cultural independence, coined in fact under the monarchy and adopted by the Islamic Republic. Turning this slogan on its head, this book will contend that modern Iran as a nation, similar to pre-modern Iran as an empire, has been culturally and intellectually "Both Eastern and Western." The Qur'anic phrase, *Neither Eastern, Nor Western,* appeared in the title of a 1974 collection of essays by Iran's leading historian Abdul-Hossein Zarrinkub, who rejected facile East–West dichotomies, calling on Iranians to create their "dialectical" synthesis, drawing on a "humanist" reading of Islamic mysticism.[13]

Second, my inversion of Zarrinkub's phrase, in the title of the present book, stresses the continuity of modern political culture, as well as its simultaneously global and local character, across the pre- and post-revolutionary divide. This means a break with nationalist, Islamist, postcolonial and postmodern insistence on the "authenticity" of pre-modern and national cultures and their "autonomy" from European or "Western" modernity. Works such as Partha Chatterjee's study of India have characterized nationalist thought as "a derivative discourse" vis-à-vis global master narratives. This, however, does not mean modern national cultures are facsimiles of a universal script, particularly if modernity is understood to have been constructed globally, rather than in "the West," and defined by its conflicts and antinomies, rather than any singular essence.[14]

This book's third major objective is to align the study of Iranian intellectual history with current debates, among world historians, on the meaning of modernity. This ongoing debate may be traced in publications such as *American Historical Review, Journal of the History of Ideas, History and Theory, Journal of World History* and *Intellectual History Review*. A 2011 issue of *American Historical Review*, for example, was dedicated to "Historian and the Question of modernity." Surveying contributions by nine leading historians, the issue's editor found a "lack of converge" among their definitions of modernity. It was clear, however, that participants in this debate, like most historians, agreed that the adjective "modern" referred properly to recent history, often a century or two before the present, as well as to specific features distinguishing this period from those preceding it. An important point emerging in this debate was that definitions of modernity hinged on our understanding of an enormously vast and complex span of "premodern" history, categorized as medieval, ancient, traditional, oriental, colonial, etc., from our own privileged "modern" perspective. Moreover, this ontological privileging becomes more problematic when modernity is defined concretely by a core ethos, for example "Critical Reason," or the "Enlightenment Project."[15] To avoid such conceptual pitfalls, this book links modernity neither to ostensibly liberating "Western" rationality, nor to discourses of European domination. Instead, modernity is treated as a malleable universal abstraction, inevitably deployed by historians to frame the recent global past in meta-narratives characterized by tension and antinomy, rather than by coherence and essentialism. Thus, modern history is the story of capitalism, as well as communism and fascism, of unprecedented gains in human well-being, as well as suffering in total wars, genocides, ecological disasters and the commodified debasing of modern politics and culture. I thus concur with international relations theorist Kamran Matin's understanding of modernity as the fluid universal encompassing social, national and global particulars, perpetually recombining, at all levels, to produce nonlinear open-ended historical trajectories. Thus, while the history of any particular society or nation, including its intellectual history, is *sui generis*, it is also shaped by, and in turn gives shape to, larger global frames. Matin's approach is in line with leading scholarship in comparative and world history, such as Sanjay Subrahmanyam's model of Connected Histories. Subrahmanyam sees early modern history as the interface of the local and regional with the global, countering nationalist historiography's attachment to "fixity and local rootedness," as well as the "methodological fragmentationism" caused by the postmodernist universalization of Europe's anti-Enlightenment philosophical tradition.[16] Last but not least, in this book's schema, "the pre-modern" is not modernity's antithesis, but epistemologically unchartered historical territory, just as "tradition" means no more than a particular pattern of collective thinking or practice with recognizable temporal continuity.

Finally, this book treats the rise of "Islamic Ideology" in Iran not as a failure of "Westernization," and "Modernization," but as a project for turning Islam into a political ideology compatible with modern "meta-religious" and secular worldviews. As a worldview, religion is a comprehensive system of ideas providing meaning and purpose to human existence, including, but not confined to, its political dimensions. It is thus similar to, but ultimately broader in normative scope and ambition than, secular political ideologies such as Marxism and nationalism.[17] This understanding of religion is typical of post-Enlightenment thought, including Marx's early writings, where religion is not merely "the opium of the people" but also "a perverted world consciousness" and "the general theory" of human suffering, oppression and distress. It is "the heart of a heartless world" and a cry of protest against this world. Proceeding from such assumptions, certain strands of Marxism have been sympathetic to religion, comparing modern socialism to early Christianity, while recognizing the religious feature of premodern revolutionary movements.[18] Thus, as several chapters in this book will note, the intellectual confluence of Marxism and religion in modern Iran is in some ways quite understandable, rather than paradoxical or enigmatic.

Within the methodological parameters outlined above, this book will trace Iran's modern intellectual history from its nineteenth-century "premodern" and prenational origins to its full articulation, via active engagement with the global discourse of orientalism, nationalism and socialism, in the twentieth century. The book's emphasis on "Eastern," in addition to "Western," features of Iranian modernity seeks to open up new paths for revisionist historiography. For example, breaking with mainstream historiography, I locate the intellectual origins of Iranian constitutionalism in nineteenth-century encounters with "the East," i.e. the Ottoman and Russian empires, rather than "the West" or Europe.[19] Similarly, I will show how twentieth-century Iranian nationalism was impacted more by Young Ottoman thought, Turkish republicanism, German counter-modernity and Russian Marxism, rather than by "Western" liberal nationalist ideologies. The book's sharpest break with mainstream intellectual history, and Iranian historiography in general, is its treatment of socialism, and particularly its "Eastern" or Soviet form, as a creative influence on the formation of Iranian modernity. With a few notable exceptions, historians have been oblivious or hostile to socialist and communist contributions to modern Iranian political culture and modernity in general. As mentioned above, a few solid historical studies of the left do exist, but their findings are generally ignored by mainstream historiography. This is rather ironic, since, as we shall see in several chapters of this book, evidence of the left's fundamental contribution to Iranian modernity, particularly in the intellectual realm, is overwhelming. State-sponsored nationalist historiography in Iran of course denies or distorts this fact due to obvious ideological reasons. Unfortunately, the same ideological bias is manifest in mainstream scholarship outside the reach of the Iranian state. It should go without saying that recognizing the left's contribution to Iranian intellectual history is not an endorsement of various socialist and communist intellectual and political projects, which are often contradictory and at odds with each other. This book is critical of the left too, without being dismissive of it or denying its significant contributions to modern Iranian intellectual history.

In addition to critically engaging with a wide range of English-language secondary sources, this book's arguments are informed by close readings of a host of Persian primary sources, including books, periodicals, memoirs, private and public archives, journalistic pieces and political tracts, translated by the author, unless referenced otherwise. What follows is a chapter summary of the book's main thematic focus and arguments:

Chapter 1, "Lineages of Authoritarian Modernity: The Russo-Ottoman Model," introduces the book's overall argument, for the specificity of Iranian modernity, by challenging conventional historiography's conceptions of "premodern" Iran. First, it rejects narratives of seamless continuity in "Iranian history," proposing instead a categorical distinction between Iran as modern nation-state and premodern historical ideas of Iran as an empire. Nevertheless, the book's treatment of Iranian modernity as highly syncretic ("Eastern and Western") fits with perceptions of premodern or imperial Iran as a cultural melting pot at "the crossroad of civilizations."[20] Second, the chapter criticizes the lingering confusions resulting from narrations of Iranian history within Orientalist paradigms of Asiatic despotism and Islamic absolutism. It argues, instead, that prenational Iranian "states" were decentralized hierarchies of overlapping authority. Equally fallacious are Orientalist notions of Iranian history's broad linkage to Shi'ism, whereas in fact premodern Iran was religiously heterodox, being the only Muslim country producing open breaches with Islam, manifest in Babi and Baha'i religions. Third, the chapter argues that the birth event of Iranian modernity, the Constitutional Revolution of 1906–11, was intellectually and politically inspired by nineteenth-century interactions with Ottoman and Russian empires, rather than "the West."[21] Iranian constitutionalism followed the path of Russo-Ottoman techno-militaristic state-building, primarily Ottoman "Islamic Constitutionalism," just as Iran's reformist and revolutionary intelligentsia followed the example of their Ottoman and Russian counterparts. Bordering the Caucasus and Anatolia, the province of Azerbaijan was Iran's center of modernizing institutional reforms and revolutionary politics, while Caucasian Azeri intellectuals, like Mohammad-Amin Rasulzadeh and Ahmad Aqaoglu, were pioneers of Iranian nationalist and socialist thought.

Chapter 2, "The Berlin Circle: Crafting the Worldview of Iranian Nationalism," locates the intellectual origins of modern Iranian nationalism and the nation-building project in the global upheaval caused by the Great War between 1911 and 1921. Conventional historiography depicts this decade as a time when foreign occupation and political chaos crushed the Constitutional Revolution's democratic aspirations, paving the way for authoritarian nation-state building during the 1920s and 1930s. This chapter, however, finds the genesis of illiberal nationalism in Iran's intellectual encounter with Russian and German socialism and counter-modernity, British imperialist ambitions, and the Bolshevik Revolution during the first two decades of the century. Prior to World War I, Caucasian and Russian social democrats had joined Iran's constitutional movement, helping turn it into a revolution and introducing what became modern Iran's core social reform agenda. The Bolshevik Revolution's spillage into Iran further strengthened this trend, providing an alternate revolutionary path to modernity. With Iran's fledgling nationhood hanging in the balance of a world war, the nationalist intelligentsia tried shifting political and ideological alignments with Imperial Germany, the Ottoman Empire and the Soviet Union. Meanwhile, a group of Iranian émigrés in Berlin labored desperately to articulate a viable nationalist ideology, anchored in a modern *weltanschauung*. This chapter traces their efforts in the pages of *Kaveh*, *Iranshahr* and *Name-ye faranestan*, nationalist periodicals published in Berlin between 1915 and the mid-1920s. Largely overlooked by historians, this Berlin intellectual circle, led by men like Hassan Taqizadeh, Hossein Kazemzadeh and Morteza Moshfeq-Kazemi, steered Iranian nationalism away from liberal constitutionalism and social democracy toward enlightened despotism and spiritual revivalism, flirting even with fascism.

Chapter 3, "Subverting Constitutionalism: Intellectuals as Instruments of Modern Dictatorship," focuses on the nationalist elite's role in making Reza Khan the country's strong-man and the evolution of his monarchy into a fully fledged modern dictatorship in the 1930s. Here, I reject two common explanations of Reza Shah's dictatorship: First, that 1920s Iran needed a strong man to save it from foreign intervention, chaos and disintegration; and second, that 1930s Pahlavi dictatorship was in line with Iran's supposedly historical patterns of "despotic and arbitrary" rule. I argue, instead, that the early Pahlavi state followed a global nation-building script that suspended constitutional government and forcibly imposed linguistic, legal, religious, educational and even sartorial unanimity on the country. Nationalist intellectuals, like members of the Berlin Circle and their cohorts in Tehran's Young Iran Society, actively served as "instruments" of a dictatorship that soon began to discard or destroy them one after another. Meanwhile, intellectuals advocating more democratic conceptions of modernity and nation building were silenced by physical elimination and political repression. These included pioneers of avant-garde trends in art and literature and revolutionary voices in political culture. Nor was the triumph of authoritarian nationalism a foregone conclusion. As late as 1921, for example, the fall of Tehran to the revolutionary militia of a Soviet republic was thwarted only by occupying British forces. A year later, the communist daily *Haqiqat* remained Tehran's most vociferous defender of press freedom and constitutional government. Soon, however, Reza Shah's nationalist dictatorship targeted the left as the enemy of the state, banning all organizations espousing "collectivist creeds." During the 1930s, the brief run of the Marxist magazine *Donya* was the most serious intellectual challenge to official nationalism and a harbinger of the coming Marxist hegemony in political culture. *Donya*'s positivist Marxism was the most radical expression of a new "scientific" ideology serving the rise of a modern-educated middle-class elite. *Donya* called for the cultural hegemony and social leadership of middle-class intellectuals, espousing an evolutionary "cultural Marxism" closer to Gramsci's than to Lenin's.

Chapter 4, "Intellectual Missing Links: Criticizing Europeanism and Translating Modernity," focuses on three thinkers, considering their understudied works of the 1930s and 1940s as the intellectual bridge between the inchoate and multifarious nationalism of the Constitutional era and the radical nationalist and anti-Western discourses of the 1960s and 1970s. The first is Ahmed Kasravi, interwar Iran's most original nationalist thinker, whose critique of "Europeanism," as the imitation of a nihilist and materialist modern European civilization, remains underappreciated by intellectual historians. Kasravi was equally critical of Iranian cultural and religious traditions, rejecting Shi'ism, mysticism and the ethics of classical Persian literature. Moreover, he launched the project of turning Islam into a modern political ideology, preaching a new religion of Reason, with the nation as its sacred object. This chapter then revisits Ruhollah Khomeini's participation in the mid-century's intellectual debates. In 1944, Khomeini published *Secrets Exposed*, a response to Kasravi and other critics of clerical Shi'ism. Oblivious to foreign thinkers, Khomeini nevertheless was in line with certain global intellectual trends, such as Traditionalism, in rejecting secular modernist thought and philosophy. *Secrets Exposed* remained primarily a refutation of anti-clerical intellectuals rather than a critique of Western cultural and

political domination of Iran, subjects that become Khomeini's preoccupation only in the 1960s and 1970s. Still, a close reading of *Secrets
Exposed* shows the kernel of a political philosophy that eventually
would evolve into Khomeini's revolutionary Shi'ism of the 1970s.
The third thinker analyzed in this chapter is Fakhreddin Shadman,
whose *Conquering European Civilization* (1948) is considered
a "liberal" response to the challenge of Iran's encounter with Europe.
Shadman believed the real problem of Iran's modernization was the
hasty imitation and shallow understanding of European civilization.
His remedy was a cultural crusade of knowledge production, literally
a national translation project, aimed at thoroughly understanding and
thus conquering European modernity.

Chapter 5, "The Mid-century Moment of Socialist Hegemony," investigates the impact on Iranian intellectual history of "Eastern," Soviet-
style, socialism. Utilizing both older and newly available primary
sources, it explains how communists launched modern Iran's most
successful political party (Tudeh), whose ideological and political legacy
deeply influenced the monarchy and its opposition in the 1960s and
1970s. Breaking with nationalist and Cold War historiography, I argue
the Tudeh Party's phenomenal impact was due primarily to the appeal of
its worldview and social reform program to middle-class intellectuals
and the laboring masses. Remarkably, within the span of a decade
(1941–1953), the Tudeh Party accomplished the *Donya* circle's project
of socialist cultural hegemony, and Shadman's project of "translating"
modernity, albeit in a Marxist-inflected version. Moreover, this chapter
shows how the 1960s and 1970s project of monarchist modernity, i.e.
"the Shah-People Revolution," was "plagiarized" from the Tudeh Party
and its offshoots, such as the Socialist League. Another example of
revisionist historiography appears in this chapter's attention to Islamic
socialism and "Islamic Marxism," obscure trends in the political culture
of the 1960s and 1970s, which made the project of an Islamic Revolution
intellectually conceivable. The chapter ends with a case study in intellectual history, revisiting the controversial legacy of Jalal Al-Ahmad, Iran's
leading writer and essayist of the 1960s. Rereading Al-Ahmad, along
with his contemporary Iranian and global interlocutors, it concludes that
his travelogues and essays, particularly *On the Services and Betrayal of
Intellectuals*, deservedly establish him as Iran's quintessential public
intellectual of the 1960s.

Chapter 6, "Revolutionary Monarchy, Political Shi'ism and Islamic Marxism," investigates the makeup of three ideological narratives contending for hegemony in 1960s and 1970s Iranian political culture. All three, it will be argued, were responding to the powerful challenge of a global master narrative, namely Third Worldist Marxism. First, the Shah-People Revolution was justified by an official ideology of revolutionary monarchism, articulated mainly via the Shah's writings and speeches, setting guidelines for national cultural planning through the state-run educational system and mass media. An overview of government publications, such as *Culture and Life*, reveals the state's systematic co-optation of the opposition's rhetoric of revolution, anti-imperialism and cultural authenticity. Second, a number of intellectual circles linked the official discourse of cultural authenticity to European counter-modernist philosophy and neo-mystical interpretations of Shi'ism. 1960s Iran's pervasive discourse of "West-struck-ness," for example, was first articulated by Ahmad Fardid, who claimed a neo-mystical reading of Islam corresponding to Martin Heidegger's critique of Western modernity. Fardid's obscure ideas paralleled those of a more influential circle of academics and clerics, led by French Orientalist Henri Corbin and Seyyed Hosein Nasr, a leader of the global Traditionalist movement. The Corbin-Nasr circle proposed an esoteric Shi'i reading of Iranian nationalism countering secular liberal and Marxist worldviews. Third, the above two ideological trends reacted largely and often explicitly to the intellectual hegemony of Marxism, reaching beyond underground dissident groups into universities and the mass media, literary and artistic production, and popular culture and entertainment. The chapter's conclusion analyzes the intellectual formation called "Islamic Marxism," identified by the regime as a chief political nemesis during the 1970s. Though polemical, this label captures the eclectic character of a potent ideological mix that anticipated the merger of Marxist and Islamist opposition factions during the 1978–1979 Revolution. The chapter ends by reassessing the intellectual production of Ali Shariati, the quintessential 1970s "Islamic Marxist," whose influential discourse oscillated between mystical existentialism, Third Worldist Marxism and anti-clerical Shi'ism.

Chapter 7, "Conclusion: Aborted Resurrection: An Intellectual Arena Wide Open to the Opposition," concludes the book by tracing the revolution's ideological makeup back to the intellectual contestations and culture wars of the prerevolutionary decade. It argues that, while neither inevitable nor predictable, the revolution's peculiar ideological makeup "made sense" only within the particular intellectual and cultural matrix of 1970s Iran. By the late 1970s, the intellectual trends outlined in Chapter 6 converged into a revolutionary ideology that occupied the political space that was suddenly vacated by the regime. Tracing contemporary sources, this chapter traces back the regime's sudden meltdown to the failure of the mid-1970s Resurrection Party project. Conceived by an odd assortment of ex-communists and US-educated technocrats, the Resurrection project did away with the façade of constitutionalism, launching instead a Shah-centered "Imperial" one-party state. When this gambit quickly floundered, the Shah reversed course and declared "the opening up of the political space," taking hesitant steps toward the restoration of constitutional government. Though aligned with the "Human Rights" turn of US foreign policy, this final corrective measure had come too late, when the political initiative was passing first to the moderates and then to the revolutionary opposition. Meanwhile, the Shah was desperately seeking a new ideological departure to halt his regime's downward spiral. To this end, he had ordered a task force of intellectuals to forge a monarchist "Philosophy of Resurrection," which, he insisted, had to be revolutionary, authentically Iranian, "neither Eastern nor Western" and rooted in the mystical "dialectic" of Shi'ism. Ironically, this precise ideological mélange, minus its monarchist component, was already in the making through the intellectual convergence of Marxist, Islamist and nativist strands within the opposition. Thus, the Shah hoped to retake the political initiative by once again appropriating his opponents' intellectual resources. This time, however, the abject failure of the Resurrection project, and its counterfeit political philosophy, cleared the path of an actual revolutionary apocalypse that brought the monarchist regime to its end.

1 | Lineages of Authoritarian Modernity

The Russo-Ottoman Model

The terms constitutionalism (*mashrutiyat*) and fundamental law (*qanun-e asai*), as well as the form of government implied by these terms, reached Iran and was adopted from the Ottoman Empire.

Hasan Taqizadeh[1]

Millat means "the People" or "the Nation," and is opposed to *Dawlat*, "the State," "the Government" or practically under the old regime, "the Court."

E. G. Browne[2]

This chapter's discussion of Iran's transition to modernity begins with a number of revisionist proposals to mainstream historiography's conceptualization of "premodern" Iran. First, it argues for distinguishing older or premodern notions of Iran as an *empire* from our modern understanding of Iran as a nation-state. Second, countering Orientalist paradigms of Asian despotism and Islamic absolutism, it conceives of the premodern Iranian "state" as a decentralized amalgam of shifting political and religious sovereignties. Third, the chapter argues that Iran's transition to modernity, via nineteenth-century reforms culminating in constitutionalism, was intellectually informed primarily through engagement with the neighboring Ottoman and Russian empires, rather than with Europe or "the West."[3]

A basic conceptual challenge facing Iranian historiography is the problem of (dis)continuity between premodern and modern conceptions of Iran. Following Orientalist scholarship, nationalist historiography has projected the idea of Iran as a *nation-state* back into premodern history, where the term "Iran" signified neither a "nation" nor a "state." While historians increasingly concede the novelty of the nation, they are less clear on distinctions between the modern "state" and premodern forms of political sovereignty. However, as historian of Iranian nationalism Afshin Marashi has argued:

We cannot assume, as the comparative-nationalism literature might lead us to, that the abstract category of "the state" was an already established presence in the social imaginary of the Iranian polity ... the bleated crystallization of the Iranian state as a technical administrative presence, and hence as an autonomous conceptual category, would have to wait until the twentieth century.[4]

Scattered references to "Iran," as both territory and polity, of course exist in premodern literary and political sources, going back to the Sasanian Empire, where they connote a political community upholding Zoroastrian religion.[5] This could be comparable to notions of Christendom and *Dar al-Islam*, the latter more closely resembling the Sasanian model of a "righteous" religious community dominating a vast multi-religious empire. Premodern Iran therefore was not a nation but an empire, similar to "Rome" or "China" in their broad imperial sense.[6] The shifting boundaries of imperial Iran encompassed all territories conquered by Sasanian emperors, stretching from Egypt to Central Asia, and from the Caucasus to India. The geographic expanse of premodern Iran corresponds to what Marshall Hodgson dubbed the "Nile-Oxus" region, where, he argued, Islam rose as a synthesis of "Iranian" and "Semitic" civilizations.[7] The vast composite makeup of imperial Iran therefore explains the multifarious and "cosmopolitan" cultural and civilizational traits often associated with premodern Iranian history.[8] More recently, however, the idea of a highly centralized pre-Islamic imperial Iran, conceived by scholars like Arthur Christensen, has been challenged by revisionist historians who see the Sasanian Empire as a loosely structured "confederation," whose internal tensions and civil wars contributed to the ease of its overthrow by smaller Muslim armies.[9]

The continuity of Iran's "national" history, tied to assumptions of "Persian-ness" as ethnicity or race, are products of nationalist historical consciousness, inspired and validated by Orientalist scholarship.[10] They are found, for example, in works by British Orientalist Ann K. S. Lambton, whose model of premodern "Persian" government and society was highly influential in twentieth-century Iranian historiography. According to Lambton, "Islamic society was 'given.' ... and the government tended to belong to the last despot who seized it."[11] Contrary to Lambton's absolutist image of Islamic government and society, recent scholarship suggests premodern Eurasian kings and emperors, whether Christian or Muslim, ruled patchworks of territories and communities with "different laws, rights, privileges, and traditions." Marked by a "multiplicity of jurisdictions," this type of premodern imperial polity allowed a conqueror to "add province after province, kingdom after kingdom to his realm and rule each as its own prince under different laws, and with varying powers." Even the so-called "absolutist" monarchies of early modern Europe "left considerable authority with the principle holders of power in the peripheries." Such "dispersal of authority" can be seen more clearly in Europe's overseas colonies, where "principle magnates also had to negotiate the terms of their governance with various regions, towns, communities, and other organized social, economic, and religious groups and institutions."[12] A similar model of governance was that of the global British Empire, including the Indian Raj.[13]

A distinct feature of premodern Iran was its large size and the political impact of its pastoral nomadic population. Beyond the reach of shahs and orthodox clerics, each tribal community was, in effect, politically and religiously sovereign in its own geographic domain. Conforming to a familiar pattern, the Qajar Kingdom (1790s–1925) was established as a tribal confederation, whereby the shah's direct jurisdiction was limited to domains belonging to his own tribe. If the Qajar Kingdom was a "state," then nineteenth-century Iran's autonomous tribes were "states-within-the state."[14] This decentralized pattern of multiple sovereignties was known as *muluk al-tawa'if*, literally meaning coexisting kingships of "tribes," or "factions," a political structure arguably comparable to Europe's feudal system of fractured authority. Historians continue to debate the applicability of the "feudal" model beyond Europe, but the Islamic system of *muluk al-tawa'if* was partly European, originating in Umayyad Iberia, and later in eleventh-century Iran and Iraq.[15] Moreover, anthropological studies suggest that *taifeh*, as the clan-based kinship structure of premodern rural Iran, persisted until the great socioeconomic transformations of the 1960s–1970s.[16]

The *muluk al-tawa'if* paradigm of premodern Iran resolves the contradictions of Lambton's model of "Persian government," arising out of her pairing royal absolutism with political instability and incessant warfare among tribal factions. According to Lambton, once in power, all of Iran's tribal dynasties followed the same basic trajectory. They adopted the administrative and revenue collection system that originated under the eleventh-century Saljuq Sultanate. This system was based on the practice of *iqta*, whereby the sultan "parceled" out land grants to tribal administrators, who collected revenue from peasant cultivators.[17] Lambton believed the *iqta* system was fundamentally different from European feudalism, since it lacked the contractual relationship between feudal lords and their vassals. Instead, she insisted on the specificity of Islamic jurisdiction and the sultanate's ownership claim to all conquered territories.[18] But the exceptionalism of her Islamic model is challenged by scholars who note that she takes at face value the claims of sultans to absolute political and territorial sovereignty.[19] Lambton's sources show the lack of centralized control by Saljuqs and other tribal-based Islamic dynasties, yet she insists on their absolutism and personal ownership of all land.[20] Commenting on a similar debate in Ottoman historiography, Suraiya Faroqhi notes how historians have used the concept of feudalism in two different senses. Defined strictly in terms of political relations between lords and vassals, feudalism appears specific to Europe. But a broader definition of feudalism, as a system whereby military elites exploit peasants by extra-economic means, makes it applicable to premodern agrarian societies in other parts of the world. [21]

In premodern Iran, local histories document patterns of "divided sovereignty," whereby Qajar princes, governors, local sheikhs, khans, landlords and powerful clerics enjoy considerable autonomy vis-à-vis the shah.[22] The decentralized character of the Qajar "state" is noted in studies of "tribe–state" relations, for example, in Arash Khazeni's *Tribes and Empire on the Margins of Nineteenth-Century Iran*, which concludes:

[T]he Qajar dynasty exhibited a flexibility that allowed for tribal autonomy and a plurality of power on the margins of empire. The state possessed a decentralized structure And the tribes remained effectively beyond its reach ... Such a system in turn allowed tribal subjects to retain political and cultural autonomy while providing nominal allegiance and services to the state, most often by paying light taxes and offering retinues to the royal cavalry. This confederate and decentralized state structure was the hallmark of the early modern state in Iran. [23]

Along with monarchist absolutism, the image of ironclad Muslim clerical authority is another Orientalist myth lingering in Iranian historiography. "Persia," according to Lambton, was first of all "a society in which no distinction was recognized between 'church' and state."[24] Moreover, Lambton claimed Iran's clerics were in perpetual conflict with sultans and shahs, due to Shi'i beliefs in the illegitimacy of secular authority during the absence of the Twelfth Imam. In contrast to this model, recent scholarship tends to see the separation of religious and royal authority as normative in premodern Muslim history, in both Sunni and Shi'i traditions.[25] Patricia Crone, for example, notes how *in theory* medieval Muslim societies formed a single religious community (*umma*), where caliphs or sultans ruled, while enforcing the Islamic shari'a. Actual historical reality, however, deviated from this ideal model toward an effective separation of religious and political authority. According to Crone and other scholars, juridical Islam barely reached beyond major cities, leaving rural and nomadic areas under the sway of folk and heterodox religion.[26] Moreover, argues Sami Zubida, the articulation and historical application of Sharia laws always takes place within the secular constraints of social power and political authority. According to Zubida, during the nineteenth century, gradual modernization increased the separation of Muslim governments from the ulema and Sharia laws. In his view, even late-twentieth-century re-Islamization of politics, in countries like Iran, have effectively installed secularized versions of the Sharia, rather than its pristine original version.[27]

In the Iranian case, the official imposition of Shi'ism under the Safavids (1500–1722) meant the Shi'i clerical establishment enjoyed greater political clout than its Sunni counterparts in the Ottoman and Mughal empires.[28] Yet, even scholars partial to Iranian Shi'ism admit its doctrinal sway to have been tenuous, seriously challenged by popular Sufi orders and numerous schismatic sects. During the nineteenth century, Qajar shahs restored orthodox Shi'ism to the dominant position it had lost with the fall of the Safavids.[29] But the political clout of Shi'i clerics did not mean they "spoke for the people" in opposition to royal abuse and tyranny.[30] As with the Ottoman Empire's Sunni ulema, Iran's Shi'i hierarchy was in charge of a particular *millet*, a pre-national "imagined community" of co-religionists in reality fractured by class, language and ethnicity. Nor did the geographic boundaries of the Shi'i *millet*, stretching from Lebanon, Syria and Iraq, across Iran and into India, correspond to any national homeland. Thus, while clerics claimed to speak for the entire Shi'i *millet*, their representation was in practice partial, slanted and locally grounded. In other words, social elites were better served by the most powerful clerics, who shared their class background and interests. Moreover, the Shi'i clerical establishment was an urban corporate elite hardly in direct contact with the vast majority of premodern Iran's population, who lived in rural and tribal areas.[31] Even by the mid-twentieth century, only about 10 percent of Iranian villages had properly trained clerics (*mullahs*), who were nonexistent in small villages, where 85 percent of the rural population lived. Lacking mullahs, most villages relied for religious services on a semi-literate local *sheikh* or *seyyed*, with no formal training or credentials.[32] Overall, historical and anthropological evidence suggests that premodern Iran's rural population conformed to global patterns in being less religiously "traditional" or "orthodox" than their urban counterparts. Indeed, it was modernity and the nation-state that vastly expanded the reach of official Islam, and other text-based religions, from the cities into the countryside.[33]

The Global Lineage of Iranian Modernity: East, West or North by North-West?

Modern civilization came to Azerbaijan primarily from two sources: Through the knowledge of the Turkish language there were intellectual ties first with Istanbul and Ottoman Territories and second with Russian territories, especially Transcaucasia.

Taqizadeh[34]

[A]s a center of both cultural reception and transmission, especially in the late nineteenth and early twentieth centuries, the Caucasus served as the playground and battleground of revolutionary ideas that permeated both Iran and Ottoman Anatolia. As such, the Caucasus served as the hinge that connected three revolutions (Russian: 1905, Iranian: 1905–11, Ottoman: 1908).[35]

Historians generally see the Constitutional Revolution of 1906–1911 as the turning point in Iran's passage into modernity, with the launch of a modern nation-state. Chapter 2 will survey the historiographic debate on the Constitutional Revolution and its place in larger narratives of Iranian modernity. Here, we will consider this debate's starting point by locating the origins of Iranian nationalism and constitutionalism within the larger matrix of global modernity. As Touraj Atabaki has observed, modernity in Iran, as elsewhere, meant increasing integration within a conflicted and dynamic global frame, rather than conformity to European paradigms.[36] Similarly, Kamran Matin shows that, in trying to remedy their weakness and "backwardness" vis-à-vis powerful European adversaries, Iran's modernizing elite, like their Russian, Chinese and Ottoman counterparts, opened up *sui generis* paths of nation formation divergent from European trajectories.[37] This chapter, therefore, will situate the genesis of Iranian modernity, understood mainly in terms of nation-state formation and its attendant ideology of nationalism, within a shifting and asymmetrical background of global interactions. In particular, it will place the generative locus of Iranian modernity within a regional matrix of south-west Asian, rather than European, interactions.

An often-mentioned inspiration for Iran's political modernizers is Japan, a small Asian country deemed exceptionally successful in its purported fusion of "Western" constitutionalism with its own indigenous cultural traditions.[38] In fact, Iranian and other Asian elites were impressed primarily by Japan's modern military prowess, allowing it to defeat the formerly much more powerful Chinese and Russian empires. More accurately, Japan's newly acquired power and stature was due to its radical break with "tradition" to embrace modern authoritarian constitutionalism, corporate-dominated industrial capitalism, aggressive militarism and an imperialist foreign policy.[39] In the end, however, the intellectual impact of Japanese modernization on Iran was marginal at best. Japan had little to no historical contact with Iran and only a handful of Iranians knew anything about its recent history. This becomes clear when contrasted to Japan's deeper and more direct influence on modernizing Ottoman intellectuals.[40]

An important study by historian Mohammad Tavakoli-Targhi emphasizes the impact of Mughal India, via its printed Persian language texts, on the crafting of Iranian modernity and "national identity."[41] Tavakoli-Targhi follows Michel Foucault's understanding of modernity as primarily an intellectual project, sustained by an "ethos" unfolding in textual discursive formations. Apart from this ideational-cultural frame, however, modernity inhabits a physical space shaped by massive social, economic and political transformations, and is feasible only via the active intervention of modernizing imperial or national states. In this broader material-cum-ideational sense, Iranian modernity begins only in the nineteenth century and is affected, due to the proximity of its geographic sites, more by the

Russian and Ottoman empires than by the British Raj.[42] Firoozeh Kashani-Sabet has argued for the crucial significance of geography, land and space for the emergence of modern Iranian nationhood. Thus, Iran's national identity was delineated within the physical parameters set by the gradual transformation of porous and uncharted territories into modern national borders.[43] This chapter therefore will focus on the physical site of Iran's emergent nationhood and modernity in the north-western province of Azerbaijan, a region immediately adjacent to both the Ottoman and Russian empires.

The best recent studies of Iran's Constitutional Revolution still attribute its origin to European Enlightenment, reaching Iran in various alterations while passing through "transregional" routes and connections. "Intellectually," writes Ali Gheissari, the Constitutional Revolution "drew on a range of ideas and orientations that in good measure were associated with the Enlightenment – either directly from European sources or, more regularly, through elaborate routes of transnational contacts, notably from India, the Ottoman Empire, and the Caucasus."[44] On the other hand, a short study by Fariba Zarinebaf, one of the very few comparative scholars of Iranian and Ottoman history, concludes: "Ottoman and Iranian modernity had a great deal more in common with each other than with the Western models."[45] English-language scholarship on Iranian modernity, nationalism and constitutionalism has paid little comparative attention to Iran's long-term interactions with the Ottoman Empire.[46] As Zarinebaf observes, "Most of the existing historiography has emphasized the role of Western thought in the development of Turkish and Iranian modernity, while local and regional influences have been ignored."[47] This oversight is apparent in pioneering English-language studies of Iranian constitutionalism, for example, those by Said Amir Arjomand or Vanessa Martin, and continues in current scholarship on Iranian nationalism and constitutionalism.[48] Yet another Orientalist residue, this "Western gaze" has been amplified by a number of foundational axioms of nationalist historiography. First, nationalist historians see foreign influence as "interference" with Iran becoming a modern nation-state "on its own." This perspective assumes a counterfactual trajectory of Iran's transition to modernity, a path which these historians presumably feel could have been followed outside the impositions of global history.[49] Second, despite its claims of normative independence, nationalist historiography tends to prefer certain global models, such as "Western" democratic politics. On the other hand, nationalist historians often consider "non-Western" models and influences, such as those of Russian and Ottoman empires, negatively.

Nineteenth-century sources, however, show that Qajar reformers and statesmen generally preferred, and often systematically emulated, Russo-Ottoman, rather than "Western," models of modernization. Similarly, nineteenth- and early-twentieth-century Iran's radical and revolutionary thinkers were more influenced by the worldview of Russian and Ottoman intellectuals than by "Western" Enlightenment. The rest of this chapter therefore locates the intellectual origins of Iranian modernity in long-term interactions not with the "West," but rather with the "North, by North-West," i.e. from the Russian Caucasus and Istanbul via Anatolia.

Clearly referenced in contemporary sources, the direct impact of Ottoman modernity on Iranian constitutionalism gradually became obscured by the rise of nationalist historiography. Hasan Taqizadeh, the prominent leader of Iran's constitutional movement, was emphatic about the movement's indebtedness to Ottoman constitutionalism. He wrote: "The terms constitutionalism (*mashrutiyat*) and fundamental law (*qanun-e asai*), as well as the form of government implied by these terms, reached Iran, being adopted from the Ottoman Empire."[50] However, Taqizadeh's acknowledgment of foreign influence on Iranian constitutionalism, and hence nationalism, was rejected by Fereydun Adamiyat, twentieth-century Iran's most influential historian of liberal nationalism and constitutionalism:

Iranian history and culture provided firm foundations for the development of a national philosophy (*falsafe-ye melli*) ... Given such proper foundation, the idea of modern nationalism developed in Iran prior to other Middle Eastern countries. Our historical evidence proves the falsehood of claims that the modern notions of "*mellat*" [nation/people] and "*vatan*" [homeland] came to Iran via the Ottoman Empire.[51]

Believing in a singular Western-style modernity, Adamiyat nevertheless insisted on the indigenous roots of Iranian nationalism:

Nationalism was not a phenomenon coming to Iran completely from the West. Before the appearance of nationalist philosophy in Europe, all of its constituent elements existed and were recognized in Iran: The idea of *Iran-zamin*, an Aryan nation, racial pride, common language and religion, and most importantly common Iranian historical consciousness and intellectual conceptions, were not imported from outside. These elements originated and grew out of our ancient history and culture. [52]

While Iranian nationalism and constitutionalism were not simply "imported from outside," comparing their origins to similar transformations in the Ottoman Empire reveals complex patterns of influence.[53] Qajar Iran was the center of an intellectual network where proto-nationalist and Islamic modernist ideas circulated back and forth between Istanbul, Beirut, Cairo, Tabriz, Tehran, Baku, Tiflis, Kabul, Herat, Bukhara, Lahore, Calcutta and Delhi.[54] Quite similar to the Ottoman case, Qajar modernizing reforms were initiated from above, in both cases by princes or sultans reacting to irreversible military defeats and territorial losses in wars with Russia. Consequently, Qajar statesmen, following their Ottoman counterparts, looked to the Russian model of strengthening an "imperial center" via top-down technological, bureaucratic and military modernization.[55] Urgent calls for Russian-style modernization are abundant in Qajar primary sources. The first major European travelogue of the nineteenth century, for example, is by Mirza Saleh Shirazi who passed through Russia in the wake of Napoleon's defeat. Like the Qajar observers who followed him, Mirza Saleh was in awe of Russian modernization. "Russia," he wrote, "is one of the world's largest countries and the most powerful one in all of Europe." He went on to credit Tsar Peter's modernizing reforms for making Russia powerful:

Peter realized that, compared to Europeans, his Russian subjects were less than human, while he himself fell short in comparison to Europe's monarchs. Europe excelled due to the prevalence of science, industry and orderliness, things which Peter's realm utterly lacked.[56]

Qajar and Ottoman attributions of European superiority to "science, industry and orderliness" echoed Europe's own positivist discourse of progress, articulated by thinkers like August Comte. Recognizing the affinity of Ottoman reforms to his own philosophy, Comte wrote in 1853 to *Tanzimat* leader Rashid Pasha, inviting him to join Europe's new "positive religion." Ottoman and Qajar statesmen, however, were more interested in the "practical application" of modern science, especially to the fields of state administration and military technology.[57] Thus, a militaristic New Order (*nizam-i jedid*) became the foundation of Ottoman Tanzimat reforms (1830s–1860s), centralizing imperial authority via the introduction of cabinet ministers, codification of secular and religious laws, and royal decrees on the legal equality of subjects. The Tanzimat also included the opening of technical academies and new schools (*rushdieh*) that supplemented traditional *madrassa* curricula with modern science and humanities.[58] By the late nineteenth century, the initially Russo-French orientation of the Tanzimat became more authoritarian and militaristic under growing German influences. During the 1880s, Colmar von der Goltz led a restructuring of the Ottoman Royal Military Academy based on the model of Berlin's War Academy. Goltz had written an influential tract, *The Nation in Arms*, describing modern warfare as a struggle for survival among entire nations. Accordingly, the nations that were fittest for survival were those that were politically led by military elites. Noting the military's pivotal role in Ottoman history, Goltz argued for the empire's revival under the political tutelage of a modernizing officer corps. By the turn of the century, a younger generation of Ottoman officers had absorbed Goltz's ideas, some eventually implementing them in the 1908 paramilitary coup of the Committee of Union and Progress. [59]

The discourse of Ottoman constitutionalism had originated in mid-nineteenth-century underground circles formed to defend the empire's Islamic character against the Tanzimat's secular encroachment. Appearing in 1859, the first of these was the Society for the Preservation of the Sharia (*muhafaza-i seriat*) or Self-sacrificers (*fedais*). It called on the empire's Muslim community (*umma*) to form an assembly dedicated to the application of Sharia laws to remedy the Tanzimat's secular orientation. In 1865, a second secret society, called Young Ottomans, proposed a constitutional government with fundamental laws (*kanun asasi*) and a consultative assembly (*majlis* or *shura*), but representing only the Islamic *umma*.[60] Henceforth, Young Ottoman thinkers, most notably Namik Kemal (1840–1888), articulated a new discourse, adapting constitutionalism to Islam. Effectively redefining familiar Islamic concepts, Namik Kemal translated *bay'a* to "consent," *ijma'* to "consensus," *mashwara* to "consultation" and *husn* to (public) "goodness/utility." More importantly, he proposed an argument that was repeated by nineteenth- and twentieth-century Turkish, Arab and Iranian modernist intellectuals, namely that Muslims had to preserve their moral (*ma'navi*) autonomy, while acquiring European modernity. "The standards of our own morality," he insisted, "are amply sufficient to meet all the requirements of modern civilization." [61]

The Young Ottoman project of Islamic constitutionalism did not seek a liberal-democratic government, something that barely existed in nineteenth-century Europe.[62] The 1876 Ottoman constitution was modeled after the 1831 Belgian constitution, drawing in part on the 1814 French Constitutional Charter and the 1871 constitution of the new German Reich. But the Ottoman text became far less liberal than the Belgian model as it heavily privileged the government's executive branch over the legislative, while eliminating the freedoms of assembly, expression and political party formation.[63] "The religion of the Ottoman State is Islam," declared the 1876 Ottoman Constitution, affirming that sovereignty belonged to God and was exercised through His earthly vice-regent, "the Emperor" (*Padishah*), who could dismiss the national assembly and suspend the constitution. Members of the national assembly took an oath of loyalty to the "sacred" person of the Padishah, who had the legal power to nullify all of their collective decisions. Similarly, cabinet ministers were responsible not to the national assembly but to the Padishah. [64]

The conflicted character of Ottoman constitutionalism was inherent in the very process of its intellectual articulation. During the debates leading to the adoption of the 1876 text, the idea of *elite* consultation (*mesveret*), which was acceptable to conservative Muslim factions, became synonymous with *mesrutiyet* (constitutionalism), while reformers like Namik Kemal used these terms interchangeably.[65] Assimilating the principle of government based on elite "consultation" into Islamic political discourse, the 1876 Ottoman text served as the model for constitutions of Egypt, Bulgaria and Serbia.[66] Similarly, the modernization of Iran's Shi'i political discourse followed in the wake of Ottoman Islamic constitutionalism. A generation prior to their Shi'i Iranian counterparts, Sunni Ottoman jurists had argued that "by *akli* [rational] as well as *nakli* [traditional] evidence" the principle of government by "consultation" (*mesverat*) was "perfectly in accordance with Islam." This claim was supported by Prophetic tradition (*hadith*), as well as Qur'anic phrases such as "consult them upon the affairs" (Surah III, verse 159) and "consult them together in kindness" (Surah LXV, verse 6).[67] Though glaringly out of context, such Qur'anic exegesis launched a modernist nomenclature and style of argumentation that soon became widespread in Muslim countries, including Iran.

In this new discourse, "*icma* meant social contract, *bia*t meant the relegation of sovereignty to the ruler by the people, *ictihad* meant parliamentary legislation, *mesveret* meant democracy, and *'ilm* meant science."[68]

An "Iranian Enlightenment": Origins of the Intelligentsia, Nationalism and Constitutionalism

Turks play the leading role in the Iranian Revolution.

Mohammad-Amin Rasulzadeh, 1907[69]

By the late nineteenth century, Iran had its own discourse of "enlightenment" or "awakening" (*roshangari* or *bidari*), which, articulated by a small but vociferous home-grown "intelligentsia," advocated for constitutionalism as remedy to Iran's "backwardness" vis-à-vis an overpowering Europe.[70] Qajar reformers followed Young Ottomans to argue constitutionalism was compatible with Islam, a contention in need of endorsement by the clerical establishment, which in Shi'i Iran was more politically autonomous than in the Ottoman Empire.

Qajar Iran's emulation of Ottoman modernization had begun earlier in the century. Almost upon its inception, the Ottoman *nizam-i jedid* was introduced in Tabriz with crown prince Abbas Mirza's launching modern infantry and artillery regiments. This was followed by two periods of administrative modernization, in the 1850s and 1870s, introducing cabinet ministers, a council of the state and a project for comprehensive law codes, all in line with the Ottoman Tanzimat. The unfolding of Tanzimat reforms was observed firsthand by Qajar reformer Mirza Hossein Khan, who served as Iran's ambassador to Istanbul for twelve years (1858–1871). As Iran's prime minster (1871–1874), Hossein Khan introduced similar administrative reforms, along with the Young Ottoman nomenclature of key terms such as "*millat*" and "*vatan*" for "the people" or "nation."[71] Soon after its inauguration, the 1876 Ottoman constitution was translated into Persian by the Iranian foreign ministry, as well as by the influential Istanbul-based newspaper *Akhtar*, which also reported the benefits of constitutional government.[72] Important too was the contribution of Qajar prince and Shi'i cleric Abol-Hassan Mirza (1848–1921) who, during his 1884–1886 stay in Istanbul, was backed by Sultan Abdul-Hamid and Ottoman officials to publish a newspaper called *Islamic*

Unity (*Itihhad-e Islam*), advocating Shi'i–Sunni unity and an Ottoman–Iranian political alliance. In 1894, Abol-Hassan Mirza proposed the same ideas in a treatise, also titled *Islamic Unity*, urging Iran's Shi'i clerics to participate directly in government, thus strengthening the monarchy in accordance with Islam. Abol-Hassan Mirza was in touch with the reformist circles of Aqa Khan Kermani and Jamal al-Din Asadabadi ("Afghani"), participated in Iran's Constitutional Revolution and became a parliamentary (*majles*) deputy.[73] The need for a legislative assembly (*majles*) was mentioned also in the 1875 essay, *al-Risala al-Madaniyya* ("The Treatise on Civilization"), by Mirza Abbas Nuri (Abdul-Baha), the leader of the Baha'i community, who lived in Ottoman exile and was familiar with Young Ottoman constitutional discourse. [74]

One of the most influential Iranian texts of Islamic constitutionalism was *A Singular Word* (*Yek kalameh*) by Mirza Yusef Tabrizi (Mostashar al-Dowleh) (1822–1895). Having served in diplomatic posts in Astrakhan, Tiflis, St. Petersburg and Paris during the 1850s–1860s, Mostashar al-Dowleh wrote *Yek Kalameh* in 1870 while in Paris. The "singular word" of the title phrase was *qanun*, i.e. the law, or constitution, prescribed as the ultimate panacea to all of Iran's ailments. The second title phrase of Mostashar al-Dowleh's book was *The Spirit of Islam* (*Ruh al-Islam*), a clear reference to Montesquieu's *Spirit of the Laws*. The less noted title, *Ruh al-Islam*, more transparently revealed the author's intention of presenting modern European laws, including texts like the 1789 "Declaration of the Rights of Man" and the 1791 French Constitution, as fully compatible with Islam.[75] Mostashar al-Dowleh himself had boasted:

For every facet of civilization and progress, I have found support in Qur'anic verses and the Prophet's Traditions (*ahadith*), so that no one can claim any of this is contrary to Islam, or that that Islam is an obstacle to civilization and progress.[76]

Mostashar al-Dowleh called on Shi'i clerics to convene an assembly and codify the Sharia as the law of the land, following the Ottoman example of codifying Islamic laws in *mecelle* codes.[77] The project of Islamic constitutionalism, however, was sharply criticized by Fath-Ali Akhudzadeh, an Azeri subject of the Russian Empire who proposed instead a thoroughly secular vision of Iranian nationalism, without fear of persecution by Qajar political and clerical authorities. Directly responding to Mostashar al-Dowleh, he retorted: "You imagine Sharia principles can help bring the French Constitution into Eastern countries. This is utterly and absolutely impossible." Rejecting all compromise with religion, Akhundzadeh went on to argue:

Freedom from despotic oppression and false beliefs is impossible without science; and science cannot be achieved without progress; and progress is not possible if you are not liberal, which means free from false beliefs. None of this is of any use, however, when your religion precludes you from being liberal.[78]

By the term "liberal," Akhudndzadeh did not mean political or economic liberalism, but something like the relative toleration of religious diversity in Tsarist Russia. The "conversation" between Akhundzadeh and Mostashar al-Dowleh took place across the border separating Iranian Azerbaijan from the Russian-ruled Caucasus. Adjacent to both Ottoman and Russian territories, Azerbaijan was the Iranian province most directly receptive to modernist influences.[79] The Turkish language facilitated Azeri reception of new ideas coming from Istanbul, while hundreds of thousands of mostly Azeri Iranian immigrants were a major cultural bridge to the Russian-controlled Caucasus. By the early twentieth century, Baku had emerged as a hub of the Industrial Revolution on Iran's doorstep. Within fifty years, a bustling oil industry had raised the city's population more than tenfold, to about 200,000. It was thus through Baku that Iran first came into contact with the newly emerging Muslim industrial bourgeois and proletarian classes and their cultural and political impact.[80] Azerbaijan's political and cultural prominence was not new. Throughout the nineteenth century, it was the country's leading province, economically and culturally, while its political leadership role would surpass Tehran's during the Constitutional Revolution. When Mohammad Ali Shah took the crown in 1907, a major uprising in Tabriz revived the constitutional movement, initiating the addition of a Supplement to the Constitution, significantly broadening the political scope of the original 1906 text. As Taqizadeh had correctly observed: "Without the uprising and agitation in Tabriz, full constitutionalism would not have been established."[81] Meanwhile, with the 1908 victory of the Young Turk Revolution, Istanbul became the main support center of Iranian constitutionalism outside the country. The Sa'adat Association in Istanbul represented the radical Provincial Association of Tabriz, linking it to constitutionalist circles in Iraq, India and some European cities, and cooperating with the Committee of Union and Progress. At the time, about 16,000 Iranians lived in Istanbul and the Iranian merchant community paid the Sa'adat Association's expenses. Following the counter-revolutionary coup in Tehran, exiled constitutionalist leaders gathered in Istanbul to launch *Surush*, the new organ of the Sa'adat Association.[82]

As we shall see in the following chapters, Azeri intellectuals would lead Iran's radical nationalist and socialist/communist movements well into the twentieth century.[83] The cultural impact of Iran's modernizing *intelligentsia*, particularly the Azeris, corresponds to similar patterns in Ottoman and Russian intellectual history. Ottoman Tanzimat reforms produced a modernizing cultural elite whose members recognized each other as *munever*, a direct translation of the French term *lumier* or "enlightener." As mentioned above, the Ottoman *munever* elite expanded the scope of Tanzimat toward an ambitious project of "cultural translation," ascribing new meanings to familiar concepts of Islamic political culture. In the Ottoman Empire's Arabic-speaking regions, the term *munever* was used interchangeably with *munuwwar al-fikr*, literally meaning "enlightened thinker." This Arabic neologism was soon adopted in Iran, where it was gradually replaced by its literal Persian translation *roshan-fekr*. A common feature of Ottoman and Russian intellectual encounters with modernity was the clash of powerful "Westernizing" ideas with a reactive discourse rejecting or questioning "Western" cultural models. In both cases, the clash is dramatically described in proto-modernist works of literature. Ivan Turgenev's *Fathers and Sons*, for example, features Bazarov, the iconoclast Westernizing intellectual, standing in contrast to the artificially Europeanized protagonist of Turgenev's *Diary of a Superfluous Man*. Ottoman literature's counterpart to the Russian "Superfluous Man" was the so-called *alafranga* (French-styled) character, whose clash with the more "authentic" *alaturka* personality became a central theme of popular late-nineteenth-century novels by Ahmed Midhat and Hossein Rahmi. (On the impact of early modernist Ottoman-Turkish literature on Iran, see Chapters 3 and 4.)[84]

More significantly, Russia's "Westernizers" were opposed by Slavophiles, Russian chauvinists and religious visionaries, who were joined by populists, socialists and anarchists, and eventually even Bolsheviks, in the belief that Russia could show the modern world an alternate "non-Western" future path.[85] According to Isaiah Berlin, the Russian intelligentsia "thought of themselves as united by something more than mere interest in ideas; they conceived themselves as being a dedicated order, almost a secular priesthood, devoted to the spreading of a specific attitude to life, something like a gospel."[86] Berlin's observation echoes in studies of nineteenth-century Iran's reformist modernizing and revolutionary thought. Hamid Dabashi has noted how Iran's modern "intelligentsia saw itself as the seer/knower/redeemer, destined to deliver the masses from the bonds of poverty ignorance, and tyranny."[87] This messianic revolutionary feature makes the Iranian intelligentsia more akin to its radical and revolutionary Russian counterpart than to the gradualist Ottoman *munevers*. Another characteristic of Iran's modernizing intelligentsia is the prominent role of religiously heterodox elements, particularly those belonging to the Azali-Babi sect. Late Qajar sources often use the word "Babi" as a synonym for terms such as atheist, anarchist, socialist, materialist and "naturist." One such contemporary observer, for example, wrote: "Europe is in chaos. Anarchists, i.e., the enemies of despotic kings in every nation, are powerful across Europe. Domestically, and especially in Tehran, the Iranian anarchists, meaning Babis, number around 50,000."[88] Though hyperbolic, such references testify to the significance of Babi political activism in Iran's constitutional movement. Following its mid-nineteenth-century violent suppression, the new Babi sect focused on underground agitation against the Qajar political and clerical establishment, rather than developing a clear religious doctrine and institutions. Consequently, the ideas of intellectuals with Babi affiliation, such as Aqa Khan Kermani (1853–1896), were quite eclectic, overlapping with secular nationalism and even socialism. Moreover, the obscurity of the Babis' presence in the constitutional movement was due to their resorting to the Shi'i practice of dissimulating true belief (*taqiyeh*). As we shall see below, such deliberate acts of self-censorship and "silencing" entered the Constitutional Revolution's "master narrative," leaving behind a historiographic legacy of "amnesia" and distortion.[89]

The turn-of-the-century transformations of Iranian, Turkish and Arab intelligentsia also show the initial fluidity of modern national identity. In the wake of the nineteenth-century Russo-Turkish and Russo-Iranian wars, millions of Caucasian Muslim refugees poured into Anatolia and Iranian Azerbaijan. "The Transcaucasian Muslim refugees of Crimean and Azeri background," writes Zarinebaf, "identified with both the Sunni Ottomans and the Shi'i Iranians and settled in both states. In both cases, these groups played an important role in forging a nationalist discourse."[90] An intriguing feature of this Transcaucasian intellectual melting pot was the case of Azeri *munevers,* who switched their national identification from Iranian to Turkish. Perhaps the most famous such figure was Mohammad-Amin Rasulzadeh (1884–1955), born into a clerical Shi'i family in Baku and initially active in Caucasian social democratic circles alongside Joseph Stalin. During the earlier phase of the Constitutional Revolution (1906–1907), Rasulzadeh began reporting on Iran in Turkish-language Caucasian newspapers. At this point, he compared Iranian constitutionalism to Russian developments following the 1905 Revolution, writing favorably of the political role of Islam and the Shi'i clergy.[91] As Iran's constitutionalist movement radicalized, Rasulzadeh began to see it as part of a broader revolutionary movement sweeping across the Russian and Ottoman empires. He also noted the important role of the Turkish language in linking together Iranian, Ottoman and Caucasian revolutionary currents. As early as 1907, for example, he wrote:

Turks play the leading role in the Iranian Revolution. Indeed, it must be so because the majority of Iranians in the Caucasus are Azerbaijani manual laborers who work alongside their Russian comrades, thus learning the ways of freedom and self-sacrifice.[92]

In 1909, Rasulzadeh came to Iran to directly observe and report on the ongoing revolutionary civil war for the Baku paper *Taraqqi*. His eyewitness accounts of revolutionary popular mobilization, in Rasht and Tabriz, are valuable primary sources showing his subsequent intellectual contribution, as the Constitutional era's leading social democratic theorist, was related to firsthand personal involvement and experience. Reaching Tehran alongside the triumphant revolutionaries, Rasulzadeh then became the editor of *Iran-e no*, organ of the Democrat Party and the country's leading constitutionalist periodical. His writings at this time show a cosmopolitan socialist perspective on the revolutionary tide sweeping the Russian Caucasus and Iran, emphasizing the role of Turkish language in linking Iran to the Caucasus and hence to the Ottoman and Russia empires. Reporting from Iranian Azerbaijan, he wrote:

Turkish is the language of communication and mutual understanding among various nations. Here, it is the international language spoken by everyone: Armenians, Kurds, Russians, French, English, Persians, Assyrians and Germans. Knowing this language allows me to communicate with people from all kinds of backgrounds. I feel fortunate being a Turk.[93]

With the ebbing of the Iranian and Russian revolutions by 1910, Rasulzadeh went to exile in Istanbul, where he drew close to Young Turk circles and incipient Turkish nationalism. Following the 1917 Russian Revolution, he returned to Baku, became the leader of the nationalist Mosavat Party and served as the head of the national assembly in the short-lived independent Republic of Azerbaijan.[94]

Another Azeri intellectual, whose contribution to Iranian nationalism is more important but less known, is Ahmed Agaoglu (1869–1939). His case is similar to Rasulzadeh's in showing how the same individual could transition from Iranian to Turkish nationalism. Born in the Karabagh region of Russian-controlled Azerbaijan, Agaoglu was educated in Tiblisi and St. Petersburg. In 1888, he went to Paris to study law and languages, attending lectures by leading Orientalists like Ernest Renan and James Darmsteter. Back in the Caucasus by the mid-1890s, Agaoglu shed his Iranian identity to embrace Pan-Turkism. After taking part in the 1905 Russian Revolution, he migrated to Istanbul and joined the Young Turks, later playing an active role in the founding of the Turkish Republic.[95] Growing up in the Caucasus, Agaoglu had learned Persian, in addition to Turkish, and considered himself a *Rus Musilman*, i.e. a Muslim subject of the Russian Empire. Later, influenced in Paris by Renan, Arthur Gobineau and other Aryan race theorists, he added Persian nationalist and Aryan layers to his initially Shi'i identity. It was during this phase of his intellectual transformation, and particularly in a series of 1891–1893 articles written in French, that Aqaoglu articulated certain arguments that became axiomatic to Iranian nationalism and its relation to Shi'ism. (As we shall see in the following chapters, Agaoglu's formulations echoed in works by Shi'i modernizers like Hossein Kazemzadeh and Orientalists like Louis Massignon and Henri Corbin.[96])

Agaoglu claimed that when the Sassanian Empire fell, its "Persian" subjects easily converted to Islam because the empire's official Mazdean religion was already unpopular. However, Persians were racially Aryan and therefore possessed a "national" identity distinct from Semitic Arabs. According to Agaoglu, Persians then reshaped Islam into Shi'ism, a religion more compatible with their national and racial identity. Thus, Persians venerate Hussein as grandson to both the Prophet Mohammad and the last Sassanian emperor. They also interjected into Shi'ism elements of Mazdean religion, such as belief in "intermediate" beings like Imams and *mujtaihids*, who link the divine and mortal realms.[97] Thus, the essence of Shi'ism was the Mazdean "belief in man's participation in the divine nature, a belief so contrary to the spirit of Orthodox Islam." Building on these premises, Agaoglu proposed the rational kernel of Iran's "national" tradition could be retrieved via modern interpretations of Shi'ism by enlightened mujtahids and implemented by a strong progressive government:

A mujtahid, venerated by the people, endowed with a will of iron, but understanding thoroughly the spirit and demands of his time, will find in the Shi'i religion powerful tools for the renewal of Western Asia.[98]

Agaolgu's ideas resonated in contemporary calls for Qajar political reform, most famously in the London-based newspaper *Qanun* (Law), published by Malkolm Khan. During the 1890s, *Qanun* advocated Islamic unity and praised Sultan Abdul Hamid's rule as a model government based on modern laws.[99] According *Qanun*, Iran needed an Ottoman-style constitutional government, whereby the Shi'i ulema joined political reformers to fashion a legal system in strict accordance with the Sharia. He wrote: "at least one hundred of Iran's great *mujtahids*, the renowned learned men, and savants of Persia, [must] be gathered in a national consultative assembly (*majles-e shura-ye melli*)."[100] Repeating Young Ottoman arguments for Islamic constitutionalism, Malkolm's *Qanun* was emphatic about the orthodox Islamic character of the modern legislature it proposed:

We are not talking about new laws at all. What we seek is the laws laid down by God and the Prophet ... Any decree issued in the great national assembly (*shura-ye kobra-ye melli*) by the Muslim *ulema* will be life-saving divine law to us.[101]

Malkolm's insistence on clerical support for constitutionalism was another case of ideological dissimulation, contradicting his earlier call for Iran's "wholesale adoption of European civilization."[102] The same was true of Aqa Khan Kermani, a proto-nationalist intellectual whose strong anti-clerical sentiments were related to his heterodox Babi background. Living in Istanbul for a decade (1886–1896), Kermani worked with Iranian exiles and newspapers like *Akhtar* and *Qanun*. When Jamal al-Din Asadabadi (Afghani) arrived in Istanbul in 1892, Kermani quickly joined his Pan-Islamic circle, helping to write hundreds of letters to Shi'i and Sunni ulema in Iran and other countries.[103] He also wrote to Malkolm, suggesting Iran's "half-alive" clerical establishment "must be called upon for limited support to possibly hasten success" by mobilizing popular backing of secular political goals. This was necessary, explained Kermani, because "the Iranian people are still philosophically backward, oppressed and in need of fanaticism."[104] At the same time, Kermani saw the ulema as politically incompetent and opposed to modern ideas. Nevertheless, he thought Malkolm's *Qanun* could lure them into believing themselves capable of managing the affairs of a modern government:

The *ulema* know nothing about politics and cannot manage it ... So they must be given assurances in this regard, i.e. *Qanun* must write that the affairs of government and the people can be handled a thousand times better by the *ulema*, who possess knowledge, religiosity and patriotism, yet consider themselves apolitical today.[105]

To Kermani, such duplicitous use of Shi'ism and its clerical establishment was a political "master stroke" (*shahkar*). Malkolm agreed, since his *Qanun* proposed a plan which uncannily anticipated the actual course of events leading to the 1906 granting of the Iranian constitution. *Qanun*'s scheme would begin with a protest movement initiated at Tehran's Royal Mosque, with "the ulema inciting the urban populace to recall wicked authorities," without the principle of monarchy being challenged. During the movement's second phase, the country's wise political elite and high clerics would gather to form "the great national consultative assembly." Once formed, this assembly would assert its full sovereignty, making laws "in accordance with the universal principles of progress."[106] This scheme broadly followed the trajectory of Ottoman constitutionalism, which was familiar to both Kermani and Malkolm.

Given their contemporary intellectual context, Kermani's "master stroke" and Malkolm's blueprint of action in *Qanun* may appear ingenious. But the real course of events quickly revealed their strategy's fundamental flaw, when a clerical backlash rejected as un-Islamic "the universal principles of progress" inserted into the Iranian constitution. Impatient for quick results, and following the Ottoman model of Islamic constitutionalism, Kermani and Malkom had resorted to the familiar Shi'i practice of dissimulation (*taqiya*), dressing their secular ideas in an Islamic garb.[107] Similar to their Ottoman counterparts, these Iranian reformers ignored the inherent contradiction in deploying religious means to achieve secular ends. Nevertheless, and despite persistent clerical opposition, the argument for constitutional government's compatibility with clerical authority became axiomatic in modern Iranian political culture. It was enshrined in the Supplement to the 1906 Constitution, whose first article declared: "The official religion of Iran is Islam and the righteous path of Twelver Shi'ism, which the shah of Iran must profess and promote." The Supplemental Law's second article clarified the first by stipulating that a committee of high-ranking ulema, in effect a clerical "supreme court," was to monitor the compatibility of all parliamentary legislation with Shi'i Islam. Moreover, several other constitutional provisions made it clear that fundamental rights and freedoms, of speech, assembly, the press and political parties, were to be curtailed by the Sharia. In the end, modern Iranian constitutional discourse theoretically had placed clerical authority above national legislative sovereignty. The clerical "guardian committee" did not formally function under the Pahlavi dynasty, but it remained an integral part of twentieth-century Iran's constitutional discourse, repeatedly evoked by politically minded clerics like Ayatollah Ruhollah Khomeini (see Chapter 4).

The shocking advent of an Islamic Republic in the 1980s forced some serious questioning of the origins of Iranian constitutionalism. Mashallah Ajudani, for example, has strongly criticized the assumption of compatibility between constitutional government and Shi'i clerical authority. According to him, this fundamental concession on constitutional government's secular democratic character paved the way for Pahlavi-style authoritarian nation-state building. Reza shah, he writes, "was the powerful champion of a constitutionalism in which democracy had been sacrificed to Iran's sovereignty and independence."[108] As we shall see in the following chapters, however, critics like Ajudani go too far when implicating twentieth-century intellectuals in the "original sin" of late-nineteenth-century constitutionalist reformers. Ottoman intellectuals also have been criticized for the confusions stemming from their assimilation of parliamentarianism to Islam.

Nevertheless, comparative studies of Iranian and Ottoman constitutionalism suggest that in both cases the advantages of assimilating constitutionalism to Islam may have outweighed their negative consequences.[109]

Historians have noted the significance of clerical support of Iranian constitutionalism, particularly from Najaf, the capitol of the Shi'i clerical establishment. The three most influential Shi'i clerics supporting Iranian constitutionalism, Mohammad Kazim Khorasani, Mohammad-Hosein Tehrani and Abadallah Mazandarani, resided in Ottoman Iraq. However, existing scholarship does not consider the impact of Ottoman Islamic constitutionalism on their ideas.[110] Vanessa Martin, for example, notes Mohammad Tabataba'i, the leading constitutionalist mujtahid in Iran, had spent at least twelve years (1883–1895) in Ottoman Iraq, where he was influenced by Jamal al-Din Asadabadi's Pan-Islamic ideas. Overlooking this immediate Ottoman intellectual background, she concludes "it was from European thought that Tabataba'i derived his views."[111] The same basic neglect of Ottoman intellectual mediation is evident too in Martin's discussion of Mohammad Hossein Na'ini's 1909 important pro-constitutionalist tract, which she notes was composed in Najaf.[112]

Meanwhile, Iran's constitutional movement had spawned a new anti-clerical discourse, attacking the clergy mainly for its alleged abandonment of "true Islam." Going farther, radical constitutionalist newspapers, such as *Mosavat,* claimed Shi'i clerics had always served despotic kings and undermined true Islam by their ignorance, dishonesty and greed.[113] Less noted at the time, but influential on future religious reformers, like Ahmad Kasravi, were those who criticized the Shi'i tradition from within (see Chapter 4). A prominent example was Ebrahim Zanjani, a constitutionalist mujtiahid who served during the first four Majles sessions, supporting, as a deputy of the Democrat Party, the separation of religion and state. Zanjani is mostly remembered as the prosecutor in the trial that condemned to death Fazlallah Nuri, the highest-ranking clerical opponent of constitutionalism. He also wrote an autobiography combining personal frankness with a radical critique of the entire Shi'i canon.[114] True Islam, according to Zanjani, had no place for clerical intermediaries between God and humanity. Throughout history, however, Islam was corrupted by "shrewd" individuals, i.e. clerics, bent on "conquering the hearts and minds of hardworking masses" to rule over them. Zanjani considered

Sunni Islam more compatible with republicanism, since Sunni jurists allowed secular political elites to decide what was in the people's best interests. Shi'is, on the other hand, believed in "personal sovereignty" (*saltanat-e shakhsi*), where both clerical and monarchist authority hinged on unverifiable divine sanction.[115]

Orientalist Narrations of Iran's Constitutional Revolution: The Browne Paradox

It is generally agreed that the ulema played a leading part in the Persian constitutional revolution of 1905–06.

(Lambton, 1970)

The role of Islam and Shi'i clerics in Iran's Constitutional Revolution has been vigorously debated by historians, especially since a clerical elite took over the leadership of Iran's 1978–1979 Revolution. Recent scholarship questions an older paradigm according to which the Constitutional Revolution was led by a trilateral coalition of clerics, merchants and reformist intellectuals. Historians now find a more fluid and conflicted revolutionary leadership, bringing together a mixture of old regime reformers, modernizing bureaucrats, big merchants, secular democrats, social democratic revolutionaries and religiously heterodox political activists, as well as an important clerical faction. Revisionist historiography thus upholds historian Fereydun Adamiyat's assertion that, although some high-ranking clerics contributed to the success of the constitutional *movement*, they did not lead the revolutionary phase of constitutionalism.[116]

Moreover, historians have been noticing how a single text, British Orientalist Edward Granville Browne's *The Persian Revolution* (1910), launched the Constitutional Revolution's enduring "master narrative."[117] Written while the revolution was still unfolding, Browne's work introduced two major interwoven tropes into modern Iranian historiography. First, it celebrated the Constitutional Revolution as the *rebirth* of Iran's ancient "nationhood," pitted against royal despotism and foreign domination. Second, to show Islam's compatibility with nationalism, Browne exaggerated the Shi'i clergy's leadership of the constitutional movement. *The Persian Revolution*'s extraordinary narrative power becomes evident in comparison to its rival contemporary account, Nazim al-Islam Kermani's *History of*

Iranians' Awakening. Written in Persian, Kermani's work is richer in detail and closer to primary sources. Nevertheless, it reads like an incoherent chronicle, lacking the modernist narrative structure that produces Browne's interpretive impact.[118]

Browne, of course, wrote for British readers, trying to shore up support for Iran's new constitutional regime, which he correctly feared the British government would sacrifice to imperial interests.[119] He was fighting an uphill battle against prevalent Orientalist views of Iran as a backward Muslim country, as well as the powerful imperialist lobby of the British Foreign Office and newspapers like the London *Times*. Within a year of *The Persian Revolution*'s publications, its author's concerns proved justified, as tsarist troops, with British consent, occupied northern Iran, effectively suspending the constitutional regime. To win over its audience, however, *The Persian Revolution* was crafted as a political drama familiar to British readers: The constitutionalists, whom Browne called the "National Party" or "Nationalists," were pitted in a heroic struggle against the forces of royal despotism (*estebdad*). Moreover, Browne claimed the nationalists were reviving "Persia" as a great "nation" that had existed since ancient times.[120] Ironically, the book's preface admits the novelty of these narrative assumptions. Still, Browne's masterfully distorted narration proved a great success, not with British readers, but with Iranians who enshrined it in their nationalist historiography. A century later, Browne's narration echoes in sophisticated studies such as Ali Ansari's *Politics of Nationalism in Modern Iran*. According to Ansari, the Iranian "framers of the Constitution were seeking a 'republic,' with representative institutions regulated by Laws ... as befits a constitution which ultimately derived from the (unwritten) English Constitution."[121]

More critical readings of *The Persian Revolution* might still admire its anti-imperialist motivation and creative contribution to Iranian historiography, while rejecting its deliberate distortions. Primarily, Browne distorted history by silencing or marginalizing the constitutional movement's secular revolutionary and heterodox religious factions. Curiously, this conforms to the time-honored Shi'i practice of *taqiya*, i.e. the religiously expedient dissimulation of truth. This kind of historiography thus becomes a "pious reading of the past," where Islam and Shi'i clerics receive undue pride of place, while secular radical and/or religiously unorthodox actors make sanitized and "air brushed" appearances. Browne, for example, was quite familiar with the crucial role of Azali Babis in the constitutional movement, particularly in its revolutionary wing. But he resorted, perhaps partly for the sake of protecting Babi activists, to the "deliberate editing" of their presence in *The Persian Revolution*, thus "de-hereticizing Constitutional memory."[122] Moreover, Browne knew of and mentioned the radical press and popular political associations (*anjomans*) appearing in 1907, but did not dwell on their crucial role in the 1908–1909 civil war and its aftermath during the Second Constitutional period. Considering internal "dissention" as a great danger to the revolution, he wanted his British readers to see a stable and successful national revolution in Iran.[123] *The Persian Revolution* thus concluded with the constitutional regime's restoration in 1910, a suspenseful triumphant moment in a narrative lacking closure. In this sense too, Browne's work differs from all subsequent narrations, which share a tragic streak as they inevitably deal with the revolution's post-1910 failures and frustrations.

In the end, *The Persian Revolution* left a deep imprint on all succeeding interpretations of the constitutional movement's background and unfolding. It was Browne who first selected, and presented in causal sequence, a series of events relevant or leading to the granting of a constitution. To this end, his book begins with the revolution's ideological preparation and its "rehearsal" via the Tobacco Protest movement of 1891–1892. The first chapter, "Sayyid Jamalud-Din, the Protagonist of Pan-Islam," places "Al Afghani" and the Iranian clergy, with Pan-Islamic ideas, in the revolution's intellectual leadership. Browne's interpretive pronouncements are evident in statements such as the following, often authenticated by referencing anonymous primary sources:

Now the effect of the influence of the clergy is fully manifest in Persia, inasmuch as it hath changed the order of government and converted it from despotic to constitutional rule … Yet none the less sayyid Jamalud-Din was the prime mover in this revolution, as he was the cause of the revolution which took place in Egypt.[124]

Again relying on an unnamed eye-witnesses, Browne claimed:

One remarkable feature of this revolution here – for it is surely worthy to be called a revolution – is that the priesthood have found themselves on the side of progress and freedom. This I should think, is almost unexampled in the world's history.[125]

In a footnote supporting this claim, Browne mentions Hassan Taqizadeh, one of his main sources and then a revolutionary social democrat, informing him how a group of "Europeanized Persians of the educated official class" had quietly "advised" the 1905 protesters, steering them to demand a constitution. But, as Taqizadeh would often do, Browne keeps such important information on the margin of his narrative, allowing instead other protagonists, including clerics, to occupy center stage.[126] Taqizadeh, in fact, had gone much farther in his assimilation of constitutionalism to Shi'ism, depicting, for example, the 1908–1909 revolutionary civil war as Islamic jihad. During the siege of Tabriz by counter-revolutionary forces, he wrote:

Today, supporting, aiding and acknowledging the jihad for freedom, carried out under the banner of Sattar Khan, the greatest of *mohjerin* and *ansar*, is tantamount to supporting the oppressed camp of Hossein son of Ali ... The religion of Islam, Iran's freedom, the country's honor, national independence and the nation's well-being, honor, morality, chastity, the sanctity of Muslim boys and girls, indeed the very survival of Islam is endangered.

Today, hearing the women of Tabriz screaming out for deliverance makes the pure spirit of the prophet Mohammad shriek and cry ... A rebellious monarch has broken his oath, bombarded the national assembly, this mosque of God and first temple in the Shi'i capital, demolished Iran's first Islamic [majles] library, burnt Qurans ... such traitorous renegade monarch, against whom Najaf clerics have declared jihad, must be eliminated.[127]

Browne's historiographic dissimulation [*taqiya*] thus launched an Islamicized narrative of the Constitutional Revolution, sustained also by its leading contemporary historians, including those who were Babi, or, like Browne himself, shared Babi sympathies. The result was what Abbas Amanat has called a historiography of "denial" and "amnesia": "The contemporary historiography of the Constitutional Revolution, whenever it cares to look back at the landscape of dissent, tended to overlook the role of the outcasts and the marginalized, and above all the heretics who contributed to Iran's vernacular modernity."[128]

Following Browne, two generations of historians struggled to explain the paradoxical role of Shi'i clergy as leaders of a modern constitutional revolution. Meanwhile "the Browne Paradox" was embedded in the most influential English-language studies of the Constitutional

Revolution, including those by Anne K. Lambton and Nikki R. Keddie. For instance, Keddie's 1966 *Religion and Rebellion in Iran* argued:

[T]he creation of an alliance between the ulema leaders and the reformers was a tactic begun by Sayyed Jamal al-Din al-Afghani, achieving its first success in the tobacco movement, and carried on through the Iranian [Constitutional] Revolution. Advanced reformers were willing to put their own liberal, freethinking, or heretical notions into the background in order to achieve an active alliance with ulema leaders against government. Afghani and others recognized that only the ulema were powerful and influential enough to lead a successful mass movement; in the absence of widespread demands for modernization, the use of religious language and appeals was necessary to move the masses.[129]

Similar to Browne's, Keddie's narrative relied in part on Taqizadeh's personal testimony.[130] Rethinking "the Browne Paradox" came only after another Iranian revolution and two generations of historiographic debate.[131]

Conclusion

This chapter critically engaged with the historiography of "premodern" Iran, trying to identify and challenge some of its paradigmatic narrative assumptions. First, it questioned the meta-narratives of "continuity" in Iranian history by distinguishing between the idea of Iran as a modern nation-state and premodern imperial conceptions of Iran. Second, it argued that, contrary to Orientalist paradigms of Asiatic Despotism and Islamic Absolutism, premodern Iran must be characterized by its decentralized political hierarchies and diverse heterodox religious belief and authority. Third, the chapter argues that Iran's pivotal moment of transition to modernity, i.e. the Constitutional Revolution of 1906–1911, intellectually and politically fits patterns set by the Ottoman and Russian empires, rather than by "the West." The chapter concludes with a critique of lingering narrative confusions in the historiography of the Constitutional Revolution, introduced by Orientalist scholarship's collapsing together the movement's reformist background and its revolutionary peak, as well as exaggerating the Shi'i clergy's contribution and obscuring the role of secular radicals and religiously heterodox participants.

2 | The Berlin Circle
Crafting the Worldview of Iranian Nationalism*

Among the least studied chapters of twentieth-century Iranian history is the decade between the restoration of the constitutional regime in 1910 and the end of the country's foreign occupation in 1921. Often labeled a time of "catastrophe" or "disintegration," this fateful decade also produced Iran's modern nationalist ideology and a project of authoritarian nation building, launched by the new Pahlavi Dynasty during the 1920s.[1] In mainstream historiography, the Constitutional Revolution ends with the 1911 Russian invasion of northern Iran, followed by the country's total loss of independence under joint Russo-British occupation during World War I. According to this familiar narrative, when foreign occupation finally ended in 1921, a "disillusioned" nationalist elite abandoned its "idealistic" notions of constitutionalism to pragmatically embrace authoritarian modernization.[2] This narrative builds on what Abbas Amanat has called the Pahlavi era's historiographic "myth of failure," portraying "the Constitutional period as a disruptive and largely failed movement," when altruistic popular participation "nevertheless triggered domestic chaos, foreign occupation and political betrayal."[3] Such narratives suggest the inevitability of authoritarian nationalism by obscuring its origins as one contender among rival ideologies of nation formation during the decade prior to 1921. In fact, no clear project of nation building or nationalist ideology yet existed when the constitutional regime was restored in 1910. The constitution and its supplements merely proposed a political frame, a potentiality whose realization was immediately preempted with the 1911 Russian invasion. Iran's constitutional experiment therefore was suspended upon inauguration, prior to any meaningful popular participation in the crafting of nationalist ideology or nation-building project. Therefore, if the nationalist elite of the 1920s were "disillusioned" with constitutionalism, they had foreclosed a political option *before* it had a chance to be put into practice. Turning away from the Constitutional

Revolution's "myth of failure," the following chapter studies the emergence of Iran's authoritarian nationalism in a broader global paradigm, defined by the upheaval of World War I, Iran's occupation by the Allies, the constitutionalist elite's temporary alliance with Imperial Germany and the impact of the Bolshevik revolution. While this volatile and fluid historical context remains to be systematically studied, this chapter proposes to locate the genesis of Iran's authoritarian nationalist ideology in an intellectual encounter with Germany, traceable in the pages of Berlin-based Iranian nationalist periodicals *Kaveh, Iranshahr* and *Name-ye Farangestan*.

Afshin Marashi notes how the first coherent articulation of Iranian nationalism emerged precisely in the "time of political disintegration" between the 1911 Russian invasion and the rise of Reza Khan in the early 1920s.[4] As seen in Chapter 1, an inchoate proto-nationalist discourse had already been launched by late nineteenth-century thinkers such as Malkolm, Akhundzadeh, Kermani, Asadabadi and Agaoglu. The constitutional movement, and its revolutionary turn, then interjected elements of liberal democratic and social democratic ideology into this fledging discourse of nationalism. As seen in Chapter 1, except for Browne's *The Persian Revolution*, no coherent narration of Iranian nationalism existed when constitutionalism was put on hold in 1911. Though noted by only a few historians, modern political parties had appeared in the wake of the constitutional regime's 1910 restoration. The country's first modern political organization was the Democrat Party (*Demokrat/Ammiyun*), acting as the parliamentary representative of a network of underground social democratic groups that had extended from Baku to a few northern Iranian cities since 1905. Though totally unprecedented, the Democrat Party's modern political agenda and organizational structure made it the prototype of twentieth-century Iran's political parties, whether leftist or rightist.[5] The party's program demanded universal suffrage, equal citizenship rights regardless of gender and religion, separation of political and religious powers, universal conscription, income tax, land reform, labor protection laws, compulsory public education, freedoms of expression, the press and associations, and the nationalization of forests, pastures and mines. Defining the core agenda of Iran's socialist and democratic parties, these demands were partly adopted during the Pahlavi regime's White Revolution (see Chapters 5 and 6) and continued to animate both secular and Islamic leftist and populist factions during the 1978–1979 revolution and its aftermath. Significantly, the Democrat Party's program included a commitment to "modernity" (*tajddod*), defined in an evolutionary Eurocentric fashion:

To the East, the twentieth century is what the seventeenth century was to Western countries, meaning it is an era of modernity, when Asia, the bulk of humanity, is on the move, its decrepit feudalism being replaced by and surrendering to the onslaught of capitalism ... An older child of humanity, Iran too is destined to experience these inevitable evolutionary transformations, its decrepit feudalism and absolute despotism, of necessity giving way to modernity.[6]

In another alignment with global modernity, Iran's first right-wing political party borrowed its name, nomenclature and part of its program directly from its leftist social democratic rival. Thus, calling themselves Social Moderates (*Ejtema'iyun E'tedaliyun*), the conservative bloc in the Second Majles adopted the "social" half of the (Social) Democrat Party's label, while dropping its democratic half, all "moderated" to fit Islamic percepts on the sanctity of property, social rank and gender hierarchy.[7] As in the case of Islamic constitutionalism, Iran's intellectual encounter with social democracy engendered another modernist ideological innovation, namely Islamic socialism (see Chapters 4–6). During the unstable post-1911 decade, however, neither Social Democrats nor Social Moderates had the chance to build a popular base or advance a distinct nation-building agenda. The Social Moderates mainly countered the Democrat Party's more coherent ideology by appealing to Islam, rather than nationalism. Nor were the Democrats strictly nationalist, since they were in fact applying European social democracy's internationalist perspective to Iranian conditions. The Democrat Party's program, for example, claimed that given its deepening links with the outside world, Iran was bound to be transformed by the forces of modernity and capitalism.[8] The party's adherence to global paradigms was reflected in a debate on whether Iranian socialists were to act within a bourgeois democratic frame or advance a socialist agenda. Participants in this debate appealed for judgment to Europe's Marxist authorities, i.e. Germany's Karl Kautsky and Russia's Gregory Plekhanov.[9] In the end, the Democrat Party's program called for no more than a bourgeois democratic transition, a proposal that was nevertheless revolutionary, particularly considering the strong conservative backlash it generated (see below).

Meanwhile, the violent intrusion of World War I forced Iran's intellectual elite to reconsider the course of nation building as rapidly shifting global realignments placed the country's very existence in peril.[10] As in other Asian countries, the war had generated significant Iranian sympathy toward Imperial Germany, which was seen as a global counterweight to Russo-British imperialism. Curiously, Germany's impact on this formative period of Iranian nationalism, as well as on modern Iran more generally, remains little noted by historians. In the aftermath of the 1978–1979 revolution, intellectual historians became interested in German linkages to Iranian modernity. But the link was seen as primarily philosophical, focused particularly on the presumed impact of Martin Heidegger on Iranian thinkers during the second half of the twentieth century. As we shall see in Chapter 7, however, Heidegger was barely read and virtually unknown in Iran prior to the 1980s, when his philosophy was found to be useful in providing intellectual gloss to the post-revolutionary regime's Islamist ideology. Adopting a broader chronological and intellectual framework, this chapter will consider the impact of German counter-modernity, of which Heidegger's philosophy was only a late byproduct, on Iranian nationalism at its moment of birth between 1915 and the mid-1920s. To better understand this crucial but neglected German–Iranian ideological encounter, we need a brief background overview of certain German intellectual trends, particularly German Orientalism, in the wake of the Great War.

Iran and Asia in German Orientalism and Philosophy of History

Recent scholarship traces the origins of "Western" claims to superiority, particularly vis-à-vis an Islamic "Orient," to a time prior to Europe's colonial domination of Asia. During the Renaissance, for example, Italian Humanist thinkers had asserted the superiority of "Western culture," particularly relative to the Ottoman Empire. Unlike what Edward Said famously critiqued in *Orientalism*, such claims could not be linked to political domination, since at the time the Ottomans were Europe's most powerful empire.[11] Similarly, nineteenth-century German Orientalism was linked to premodern conceptions of German culture, predating the rise of Germany as a unified political entity. In these conceptions, German culture occupied a "middle ground" between the Orient/East and the Occident/West. The German Orient began with the Slavic and Islamic worlds, where

German-speaking communities had fought in the Crusades and, later, against the Ottoman Empire's expansion into central Europe. Premodern German images of the Orient, therefore, were largely negative, involving tropes of Muslim/Turkish aggression, violence, lasciviousness and deceit.[12] In the course of the eighteenth century, fearful images of the Orient gradually subsided as the relative decline of Ottoman power coincided with the Enlightenment's more positive appreciation of non-European cultures. Perhaps most significantly, nineteenth-century classical German Orientalism developed, unlike its British and French counterparts, without colonial linkages to Asia or the Ottoman Empire.[13]

Known for exceptional intellectual rigor, German Orientalism was intimately linked to nineteenth-century German-language studies of culture, history and philosophy. In particular, the German idea of "culture" focused on intellectual achievements shared through a common language and serving as the foundation of national identity. As Norbert Elias noted, the German preoccupation with culture classified the world's inhabitants according to essential "cultural" distinctions preceding modern national identities. This differed from French and British focus on notions of "civilization," which tended to assimilate cultural diversity to universal patterns, typically achieved within imperial frames. Broadly, in German perspectives, "culture" meant particularity, authenticity, autonomy and youthful vigor, while "civilization" was linked to domineering universalism, conformity and decadence. Ideologically, the culture-versus-civilization dichotomy served Germany's national unification, as it upheld the autonomy of German "culture" vis-à-vis the continental sway of French "civilization."[14] Originally, German notions of culture had anti-imperialist overtones, a feature that receded into the background when the Second German Reich developed its own grand imperial ambitions.[15]

Historiography, and particularly the field of world history, was another intellectual arena where German ideas had far-reaching ideological and political consequences. During the eighteenth century, Gottfried Herder (1744–1803) articulated a culture-based paradigm of world history that became widely influential in modern European historiography and early social science discipline formation.[16] Herder described the historical process in terms of birth, maturation and decline cycles of cultures. In his developmental scheme, the core ethos or spirit of each culture was the storehouse of its unique historical experience. Moreover, world history itself had a developmental design, unfolding in both time and space. It was born in the Orient and matured in ancient Greece and Rome, moved westward during Europe's middle ages, to be revived with the rise of the Germans. Herder, following the Roman historian Tacitus, depicted the Germans as a warlike people who carried the torch of civilization westward from Asia, while defending Christian Europe against Oriental invaders.[17] Explaining the decline of Asia, Herder believed India's brilliant ancient civilization had grown stagnant under the yoke of Oriental despotism, while ancient Iran's prominence continued into the Islamic era in Persian cultural production, such as the poetry of Sa'di. Herder thus "opened up the gate of Persian poetry to German literature," initiating a German Orientalist trend that identified Iran primarily with the glories of Persian literature. Building on Herder's theory of "national literature" as the core of national identity, Johann Wolfgang von Goethe (1749–1832) championed non-European national cultures, urging his followers to "compare them with themselves, respect them in their own context, and forget that Greeks and Romans ever existed." Relying on recent German translations of medieval Persian poetry, Goethe became an enthusiast of Hafiz, the inspiration of his famous *West-Eastern Divan*. He also found affinity with Shi'ism, seen as "Iranian Islam," for its purported qualities of tolerance, sophistication and esotericism.[18]

In a broader perspective, German thinkers were on the forefront of the "Oriental Renaissance" that swept post-Enlightenment Europe during the 1780s–1850s. Inspired by breakthrough translations of Sanskrit texts, this intellectual movement shifted Europe's admiring gaze Eastward, especially toward India. Prominent nineteenth-century German philosophers elevated ancient India's intellectual standing near or above the Greco-Roman and Judeo-Christian traditions.[19] Arthur Schopenhauer identified the Hindu-Buddhist tradition as the source of his own "transcendental idealism," a philosophical stand rejecting the "illusion of existence and personality," upholding instead "the will to live" in defiance of a material world of pain and decay. He also declared preference for India's malleable pantheism over the rigid monotheism he believed both Christianity and Islam had inherited from Judaism.[20] Schopenhauer's appreciation of "Oriental Wisdom" was shared by Friedrich Nietzsche, who returned to Pre-Socratic philosophy, aligning with a Dionysian Orient in opposition to Europe's heritage of Greek rationalism. Hence, in *Thus Spake Zarathustra*, an ancient Persian prophet became Nietzsche's mouthpiece to pronounce the death of the Judeo-Christian God, allowing his Superman's "Will to Power" to transcend the world of illusions and false idols.[21]

Kaveh's First Series: German-style Nationalism, Socialism and Orientalism

In an important sense, the history of Iranian nationalism began with the publication of *Kaveh*.[22]

By the second half of the nineteenth century, European theories of Indo-European linguistic affinities gradually acquired racial overtones. Thus, Germans were tied to an ancient "Aryan" race, originating somewhere in the Orient, i.e. the Caucasus or north India, and linked to "Iran," a term made synonymous with "the land of Aryans." In such schemes, the cultural achievements of Indians and Iranians were due to their supposedly Aryan racial origins, which made them superior to Semitic Arabs. This new racialist Orientalism, notes Rudi Matthee, then became "an internalized axiom of Iranian nationalism."[23]

The rise of Aryan race theories coincided with global European colonial domination, including that of almost all of Asia. The Asian sympathies of the Oriental Renaissance were now countered by a rigid discourse of European/Western superiority, explained in terms of racial and civil hierarchies. Meanwhile, following Europe's failed 1848–1849 revolutions, pan-German sentiments turned inward and chauvinistic, serving the rise of an aggressive Second German Reich. The Orient now was the target of German imperial expansionism, on a path through Slavic Poland and Eastern Europe, the Balkans, Crimea, the Caucasus, the Near East and Iran, to ultimately reach India. The Berlin–Baghdad railway was to be built on this path, pointing to larger imperial designs behind Germany's economic, political and military ties with Istanbul. Having suffered a long history of Russian, British and French imperialist aggression, the Ottoman Empire eventually aligned itself with Imperial Germany in World War I. In addition to its considerable military value, wartime alliance with Istanbul allowed Berlin to directly sponsor anti-colonial movements, and particularly Pan-Islamism among Ottoman subjects and all the way to India. Pan-Islamism, or more accurately "Islamic Unity" (*Ettehad-e Islam*), was a political movement initiated by Namik Kemal and Young Ottoman intellectuals of the 1870s in reaction to Russia's Pan-Slavic propaganda among the Orthodox Christian subjects of the Ottoman Empire.[24]

Awash with anti-British and anti-Russian sentiments, Iran too was ripe for a German alliance when World War I broke out. Though officially neutral, Iran was occupied by Russian, Ottoman and British armies, leading its semi-suspended constitutional government to welcome German support. Thus began a brief but significant partnership between Imperial Germany and Iran's fledgling constitutionalist nationalism. When Russian armies threatened to capture Tehran in the fall of 1915, a mostly Democrat Party faction of Majles deputies left the capital and soon formed a German-backed "provisional government" in Kermanshah. Financed by Germany and militarily backed by advancing Ottoman armies, this provisional national government then conducted a series of protracted military operations against the Allied occupation of Iran.[25] Politically, the provisional government was a coalition of pro-German Democrats, pro-Ottoman Pan-Islamists and nationalists with less clear-cut international affiliation. Hasan Taqizadeh and a few other Democrat leaders had been ideologically aligned with Germany's Social Democratic Party (SPD) before the war. Though it was Germany's largest political party, the SPD had little influence on foreign policy, which was decided by the Kaiser and a small military-bureaucratic elite. Cowed by this militaristic clique, SPD leaders had capitulated to support Germany's war effort. Backed by the SPD, the German government reached out to Asian socialists, as well as nationalists and Pan-Islamists, to forge a grand anti-Entente alliance. In 1914, Taqizadeh, who then resided in the US, was contacted by the German consulate in New York. He and his friend Reza Afshar agreed to help with pro-German propaganda among the Muslim subjects of the British Empire. The main target of this propaganda was India's anti-British Muslim activists, whose Berlin-based "revolutionary committee" had recommended Taqizadeh's recruitment. These Muslim revolutionaries received military training in preparation for an anti-British uprising in India, to be backed by a German–Ottoman invasion via Iran. At first, Taqizadeh and Afshar were to work as part of the India "revolutionary committee," but Taqizadeh insisted on setting up an independent committee of Iranians. Thus, shortly after his January 1915 arrival in Berlin, he began inviting Iranian nationalists in Istanbul and across Europe to join him in "the Iranian Committee for Cooperation with Germany." His call was answered by the cream of Iran's intellectual and political elite who then resided in Europe as exiles or for other reasons. The most famous of these were journalist Hosein Kazemzadeh, eminent scholars Mohammad Qazvini and Ebrahim Purdavood, pioneering modern fiction writer Mohammad-Ali Jamalzadeh, socialist parliamentarian Abdol-Hosein Sheybani (Vahidolmolk), parliamentarians Hosein-qoli Navab and Mirza Ali Farzin, revolutionary socialist Heydar Amuoghli, journalist and former minister Mohammad-Reza Mosavat, socialist educator Mohammad-Ali Tarbiat and parliamentarian mujtahid Faz-Ali Tabrizi.[26]

According to Taqizadeh, the activities of this "Berlin Circle" of Iranian nationalists were generously funded by the German government, which also paid its members living stipends.[27] In retrospect, such blatant sponsorship by a European power of Iran's nationalist elite might appear odd, if not embarrassing. Addressing this point, the only Persian-language study of the Berlin Circle has noted:

Most of this first generation stayed social democrat and committed to Enlightenment ideas. They had come to Berlin as nationalist and constitutionalist followers of a social democratic party. Their cooperation with Germans was for the cause of Iranian freedom and not German expansionism.[28]

The Berlin Circle's original socialist leaning is correctly recognized here. Unexplained, however, is the enormous challenge these intellectuals faced in trying to reconcile their fledgling Iranian nationalism to Pan-Islamism and socialism, as well as to German and Ottoman war aims. Given this highly conflicted agenda, and in the midst of an unprecedented global upheaval with unforeseeable consequences, the Berlin Circle began to articulate a comprehensive Iranian nationalist worldview in its flagship periodical *Kaveh*.[29] This remained a somewhat disingenuous endeavor as *Kaveh* tried to anchor its nationalism within rapidly shifting global geopolitics. Thus, the journals' first issue declared support for Imperial Germany's war effort,[30] followed by the second issue's call for creating a modern Iranian army staffed by German officers, devoting an entire article to the Kaiser's birthday celebration:

The victory of Germany and its allies being our greatest goal, as well as in our best interest, we Muslims pray to God, on this day of His Majesty Wilhelm II's birthday, wishing this beloved German Emperor longevity of life and reign, and asking for the final triumph of German armies, joined by the first independent Muslim monarchy, i.e. the great Ottoman government.[31]

Kaveh was equally deferential to German intellectual authority, and particularly Orientalist scholarship. The choice of the journal's title, for example, was explained in a first issue article, "Kaveh and His Flag," by Oskar Mann, a German scholar of Kurdish dialects. In addition to naming the journal after the legendary hero of Ferdowsi's *Shahnameh*, Mann proposed the changing of Iran's modern tricolor flag to "a form closer to historical truth." The flag's Lion and Sun emblem, presumably linked to Seljuk Turks, he argued, were to be dropped and its colors changed to red, yellow and purple, corresponding to Kaveh's flag, as described in *Shahnameh*.[32] Moreover, Mann edited *Kaveh*'s content, making sure it was in line with German war aims, a job that was taken over by another Orientalist, Sebastian Beck, when Mann died in 1917.[33] Taqizadeh's covert cooperation with scholars like Mann and Beck, who acted as political agents of their government, meant he was resorting to dissimulation (*taqieh*) when defending the impartiality of Orientalist scholarship. In 1918, for instance, *Kaveh* ran a series of articles, titled "The Best European Works on Iran," praising European scholars' discovery of Iran's historical identity and ancient nationhood. Addressing the allegation of linkage between Orientalism and European colonialism, the first of these articles argued:

Such interactions, between the East and the West, opened up a broad field of knowledge, called Orientalism (*sharq-shenasi*) ... Some Orientalists specialized in Arabic works and Arab civilization, while others focused on India and Iran, that is to say, the civilization of Aryan races ... According to some politically-minded Easterners, Orientalists have led their governments on the oppressive and shameful path of conquering and dominating Eastern countries ... In our opinion, while some Orientalists are biased and political, most dedicate their research and studies to furthering knowledge, truth and civilization ... A few have made sincere and honest sacrifices to champion weak nations and the Eastern civilization, even writing and acting against their own governments ... We must admit many of them know more about Iran and our ancestors' history, culture and religion than we do. Not a single Iranian knows Old Persian, Sanskrit or Avestan, whereas each of these languages is mastered by several European experts ... whose knowledge allows us to know about our ancient kings and ancestors ... The best way a nation can be politically educated and morally uplifted is to learn the history of its own ancient civilization. This is true particularly of a nation like Iran, whose Iranian spirit has endured despite thousands of years of foreign domination.[34]

While defending the intellectual integrity of European scholarship, such passages show the imprint of German Orientalist theories tying together language and race to history and nationhood. Crucially important is the German idea of a mystical "Iranian spirit" sustaining the nation's primordial existence. It must be noted that such deference to European intellectual authority was shared by almost all of Taqizadeh's collaborators in *Kaveh*. The outstanding exception was Mohammad Qazvini, who mostly agreed with *Kaveh*'s politics, but had a low estimation of Orientalist scholarship. Qazvini had lived and worked in Europe longer than Taqizadeh and was more familiar with modern European scholars. Consequently, he considered himself far superior, in knowledge of Persian and Arabic, as well as Islamic and Iranian history and literature, to his European peers.[35] In 1923, for example, he opined to Taqizadeh that "in no field of modern European sciences can we find as many charlatans as among the Orientalists, where charlatans abound a hundred times more than in any other field."[36] As a specific example, he cited French scholar Louis Massignon's study of Muslim mystic Al-Hallaj as utterly worthless.[37] Massignon, of course, would become a highly influential figure in Islamic studies, with his work on Hallaj being particularly appreciated by Iranian intellectuals like Ali Shariat'i (see Chapter 6).

The least noted feature of *Kaveh*'s first series (1915–1919) is its socialist orientation. During the war, *Kaveh* had displayed open affiliation with German social democracy, reporting on its own editors' and writers' participation in the activities of the Socialist International. For example, one of its summer 1917 lead articles covered the peace conference that factions of the Socialist International had tried to organize in neutral Sweden. Taqizadeh and Abdol-Hosein Sheybani had gone to Stockholm to represent Iran in "discussion with socialist leaders who embody the world's greatest power and are perhaps its future rulers."[38] A former socialist Majles deputy, Sheybani was commissioned by the Iranian embassy in Berlin to present a resolution at the Stockholm meeting, asking European socialists to support Iran against foreign intervention.[39] While the conference never convened officially, Sheybani and Taqizadeh were able to meet with socialist delegations from other countries, including members of Russia's provisional revolutionary government, who promised to reverse tsarist policies toward Iran.[40] This promise was soon fulfilled by the Bolshevik regime's renunciation of secret Entente treaties, including partition plans for Iran and the Ottoman Empire. Subsequently, Iran's independence and territorial integrity was recognized in the 1918 Soviet-German Brest-Litovsk peace treaty.[41] *Kaveh*'s January 1918 editorial hailed the Brest-Litovsk treaty as "a promise of life" for Iran, calling for "a day of national celebration." Consequently, *Kaveh* redoubled its demand for British withdrawal from Iran and Britain's recognition of Iranian sovereignty.[42] Imperial Germany's 1918 collapse made its political commitments irrelevant, but the Bolshevik pledge, at Brest-Litovsk, to Iran's independence was reiterated by Lenin and eventually incorporated into the 1921 Soviet-Iranian Treaty.[43] The latter treaty and Bolshevik diplomacy helped preserve Iran's independence at a time when British attempts at turning Iran into a semi-protectorate were resisted by Iranian nationalists.[44] *Kaveh*'s positive appraisal of the Russian Revolution's contribution to Iranian independence echoed in Iranian historiography, including even in Pahlavi-era textbooks.[45] Decades later, Taqizadeh still argued:

The fall of the Tsarist Empire due to the Russian Revolution was the greatest historic event affecting Iran during the past 150 years. Without a doubt, if not for the Russian revolution neither Iran nor Turkey would have existed after World War I.[46]

Similar estimations of Soviet contribution to Turkish independence are acknowledged by historians of the Ottoman Empire's transition to the Turkish Republic. In 1920, Lenin began correspondence with Mustafa Kemal, leading to Soviet recognition of Turkey's National Pact and a 1921 Turkish-Soviet treaty of friendship, settling border disputes and providing the Ankara regime with arms and financial help.[47] During his brief tactical alliance with Bolshevism, Mustafa Kemal even claimed to be a "Muslim communist," adopting the rhetoric of Central Asia's "national communists" like Mirsayet Soltangaliev. He wrote to the Soviet authorities about Turkey aligning with other Muslim countries to join "the enslaved people of Asia and Africa" in rising against

European capitalist imperialism, while declaring to Ankara's Grand National Assembly that "Bolshevism includes the most exalted principles of Islam."[48]

The rise of Bolshevism, followed by Germany's collapse and postwar revolutionary upheaval, forced Taqizadeh and his Berlin group to redefine Iranian nationalism in a reconfigured global context. Mohammad Qazvini, for example, had witnessed Berlin's 1919 worker-soldier soviets and revolutionary socialist government. Commenting on the simultaneous collapse of German, Russian and Austro-Hungarian empires, he wrote: "Now comes the turn of the socialists ... Europe's three emperors are destroyed, while Bolshevism is spreading everywhere like an oil stain."[49] The last issues of *Kaveh*'s first series thus reflected the Berlin Circle's growing sense of unease and bewilderment. Suddenly, the great expectations they had pinned on the triumph of Imperial Germany had come to naught. By early 1919, Sheybani, who also was observing the German revolution firsthand, reported of the Berlin Circle's demise and its members return to Iran:

We rightly assumed Germany's defeat of Russia and Britain, powers with a long history of intervention against Iranian independence, would be beneficial to our country ... Unfortunately for Iranian nationalists and democrats, after about five years of bloodshed, destruction and chaos, the war's outcome dashed our hopes.[50]

The March 1919 issue of *Kaveh* featured a lead article on "the Victory of Social Democrats in Germany," providing a brief but accurate account of German socialism, covering the fall of the Second Reich, the failure of Germany's socialist revolution and the emergence of a moderate social democratic republic.[51] In the aftermath of these developments, socialist and pro-German tendencies diminished in *Kaveh*'s second series, while the search for an alternative worldview that could globally contextualize Iranian nationalism continued.[52]

Kaveh's Second Series: Surrendering to Europe and Its Enlightened Despotism

Kaveh's wartime socialist and pro-German orientation reflected Taqizadeh's and his cohorts' desperate need for a powerful global benefactor, rather than ideological convictions. While the war continued, and especially after the fall of Imperial Russia, *Kaveh*'s anti-British rhetoric became more pronounced, with its lead articles attacking British presence not only in Iran but in India and elsewhere. However, the sudden postwar shift in the European balance of power caused a corresponding ideological realignment in *Kaveh*. In August 1919, *Kaveh*'s first series folded and, in January 1920, Taqizadeh and a few former Berlin associates launched the journal's second series, which lasted until 1922. The radical new departure of *Kaveh*'s second series was summed up in its first issue by Taqizadeh's (in)famous proposal of "the unqualified acceptance and adoption of European civilization."[53] As we shall see in the following chapters, this idea soon became anathema to Iranian nationalism. Decades later, Taqizadeh explained his own "throwing the first bombshell of surrender to the West" as a desperate reaction to the urgent need for catching up with Europe.[54] In his 1960 retrospective, Taqizadeh claimed to have adopted the idea of total surrender to Europe from Ottoman reformers like Abdullah Cevdet.[55] This is quite plausible, given the drift of Cevdet's writings, such as the following passages published in 1912 in the journal *Ijtihad*:

The relation between Europe and us is the relation between strength and weakness, between science and ignorance ... Yes, Europe means supremacy; let hatred for it be far from me. My hatred is turned against those things that are the obstacles to our attaining power equal to that of Europe ... Our mortal enemy is our own inertia, ignorance, fanaticism, and our own blind following of tradition ... The West is our teacher; to love it is to love science, progress, material and moral advancement ... To be an industrious and thankful disciple of the West – that is our lot! ... The West slapped Japan only once; it awakened. We have been slapped a thousand times; if we are still not awake, is it the West's fault? ... Let us face the mirror and look at ourselves courageously ... We have to understand one thing – there are not two civilizations, there is only one to which to turn, and that is Western civilization, which we must take into our hands whether it be rosy or thorny.[56]

Whether originally following the Young Ottomans or not, by the early 1920s, Iranian nationalists held the same beliefs concerning the necessity of emulating Europe. According to the writer Jamalzadeh, members of the Berlin Circle "agreed unanimously that, except in religion and language, Iranians must follow Europeans in every way."[57] This conviction was shared by conservatives like Qazvini, who confided to Taqizdeh: "One must fearlessly pursue this task, which like a sharp sickle quickly cuts out the weeds of superstition at their roots."[58] But the Iranian idea of "total surrender to Europe" was not an innovation of 1920s émigré intellectuals. It had in fact originated a few decades earlier, in modernizing circles affiliated with the Qajar court, exemplified by the father and son intellectual team of Mohammad-Hosein and Mohammad-Ali Forughi. Around the turn of the century, the Forughis had co-authored "the most widely read history textbook of early twentieth-century Iran," *An Elementary Overview of World History*.[59] Dedicated to Iran's last pre-constitutional monarch, Mozaffar al-din Shah, this text served as master narrative for the state's modern history education project. Among the book's features was a novel approach to the narration and periodization of Iranian history, based on structures and divisions proposed in eminent British Orientalist Edward Browne's *Literary History of Persia*.[60] Admiring European civilization for achievements in science and learning, the Forughis also embraced a "survival of the fittest" civilizational approach to contemporary global history. According to them, following the eclipse of its once brilliant civilization, Iran, like the rest of the world, had to adopt modern European civilization, or be annihilated:

[History] placed the regions of the globe in the hands of the people of Europe ... Whoever has money, power, and knowledge does as he wishes. After this, the most that other peoples and nations can do is to protect themselves and this is not possible except by one means—in other words, by accepting modern civilization (*tamaddon-e jadid*). Every country and nation that wants to avoid destruction and annihilation ... must make haste in accepting the civilization of the age (*tamaddon-e vaqt*) because the basic pretext of European conquest is to introduce civilization.[61]

Thus, by the early twentieth century, the necessity of surrender to modern European civilization was axiomatic among Iranian intellectuals, the only caveat being its extent and the problem of its grafting onto "native" Iranian culture. In the aftermath of the Great War, the politics of this "civilizational surrender" became manifest when Prime Minister Vosuq al-Dowleh's cabinet came close to signing a formal treaty turning Iran into a virtual British protectorate. The proposed 1919 Anglo–Iranian agreement called for strengthening Iran's central government, a top priority of Iranian nationalists. At the same time, it would have placed Iran's military, finances and foreign relations under the supervision of Britain, an occupying power opposing Iran's participation at the Versailles peace conference.[62] The mood of despairing capitulation to British demands is reflected in contemporary sources, exemplified in comments by Mohammad-Ali Forughi, soon to emerge as the early Pahlavi era's most prominent intellectual statesman. In 1919, while serving on the Iranian delegation to the founding meeting of the League of Nations, Forughi wrote:

No one says we should go against what Britain wants. The point, however, is the extent of subservience to the British, which should not go so far as our begging them to come put leashes around our necks.[63]

In the end, however, the 1919 agreement could not be ratified due to nationalist opposition, backed by Moscow's new Bolshevik regime. Meanwhile, Taqizadeh was calling on émigré nationalists in Europe to look to the US, as Iran's new foreign benefactor. In a 1921 letter to fellow nationalist Mahmud Afshar, for example, he wrote:

To set things on a proper path, the main point, in my view, is attracting Americans to Iran and handing them the administration of affairs. Utmost efforts must be made to draw the U.S. into Iran. Concessions should be granted and American advisors must be hired for financial and public projects, agriculture, trade, transportation and telegraph, while American schools must be fully supported.[64]

By the end of World War I, the US had emerged as a powerful game-changer in international relations, echoing the Bolsheviks' call for a new global order, where every nation could enjoy the right of self-determination. This promise was the most important of President Woodrow Wilson's Fourteen-Point program, which was especially resonant across the Asian and African colonial world. But the "Wilsonian Moment" of Afro-Asiatic optimism toward US global intervention quickly passed as Wilson himself acceded to the Anglo-French revival of the colonial order at the Versailles Peace Conference.[65] Taqizadeh's enthusiasm for drawing Americans into Iran, however, was not a mere reaction to the so-called Wilsonian Moment. Rather, it was his relapse into the familiar pattern of searching for a third power to counter-balance Anglo-Russian intervention in Iran. At any rate, while *Kaveh* did not explicitly mention the US, the call for hiring foreign advisors became one of its constant refrains.

It was prominent in an important list of demands published in a January 1921 issue and included among the "urgent reforms" recommended in a December 1921 issue. *Kaveh*'s January 1921 reform agenda was important because its key parts coincided with similar nationalist proposals inside Iran, soon to be officially adopted under the new Pahlavi Dynasty (see below and Chapter 3). Arranged "according to significance," these demands were:

1) Ceaselessly promoting public education; 2) Publishing useful books and translating European books; 3) Accepting unconditionally the principles of European civilization; 4) Spreading European-style physical education; 5) Maintaining Iran's national unity; 6) Safeguarding Persian, as national language, from corruption; 7) Waging merciless war on opium and alcohol; 8) Struggling against prejudice and for full legal equality among followers of different religions; 9) Waging war on contagious diseases, especially malaria, tuberculosis, typhus, venereal and childhood diseases; 10) Safeguarding Iran's independence; 11) Renovating Iran along European lines, especially by importing machinery; 12) Women's liberation, their education and cultivation, and accomplishing their rights; 13) Waging war on lying and deceit; 14) Wiping out the corrupt practice of "diplomacy" [careerism and nepotism]; 15) Wiping out the shameful practice of unnatural [same sex] love, one of our people's oldest vices and an obstacle to civilization; 16) Waging war on frivolousness, mockery and hyperbole; encouraging instead public seriousness; 17) Reviving beneficial old Iranian national customs and traditions.[66]

This program's call for the "unconditional acceptance of the principles of European civilization" is repeated several times and in various ways, along with an emphasis on Iran's independence and national unity. But the only feature of Iranian culture deemed worth "safeguarding" is Persian as the "national language," whereas the revival of unspecified "old Iranian national customs and traditions" is mentioned at the bottom of the list. More importantly, *Kaveh*'s abandonment of socialist or democratic commitments is evident in the above agenda's lack of reference to social reform or constitutionalism. Instead, several articles justify *Kaveh*'s "cultural turn" by arguing that, without prior moral cultivation no nation could secure political sovereignty. *Kaveh*'s new nation-building project therefore had become a culture war, similar to those underway in Ottoman and Republican Turkey and the Russo-Turkish *Jedid* project. In Chapter 3, we shall see how the majority of interwar Iran's statesmen and nationalist thinkers embraced *Kaveh*'s nation-building project. At the very top of *Kaveh*'s agenda was a single (Persian) language educational system, *teaching* the nation mental and physical "fitness," while purging its "infirmities" of contagious disease, substance addiction, frivolousness and "unnatural" sexuality. Noting the centrality of education to the cultural project of nation building, Afshin Marashi has described the modern Iranian state as "pedagogical." This is apt if pedagogy is understood as a *political* process whereby the state forcibly acculturates diverse populations into a homogenous national community. It also must be emphasized that according to *Kaveh*'s "pedagogical" agenda, a modern Iranian nation becomes possible only through its "unconditional" conformity to European cultural standards.

At another level, *Kaveh*'s 1921 program hints at the secularist impetus that would become more pronounced in Pahlavi-era nationalism. This was explicit in the call for "equality among followers of different religions," a sensitive point *Kaveh* had to clarify in subsequent issues. Responding to readers' criticism, a March 1921 article insisted that "none of *Kaveh*'s writers are Babi, Baha'i or Isma'ili, follow religions other than Islam, or believe in changing Iran's religion." *Kaveh*, it was claimed, was merely restating Iran's "constitutional principle of equality among followers of different religions." However, the same article mentioned *Kaveh*'s belief in "reforming" Islam by purging it from what was contrary to "reason, science and civilization" (*aql, elm va tammadon*).[67] In a "Protestant" posture, *Kaveh* insisted that making Islam compatible with reason meant the restoration of the religion's original "purity."[68] As we shall see in Chapter 4, this would become a central argument of 1930s–1940s Shi'i reformers, like Shari'at Sangelaji and Ahmad Kasravi.

In sum, *Kaveh*'s retreat from constitutionalism anticipated the rise of 1920s–1930s Pahlavi-era authoritarian nationalism. Ejecting both socialist and democratic perspectives, the 1921 program completely ignored the dire needs of the urban and rural lower classes or the political empowerment of citizens. Nor did the program's obligatory mention of "women's liberation" propose any specific rights or beneficial programs for women. In fact, *Kaveh* circumvented politics by claiming its desired reforms could be accomplished by "the Iranian people themselves" without recourse to state officials or parliamentary legislation. At the same time, it recommend working "in line with government politics," in order to "strengthen existing governments" (*taqviyat-e hokomat-e vaqt*) and "creating security" (*tolid-e amniyat*). Once a strong central government was established, *Kaveh* further argued, it had to accomplish the following: First, the disarming and settlement of the tribes; second, ending "brigandage" and purging politics of corruption; third, establishing political freedom and equality ("democracy") and improving the peasants' lot by bringing education, agricultural credit and machinery to the countryside, as well as by strengthening "the villager's right in his own land"; fourth, punishing all transgression, particularly in public affairs; fifth, fighting against corrupt and careerist politicians, parliamentarians and journalists.[69] Once again, *Kaveh*'s references to "democracy," "freedom" and "political equality" remained rhetorical flourishes, without specific definition and content. Similarly, its passing reference to "strengthening the villager's rights in his own land" was far from the Democrat Party's demands for land reform and advocacy of rights for laboring rural and urban classes.

By the end of its run, therefore, *Kaveh* was advocating "enlightened despotism" rather than "social democratic revolution."[70] The journal's 1921 nation-building proposal was a project of cultural transformation imposed on "traditional society" by a centralized state monopolizing political authority. Aligning with illiberal notions of sovereignty gaining ground in Iranian nationalism, *Kaveh*'s last words on politics were unambiguous:

We believe only three options exist for ruling Iran. First, benevolent despotism, prompting progress and civilization, in other words what Europeans call "enlightened despotism," similar to the rule of Peter the Great in Russia, the Mikado in Japan, and, to some extent, Mohammad Ali Pasha in Egypt. Second, malevolent despotism, which most despotic governments, with a few exceptions, actually are. Third, flawed and imperfect constitutionalism. A fourth option, i.e. a benevolent perfect constitutionalism, is undoubtedly preferable to all of the above. But that is possible only in progressive countries and not in Iran, and hence irrelevant to our discussion.[71]

According to this article, Iran's best option was "a patriotic, civilized, and domineering despot." But finding this kind of enlightened despot was improbable in Iran, where old-fashioned despotism was deeply entrenched and hence likely to continue.[72] *Kaveh* hence concluded:

Therefore, Iran's choices are only between a dark, corrupt and vicious despotism ... and an imperfect, mixed up peasant-style (*dehati*) constitutionalism ... Undoubtedly, imperfect constitutionalism, even ten times worse than ours, is preferable to ... despotism. We owe every existing or potential facet of progress and civilization only to constitutionalism.[73]

Thus, while paying lip service to "backward peasant constitutionalism," Taqizadeh and his *Kaveh* collaborators admitted their preference for "a patriotic, civilized, and domineering despot." This political perspective was articulated in Weimar Berlin, where Germany's nascent liberal democracy seemed shaky in comparison with Europe's rising modern dictatorships in Italy and the Soviet Union. It is important to note that *Kaveh*'s authoritarian nationalism was framed within an innovative modernist worldview. The need for a revamped "worldview" was specifically broached in a 1921 article titled "Indian and Greek Worldviews," which proposed the Persian term *"binesh"* for "worldview," equivalent to *"conception du monde"* in French and *"Weltanschauung"* in German. According to this article, "Eastern" (*sharqi*) worldviews were spiritual and metaphysical, while the West (*gharb*) had developed a more secular, rational and materialistic worldview:

Locating these two different notions in India and Greece, we can call the Eastern one an "Indian worldview," whereas Western ideas and reasoning correspond to a "Greek worldview."

The Indian worldview had shaped Asia's Aryan and Semitic cultures, while Europe's Roman, German and Latin cultures were informed by the Greek worldview. Despite its spiritual depth, the Indian worldview eventually succumbed to the material strength sustained by Britain's Western worldview. Iran's historical "misfortune," it was further argued, was related to the Indian "origin and essence of its worldview and civilization." Iranians, like Europeans, were racially Aryan, but the vicissitudes of their long history had cut them off from the Greek worldview, i.e. "the sun and fountainhead of universal knowledge and cultivation." Iran's break with the West, according to *Kaveh*, originated in the Greco-Persian wars and solidified with the coming of Islam, a Semitic religion. In contrast, Europe was set on a progressive path by adopting the Greek worldview, to which Christianity was assimilated, despite its Semitic origin.[74] The article's conclusion repeated Taqizadeh's call for the wholesale acceptance of modern European civilization, an argument now backed by *Kaveh*'s embrace of a superior "Western Worldview." Enormously influential in subsequent decades, this foundational *weltanschauung* of Iranian nationalism found its first articulation in the political and cultural milieu of Weimar Berlin. Equally remarkable, as well as scarcely noted by historians, is the fact that the powerful "anti-Western" intellectual strand of Iranian nationalism also originated in Berlin and in the pages of *Iranshahr,* the periodical that succeeded *Kaveh* in 1922.

Iranshahr's Weltanschauung: The Decline of the West and Iran's "Spiritual Revolution"

We have said repeatedly that Iran should not become Europeanized, in essence and appearance, nor should it remain in its present unfortunate state. Instead, it must make progress by creating a civilization that can be called Iranian.

Iranshahr, *1924.*[75]

Kaveh finally ceased to publish when Taqizadeh and most of its original staff returned to Iran. Those who remained in Berlin then launched the periodical *Iranshahr,* which published forty-eight issues between 1922 and 1927. Except for an important 2002 article, Iranian historiography has paid scant attention to *Iranshahr*'s pioneering advocacy of a nationalist discourse combining a radical critique of European civilization with the call for an Iranian "spiritual revolution."[76] As we saw, *Kaveh*'s nationalism was contradictory and shifting, relying haphazardly on European intellectual authority and finally "surrendering" to it completely. *Iranshahr,* on the other hand, signaled a radical intellectual departure by rejecting, at the very outset, *Kaveh*'s "Western Worldview" and "surrender" to European civilization. Ironically, *Iranshahr*'s nationalist ideology was more firmly rooted in a European, and particularly German, intellectual background. Basically, *Iranshahr* originated a discourse that tied together three foundational axioms of Iranian nationalist ideology. First, it argued that modern nation building was predicated upon the regeneration of a "national spirit," via a *moral and religious revolution.* This was in line with the ideas of Ottoman-Turkish nationalist intellectuals such as Zia Gokalp, who were in turn influenced by European social thinkers, particularly Emile Durkheim.[77] Second, and again showing the imprint of contemporary European thought, *Iranshahr* located the origin of Iran's "national spirit" in its pre-Islamic past and "Aryan" racial affiliations. Third, and perhaps most importantly, it defined Shi'i Islam as the religion adapted historically to Iran's "national spirit" and hence most conducive to its modern revival. As noted in Chapter 1, Ahmed Aqaoglu, following Orientalist scholars, had first suggested somewhat similar ideas, but *Iranshahr* fused them together into an elaborate synthesis linking Iran's "national spirit" to racial Aryanism, mystical Shi'ism, and archaic-imperial historical memory. *Iranshahr*'s most original contribution to nationalist ideology was its linking of a radical critique of European modernity to the moral-religious revival of indigenous culture. As we shall see in Chapter 4, this new perspective deeply influenced Iran's major nationalist thinkers, most notably Ahmad Kasravi.

Iranshahr's ideological innovation was firmly rooted in Weimar Germany's cultural milieu, something that historians of Iranian modernity, following *Iranshahr*'s claims to originality, have ignored or downplayed.[78] To properly appreciate this intellectual linkage, a brief foray into the creative intellectual cauldron of 1920s Germany is necessary. Most German intellectuals and academics had welcomed the Great War as a moral crusade pitting their own supposedly superior culture against British "shop-keeper" capitalism as well as decadent French universalism and socialism.[79] Imperial Germany's legacies of authoritarian politics, militarism and cultural chauvinism survived under the Weimar Republic. Conservative intellectuals saw the Weimar regime as an imposition by Germany's enemies and too weak in facing the challenge of Bolshevism. This deep-rooted right-wing trend in German political culture formed the intellectual foundation of Nazi ideology.[80] In the Great War's immediate aftermath, belief in German culture as panacea to Europe's ongoing instability was most famously articulated in Oswald Spengler's *The Decline of the West*.[81] Heir to Herder's tradition, Spengler saw global history as a chaotic battleground where cultures and civilizations, each driven by its vital core values, competed and clashed. In Spengler's normative taxonomy of old and new civilizations, modern Europe was labeled "Faustian," because it had traded off its moral "soul" for material gain and worldly domination. More specifically, and similar to Marxists, Spengler saw capitalist imperialism as the peak of

European civilization's predatory global domination, as well as its "winter season" of decay and fall.[82]

The Decline of the West caused a sensation in Germany and across Europe; its Russian translation, for example, set a sales record in the Soviet Union and elicited comments from Lenin.[83] In a crucial difference, however, Spengler rejected Marxist internationalism, believing instead that humanity could be saved only by following German standards of high culture.[84] His book's second volume (1922) advocated the revitalization of the German nation through a "spiritual revolution."[85] While this German cultural chauvinism was not universally welcomed, Spengler's vision of a decaying Western civilization resonated well with similar intellectual convictions prevalent in Europe during the period between the two World Wars. In addition to Marxists, influential thinkers across the political spectrum – including Max Weber, Arnold Toynbee and Sigmund Freud – were pessimistic about European civilization's rationality, future prospects and even its short-term survival.[86] They were joined by Christian moralists who also preached against the West's secular materialistic drift, some warning of its vulnerability vis-à-vis rival religions and civilizations, particularly Islam.[87]

Following Germany's defeat in World War I, Spengler advocated a nationalistic form of socialism. *The Decline of the West* was no Nazi manifesto, but its central themes and sentiments could develop in proto-fascist directions.[88] In 1920, Spengler published *Prussianism and Socialism*, calling for a "national socialist" regime, uniting German workers, soldiers, technocrats and intellectuals to overthrow the Weimar republic and contain Bolshevism.[89] The same year, Adolf Hitler crucially added the adjective "National" to the name of the Socialist German Workers' Party, an obscure organization he had recently joined.[90] While Spengler kept a critical distance from Nazism, his philosophy of history, like jurist Carl Schmitt's "Friend-Foe" theory of politics and Martin Heidegger's metaphysics of the "Authentic Being," provided Nazism with intellectual and philosophical gloss.[91] Schmitt's two short books, *Dictatorship* (1921) and *Political Theology* (1922), depicted modern political sovereignty as ultimately arbitrary and dictatorial. The modern state, according to Schmitt, emerges when inherently unstable liberal constitutionalism is replaced by a political faction imposing its binding "decision" on all contenders.[92] He also agreed with Spengler's condemnation of modernity and the West for being "capitalistic, mechanistic, relativistic; a world of traffic, technique and organization."[93] Similar themes and concepts, such as "nihilism," "the spiritual decline of the earth," "the darkening of the world," "the emasculation of the spirit" and "technological frenzy," permeate Heidegger's early writings. Like Spengler and other German conservatives, Heidegger equally loathed modernity's Bolshevik and Anglo-American variants, finding political "authenticity" only in German culture.[94]

There is no indication that Iranian intellectuals in 1920s Berlin had read or even heard of Spengler, not to mention Heidegger or Schmitt. Nevertheless, *Iranshahr*'s radical anti-Western departure reflects the intellectual imprint of contemporary German critique of Western modernity. *Iranshahr*'s writers more likely were exposed to German counter-modernity as it resonated in contemporary Ottoman-Turkish nationalist thought. As we saw, *Kaveh*'s embrace of "Western Civilization" was affiliated with intellectual trends, such as those set by Zia Gokalp. But another strand of Ottoman-Turkish nationalism followed thinkers such as Spengler, Toynbee and Henri Bergson to see Western civilization in crisis and decline. This trend began in the late nineteenth century and overlapped with official Pan-Islamic sentiments. A version of it was adopted by Sultan Abdulhamid, who also saw Western civilization as a combination of two basic components: "technology" and "ideas." To strengthen themselves, the Ottomans needed to adopt Western technology, but they had to reject "poisonous" Western "ideas," returning instead to Islam.[95] Cemil Aydin has shown how modernist Ottoman political culture changed its earlier emphasis on selective emulation of Europe to an "anti-Western" stance around World War I. Ottoman intellectuals had in fact preceded Spengler in their diagnosis of European civilization's deep crisis, looking instead to Asia, and particularly Japan, for successful models of self-strengthening. Just prior to the outbreak of World War I, influential Pan-Islamist Ahmed Hilmi (1865–1914) had criticized Western civilization's immorality, crass materialism and Social Darwinist politics, predicting a destructive upheaval in Europe. Celal Nuri (1882–1936) proposed a Realpolitik conception of Pan-Islamism in international relations, his 1913 *Islamic Unity* foreseeing a European war that would accelerate Asia's "awakening" with a colonial revolt against Western imperialism. Similarly, Ismail Naci in several works, all written before World War I, defined Pan-Islamism as a grand strategy of

Ottoman self-strengthening via a new geopolitical orientation beyond the loss of the Balkans and toward Muslim territories in Asia. These late Ottoman Pan-Islamists, however, were neither religious anti-modernists, nor doctrinally "anti-Western." Most of them condemned Western imperialism while appreciating European Enlightenment, and some even proposed an Anglo-French alliance in the coming war.[96]

Going back to 1920s Berlin's Iranian nationalist circles, the change from *Kaveh*'s Eurocentric worldview to the Iran-centered *weltanschauung* of *Iranshahr* is apparent in the very names of the two periodicals. *Kaveh* was named after the blacksmith leader of *Shahnameh*'s famous uprising against royal oppression, a choice hinting at the periodical's initially socialist leanings. *Iranshahr*, on the other hand, meant "Imperial Iran," declaring identification with pre-Islamic imperial glory and grandeur. Characteristically, *Iranshahr*'s editor, Hasan Kazemzadeh (1883–1962) later would change his own surname to Iranshahr. Born in Tabriz, Kazemzadeh was yet another Azeri pioneer of Iranian nationalism, whose intellectual pedigree was more cosmopolitan than Taqizadeh's. He had studied in Istanbul (1904–1910) and then lived in France, England and Belgium, where he became involved in socialist activities. A veteran constitutionalist, as a Democrat Party member, Kazemzadeh joined *Kaveh*'s staff in 1915 and was dispatched to Iran as the journal's representative in the pro-German "provisional government" of Kermanshah. Following his participation in German-sponsored political and military campaigns, he was exiled to Ottoman territory, whence he returned to Berlin in 1917. When *Kaveh* finally folded, a small and mostly scholarly group of Iranians remained in Berlin to help Kazemzadeh publish *Iranshahr*. The most famous of these were eminent literary scholar Mohammad Qazvini, historians Gholam-Reza Rashid Yasami and Abbas Eqbal-Ashtiani, fiction writer Morteza Moshfeq Kazemi (1902–1977) and future Marxist intellectual Taqi Arani (1903–1940).[97] *Iranshahr*'s very first editorial declared a new agenda for saving Iran in the midst of an endemic global crisis:

We start publishing this magazine at a time when the entire world, and particularly Germany, is shaken by an economic and social crisis … *Iranshahr* magazine will strive to prepare the grounds for the cultivation of the spirit of a young and free Iran. It will strive to create the free and pure conditions for the spiritual growth of a new Iranian race. It will expose the secrets of the European nations' progress, explaining what Iran really needs to take from European civilization.[98]

The first issue also featured an article, titled "Orientalism and Occidentalism," which literally reversed *Kaveh*'s "Western world-view," calling on Iranians to adopt instead an "Eastern perspective," labeled "Occidentalism" (*ghrabshenasi*).[99] The break with *Kaveh* deepened in issue no. 3, with an article on "Science and Morality," featuring a strong moral condemnation of Western civilization. The article credited science and technology for freeing humanity from "superstition, illusions, and savagery," providing benefits such as railroads, telegraph, telephone and steam ships. It then asked whether modern people felt more content than those of previous times. Lacking modern material comforts, the author argued, people in the past found solace and contentment in ethics and morality. In contrast, and despite great scientific and technological progress, contemporary Europeans were less content, due to modern life's moral failings and deficiencies:

Today, no European nation considers itself fortunate, and no one is content with the life they live. Misery and discontent with life are an epidemic disease, while moral corruption is fast spreading among all of these nations ... Unless their governments find a solution, European nations will become like Iran, because science and technology will not be able to contain moral decline.[100]

From the outset, therefore, *Iranshahr* forcefully argued that without a fundamental "reform of social morality," the mere adoption of European science and technology would ruin Iran.[101] As we shall see in the following chapters, this moral critique of Western civilization was to become axiomatic in the 1930s–1940s writings of Ahmad Kasravi and later embraced by a host of secular and religious Iranian intellectuals during the 1950s–1970s. Back in the early 1920s, *Iranshahr* quickly had moved from critiquing Western modernity to its complete rejection as a model for Iran. A 1923 article warned against the idea of importing European civilization as an "antidote" to Iran's ills:

This antidote of Western civilization (*nushdaru-ye tamaddon-e gharb*), which is to save our new generation, is itself polluted by poison, causing the murderous annihilation of entire societies and leading to the current downfall of humanity. This is a mystery crying out to be resolved, something that is among our main tasks.[102]

In the next issue, Kazemzadeh sketched an outline of European history, criticizing both traditional religion and modern secularism. The Enlightenment and modern scientific progress, he argued, had weakened organized religion and clerical power, but they also created materialistic capitalism, the new bane of Western civilization:

During the past centuries, the greatest inspiration of European nations has been capitalism, meaning the sovereignty of wealth or capital, something which is born of materialism, meaning the worship of material things. Having accumulated all power, capitalism has replaced the dominance of kingship, religion, and all that previously inspired and moved humans. It also caused the recent World War, turning Europe into a battleground of greed, hatred and prejudice.[103]

He continued with a vivid condemnation of Europe's obsession with materialism:

Western civilization has drowned humankind in materialism, allowing no outlet for humanity's spiritual exaltation. Western civilization has dragged human life down to a bestial level, and in some ways even below that. Millions of humans are daily dispatched to factories, toiling like animals or machines, returning to homes or taverns each night, only to resume the same routine the next day. How are they different from sheep and cattle daily taken to pasture by shepherds? Because of this civilization, people are drowned in greed and thirst for blood; in pursuit of wealth and material pleasure, they violate the rights of others, deceiving each other and knowing no other kind of life; like fish immersed in water, they are incapable of conceiving a different and better world.[104]

If Iran were not to follow in the destructive path of modern Europe, argued *Iranshahr*, it had to accomplish its potential for authentic "nationhood" through a "spiritual and moral revolution":

To shake up a sleepy depressed Iran, to make it bounce back to life from its death sentence, to give it a new spirit, and to pump warm young blood in its veins, we must inject a powerful life-giving messianic elixir into its social body .... History itself and the experience of many nations testify that the one and only potent goal and inspiration for the Iranian nation is indeed "nationhood" (*melliyat*) ... Our nationhood is defined by our being Iranian (*Iraniyat*), which includes all we possess ... The sacred all-encompassing concept of "being Iranian" covers under its spirited wingspan every member of the Iranian nation, regardless of religious or linguistic differences. Whether Kurdish, Baluchi, Zoroastrian or Armenian, those of Aryan blood, who consider Iranian soil their land, must be called Iranian.[105]

Elaborating the above theme, Kazemzadeh's 1923 article on "Iran's Nationhood and National Spirit" claimed that centuries of subordination to "savage foreign nations" had caused Iran to lose its "national religion" and traditions. Nevertheless, he insisted, "the Iranian spirit is still alive, retaining the same innate attributes it possessed two thousand years ago … the Iranian nation has not lost its racial capability and Aryan astuteness." The core attributes of Iran's national spirit, he surmised, were "ambition" and "grandiosity." These two core qualities allowed Iranians to survive centuries of foreign domination and even to "create an exalted Iranian Islam." While highly critical of Shi'i clericalism, Kazemzadeh believed Shi'ism could be reformed to serve Iran's spiritual renewal. To this end, he repeated the arguments of thinkers like Aqaoglu, who claimed Shi'ism was Iran's national religion:

In my view, the Shi'i religion has two distinct attributes making it capable of adopting all features of modernity and civilization. First is the openness of the gate of ijtihad in Shi'ism … and second is the fact that for over a thousand years Iran has taken ownership of Islam, tuning Shi'ism into an Iranian national religion, conforming to the Iranian spirit.[106]

Despite such pronouncements, Kazemzadeh's overall estimation of Shi'ism remained inconsistent. While claiming Shi'ism was Iran's "national religion," he strongly condemned Shi'i clerics for causing political discord and moral confusion in Iranian history. He also argued the dispersal of juridical authority (*ijtihad*) among Shi'i clerics was a setback in comparison to the Sunni closure of ijtihad, which allowed the Ottoman Empire's centralization of religious affairs under a Shehykh al-Islam, who served as cabinet minister in a basically secular government.[107] Turning to politics, another *Iranshahr* article claimed Iran's ruling aristocratic, governmental and clerical elite could not understand the country's old order was on the verge of collapse. Iran's salvation, however, could not come through a "political revolution," which was doomed to failure, as recent upheavals in Azerbaijan (1920) and Khorasan (1921) had shown. Citing French social psychologist Gustav Le Bon, the article concluded, "for a political revolution to succeed, the nation must first be armed by an intellectual and spiritual revolution." Iran's impending "spiritual revolution" was to be led by the urban "middle classes" (*tabaqat-e motevasset*), the only social force capable of moving the bulk of the population, made up of "savage, tent-dwelling and pilfering tribesmen" and "hungry, naked and enslaved peasants," ruled by a "physical and spiritual aristocracy."[108] This "spiritual revolution" could be achieved only through a program of "social education," with the following items on its agenda:

Compulsory education; Scientific and literary association for spreading modern ideas; Dispatching teachers and preachers to the countryside to educate the peasants; Publishing booklets teaching modern ideas in simple language; A modern press spreading technical knowledge, especially geared to the middle classes; Compulsory physical education in schools; Serious education of girls and preparing women for modern life; Jihad against alcohol, opium and idleness, Iran's three worst "national diseases;" Hiring educators and teachers from Europe and especially from the Parsees of India; and setting up public libraries in every city.[109]

Similar to *Kaveh*'s 1921 program, this was a project of inculcating national culture via education, but there were major differences. Most significantly, *Iranshahr* had dropped *Kaveh*'s call for the "unconditional acceptance of European civilization," admitting only the need for hiring "educators" from Europe. The latter were to be supplemented by educators from India's Parsi (Zoroastrian) community, who presumably still possessed their "Iranian spirit." In some ways, *Iranshahr*'s agenda was less authoritarian than *Kaveh*'s, since, for example, it did not insist on national unification via the imposition of Persian language. Nevertheless, *Iranshahr* shared the emerging consensus that nation building could be accomplished only by a powerful centralizing state. Kazemzadeh approved of Reza Khan's 1923–24 republican campaign as a project in line with the emergence of republicanism in Turkey and the Caucasus. Still, he remained consistent in arguing the centrality of a "moral revolution" to nation formation in Iran. "Republicanism and freedom are useless," he wrote, "until a nation has reached a stage of social evolution, capable of changing its morality, heart and soul."[110] Moreover, while endorsing Reza Khan's political ascent, *Iranshahr* did not advocate for its ideal "moral revolution" to be implemented by a modernizing dictatorship.

This was evident, for example, in *Iranshahr*'s disagreeing rejoinder to a long article calling for a modernizing despot to dominate Iran's parliament and government bureaucracy, "forcibly" separate politics and religion, educate men and women, and impose uniformity of dress.[111] Similarly, *Iranshhar* did not endorse frontal attacks on Shi'ism and the clergy, such as those advocated in *Name-ye Farangestan* (see below) or occasionally in its own pages.[112]

In the end, *Iranshahr*'s basic conservatism was manifest in a series of articles dealing with women, marriage and family. A few of these were written by women and many focused on the topic of marriage between Iranian men and European women, with a view to "improving" Iran's cultural and racial (Aryan) character. Kazemzadeh's own verdict was summed up in the motto: "Women must remain women!" According to him, modern European civilization had brought women more social, economic and political equality. Nevertheless, he believed such changes distracted women from their three "natural" duties of being mothers, homemakers and comforters of men. These "sacred duties" elevated women to high social standing, while they fitted the "natural" feminine traits of emotionalism, kindness and attractiveness.[113] As with his advocacy of a "moral revolution," Kazemzadeh's views on women and family, minus their racial tone, would echo in Kasravi's writings (see Chapter 4).

Both Eastern and Western: Toward a Unitarian Conception of Iranian Civilization

The sad problems of Western society turn us to seek a higher solution in Indian religion and Chinese ethics. The very trend in Europe itself, in German philosophy and Russian spirituality, in its last developments, toward the East, assist us in the recovery of these nations themselves nearer to the stars in the night of their material oblivion.

Japanese thinker Tenshin's 1903 Ideals of the East[114]

By the mid-1920s, *Iranshahr*'s advocacy of "moral revolution" was acquiring gnostic and mystical features, showing a fascination with the recovery of Eastern spiritual wisdom. A 1924 article by Kazemzadeh, entitled "Love and its Manifestations in Social life," resurrected Iran's "Illumination School of Philosophy" to explain how "every single particle in this world possesses a force or spirit drawing it toward beauty and perfection." This mystical force was the power of "love." *Iranshahr*'s mystical turn aligned it with contemporary global movements, such as Theosophy and the Parliament of the World's Religions, calling for the spiritual unity of "Eastern and Western" religious traditions.[115] Similarly, *Iranshahr* preached belief in a single core truth uniting the world's religions, something supposedly compatible with modern science as well. Thus, according to Kazemzadeh, "we must unify the beliefs of philosophers and mystics, that is to say the essence of reason and spiritual power must be cultivated together and used jointly ... meaning we must place materialism and spiritualism on the same plane."[116] This balancing of materialism and spiritualism, he proposed, would allow for the merging of "Eastern and Western" worldviews into a uniquely Iranian "civilizational" synthesis:

We must scrutinize both Eastern and Western civilizations, accept their vitalizing maxims and laws, and establish a new "Iranian civilization." Based on a foundation incorporating the merits of Eastern and Western philosophies, this civilization can be called "Unitarian (*tawhid*) Philosophy."[117]

Kazemzadeh therefore admitted the innovative modern character of his idealized "Iranian civilization," as well as its partial derivativeness from both Eastern and Western models. At the same time, and like nationalists everywhere, he insisted this syncretic new national identity would revive an unchanging trans-historical "national spirit." *Iranshahr* thus reaches beyond *Kaveh*'s explicitly Eurocentric intellectual frame, to give modern Iranian nationalism its classical articulation, laying bare its fundamental contradictory claim of being both "Eastern and Western," while also authentically and unchangingly Iranian.

During the second half of its run, i.e. from 1924 to 1927, *Iranshahr* featured more articles on neo-mysticism, occult sciences, personal magnetism, hypnosis, clairvoyance and "spiritism." This genre of writing supposedly vindicated Kazemzadeh's claims for the compatibility of modern science with insights from Eastern religions and mysticism. Despite their dubious intellectual merit, such arguments reversed *Kaveh*'s negative estimation of "Eastern" worldviews. Instead, they redirected Iranian nationalist discourse Eastward, specifically toward India, presented as the font of an archaic mystical knowledge that the West lacked or had forgotten. The idea of a return to "Eastern" or Asian identity was already popular among

Ottoman, Indian, Chinese and Japanese thinkers. In 1903, for example, Japanese intellectual Okakura Tenshin (1862–1913) published *Ideals of the East* (1903), a plea for Asia's return to Eastern spirituality in the face of a European civilization hopelessly mired in materialism, aggression and greed.[118] By the early twentieth century, there was also a new and growing Euro-American fascination with India, manifest in movements such as Traditionalism or scholarly works such as those by Mircea Eliade, who found a sacred common core to all religions, particularly in Hinduism and mystical Christianity.[119] (For the impact of these ideas on mid-twentieth century Iran, see Chapter 6.) Iranian nationalists' interest in India began with nineteenth-century discoveries of ancient Iran's "living traces" in India's Parsi (Parsee) or Zoroastrian community. Works such as Dosabhoy Framjee's *Parsees: Their History, Manners, Customs, and Religion* (1858) and Maneckji Hataria's *A Parsee Mission to Iran* (1865) intended to elevate the Parsees, in British eyes, by presenting them as the living embodiment of ancient Iran's Aryan religion and civilization. Ironically, such "indigenous" testimonies sought to establish their superior cultural pedigree by appealing to European theories of racial and religious hierarchy.[120] Influenced by such works, early twentieth-century Iranian intellectuals, like the ultra-nationalist scholar Ebrahim Purdavud and pioneering modernist fiction writer Sadeq Hedayat, would travel to India in search of ancient Iran's surviving Zoroastrian roots.[121] Official Pahlavi nationalism also acknowledged India's significance, famously exemplified by the 1932 invitation of Indian poet and philosopher Rabindranath Tagore, who was received in Iran as the "living personification of the ancient Iranian heritage."[122]

Iranshahr's search for "Eastern" dimensions of Iran's "national spirit," however, was cut short when it ceased publication in 1927. Kazemzadeh remained in Berlin, briefly serving as official supervisor to Iranian students in Germany. His contact with Iran gradually diminished and he eventually settled in Switzerland where, during the 1940s, he set up a "School of Inner Mysticism," teaching his students physical and spiritual discipline. His theosophical pedagogy was based on "the unity of science, religion and industry" for the purpose of brining "man's body and soul into harmony." He also published a newspaper called "Harmony" in both German and French.[123]

Name-ye Farangestan: Between Fascism and Modernizing Dictatorship

Today the East is dead ... its resurrection can only come from the West.

Name-ye Farangestan, Nos. 11–12

The Berlin Circle of Iranian intellectuals briefly launched a third organ, whose radical agenda of European-style authoritarian modernization verged on fascism. *Name-ye Farangestan* (*European Letter*) published only twelve issues (May 1924 to April 1925) as it was banned in Iran due to its radical tone and blatant anti-clericalism. Its staff included Moretza Moshfeq-Kazemi, Ahmad Farhad, Gholam-Hossein Foruhar, Ebrahim Mahdavi, Parviz Kazemi, Hasan Nafisi and Taqi Arani. Some of these men also wrote for *Iranshahr*, but their contributions to *Name-ye Farangestan* converged on a different worldview with radical political implications. The paper's editorials were written mostly by Moshfeq-Kazemi, the young author of *Terrible Tehran* (1922), often considered Iran's first social novel. Essentially, Moshfeq-Kazemi and his colleagues called for the kind of dictatorial nation building that soon was implemented under Reza Shah, but they insisted on its conformity to European fascist models. Thus, the journal's first editorial declared:

We want to Europeanize Iran and flood it with modern civilization. While preserving our innate Iranian moral qualities, we will follow this sagacious command: Iran must be come Europeanized in body and spirit, as well as in essence and appearance.[124]

Endorsing Taqizadeh's "sagacious command" on wholesale Europeanization, *Name-ye Farangestan* agreed with both *Kaveh* and *Iranshahr*, that building a modern Iranian nation was predicated on a major cultural transformation:

As long as the national spirit is dormant and quiet, and when, instead of loving life, Iranians indulge in typically Oriental superstitions, infirmity, idleness, and dervish-like reclusiveness, neither railroads nor factories can cure our innermost afflictions ... What Iran suffers from is spiritual backwardness.[125]

However, a modern "national spirit" could only be imposed on Iran forcibly by an "enlightened dictator" like Mussolini. As Moshfeq-Kazemi put it in *Name-ye Farangestan*'s first issue:

> The current Italian Prime Minister, Mussolini, is a dictator ... He possesses both knowledge and determination ... He is indifferent to monarchism or republicanism, as long as fascists are in power ... He pretends to believe in the parliament, but when necessary, uses threats to produce his own parliamentary majority ... Iran too needs such a dictator.[126]

Name-ye Farangestan's hyper-elitist nationalism was based on the belief that the great majority of Iranians were hopelessly backward and utterly incapable of understanding what the country needed. Forever prone to manipulation by clerics and politicians, the ignorant masses were not worthy of freedom and political rights:

> With the help of educated individuals, take existing freedoms away from a people who are nothing but tools in the hands of others. These decaying fossils, belonging to a nation where five out of seven people are mentally equal to cavemen and their ape-like ancestors, do not deserve freedom.[127]

Naturally, *Name-ye Farangestan* admired Mustafa Kemal's top-down secularizing reforms in the new Turkish republic. Following Turkey's example, it insisted, an Iranian "enlightened dictator" had to forcibly separate religion from politics, allowing clerics only to be moral guides to their fanatical followers. A small, educated minority of men and women were entitled to social and political rights, while the bulk of the population had to be indoctrinated in patriotism and disciplined, as conscripts, in military barracks. Public education had to eradicate all difference in beliefs and ideas, which was detrimental to national unity. Significantly, *Name-ye Farangestan* differed from *Kaveh* and *Iranshahr* in its advocacy of an "agrarian revolution," to be accomplished through radical state intervention in the economy. Agriculture was the backbone of Iran's economy, but it remained backward and exploited by the Qajar ruling family, other large landlords and religious foundations. The solution was for the state to take over, parcel out and sell all land to peasant cultivators. At the same time, agriculture was to be modernized and mechanized, while rural children were to receive some basic modern education, applicable to rural labor. Meanwhile, neither the rural nor urban masses could have voting rights until they became sufficiently literate.[128]

Name-ye Farangestan therefore was more open and consistent than both *Kaveh* and *Iranshahr* in embracing European models of nationalism and modernity, as well as in rejecting "traditional" Iranian culture. Moreover, *Name-ye Farangestan*'s nationalism was more explicitly class-based, as shown, for example, in its restriction of political rights to a minority of elite men and women.[129] Yet, despite its advocacy of a fascist-type dictatorship, *Name-ye Farangestan* showed no serious intellectual engagement with Nazism or Italian fascist ideology. Moshfq-Kazemi himself was clear on this point:

I read in the papers how Mussolini had accomplished great reforms in Italy, putting an end to that weak country's deplorable conditions. Gradually, I came to believe that Iran too could be shaken up only by a strong-armed man, with awareness of both world affairs and Iranian conditions... Influenced by such ideas, I wrote in *Name-ye Farangestan* of the need for an enlightened dictator ... who could save Iran.[130]

The only truly fascist writer of *Name-ye Farangestan* was Gholam-Hossein Foruhar, who actively participated in Nazi Party demonstrations and street clashes with communists.[131] The less doctrinaire Moshfeq-Kazemi returned to Iran in 1926, joined the Young Iran Party and wrote for its organ *Iran-e javan*. Basically a political club of Tehran's European-educated elite, Young Iran proposed a nation-building project that was adopted by Reza Shah (see Chapter 3). Embracing this project, Moshfeq-Kazemi wrote: "I was totally in agreement with the reforms that were underway, especially seeing the gradual implementation of what we had advocated in *Name-ye Farangestan*."[132]

Conclusion

During the early 1920s, the idea of modern nation building by an enlightened dictatorship was gaining ground among the nationalist intelligentsia in Iran and abroad. Some veteran constitutionalists, like social democrat poet laureate Mohammad-Taqi Bahar, hoped a government "acting like Ataturk and Mussolini" might be set up "by wise and freedom-loving men, not a bunch of Cossacks."[133] They thus supported Reza Khan's strengthening of the central government, while opposing his moves toward a personal dictatorship. However, as we shall see in Chapter 3, Bahar and his "semi-constitutionalist" faction was quickly forced out of politics by nationalist intellectuals who advocated or accepted a modernizing dictatorship.

This chapter located the genesis of Iran's authoritarian nationalist ideology in a global encounter between Iranian émigré intellectuals and

German political culture in 1920s Berlin. The specific site of this productive encounter was the pages of Berlin-based periodicals *Kaveh, Iranshahr* and *Name-ye Farangestan.* Taqizadeh and his colla-borators in *Kaveh* gave up their vaguely liberal or social democratic convictions to advocate illiberal blueprints of nation building, justified according to a haphazardly conceived "Western" worldview, urging "surrender to European civilization." A rival intellectual trend appeared in *Iranshahr*, rejecting *Kaveh*'s blatant conformity to European standards to propose instead a nation-building project within a modern "Iran-centric" worldview. Despite its purported rejec-tion of Eurocentrism, *Iranshahr* was more deeply influenced by European thought, as it embraced the German critique of Western modernity's moral nihilism, rampant social conflict and urge to global domination. *Iranshahr* followed *Kaveh*'s drift toward illiberal politics by endorsing nation building through the imposition of a homogenized national culture. Arguably, *Iranshahr*'s most important intellectual legacy was its launch of a discourse that tied Iranian nationalism to global ideologies highly critical of Western modernity. Moreover, its call for national regeneration via a "moral revolution," linked to Shi'i modernization, anticipated the creative merger of nationalist and reli-gious thought that began with Kasravi and, as we shall see in the flowing chapters, continued to reverberate into the 1960s–1970s and beyond.

3 | Subverting Constitutionalism: Intellectuals as Instruments of Modern Dictatorship

There is no Iranian nation; and Iranians don't want to be human beings.
> Foroughi, Reza Shah's intellectual prime minister.[1]

Iranians would not become human beings voluntarily. Salvation must be forced on Iran.
> Davar, architect of Reza Shah's legal system.[2]

By the second half of the 1920s, almost all members of Berlin's Iranian nationalist circle had returned home, where the political instability of the first post-constitutional decade was settling into a semi-military dictatorship. Reza Shah's dictatorship conformed to interwar global patterns, most closely to Republican Turkey, whereby a modernizing elite implemented top-down nation building via an authoritarian state. As noted in Chapter 2, Iranian historiography tends to explain the rise of Reza Shah in terms of the "catastrophist" conditions of the decade from 1911 to 1921. In this narrative, the "failure" of constitutionalism and Iran's wartime "disintegration" led the nationalist elite to back to a strong-man "savior" of the country. According to Homa Katouzian, for example: "By the end of World War One, the chaos caused by the Constitutional Revolution had brought Iran to the verge of disintegration, leading Taqizadeh and many other intellectuals to conclude Iran needed a strong centralized government."[3] Originating with the British instigators of the 1921 coup, the narrative of "national salvation" from post-constitutional "chaos" became semi-official in Pahlavi-era historiography and foreign scholarship.[4] The longevity of this "catastrophist" narrative, however, is partly due to the feebleness of alternative explanations of Reza Khan's rise as either a British "conspiracy" or Iran's relapse from "chaos" to "arbitrary rule."[5] The British instigation of the 1921 coup has been questioned, on the grounds that it was decided not by the "British government" in London, but by its diplomatic and military personnel in Iran.[6] This argument ignores the typical pattern of British imperial intervention via the initiative of overseas functionaries, which in 1921 in Iran meant the commanders of an occupying British army. Challenging such prevalent historiographic assumptions, this chapter will explain 1920s Iran's authoritarian nation-state building primarily in terms of the intellectual elite's abandonment of constitutionalism to embrace illiberal nationalism. At the same time, it will be argued that the triumph of authoritarian nationalism was not an inevitable outcome of Iranian history, but the result of an intense and often violent political struggle whereby more democratic projects of nation building were suppressed.

To begin, the "catastrophic narrative" misses the point that the nationalist elite converged on calling for a hyper-centralized state in the early 1920s, when the "chaotic" conditions of war and foreign occupation had actually passed. By 1921, constitutional government was more or less functional again, while the country's "disintegration," caused by foreign occupation, was no longer an issue. A comparison with the emergence of the Turkish Republic, out of the total collapse and dismemberment of the Ottoman Empire, is instructive. Whereas Mustafa Kemal's nationalist forces fought foreign armies to salvage the core of a dismembered empire, Reza Khan's military campaigns targeted only provincial power centers across Iran. Moreover, none of Reza Khan's main political rivals, i.e. the autonomous regimes in Khorasan, Gilan and Azerbaijan, threatened Iran with "disintegration," while all of them were more committed to constitutionalism than he was. By the end of 1921, all three contenders to the new Tehran regime were crushed, while the Soviet-Iranian treaty and British military withdrawal finalized both powers' recognition of Iranian independence. In other words, the post-1921 line-up of the nationalist elite behind Reza Khan's creeping dictatorship occurred precisely when Iran's independence, and potential for restoring constitutional government, had become more secure than during the previous decade. Thus, moving beyond the fatalism of "catastrophist" and "perpetual despotism" historiographic narratives, we need to explain why so many 1920s nationalist intellectuals preferred a dictatorship to a flawed but semi-functional constitutional regime. This is all the more necessary because the 1920s project of top-down nation building was clearly an elite imposition, unpopular with, and often resisted by, significant segments of both the rural and urban population.[7]

"The School of Taqizadeh": Rationalizing Capitulation to Dictatorship

"I annihilate you," was Reza Shah's constant refrain.

Taqizadeh[8]

The greatest consequence of Iranian constitutionalism was the appearance of a powerful and patriotic man who, in the midst of revolutions and misfortunes, rose up to save the country, creating a new era that was to be named (Pahlavi) after him.

1927–8 Iranian Government Almanac.[9]

The nationalist elite's capitulation to Pahlavi dictatorship is exemplified in the case of Hasan Taqizadeh, the leading intellectual champion of the Constitutional Revolution. As described in Chapter 2, up until leaving Germany in 1922, Taqizadeh and his collaborators in *Kaveh* preferred "flawed and imperfect constitutionalism" to "enlightened despotism."[10] Returning to Iran, Taqizadeh was dispatched by the Iranian government to Moscow, where he spent more than a year as head of a trade delegation, and then to London to negotiate with the new British Labor government. Both assignments seem related to his former socialist credentials, yet Taqizadeh remained aloof of the Socialist Party's parliamentary faction when returning to serve as Majles deputy in 1924. Instead, he joined a small circle of the capital's political elite acting as advisers to Reza Kahn, who was both prime minster and armed forces commander. In addition to Taqizadeh, the circle's most prominent members were the future prime ministers Mohammad Mosaddeq and Mohammad-Ali Forughi, as well as historians Hasan Pirnia and Yahya Dowlatabadi. According to Taqizadeh, the circle sought to steer and harness Reza Khan's personal ambitions toward serving the country.[11] This claim is unconvincing, since by 1924 Reza Khan had proven himself an enemy of constitutional government, in relentless pursuit of personal dictatorial power.

A year later, however, Taqizadeh took a final principled stand as one of four Majles deputies, including Mohammad Mosaddeq, who voted against the transfer of monarchy to the Pahlavi Dynasty. He boldly declared: "I say, to history and future generations, this is not done according to the country's constitution, neither does it serve the country's best interest."[12] Yet, as Mosaddeq would put it years later, Taqizadeh quickly "enslaved himself to the very monarchy he had deemed un-constitutional," serving in a succession of high positions.[13] Taqizadeh's darkest moment arrived when, as finance minister, he signed the 1933 renewal of the Anglo-Persian oil agreement. The new agreement was highly unfavorable to Iran, something Taqizadeh later admitted, while claiming he had acted merely as Reza Shah's "instrument," and was therefore blameless.[14] Offered as self-defense, this was in fact a disingenuous admission that his political career choices had turned him into an instrument of dictatorship.[15] Their dubious benefits to the country notwithstanding, Taqizadeh's political choices served him well, as he continued to hold high political and diplomatic posts, while expressing some remorse toward the end of his life.[16] A definitive judgment of Taqizadeh's career is not easy, but it is hard to agree with commenters like Katouzian who claim he "wanted a democratic but powerful government, something like English democracy, or modernity in its deep true sense of the word."[17]

A less noted but important legacy of Taqizadeh is his mentoring of younger intellectuals who learned the art of political conformity at the "School of Taqizadeh." Back in Tehran during the mid-1920s, Taqizadeh had opened a small bookstore, where his Berlin colleagues mingled with the capital's nationalist intellectual elite. Enlisting the country's leading historians, political scientists, jurists and literary scholars, this cohort included Ali-Akbar Dehkhoda, Abbas Eqbal-Ashtiani, Yahya Dowlatabdi, Vahidolmolk Sheybani, Ahmad Kasravi, Fakhr al-Din Shadman, Ebrahim Purdavud, Mahmud Afshar, Abdulrahman Faramarzi and Mojtaba Minovi.[18] Converging on a nation-building project similar to the common agenda of *Kaveh, Iranshahr* and *Name-ye Farangestan*, the more politically articulate of these intellectuals had formed the Young Iran Party, whose 1921 program called for:

Establishing a secular government in Iran and fully secularizing the legal system; Disenfranchising illiterate citizens; Ending capitulations and revising foreign trade agreements; Progressive taxation; Adopting the better parts of European civilization; Sending male and female students to Europe; Paying special attention to education, including compulsory elementary education, secondary and technical-industrial education, and changing the Persian alphabet; Removing all barriers to women's liberation; and constructing railroads, museums, libraries and theatres.[19]

Young Iran was in fact not a party, but a political club of the capital's European-educated elite, led by Ali-Akbar Siasi (1896–1990) and

Mahmud Afshar (1894–1984). With a doctorate in education from France, Siasi would go on to serve as minister of education, foreign minister and chancellor of Tehran University. Afshar, who had a doctorate in political science from Switzerland, became an influential nationalist ideologue, without pursuing a political career. According to Siasi, upon Young Iran's formation in 1921, its leaders were invited to meet with the new war minister Reza Khan, who wanted to know what these "European-educated youths" were proposing for the country. After reading their nation-building program, Reza Kahn told Siasi and his friends to continue advocating their agenda, but leave its implementation to him.[20] This story conveys a presumed tension between Young Iran's "progressive" nationalist agenda and its dictatorial actualization by Reza Shah. It can be argued, on the other hand, that the authoritarian character of Young Iran's program fitted Reza Khan's barracks-style approach to politics. By the mid-1920s, Young Iran's brand of nationalism was gaining ground among the country's European-educated intellectual elite. It was forcefully propagated in *Ayandeh* (The Future), a periodical launched in 1925 by Mahmud Afshar, with the cooperation of Taqizadeh, Siasi and Moshfeq-Kazemi.[21] Penned by Afshar, *Ayandeh*'s first editorial clearly articulated the vision these men shared together:

Our social goal and ideal is the preservation and perfection of Iran's national unity ... What we mean by Iranian national unity is the political, moral and social unity of the people who live within the present boundaries of Iran. This notion has two other aspects, which are the preservation of Iran's political independence and its territorial integrity. Perfecting national unity means the spread of Persian language throughout the country, getting rid of "fractured sovereignties" (*muluk al-tawa'efi*) and regional differences in behavior, appearance, etc; and making Kurds, Lurs, Qashqais, Arabs, Turks and Turkomans speak the same language and dress the same ... We believe that until national unity in language, morality, dress, etc., is achieved, our political independence and territorial integrity is constantly in danger. Unless we can make uniform all of Iran's various regions and different ethnicities, in other words, making all of them truly Iranian, we face a dark future.[22]

This nation-building agenda fundamentally differed from what the leading intellectuals of the Constitutional era, such as those gathered in the Democrat Party, had proposed. Afshar, Siasi and their cohorts in *Ayandeh* now insisted that Iran's "national unity" required cultural homogenization, a different argument from saying the country had to be saved from disintegration caused by foreign intervention. Scholarly backing for this new kind of "national unity" agenda is found in Siasi's doctoral dissertation, entitled "Iran and the West," which was submitted to the University of Paris in 1931. Justifying Iran's 1928 imposition of a national dress code for men, Siasi claimed that "Persians, although of the same race, and with a few exceptions, of the same language and religion," used to be separated from each other by different "mores, customs and costumes." Therefore, a "national Persian costume, ... precisely because it is superficial and visible, will bring together the different groups of Persians – the Turks of Azerbaijan, the Kurds, the Lurs, the Arabs of Khuzistan, the Baluchis, etc."[23] Authoritarian nationalists, like Siasi and Afshar, openly admitted their ideal of "national unity" could be realized only through the forcible eradication of existing diversity in ethnicity, language, culture and sartorial style. Inspired by Orientalist historiography and Euro-American race theories, they sought to transform Iran's *actual* linguistic, ethnic and religious diversity into an "imagined" national community shaped by a "common" Persian language, Aryan race and proud imperial history. According to Afshar:

Several millennia of glorious history, as well as Aryan racial superiority, distinguish Iran's nationhood from those of its yellow-skinned Turanian and Semitic Arab neighbors. Nevertheless, our national unity is deficient linguistically, due to language differences among Azerbaijani Turkish-speaker, Khuzistan's Arab-speakers and Persian-speakers in other regions.[24]

The identification of Iran with the Aryan race originated with Orientalists like George Rawlinson and Arthur Gobineau, who influenced proto-nationalist thinkers like Akhundzadeh and Aqa Khan Kermani. The purported Aryan lineage of ancient "Persians" then became a tenet of Iranian nationalist discourse, appearing to various degrees in paradigmatic works by historians, statesmen and educators like Hasan Pirniya (1871–1935), Isa Sadiq, Mohammad-Ali Foroughi and Abbas Eqbal-Ashtiani.[25] The significance of race to Pahlavi-era nationalism was underscored, for example, in the speech delivered, on the occasion of Reza Shah's coronation, by Prime Minister Mohammad-Ali Foroughi, the most erudite intellectual statesman of his generation. "The Iranian nation," he said, "knows that today it has a monarch who is pure-bred (*pakzad*) and of Iranian race (*Irani nezhad*)."[26] The Aryan purity of native Persian-speaker Reza Pahlavi thus certified his dynasty's Iranian authenticity and racial superiority, compared to the Turkish-speaking and hence inferior non-Aryan Qajars.

The case of Young Iran shows how prominent European-educated intellectuals, like Siasi and Afshar, followed Taqizadeh in adapting illiberal nationalism to the exigencies of political dictatorship. In 1927, Young Iran was dissolved so that its members could join New Iran, a fascist-style party led by court minister Abdol-Hosein Taimurtash (1883–1933), who argued a single-party political system was a requirement of modernity (*tajaddod*). Dissolving all other parties into New Iran, according to him, was necessary because:

small and scattered, the country's modernity-seeking (*tajaddod-khah*) forces were always in retreat, unable to resist the unified forces of reaction. Today, when His Majesty's modernity-promoting monarchy (*saltanat-e tajddod-parvar*) has established suitable conditions for the spread of modernity-seeking ideas (*aqayed-e tajaddod-khahaneh*), it is incumbent on all modernist elements (*anaser-e motejadded*) to unite, leave minor differences aside, and lead the country toward progress and civilization.[27]

Obsessed with *tajaddod* (modernity), this passage typifies the mindset of 1920s–1930s nationalist intelligentsia and statesmen. Tajaddod was also the name of a short-lived (1925–1926) political party Taimurtash had co-founded in order to force the Majles to oust the Qajars and install Reza Khan as Iran's dictator, initially as president and then as a new dynast.[28] The equally short-lived 1927 New Iran Party closed the authoritarian cycle by officially terminating the Constitutional era's experience of party politics. Ironically, the assault on constitutional government in the name of modernity was led by Taimurtash, Iran's most cosmopolitan diplomat, who was intimately familiar with European culture since his student days at the military academy of St. Petersburg. More intellectually steeped in European modernity was the co-leader of Tajaddod Party, Ali-Akbar Davar (1885–1937), who had also spent many years living and studying in Europe. Together, these two men played the most pivotal role in shaping Reza Shah's new dynasty into a modern European-style dictatorship. During the Pahlavi dynasty's first decade, Davar was in charge of crafting Iran's modern legal system, while Taimurtash managed both domestic politics and foreign affairs.

While the flamboyant Taimurtash took the spotlight as the more consummate diplomat, Davar quietly labored as the intellectual architect of 1920s–1930s Iran's modernizing dictatorship. He had returned home soon after the 1921 coup, having spent eleven years in Europe, where he completed a doctorate in law and political science at Geneva University. Davar shared the proto-fascist ideological assumptions prevalent in 1920s–1930s Europe, especially in Italy and Germany. He was perhaps influenced directly by Vilfred Pareto, who taught at the University of Lausanne when Davar was studying in Switzerland.[29] In 1923, Davar became a Majles deputy, established his own Radical Party and launched the daily newspaper, *Mard-e Azad* (Free Man). Davar's newspaper espoused the 1920s' most coherent authoritarian nationalist ideology, defined by a fanatical belief in economic and technological determinism. Endorsing Taqizadeh's call for total Europeanization, Davar went farther to insist, similarly to *Name-ye Farangestan*, that modern nation building through parliamentary politics and gradual cultural and educational reforms was futile. According to him: "Western civilization is not rooted in schools, libraries and scientists. These are the branches and fruits of a superior civilization, which is rooted in the railroad." Or, he would argue, "contemporary Western civilization is the product of the Industrial Revolution. If we want this civilization, we must first acknowledge and try to secure its prerequisites." This could be accomplished only by "those who wish and are capable of imposing their politics on society, in defiance of existing conditions."[30] A modern European-style dictatorship therefore was necessary since "Iranians would not become human beings voluntarily. Salvation must be forced on Iran." And even more blatantly: "Someone must be found to educate Iran under the whip, obliterate this babbling generation, force people to work and build railroads across Iran."[31] The perfect candidate for this job of course was Reza Khan, who was, by 1923, already acting as Iran's dictator, simultaneously being prime minister and minister of war. By 1924–1925, therefore, Davar was a leader of the nationalist elite circle working to institutionalize Reza Khan's dictatorship, either in a republic or as the head of a new dynasty. In the end, and as was the case with Taimurtash and Reza Shah's other top statesmen, Davar's political career and life were terminated by the dictatorship he had helped install. In 1937, Davar committed suicide when faced with the infamously murderous wrath of Reza Shah.[32] The elaborate modern legal system he had constructed could not provide the minimum protection, even to its own architect.

Silencing Modernity's Revolutionary Voices in Politics and Culture

If you are poets and literati, know that you must be leaders not followers. You must swim upstream, against the current … write for tomorrow.

Revolutionary Azeri poet Taqi Raf'at, 1918.

The ideological legacy of intellectuals like Davar, Siasi, Taqizadeh and Foroughi is an enduring historical narrative suggesting dictatorship was the only viable path of modern nation building in 1920s Iran. On the contrary, the historical record shows that 1920s Iranian modernity spoke in a plurality of voices, all of which were silenced by the dictatorship authoritarian nationalists were building. Reza Khan's relentless drive toward replacing constitutional government with a semi-military dictatorship was in fact opposed by a diverse coalition of liberal and conservative nationalists, backed by a segment of the left. Constitutional government was defended famously by prominent Majles deputies like the Swiss-educated doctor of law Mohammad Mosaddeq, veteran clerical politician Hasan Modarres and social democrat poet laureate Mohammad-Taqi Bahar. These men supported Reza Khan's strengthening the central government, while opposing his dictatorial ambitions. The left's overall response to Reza Khan was more ambiguous. By the 1920s, Iran's already splintered social democrats were divided further into a Socialist Party and a pro-Bolshevik Communist Party. The Socialist Party's parliamentary faction supported Reza Khan, considering him a progressive centralizer and modernizer. Confounded by a shifting Bolshevik policy toward Iran, the communists were divided into supporters and opponents of Reza Khan. In the end, after a few years of resistance to Reza Khan's creeping dictatorship, all of these factions were forcibly removed from the scene.

The political struggles of the 1920s were paralleled by equally intense contentions over the meaning of cultural modernity, which was debated mainly in literature. As in politics, these literary-cum-cultural debates were carried out almost entirely in Persian, which for centuries had been the language of power in governance and high culture. Conforming to global patterns, however, most of Iran's inhabitants did not understand the language of their rulers or the literate elite. Yet, by the end of Reza Shah's rule, Persian was imposed on all Iranians as the "national language," effectively creating a "Persian/Iranian" variant of cultural modernity. But this particular outcome emerged only after a fierce but now forgotten civil war within the modernist cultural camp.

In the wake of the Constitutional Revolution, pioneering modernist experiments in journalism, fiction, poetry, theatre and opera challenged the hallowed conventions of Persian-language high culture. The most venerable of the latter was the millennium-old tradition of Persian literature (*adab*), already certified by Orientalist scholarship as the expression of Iranian "national" character. As seen in Chapter 2, ever since the Oriental Renaissance, European scholars had celebrated Rumi, Sa'di and Hafez as Persian literary masters, thus designating Iran as "a nation of poets," with Ferdowsi's *Shahnameh* as its "national epic."[33] Historically, however, Persian-language *adab* was linked not to any "national" tradition but to the courtly culture of Perso-Turkish empires successively ruling parts of a region extending from the Balkans and Anatolia to Iran, India and Central Asia. Hamid Dabashi finds in the Persian *adab* tradition a "literary humanism" subversive of both its own courtly patronage and the linguistic hegemony of Arabic in the Islamic world. Medieval Persian *adab*, contends Dabashi, was "humanist" because its mystical lyricism carried a "cosmopolitan worldliness" focused on notions of *admai* (man/human) as "a decentered subject" reaching out for meaning and agency.[34] The collapse of courtly patronage, during the nineteenth-century onslaught of European imperialism, allowed the Persian literati to transfer their intellectual and moral allegiance to the emergent "public space" of the nation. At the same time, the destabilizing power of global modernity plunged "Persian literary humanism" into a "chaotic" state, which created new forms of subjectivity in literature and the arts. According to Dabashi, the creative chaotic phase of "Persian literary humanism" defies all theories of modernity and therefore is itself an "alternative theory to modernity."[35] This reading overstates both the subversive "humanist" aspects of traditional Persian *adab* and its purportedly creative postmodern agency and subjectivity. Nevertheless, Dabashi's intervention reopens an old debate on the "worldview" and moral compass of the Persian *adab* tradition and its role in modern nation formation within the matrix of Eurocentric modernity, and particularly Orientalism.

As discussed in previous chapters, the encounter of Orientalism with Iranian nationalist consciousness was not a simple process of one side dictating to the other. Recent historical research shows that Orientalism itself, as a system of knowledge production, developed in a global frame of intellectual exchange between European and non-European actors. The Iranian case of this exchange is exemplified by the intricate scholarly collaboration of Edward G. Browne and his intellectual associates in Iran. As Browne's *The Persian Revolution of 1905–1909* had done for nationalist historiography (see Chapter 1), his multi-volume *Literary History of Persia* provided a "master narrative" for the categorization and canonization of Persian literature. In both cases, the ultimate "narration" was Browne's, but the source material and its original interpretation came from Iranian and Indian experts and scholars. Browne's closest and best-informed intellectual collaborators were Hasan Taqizadeh and Mohammad Qazvini, but he also consulted numerous other Iranians during decades of regular correspondence. Browne's scholarship, and particularly its collaborative epistolary character, thus fits what Pascale Casanova describes as a "World Republic of Letters," whereby global networks of intellectual exchange, including translation, facilitate "national identity" formation through the categorization and canonization of "national literatures."[36]

Going back to Iran's culture wars of early modernity in the 1920s, we find it was precisely the established canons of Persian literature (*adab*), tying poetics to morality and politics, which the modernist avant-garde saw as their greatest challenge and obstacle. Similar to the evolution of the constitutional movement's political discourse (discussed in Chapters 1 and 2), the Iranian movement of literary modernity (*tajaddod-e adabi*) followed a path that had already been blazed in the Ottoman Empire. During the 1890s, Istanbul had been the site of a "new literature" (*edebiat jedid*), rejecting old and "decadent" Ottoman canons in favor of contemporary French literary standards. A famous turn-of-the-century modernist poem, "Fog," for example, alluded to intellectual conservatism as "a stubborn smoke," shrouding Istanbul and turning it into a dark city. A few years earlier, modernist author Semseddin Sami had called for a European-style overhaul of Persian-Turkish literary styles:

If the West were deficient in culture it could not develop its material civilization ... Those who know European languages and literatures will realize that our own language and literature are deficient and underdeveloped. A Turkish poet acquainted with European literature cannot sing any longer of those *mugh-beche's, pir-mughans, kharabat,* etc ... We too ought to have in our literature, the verse, the story, the drama, and the novel of the type of Western literature.[37]

Going farther, another writer, Huseyn Cahit, rejected the entire Arab-Islamic historical and literary legacy in favor of the wholesale adoption of European models:

We are bound, whether we like it or not, to Europeanize. Just as the pantaloons we wear came from Europe, our literature too ... ought to come from there ... We are bound to turn to Europe even if all the history books of the Arabs are translated; still we have to learn antiquity and pre-history from European science.[38]

The Young Ottoman revolt against traditional literature had echoed in Iran via works by Azeri modernizers like Akundzadeh and Aqaoglu (see Chapter 1). In 1910, Aqaoglu contributed to the Istanbul-based Iranian constitutionalist paper *Sorush*, while also writing about Iran in the Istanbul paper *Serat al-mostaqim*. According to him, repressive Iranian rulers, like the Qajars, had endured for centuries because of an entrenched worldview of submissiveness and surrendering to destiny, espoused by medieval Muslim literati like the great poet Sa'di. In a rapidly changing modern world, he argued, Sa'di's perspective was irrelevant, and bound to be challenged by Iranian intellectuals. "We are still oscillating between Iran and Europe," wrote Aqaoglu, "but inevitably will prefer Rousseau to Sa'di."[39] A few years earlier, Agha Kahn Kermani similarly had blamed "Muslim poets" for the moral and political corruption of Iran's rulers and their subjects, from the Abbasids down to the Qajars. He claimed: "It was the love lyrics of Sa'di and Homam and their cohorts that corrupted the morals of Iranian youths." Judging traditional Persian literature by contemporary European standards, he proclaimed:

Poetry ought to lead the people along the path of perfection, virtue, and moderation, not to that of evil and vicious deeds, etc. The only Persian poet whom the *litterateurs* of Europe admire is Ferdowsi of Tus, whose poems in *The Shahnameh* –even if they are not free from exaggerations– inculcate love of nationality, courage, and bravery to an extent.[40]

The critique of classical Persian literature became more direct during the Constitutional Revolution. Perhaps most prominently, Tehran's radical socialist weekly, bearing the messianic title *Sur-e Esrafil* (Seraphim's Trumpet Call), advocated a "literary revival," asserting that centuries of literary "stagnation and decline" was proof of Iran's moral decadence. According to the paper's co-editor Ali-Akbar Dehkhoda:

Our literature in general and our poetry in particular have remained stagnant or have declined, and our men of letters have engaged themselves only in slavish imitation of the classics ... this stagnation or decline, which without any notable exception has continued for five centuries in Iran, has, with the clarity of a mirror, made manifest the literary demise and moral decadence of the nation.[41]

Echoing the Enlightenment's famous dictum, *Sur-e Esrafil* insisted human beings were "autonomous agents" (*fa'el-e mokhtar*), capable of unlimited "progress," once freed from the moral and intellectual tutelage of others. But the paper's radical questioning of traditional authority caused a strong reaction among supporters of the old regime and especially the clergy. Consequently, *Sure-e Esrafil* was forced to backtrack, claiming it had not questioned Islam's original perfection, but its corruption and abuse throughout history. Repeating Muslim reformers, it argued that, despite its perfect core principles, Islam had to be reinterpreted according to the exigencies of every age.[42] As was done earlier with constitutionalism (see Chapter 1), *Sure-Esrafil* now presented socialism in the vernacular of Islam, claiming the two were fully compatible.[43] The paper's brief run, however, ended with the 1908 royalist coup, during which one of its two editors, Mirza Jahangir Khan, was executed on the shah's orders, while Dehkhoda managed to escape, returning to politics with the restoration of the constitutional regime. *Sur-e-Esrafil*'s most popular column was Dehkhoda's satirical "Balderdash" (*charand-o-parand*), a brilliant pioneer of literary modernity in its use of lowbrow colloquial Persian for hard-hitting social and political criticism.[44] Showing trans-Caucasian affinities, *Sure-Esrafil*'s politics and literary modernism were similar to those of its contemporary Tiflis-based Turkish paper *Molla Nasr al-Din*. The two papers referenced each other and *Dehkohda* wrote for *Molla Naser-din* as well.[45]

Despite their brevity and limited reach, revolutionary experiments in literary modernity, such as *Sure-Esrafil*'s, caused major cultural ripples beyond the pro-constitutionalist camp. Toward the end of World War I, pro-constitutionalist classical poet Mohammad-Taqi Bahar launched the magazine *Daneshkadeh* (Academy), advocating a "literary revolution" as corollary to Iran's ongoing political revolution. *Daneshkadeh* wanted "to promote new ideas in traditional forms of poetry and prose, introduce standards of eloquence and perimeters of literary revolution, while respecting traditional literary masters and adopting the best features of European prose."[46] In practice, Bahar and his circle remained within traditional canons, while selectively borrowing from European literary styles. *Daneshkadeh*'s cautious modernity, however, was challenged when a literary debate erupted in response to an article in the social democratic paper *Zaban-e Azad* (Free Language). Provocatively titled "The School of Sa'di," the article questioned the contemporary relevance of Sa'di's poetry and prose and, by implication, the entire corpus of classical Persian *adab*. A furious traditionalist backlash led to the closure of *Zaban-e Azad*, while Bahar intervened to defend Sa'di, claiming the moral compass guiding modern life could be found in the poetry of Rumi, Sa'di and Hafez.[47]

Subsequently, Bahar's claim of seamless continuity between Persian *adab* and the cultural norms of European modernity was strongly challenged by Taqi Raf'at, editor of the periodical *Modernity* (*Tajaddod*), published in Tabriz by social democrat Majles deputy Mohammad Khiabani (1880–1920). Raf'at seized the occasion to call for a "revolt" against Sa'di and the entire moral and political teachings of traditional Persian *adab*:

We have needs that did not exist in Sa'di's age. We suffer national and political calamities that would have been unimaginable to Sa'di ... Today's thirteen-year old school children know more about the arts and sciences than Sa'di ever did ... It is our spiritual privation that sparks this revolt [against Sa'di]. Along with all old poets and literati, Sa'di, Hafez and Ferdowsi must face up to this revolt ... So, stop preaching Sa'di, Hafez and Ferdowsi to restless reflective youths in this age of awakening. [Instead], tell us the meaning of life ... Remove this nightmare of decadence and decline from our view.[48]

Citing familiar adages from Sa'di's prose masterpiece *Golestan*, Raf'at challenged Bahar to defend the book's moral perfection:

The first fable in *Golestan* teaches us: "A well-meaning lie is better than an insidious truth." Its fourth fable preaches: "No amount of education can cure inborn criminal traits." The eights suggests kings must ruthlessly eliminate those they perceive as threats; etc.[49]

Raf'at thus pushed the debate on literary modernity farther than *Sur-e Esrafil* had, boldly storming the hallowed grounds of traditional poetics and politics. The debate peaked in 1918 after *Daneshkadeh* published a manifesto on literary modernity, declaring Bahar's position:

We follow a basic program of a malleable step-by-step modernity, not yet daring to tear down the historical edifice (*emarat*) built by our poetic and literati forefathers. Thus, we will repair this edifice, while laying down, next to it, new foundations, upon which walls will rise in an evolutionary manner.[50]

Immediately responding in *Tajaddod*, Raf'at rejected the very idea of "malleable" modernity, mocking Bahar's "structural" metaphor of becoming modern by gradually "repairing" an ancient edifice:

No architect or mason follows this sort of plan. Such notions will lead you to failure. Would you apply twentieth-century cement to patch up cracks in Persepolis? ... Can you imagine what a bizarre structure will result? ... Constructing modernity in literature, especially in Iranian literature with its celebrated classical past, is no easy task ... Certainly, there is no danger of a single modernist figure suddenly rising up to pronounce prematurely the last word on modernity, performing overnight what took a hundred literati a century to accomplish ... [Nevertheless], modernity is like revolution; it can't be poured into people's eyes with a dropper.

If you are poets and literati, know that you must be leaders not followers. You must swim upstream, against the current ... write for tomorrow ... Today, Sa'di stands in your way. His sarcophagus is crushing your crib. The seventh century dominates the fourteenth century. The very same ancient age tells you [in Sa'di's words]: "Every newcomer builds a new edifice ... " Yet, you plan merely to repair what others have built ... Be at least as innovative and modern in your time as the Sa'dis of the past were in theirs. Do not let the weight of seven centuries crush you. Prove your own presence. Nothing in this world precludes the existence of other things.[51]

Bahar's defense was feeble and vacillating. He claimed not to have called for "preserving old habits, ethics and beliefs," since the ancestral "edifice" in question referred merely to "lexical and formal principles and norms."[52] He then asked, rather lamely:

If you modernists see Iran's literary lexicon, expressions and compositions as ancient ruins, then say so directly, and have no fear. We will not fight, but only ask of you to lead us to the quarry of stones and bricks to use, replacing the particularly solid foundations and building material already at our disposal.[53]

But this fascinating debate was halted mid-way with *Daneshkadeh*'s closure in 1919, thus giving the last word to *Tajaddod*, which in turn was forced to close about a year later. Raf'at's final words echo the silenced voice of revolutionary cultural modernity:

We declared our views in previous articles. This is not merely a literary debate but a fundamental social and national one. A nation's literature is a mirror to its civility. If Iranian civilization in this fourteenth Islamic century is praiseworthy and admirable, so must be its literature. Considering contemporary Iranian literature as suitable to this age means accepting the social and political conditions prevalent in our debased and ruined country.

Even worse, if returning to the literature of six centuries ago is a reasonable literary tactic, the adoption of that era's corresponding civic, governmental and social arrangements must also be equally acceptable as civic revolutionary tactics. None of the above is acceptable to us. [54]

Raf'at remained true to these words. In 1920, he became an active supporter of an autonomous revolutionary government formed in Azerbaijan, led by Mohammad Khiabani and his splinter faction of the Democrat Party. Similar to its contemporary revolutionary regime in Gilan, the autonomous government of Azerbaijan defended Iranian constitutionalism vis-à-vis a Tehran government propped up by occupying British armies. But these two alternate nationalist and constitutionalist regimes, as well as a third one in Khorasan, remained weak and isolated from each other. Refusing to cooperate with Gilan's Bolshevik-backed revolutionaries, the autonomous government of Azerbaijan was easily crushed by a few hundred Cossacks dispatched from Tehran. Its leader, Khiabani, was killed and soon thereafter a despondent Raf'at committed suicide.[55] Thus, in the wake of World War I, three revolutionary projects of nation building and cultural modernity had appeared in Iran's provincial centers, but all three were crushed by the Cossack armies of Tehran's British-backed government. Khiabani's ethnic Azeri sympathies allowed Tehran's conservative nationalists to falsely accuse his movement of "separatist" designs. In fact, the bilingual (Azeri/Persian) conception of cultural modernity, promoted by Khaibani and Raf'at, showed an alternate path of multiethnic, and hence more democratic, nation building. The forced closure of such bilingual and multiethnic modernist projects allowed for the consolidation of Persian as Iran's sole national language of modernity. As we shall see in Chapter 4, this was no "natural" development, but an ideological choice favored also by certain Azeri intellectuals, like Ahmad Kasravi, who shared a monolithic conception of Iranian modernity and nationhood.

In the end, the post-1921 rise of Reza Khan epitomized a broader political process that within a few years violently eradicated pluralism and dissent in politics, as well as the potential for multi-linguist diversity in modernist culture. The violence of this process is perhaps best remembered in the case of radical nationalist poet Mohammad-Reza Eshqi (1894–1924), who was assassinated due to his vociferous opposition to Reza Khan's 1924 republican campaign. A warning to all dissident intellectuals, Eshqi's murder occurred at the brink of his national recognition as a revolutionary modernist poet, dramatist and journalist. Believing, like Raf'at, in the fusion of literary modernism and revolutionary politics, Eshq'i had written:

I began versifying poetic thoughts in an unprecedented manner [*shekl-e nowzohur*], believing that the literary revolution of the Persian language must be undertaken in such a way ... Forgive my shortcomings, since the work has just begun.[56]

About a fifth of Tehran's total population of 150,000 reportedly attended Eqshqi's funeral, turning it into a mass protest against Reza Khan's openly terroristic machinations, which nevertheless continued unabated. A month after Eqshqi's assassination, three leading deputies, including the influential cleric Hassan Modarres, were physically assaulted in the Majles after criticizing Reza Khan. Within a year, Bahar narrowly escaped assassination, when a man resembling him was murdered in his place, once again during a Majles session.[57] Like Mustafa Kemal's arranged murder of Turkish communist leaders, or fascist Italy's assassination of parliamentarian Giacomo Matteotti, Reza Khan's "modernist" use of extra-juridical violence was quite effective in silencing the opponents of his dictatorship.[58]

Arani's Positivist Marxism: Hegemonic Intellectuals and Sacred Masses

You are bound to follow Western civilization in every facet of your life. Your clothing, eating habits, dwelling, and legal and juridical principles, are all imitations of the West.

Taqi Arani's defense in Reza Shah's military tribunal

Along with constitutionalism and liberal democracy, socialism was another political option, within the conflicted range of global modernity, whose pursuit in Iran was effectively subverted in the 1920s and criminalized by the 1930s. As noted earlier, radical constitutionalist papers, like *Sur-e Esrafil* and *Iran-e no*, had introduced a Russian populist version of socialism, arguing for its compatibility with Islam. Iran's first social democratic "party" (*ejtema'iyun ammiyun*) began as a network of small groups, without a unifying organization or political program. The membership of *ejtema'iyun ammiyun* never reached above a hundred, although during the 1908–1909 civil war, its ranks were bolstered by hundreds of Armenian, Georgian, Azeri and Russian armed revolutionaries dispatched to Iran from the Caucasus. Ironically, these internationalist defenders of Iranian constitutionalism, along with a few thousand Iranian militias, came to be known as *mojahedin*, a Qur'anic term that became synonymous with *ejtema'iyun ammiyun*, a literal translation of "social democrat."[59] The great majority of these "social democratic" *mojahedin* therefore were militant defenders of the new constitutional regime, rather than socialists.[60] Nor do famous Iranian "social democrat" leaders, such as Taqizadeh, appear to have been seriously familiar with socialism or Marxism. The first clear and systematic exposition of Marxism in Persian is *The Critique of Social Moderates* (1910) by Mohammad-Amin Rasulzadeh, who spent only a few years in Iran and later abandoned Marxism for Pan-Turkism.[61]

As argued in Chapter 2, following the 1910 revolutionary restoration of the constitutional regime, the political program and organizational model of the (Social) Democrat Party set a crucial precedent for modern Iran's ideological and political movements. But the impact of Marxist socialism became tangible, and potentially decisive, only when the Bolsheviks consolidated power in the neighboring Russian empire. In 1920, a newly formed Iranian communist party joined armed constitutionalist rebels in the southern

Caspian province of Gilan, where a small Red Navy detachment, in hot pursuit of White forces, had landed, soon to become involved in the launch of a soviet socialist republic. Tragically fractured from the start, Gilan's soviet republic quickly unraveled as armed clashes broke out between nationalist and communist factions.[62] Nationalist, Islamist and Cold War historiography converge on considering the Gilan republic's failure as proof of communism's incompatibility with Iranian conditions. This interpretation, however, ignores the evidence that, despite their disarray, Soviet-backed Gilani revolutionaries were prevented from taking Tehran only because a British-occupying army held the capital. According to an official report, filed in September 1920 by Herman Norman, British minister to Iran:

[Tehran was] seething with Bolshevik intrigue, and invitations to occupy it were being sent to Resht from many influential quarters. Had Bolsheviks responded in time, their advance might well have been assisted by a rising here, and they would, *failing an occupation of Tehran by British troops*, have received welcome from a large section of the population, chiefly of lower classes [emphasis added].[63]

Beyond nationalist and Cold War historiography, even some leftist historians consider the 1920–1921 Bolshevik intervention as the "original Sin" of Soviet-style Marxism in Iran.[64] Such judgments, however, deflect agency and responsibility from Iranian revolutionaries, portraying them as mere dupes and victims of Bolshevik intrigue. In reality, while the Gilani rebels had no clear understanding of Bolshevism, they eagerly welcomed Soviet military assistance, just as they had accepted similar German and Ottoman offers. The subsequent Bolshevik abandonment of Gilan rebels occurred in the context of a Tehran-Moscow rapprochement sealed with the 1921 Soviet-Iranian treaty of friendship and non-aggression. Well received by Iranian nationalists, this treaty was related to a larger Anglo-Soviet accord ending their armed hostilities in Eurasia and terminating the British occupation of Iran (see Chapter 2). Fighting for survival, the Bolsheviks nevertheless had acted opportunistically, but the 1921 settlement in Iran, i.e. the crushing of revolts in the northern provinces and the restoration of Tehran's control under Reza Khan, was due to British rather than Soviet intervention. However, as we shall see below and in the following chapters, the 1920–1921 events signaled the origin of a twentieth-century "traumatic" relationship of mistrust and acrimony, as well as mutual influence and attraction, between Iranian Marxism and nationalism.

After its inauspicious debut during the Gilan rebellion, the small Iranian Communist Party continued with an inconsistent record of activities, its own confusion and factionalism being exacerbated by the vicissitudes of Moscow's policies toward Reza Khan. Following a contradictory Soviet line, one party faction considered Reza Khan a progressive "bourgeois nationalist," while another attacked him as a British puppet and would-be dictator. The pro-Reza Khan communist faction was close to the Socialist Party that had replaced the (Social) Democrat Party of the earlier Constitutional period.[65] On a more pragmatic course, communists had forged ties to an incipient labor movement, making some headway beyond middle-class intellectual circles. By 1922, the communist-affiliated Central Council of Professional Labor Unions claimed to have organized 20,000 workers, roughly 20 percent of the country's new industrial labor force. The same year, this organization's official organ *Haqiqat* (The Truth) became one of Tehran's leading dailies, showcasing the appeal of left-wing pro-Soviet constitutionalism. *Haqiqat*'s editorials and articles were mostly written by Mir-Ja'far Pishehvari, an Azeri intellectual from a working-class background. Pishevari introduced his readers to a fairly systematic Marxist worldview, analyzing Iranian and international affairs in a crisp modernist Persian prose. Ironically, it had fallen to Tehran's openly communist daily to champion the cause of constitutionalism and press freedom against the systematic encroachments of war minister Reza Khan. Forced to close down by late 1922, Haqiqat lost the battle, as did one independent journal after another, while Reza Khan consolidated his virtual dictatorship.[66] Shortly after Reza Shah's accession to the throne, labor unions were banned and their leaders, along with communist activists, were imprisoned.[67] In 1931, communists became the main target of new legislation that outlawed organizations opposed to monarchy and/or espousing a "collectivist creed" (*maram-e eshteraki*), condemning their members to as many as ten years in solitary confinement.

Against such formidable odds, a small group of intellectuals launched an ambitious project to systematically introduce Marxism into Iran. Their leader, Taqi Arani (1902–1940), already enjoyed some recognition in Tehran's nationalist and academic circles. What distinguished him from nationalist intellectuals like Taqizadeh, however, was his principled defiance of dictatorship, combined with a selfless dedication to the cause of the poor and working classes. Staying in prison until Reza Shah's fall, Arani's famous "Group of Fifty-three" became modern Iran's iconic prototype of committed intellectuals, daring to speak truth to power at the risk of incarceration, torture and death. More than all of them, Arani's Socratic stature was sealed when the public learned of his powerful defense in military court, brave conduct in prison and eventual "martyrdom." Neglected by intellectual historians, Arani and his circle are long overdue the recognition they deserve. To begin with, Arani was yet another Azeri pioneer of Iranian modernity, transitioning from ardent nationalism to Marxism. Born in a humble Tabrizi family, he grew up in Tehran and spent about six years (1922–1928) in Germany, completing a doctorate in chemistry. Originally a philosophy student, he gravitated to science at Berlin University, reportedly attending lectures by Albert Einstein and Max Planck.[68] By 1924, he was writing hyper-nationalistic articles in *Iranshahr* and *Name-ye Farangestan*. One article, for example, described Azerbaijan as "the most important cradle of Iranian civilization," whose original Iranian language was forcibly replaced by Turkish. Another praised Persian as an "Aryan language," corrupted after Arab Islamic conquests, and therefore in need of purification.[69] While typically nationalistic, these articles were distinctly attentive to the progressive social impact of science, showing a positivist mindset at odds with *Iranshahr*'s romantic mystical drift.[70]

By 1926, Arani had joined a small Berlin-based Marxist group called the Revolutionary Republican Party of Iran. The group's leader, Morteza Alavi, was soon expelled from Germany and took refuge in the Soviet Union, where he later perished in the Stalinist purges. The organization's representative in France was Iraj Eskanadri (1907–1986), a law student and later a founder and general secretary of the Tudeh Party (see Chapter 5). Arani and Alvai were in contact with the Communist International and participated at the 1927 Brussels Congress of the League Against Imperialism.[71] In 1929, Arani returned home to teach science at the Ministry of War and began writing textbooks in physics, chemistry, psychology, biology and scientific methodology.[72] In 1934, he founded the magazine *Donya (The World)*, which featured many of his previous writings in a condensed didactic format. Arani's main collaborators in *Donya* were Iraj Eskandari and Morteza Alavi's younger brother Bozorg

Alavi (1904–1997), another former student in Berlin, soon to become a famous modernist fiction writer.[73]

The precise ideological makeup of Arani's *Donya* circle remains in dispute. The journal's intellectual import was immediately recognized by contemporaries, but the specificity of Arani's thought was obscured when the Tudeh Party claimed him as the progenitor of its own Stalinist brand of Marxism. The Tudeh Party's ownership claim to Arani and *Donya* covered up facts such as the cooperation of future party leader Abdolsamad Kambakhsh with the police in framing the Group of Fifty-three and passing the blame to Arani.[74] (In 1937, members of the Arani circle were arrested, tried and most of them received long prison sentences. Arani's sentence was the maximum ten years, but he was murdered in prison shortly after being sentenced.)[75] Beyond Tudeh Party distortions, Arani's intellectual credentials and particularly his creative adaptation of Marxist thought to 1930s Iranian conditions show he was no typical Stalinist toeing Moscow's line. In his memorable courtroom defense, Arani noted the historical significance of his group's trial, accusing the judges of betraying what the Constitutional Revolution had "purchased with the blood of the nation." Condemning the 1931 anti-collectivist law, he argued:

The more civilized a nation, the less it restricts the freedom of belief and opinion. The most civilized countries, such as the U.S., Great Britain, France and Switzerland, do not stifle public opinion . . . As *Donya* has explained, you are bound to follow Western civilization (*tamaddon-e ghrab*) in every facet of your life. Your clothing, eating habits, dwelling, and legal and juridical principles, are all imitations of the West. Don't you openly declare yourselves followers of democracy and democratic countries? Then why in this particular case you follow those Western nations that temporarily have lapsed into reaction?[76]

As he expected, the court gave Arani the maximum sentence of ten years imprisonment. "A society must be ashamed of itself," his defense had concluded, "when it so harshly punishes those who speak up for the oppressed and their rights." True to his principles, and taking the blame even for charges against his friends, Arani endured solitary confinement, torture and malnourishment, finally expiring after deliberate exposure to typhus.[77]

Arani's moral and political stance thus differed markedly from that of intellectuals like Taqizadeh, Davar, Foroughi and Siasi, who served a dictatorship in the name of nationalism, modernity and progress. In line with the pro-constitutionalist Marxist newspaper *Haqiqat*, the project advanced by *Donya* diverged from Stalinist flirtations with "progressive" dictatorships. In another contemporary comparison, *Donya* was unlike *Kadro* (Cadres), a periodical published by left-leaning Turkish intellectuals who supported Kemalism as a progressive nationalist ideology.[78] Only implicitly political, *Donya*'s project was deliberately cultural and intellectual, aiming to create a hegemonic Marxist trend in Iranian modernity. To that end, Arani in 1934 had filed an official request to edit and publish a monthly magazine probing "scientific, economic, industrial and social" questions. A few proposed titles, including "Materialism," were rejected because of their foreign origin. But the familiar Arabic/Persian term *Donya* (The World), apparently chosen in homage to the prestigious French daily *Le Monde*, was allowed.[79] Donya was then launched officially as a "scientific" journal, the cover of its first issue showing the splitting of an atom, with a caption reading: "Science dissects the indivisible particle." The cover also announced: "*Donya* discusses scientific, industrial, social, and artistic issues from a materialist point of view."[80] Despite such auspicious beginnings, only twelve issues of *Donya* were ever published, from February 1934 to June 1935. Its publication ceased when Arani left for Germany, returning via a stop in Moscow, presumably to plan communist activities back in Iran. Already facing financial problems, *Donya* apparently closed down once Arani decided to vacate the spotlight as the editor of a thinly disguised Marxist publication.

As historian Baqer Momeni has noted, *Donya* was the first open advocate of a systematically "scientific materialist" worldview in Iran. "Materialist ideas," the magazine insisted, "form the only general theory capable of bringing science and industry into harmony with contemporary human society." *Donya*'s "historical role" therefore was to prove "such ideas inevitably must reach Persian speakers."[81] Though implicitly stated, this meant the propagation of a comprehensive Marxist worldview, something that was against the law. Hence, *Donya* avoided discussions of Marxism, politics, class struggle and revolution, relying instead on an indirect philosophical and cultural approach. This paralleled the project of Italian Marxist Antonio Gramsci, who wrote under fascist censorship in prison during the 1930s.[82] In both cases, however, the cultural and philosophical approach to Marxism was more than a tactical imposition. Arani, like Gramsci, insisted that political ideologies, including Marxism, were built on philosophical foundations, affecting society differently at various levels of popular and elite culture. Unlike Gramsci, however, Arani's epistemology was positivist, his Marxism being a "unified field" theory that fused history, politics, economics, laws, ethics and religion into a single materialist philosophical frame, sustained by the methodology of physical sciences.

Despite being shorn of obvious Marxist references, *Donya*'s aggressively secular scientific worldview was provocative in an Iranian intellectual milieu where "materialism" was synonymous with Bolshevism, atheism and apostasy from Islam. Yet, by the mid-1930s, the Pahlavi state's creeping secularization had made sufficient inroads to allow for the open discussion of materialism, at least in academic and philosophical forums. At the same time, a more diffuse "scientific worldview" was being promoted by the country's European-educated elite. Upholding a "scientific" positivist take on modernity, nationalist intellectuals like Siasi, Davar, Isa Sadiq and Qasem Ghani were leading a *kulturkampf* to purge education, religion and the law from "useless knowledge" and "superstition." In line with global trends, the nationalist elite's "scientific worldview" included blatant ideological distortions such as "scientific racism." This was evident, for example, in 1940s and 1950s periodicals such as *Yadegar*, edited by influential nationalist historian Abbas Eqbal-Ashtinai. In a special section devoted to "scientific discussion," for instance, *Yadegar* featured a series of articles on "Race Improvement" (*eslah-e nezhad*). Following contemporary Euro-American race theories, the author Qasem Ghani argued: "The purity of lineage (*paki-ye nasl*) is among the great critical issues facing humanity."[83] As Cyrus Schayegh has argued, during the first decades of the twentieth century, an emerging modern Iranian middle class was deploying the rhetoric of science to bolster its own social and political standing. Noting similar studies for India, Schayegh shows how European scientific knowledge was the "cultural capital" whose possession allowed middle-class elites to enhance their ideological hegemony within the nation-building project. Schayegh's important study, however, mentions Arani in passing, missing *Donya*'s role in articulating the most radically science-based worldview of 1930s Iran.[84]

Donya's embrace of scientific materialism underpinned its commitment to a global yet Euro-centric Marxist paradigm of modernity. Its first issue declared Iran was to follow Euro-American modern civilization in an inevitable evolutionary manner:

Iran, like the rest of the world, is constantly evolving, becoming more civilized. On this path to progress, Iran follows Europe and the U.S. This is a historical inevitability. It must and will be so, no matter how much a bunch of reactionary opium-addicts protest against European civilization, praising instead ancient Iranian and Indian civilizations. The nightingales, roses and rivers of Shiraz, Sa'di's *Rose Garden*, Avicenna's medical treatises, cursive writing and caravan travel will be museum pieces, replaced by Beethoven's music, Latin alphabet, typewriters, automobiles, radios, airplanes, dialectical principles and Einstein's Theory of Relativity.

But European civilization itself is mired in conflict and discord, to which materialist principles respond by harmonizing societal, scientific, industrial and artistic life. Naturally, and as with other features of European civilization, such [materialist] ideas will impact Iran too.[85]

As the above passage shows, *Donya's* worldview merged several ideological strands of 1920s Iranian modernity into an eclectic Marxist synthesis. It accepted Taqizadeh's call, in *Kaveh*, for total Europeanization, sharing to some extent the epistemological positivism of *Name-ye Farangestan*. To these, it added *Iranshahr*'s radical critique of European modernity, replacing its romantic spiritualism with the ironclad certainties of scientific materialism. At the same time, *Donya* creatively applied Marxism as a universal theory of cultural modernity, adapted to specific Iranian conditions of nation building, rather than a project of transition to socialism. While this worldview was unabashedly Euro-centric, Arani's open acknowledgment of European sources showed more intellectual integrity than the denial of indebtedness to Europe by nationalist thinkers like Kazemzadeh and Ahmad Kasravi (see Chapters 2 and 4). Finally, *Donya*'s global perspective was distinct and enriched by its appreciation of the Soviet experiment as a project of building an alternate modernity, a monumental historical event that nationalist thought invariably failed even to consider.

An indication of *Donya*'s intellectual maturity was its understanding that modernity had to be built within in a national tradition, whose reference point in Iran was the Constitutional Revolution. Hence, the journal's discussions of literature and the arts show direct continuity with the views of members of the Constitutional-era avant-garde, such as Taqi Raf'at. An article by Bozorg Alavi, on "Materialism and Art," for example, argued that within the broad sweep of history, classical Iranian literature and the arts reflected "obeisance to dominant powers." But Alavi also claimed great literary figures and artists of every age had some positive social impact. Thus, the preaching of blitheness in life by Sa'di may have been a comforting reaction to the chaos and insecurity of post-Mongol times. "In his own time," Alavi retorted, "Sa'di performed his social role properly." But in the twentieth century, "Sa'di, his *Golestan*, ideas and writing style, along with his wardrobe, belong to museums." Similarly, he claimed, Ferdowsi's *Shahnameh* served the interests of Iranian feudal magnates, asserting their independence vis-à-vis an Arab caliphate. Alavi in fact pushed this argument to the point of claiming Ferdowsi had composed the *Shahnameh* for monetary gain.[86] Interestingly, this interpretation was countered by Tehran University Professor Fatemeh Sayyah, who was educated in the Soviet Union.[87] *Donya* thus revived the 1920s modernist avant-garde debates on the historicity and political relevance of literature and the arts, with an added Marxist gloss of sophistication.

Class Struggle and the Cultural Hegemony of "Leading Intellectuals"

The only sacred law is that which serves the interests of the masses.

Arani's defense in military tribunal.[88]

Donya's most innovative contribution was its application of Marxist class analysis to contemporary Iranian society, with particular attention paid to modern culture and the role of intellectuals. This was clear in the magazine's choice of its target audience, pedagogical mission and didactic style. According to *Donya*, 1930s Iran was "a nation of peasants," where modern urban life and industrialization had barely begun. The bulk of the country's roughly ten million inhabitants consisted of poor illiterate tribal and rural people, "mentally enslaved by prejudice and superstition," and therefore beyond *Donya*'s reach. Of the remaining four million, about half were classified as artisans, shopkeepers and laborers, while the rest belonged to the urban middle and upper classes. A small segment of this latter category was literate,

while it too had to be subdivided into a hopelessly conservative majority and a minority of "intellectuals," finally identified as *Donya*'s
interlocutors.[89] Further refining its sociology of knowledge model,
Donya carefully defined intellectuals as "individuals whose fields of
perception are broadened due to literacy, education and schooling,
accessible to them because of their particular (generally middle class)
social position." This definition includes the three most often-noted
characteristics of modern intellectuals, i.e. their relatively privileged
social position, access to systematic education and ability to broadly
and critically reflect on society. Contrary to what would soon become
axiomatic in Iranian political culture, *Donya* did not consider intellectuals as generically progressive. Instead, and similar to Gramsci and
Karl Mannheim, it saw intellectuals as politically and ideologically
divided and stratified.[90] The main distinction was between "corrupt
intellectuals" (*monvvar al-fekr-e fased*) and "leading intellectuals"
(*monavvar al-fekr-e rahbar*). The first group had a fairly realistic
understanding of the modern world, yet followed their "class and
social interest" in pursuit of material gain and high status. With
fatalistic optimism, *Donya* claimed such conservative intellectuals
had little cultural and political impact, because of their "lack of
moral and social authority." The other intellectual category consisted
of those "not yet corrupted, and, due to their social position, interested in [social] struggle and progress." These were of course
Donya's intended readers: "The social role of uncorrupted intellectuals, whom we call leading intellectuals, is to elevate Iranian civilization and transfer the benefits of European civilization to Iran."[91]
Presently a very small minority, these intellectuals would in time
become strategically influential as educators and therefore leaders of
the entire nation. Moreover:

The leading role of this group is of course provisional, because history
inevitably pushes peasants to the city, diminishing differences between
rural and urban life, and brining literacy to the masses. The contribution of
leading intellectuals to civilized nations and historical evolution will have its
decisive impact on the progress of Iranian society. Thus, *Donya* will
constantly expand its intellectual leadership among the masses, until
the day when it reaches the entire public.[92]

Donya specifically included "young educated women" among "leading
intellectuals," offering a radically more gender-egalitarian perspective

than Iran's nationalist and official discourse on "Women's Liberation."[93] This socialist perspective was articulated, for example, in Bozorg Alavi's article on "Women and Materialism":

Talking of "Women's Liberation" is meaningless as long as women remain materially dependent on men ... According to materialist beliefs, society is responsible for providing all of its members with the means of subsistence. Here, there is no difference between men and women. But society can feed only those members who perform useful work. Therefore, women too must be compensated for their work. This means they must be freed from material dependence on men and instead perform other social tasks ... Idealist thinkers place women on an artificially scared pedestal, making them responsible for raising children. But child-rearing within the family serves only the interests of individual families, whereas materialist beliefs place societal interests above those of individuals and families. Therefore, neither women nor families, but society itself, must be responsible for raising children.[94]

Alavi concluded: "Materialist principles do not recognize any difference between men and women ... Just as it does for men, society must create suitable employment for women, thus freeing them from domination by men, on whom their livelihood depends at present."[95] (On Alavi and the women's rights campaign, see Chapter 5.)

In sum, *Donya*'s basic conception of modernity was one in which an intellectual elite, armed with a scientific materialist worldview, led the masses toward this society free from class and gender hierarchies. According to his confidently positivist narrative, scientific advances would inevitably bring about social progress and human emancipation. This kind of Marxism was not Leninist, since it did not call for a professional revolutionary elite to seize power via a vanguard political party. The pivoting of class struggle on the cultural leadership of intellectuals made *Donya*'s project similar to Gramsci's Marxism of cultural hegemony, albeit with a strong positivist determinist distinction. Arani of course sympathized with the Soviet Union and had contacts with the Moscow-led Communist International. But *Donya*'s advocacy of middle-class intellectual hegemony, rather than immediate working-class political mobilization, implied the assumption that Iran was not yet ready for socialism. Somewhat at odds with this evolutionary view of intellectual progress, *Donya* insisted that only its own "Materialist worldview," i.e. Marxism, was relevant to the social realities of 1930s Iran. This intellectual overconfidence was perhaps related to the fact that Reza Shah's dictatorship did not allow contending political ideologies, such as liberal-democratic or populist nationalism, to have a viable presence. But *Donya* underestimated authoritarian nationalism itself, which was powerfully present as official state ideology, as well as in semi-official versions. This underestimation of nationalism may have been due to *Donya*'s deterministic expectations that Iran's transition to capitalism would inevitably weaken nationalist sentiments. On the other hand, *Donya* proved surprisingly prescient in its anticipation of Marxist hegemony in modern Iranian political culture, something that was realized within a decade and lasted into the 1970s (see Chapters 5–7). This timely anticipation of a powerful Marxist intellectual presence may explain why, despite its brief lifespan, the magazine made a powerful impression on contemporaries. Ahmad Kasravi, an ardent nationalist and opponent of philosophical materialism, for instance, praised Arani's intellectual contribution, claiming to have shared "the same goals" with him:

Arani was a young scientist whom I befriended, especially before his imprisonment. Everyone knows Arani and I did not share the same ideas. Despite many differences, however, our goals were the same ... Arani had spent years studying various branches of knowledge, well prepared to write books and train students, thus benefiting the country ... Already familiar with vulgar accounts of subjects like "Dialectical Materialism" or "Mysticism and Materialist Principles" [titles of Arani's books], I was eager to read about them in books, written by an expert.[96]

As Kasravi indicates, *Donya*'s launch of a "scientific" materialist worldview caused ripples in Tehran's religious and secular intellectual milieu, already challenged by the positivist rhetoric of science as harbinger of social progress. Dabashi has noted how influential Muslim thinkers felt compelled to respond to *Donya*'s open advocacy of materialism. By the mid-1940s, Ayatollah Mohammad-Hosein Tabataba'i was including refutations of materialism in the philosophy curriculum he taught in Qom, the center of Iran's clerical establishment. According to Tabataba'i, although high-ranking clerics frowned upon such subjects, young seminarians were attracted to them. Conceding the inadequacy of traditional Shi'i teachings, Tabataba'i identified materialism as the greatest intellectual challenge to the younger generation of Shi'i clerics and seminarians:

> The reason I have come to Qom from Tabriz is to correct the [seminary] students' ideas according to truth, and to struggle against the unrighteous ideas of the materialists and their cohorts ... nowadays, every [seminary] student who enters through the city gates of Qom comes with a few suitcases full of doubts and questions. Nowadays, we have to attend to the students' needs. We have to prepare them for struggle against the materialists.[97]

Tabataba'i seminary curricula became the foundation of an influential text titled *The Principles of Philosophy and the Realist Method* (1953). His student Morteza Motahhari, Iran's leading clerical intellectual of the 1960s and 1970s (see Chapter 6), wrote the book's introduction, citing Arani's work more than fifty times. According to Motahhari:

> In our references to materialist ideas, we mostly rely on Arai's writings ... Fifteen years after his death, Iranian proponents of Dialectical Materialism still cannot improve upon his writings ... Arani's familiarity with the Persian language and literature, as well as with Arabic, enabled him to present [to us] Dialectical Materialism better than Marx, Engels, Lenin and others. Thus, his philosophical works are superior to those of his predecessors. That is why, despite numerous other writings and translations existing in this field, we mainly refer to Arani's discourse.[98]

Motahhari's near-obsession with Arani's challenge is explained clearly in his revealingly titled *Why Materialism Attracts*:

> In 1943, I began studying the rational sciences, always feeling inclined to gain an intimate knowledge of materialist thinkers' ideas and reasoning, as presented in their own books ... I carefully studied any book I could find by Taqi Arani, rereading them, taking notes and referring to other books, having difficulties with new philosophical language and ideas. I had read some of Arani's books so many times that I knew their sentences by heart.[99]

Conclusion

This chapter made a number of revisionist interventions within ongoing debates on Iranian intellectual history, nationalism and nation building during the 1920s and 1930s. First, it argued that the authoritarian nationalism and dictatorial nation-building project of the 1920s–1930s were the results of an illiberal consensus in early

Iranian nationalist thought. This was in line with and influenced by similar regional and global patterns, rather than being the product of supposedly perennial patterns of Iranian "despotism." Secondly, the chapter showed authoritarian nationalism became hegemonic only after defeating contending nationalist trends that were liberal democratic, constitutionalist or revolutionary populist. As well as in politics, this contestation was traced in the arena of literary production where prominent democratic and revolutionary modernist voices were shown to have been forcibly silenced. Third, the chapter focuses on the mid-1930s Marxist intellectual challenge to official and unofficial Pahlavi nationalism. Though quickly suppressed, the small intellectual circle that briefly published the magazine *Donya* had a deep impact on contemporaries, establishing the foundation of a phenomenal Marxist intellectual presence in political culture during the following four decades.

4 | Intellectual Missing Links
Criticizing Europeanism and Translating Modernity

> The East had fallen into infirmity and stupor for centuries. It is awake and moving now, but on a path leading only to greater misery. This path follows Europe, which Eastern countries are trying to catch up with. But Europe itself is lost, sinking ever deeper into misery. Thus, Easterners who finally catch up with Europe will face the same misery, but only when it is too late for regrets.
>
> Kasravi in *Peyman*[1]

Ahmad Kasravi (1890–1946), Iran's most original nationalist thinker of the interwar period, was also his generation's greatest historian, linguist and cultural/religious reformer. Yet his contribution to the modernist discourse of cultural and religious reform, particularly his critique of "Europeanism," remains obscure and underappreciated. Admired and vilified for his bold anti-clericalism, Kasravi was accused of apostasy and murdered by Muslim fanatics. Yet, he was considered "well versed in history and also a good writer" even by Ayatollah Ruhollah Khomeini, who angrily denounced his anti-clericalism in the 1940s[2] (see below). This chapter first reexamines Kasravi's intellectual contribution, locating his nationalism within a worldview radically critical of both European modernity and Iran's traditional Islamic culture. Curiously, his rejection of European modernity was coupled with a radical Protestant-style "purification" of Islam, followed by the launch of a new "rational" religion, with himself as its prophet. The chapter then reconsiders Khomeini's response to Kasravi, identifying it mainly as a defensive reassertion of clerical claims to moral/intellectual authority. Absent in Khomeini's discourse at this time is the project of turning religion into an ideology of resistance to "the West," a legacy Kasravi bequeathed to the next intellectual generation, including Khomeini himself. Finally, Kasravi's radical refutation, and Khomeini's dismissal, of European modernity will be contrasted to Fakhreddin Shadman's "liberal" proposal for the appropriation of modernity's positive side via a massive translation project. Along with Arani's Marxist legacy, the chapter concludes, the contributions of Kasravi, "young" Khomeini and Shadman are prototypical "missing links" in Iranian modernity's intellectual transition from the first to the second half of the twentieth century.

Populist Historiography, Anti-clericalism and Religious Revolution

My son, Mir Ahamd, should be educated ... But he should not make a living as a cleric. That would be apostasy.

Kasravi's father on his deathbed.[3]

Acknowledging indebtedness to Kasravi, the quintessential intellectual of 1960s Iran, Jalal Al-Ahmad, would write:

We live in times when the absence of Kasravi, as historian and linguist, is a heavy loss. He was an honest and forthright man of probing and independent judgment, detached from our wretched times, whose historiography of constitutionalism alone is worth more than the entire literary and historical production of the 1920s–1930s.[4]

Al-Ahmad's selective tribute in fact conceals the intellectual indebtedness of his own highly influential concept of "West-struckness" (discussed in Chapter 6) to Kasravi's critique of "Europeanism." As Mohammad Tavakloi-Targhi notes, such treatments of Kasravi are examples in a pattern of "historical amnesia" persisting in studies of Iranian modernity.[5] While this often has political reasons, the neglect of Kasravi's pioneering role as a critic of European civilization, and specifically his anticipation of the "West-struck-ness" discourse of the 1960s and 1970s, shows glaring "disremembering" in the genealogy of intellectual modernity.[6] Scholarly attention to Kasravi began in the early 1970s when Ervand Abrahamian noted his writings converged on a highly "integrative" form of nationalism. Without focusing on his critique of "Europeanism," Abrahamian nevertheless drew attention to Kasravi's project of turning religion into a modern ideology.[7] Two decades later, however, Hamid Dabashi's study of pre-revolutionary Iran's "Islamic ideology" was dismissive of Kasravi, considering his ideas a "side step" on the mid-century intellectual path to Marxism.[8] Similarly, Mehrzad Boroujerdi's study of Iranian intellectuals focused on Shadman, rather than Kasravi, as "the missing link between the earlier staunch supporters of the West and its late arch-critics."[9] Finally, an important 2002 article by Tavakoli-Targhi recognized Kasravi as the intellectual link between the 1920s project of "spiritual revolution" (*enqelab-e ruhani*) and the politicized revolutionary readings of Shi'ism later in the century.[10] Tavakoli-Targhi also pointed out the deliberate historiographic amnesia concerning Kasravi's intellectual contribution:

> Kasravi's writings on Europe and Europeanism undeniably impacted and shaped the ideas of Ahmad Fardid, Ataollah Shahabpur, Fakhreddin Shadman, Gholmreza Saidi, Jalal al-Ahmad, Ali Shariati and the Islamic movement's leaders, including Ruhollah Khomeini. Influenced by the intellectuals of the Constitutional Revolution and its following two decades, his works launched a discourse that eventually became manifest in the Islamic Revolution. Yet the dis-remembering of Ahmad Kasravi has de-familiarized this discursive and ideational continuity. Such dis-remembering turns Iran's modern intellectual history into a chain of unrelated events.[11]

Kasaravi's widely recognized achievement is his narration of constitutionalism as the biography of the Iranian nation reborn in the crucible of a popular revolution. As noted in Chapter 1, Edward Granville Browne's *The History of the Persian Revolution* (1910) provided Iranian nationalism with its first modern historical "master narrative." But it was Kasravi's richly source-based *History of Iran's Constitutional Movement*, and its companion *The Eighteen-year History of Azerbaijan*, that launched Iran's populist-nationalist tradition of historiography.[12] Standing between traditional chronicle and modern narration, Kasravi's historiography depicted the constitutional movement as the epic tale of a failed national and popular revolution. In his account, the people's revolutionary struggle for national sovereignty was betrayed by leaders who compromised with a corrupt old order and its foreign (Anglo-Russian) backers. As Farzin Vejdani has noted, it was Kasravi who first narrated the Constitutional Revolution as a nationalist "morality tale," with the people, or in his words "the mass," writ large as the main protagonist, defeated and betrayed, but left on the stage to continue the struggle.[13] Significantly, Kasravi's writings helped popularize the Persian term *tudeh*, or "the mass," as a widely used equivalent for both "the people" and "the nation."

Kasravi's 1930s historiography anticipated a narrative closure to be accomplished with the nation's achievement of full political sovereignty, coterminous with moral perfection. Responding to the ideological upheavals of the post-Reza Shah era, he assumed the role of a modern prophet, calling for radical religious and moral reform beyond Islam. Braving the burden of this new role, he endured vehement clerical denunciation, which eventually led to his assassination by Muslim terrorists. To the political generation coming of age during the 1940s, however, Kasravi's devastating criticism of traditional religion paved the way for a hasty transition to atheism and communism. Less apparent was the long-term intellectual impact of Kasravi's blending of populist nationalism with a radical critique of both "Europeanism" and traditional Shi'ism. As we shall see in Chapters 6–7, this deeper imprint of Kasravi's ideas echoes in the ideological projects of the 1960s and 1970s that merged Marxism, third-world nativism and revolutionary readings of Shi'ism, producing the peculiar eschatology of Iran's 1978–1979 revolution.

As with his intellectual legacy, the genesis of Kasravi's worldview, as a historian, nationalist and moral crusader, remains obscure. Being an "epistemological nationalist," he was obsessed with intellectual originality and thus loath to admit foreign, and particularly European, influences on his own thoughts. Nevertheless, his historiography fits the genre of nineteenth-century Europe's populist-nationalist historians, showing striking similarity to the works of Jules Michelet. The history of France, for Michelet, was centered on "the people," whose divisions into modern social classes had to be overcome by their unification into an organic national body. His influential work, *The People* (1846), idealized France's small property-holding peasant majority, whom he called "the mass" (*la foule*). Michelet also preached a kind of "peasant socialism," based on the equitable distribution, rather than abolition, of private property. Later in life, he came to fear the rise of "machines," anticipating the technological drift of modern industrial capitalism.[14] Moreover, he believed modern society exploited working women both economically and sexually. Women, he believed, were naturally unequal to men, and thus were fitted to serve society as men's "comforters" by staying at home and raising children under their husbands' moral and intellectual guidance.[15] Finally, Michelet was simultaneously anti-materialist and anti-clerical. Breaking with the Catholic Church, he wrote *Bible of Humanity* (1864), casting himself as the prophet of a new secular religion, derived from Enlightenment ideals.[16] As we shall see below, Kasravi's views on all of these subjects are quite similar to Michelet's.

Ironically, Kasravi's posture of intellectual autonomy is related to his being the first Iranian whose modern scholarly contribution was recognized in Europe. During the early 1920s, his original research was translated into English and Russian, he wrote for *The Encyclopaedia of Islam*, and joined the Royal Asiatic Society and other European and American scholarly associations. At the same time, he had found errors of translation and interpretation in the work of E. G. Browne, the best-known and most revered Orientalist among Iranians.[17] Having praised Browne's *The Persian Revolution*, Kasravi castigated his four-volume *A Literary History of Persia* (1902–1924). Unlike *The Persian Revolution*, he argued, the latter work diverted its readers' attention away from Iran's contemporary predicaments, toward the mystical realm of classical Persian literature. Going farther, he accused Browne's Iranian associates, especially Taqizadeh and the Forughis (father and son), of colluding with Europeans in preaching moral laxness to Iranians, thus weakening their nationalist and revolutionary resolve. Specifically attacking Taqizadeh, he wrote:

We all know about the man who after forty years of being nourished by Iran, and boasting of being Muslim and Iranian, took a European wife and to please Europeans and prove his own superiority over other Iranians began praising Europe to the extent of arguing Iranians must become Europeanized thoroughly and in every way ...

At the time, Iran was in a weak and hopeless condition, with many people ready to sell their country to Europeans. This man and his collaborators had the same intent, offering their agenda to victorious European governments, claiming they could Europeanize Iran inside and out.[18]

His judgment on the Forughis was equally harsh:

The people's passions had to be cooled ... This task was to be done by the alignment of the Forughi family with Browne and his cohorts in Europe. Dishonestly, they claimed Europeans recognize Iran through Sa'di, Hafez, Khayyam and Ferdowsi. Iranians were to follow suit ... Hence, Browne's *Literary History of Persia* and his other books were dispatched from Europe ... Streets were named after poets. Sa'adi, Hafez and Ferdowsi were called our "national pride."[19]

Prematurely postcolonial, Kasravi was radically rejecting Europe's intellectual authority, insisting that Orientalist scholarship was politically prejudiced against "Easterners," particularly Muslims and Iranians:

Most Orientalists, whom we consider objective scientists, have been Europe's political agents, systematically sewing discord and wrong-doing in the East. That is why they are always interested in subjects promoting religious innovation and spreading divisiveness among Easterners.

If not for such purposes, why should a French scholar sacrifice many years to research the life of Mansur Hallaj? Why so much debate on the Gataha and Yashtha of Zoroaster, an Iranian prophet of past millennia? Why are Europeans so interested in the Batinis and in reviving their literature? Are the Rubayat of Khayam as praise-worthy as these Orientalists claim? Is there any rational philosophy in the Rubayat?

Without considering all Orientalists as Europe's political agents, we are certain their pursuit of the above subjects shows nothing except malevolence toward Easterners, especially toward Muslims.[20]

This radical critique of Orientalism, however, was coupled with an equally harsh assessment of the worldview embedded in Iran's classical literary tradition (*adab*). Kasravi, like his immediate predecessor Taqi Raf'at (see Chapter 3), believed the powerful mystical bent of classical Persian poetry sewed irrationality, moral degeneration, other-worldliness and sociopolitical escapism. To survive in the modern world, he argued, Iranians had to be unified in a culturally cohesive and politically sovereign nation, with a singular national will, based on reason, worldliness, moral vigilance and communal responsibility. What distinguished Kasravi from intellectuals like Taqizadeh and Foroughi, as well as Raf'at, was his belief that Iran's national regeneration was predicated upon a radical "double critique" of both its own indigenous cultural tradition and modern European culture.

Though iconoclastic in 1930s Iran, Kasravi's ideas were in line with global intellectual trends, especially among Asian thinkers. Juxtaposing the nihilist "Western" culture of "materialism" and "the machine" to "Eastern" spirituality was a major intellectual preoccupation in interwar Europe and Asia. Partly inspired and confirmed by European thinkers like Oswald Spengler, as well as by Marxists, such negative appraisals of European civilization were prevalent among Indian thinkers like Muhammad Iqbal, Mahatma Gandhi and Rabindranath Tagore, as well as Chinese, Japanese and Ottoman/Turkish intellectuals.[21] Kasravi, who read Turkish, Arabic, French and English, must have known about his fellow "Eastern" critics of the modern world, though his works do not show engagement with them. He certainly was familiar with Gandhi's ideas and must have been at least exposed to Tagore's, whose 1932 visit to Iran became a nationally celebrated occasion.[22] During the 1930s Kasravi had shared Gandhi's negative view of large-scale industry and mechanization, believing they contributed to mass unemployment and workers' misery. By the early 1940s, however, he wrote:

Regarding machinery, the Indian leader's idea is not acceptable. It is true that in present conditions machines are harmful because their spread everywhere has made life more difficult ... But we must change these conditions, instead of discarding machines ... Like other European inventions, machines are products of the world's progress, and therefore they cannot and should not be opposed. If machines were not to be used, the Indian leader's wooden (spinning) wheel is yet another human-made machinery that is to be discarded.[23]

Kasravi must have been familiar too with Mohammad Iqbal (1877–1938), India's renowned Muslim intellectual of the interwar period. Iqbal's decades of intellectual production, in Persian, Urdu and English, culminated in his influential *The Reconstruction of Religious Thought in Islam* (1930). Directly engaged with modernist European thought, Iqbal had criticized, for example, Oswald Spengler's characterization of Islam as a messianic "Magian" religion, focused on the cosmic struggle of good and evil. Instead, he proposed a modernist Islamic spirituality, appealing to scientific "indeterminacy" and relativity physics to challenge Europe's nihilistic materialism. More specifically, Iqbal's *khodi* (self/selfhood) philosophy modernized Islamic mysticism by arguing that the individual's growing knowledge of God enriched selfhood and subjectivity, rather than causing their dissolution (*fana*) in God. Moreover, he saw Islam's reconstruction as an integrative modern ideology/world view "uniting religion and state, ethics and politics, in a single revelation much in the same way that Plato does in his *Republic*."[24] Iqbal's anti-positivist philosophy of Islamic subjectivity, as well as his integrative moralistic conception of the self, society and politics, parallel but also differ from Kasravi's ideas.[25]

Kasravi's Critique of Europeanism

How does our Europeanism benefit Europe? It benefits Europe greatly by making Easterners feel lowly and worthless, thus incapable of resisting

Europe's agenda of world-domination. What benefit could be greater than our following European life-styles, making the East a lucrative market for Western commerce? Thus a handful of contemptible lackeys accomplish for Europe what massive armies and huge expenses fail to do.

Kasravi in *Payman.*[26]

Foreign influences on his thought notwithstanding, Kasravi's peculiar articulation of an "Eastern" worldview was a unique intellectual contribution in 1930s Iran. A sharp critique of European culture also distinguished his advocacy of "reason" (*kherd*) from a contemporary Turkish nationalist "cult of reason" that closely identified with Western civilization.[27] Arguably, therefore, Kasravi's salient intellectual contribution is his largely forgotten critique of "Europeanism."[28] The Persian term he used, i.e. *Orupa'i-gari*, was his own invention, literally meaning "acting like Europeans." A similar term, *farangima'abi*, literally meaning "following European manners," already existed in Persian. But, as was his wont, Kasravi replaced it with *Orupa'i-gari*, a neologism stressing the particular nuance he intended. In a broader linguistic contribution, he had proposed the Persian suffix "*gari*" as equivalent to "ism" in modern French and English, conveying "the acceptance and upholding of something," including a creed or belief system. Therefore, as defined by Kasravi, *Orapa'i-gari* meant "accepting, preferring and following Europe's life-style."[29] In his small 1943 book, *On Philosophy*, Kasravi described the critique of *Orupa'i-gari* as the foundation of his life's "endeavors":

Twelve years ago, I was moved to begin a series of endeavors toward spreading goodness in the world. At that time, Iranians were bewildered by Europeanism. You may not know the meaning of Europeanism. People saw Europe differently, believing Europeans had reached the pinnacle of progress, following a straight clear path in life. Easterners therefore had to follow Europeans, considering everything they offered to be positive ... Europe and the U.S. were called "the civilized world," whereas Easterners were understood to be uncivilized ... You know of Mr. Taqizadeh's advice, in *Kaveh*, i.e. that "Iranians must become Europeanized in essence and appearance."[30]

Kasravi's point of departure, therefore, was the rejection of Taqizadeh's advocacy of total "surrender" to European civilization (see Chapter 2). He was quite familiar with both *Kaveh* and *Iranshahr*, having written for both.[31] However, his own critical views on Europe began to appear in the periodicals *A'in* (Creed), launched in 1932, and *Peyman* (The Pact), published throughout the 1930s. In many ways, Kasravi followed Kazemzadeh's lead, whose 1920s *Iranshahr* had urged Iranians not to emulate modern Europe (see Chapter 2). Perhaps most importantly, he echoed Kazemzadeh's belief that modern science and technology had neither created a better world, nor improved life for Europeans. But he also disagreed with Kazemzadeh, for example, in rejecting racist Aryanism as a negative feature of Europeanism.[32] Both men thus saw the value system guiding human society as more important than techno-logical or material progress. Significantly, Kasravi agreed with Kazemzadeh, Iqbal and their manifold Asian and European cohorts in condemning Europe's "materialism" as the epitome of its moral bank-ruptcy. At the same time, he agreed with Iqbal's positive estimation of modern science, because it discovered nature's laws, allowing humans mastery over them. In line with Asian and European anti-positivist thinkers, however, he denied that physical science models could serve as normative guidelines for social life. Indeed, Kasravi categorically rejected the use of scientific knowledge as the foundation of a "materialist" philosophy of social life. Thus, his rare references to European thinkers include citations of Nietzsche and Schopenhauer as philosophers who showed the moral vacuity of science-based sociology of knowledge.[33]

Whether knowingly or not, Kasravi's critique of European moder-nity's dichotomous split into moral and material sides echoed the views of anti-positivist Ottoman intellectuals. In 1891, for instance, Mahmud Es'ad had written:

A civilization has a spiritual and a material side, the first consists of its moral acquisitions. The material aspects of civilization include those things ranging from sewing machines to railroads and battleships; in short industrial inventions ... Which is the aspect of [Western] civilization that we want to take over? If it is the first, we do not need it because we are not devoid of civilization in that particular sense. We do not need that aspect of civilization which is already laden with innumerable shortcomings. Our own moral civilization is ample enough for our needs, let alone that it is far superior to that of the European moral civilization.[34]

Kasravi, however, would go farther than the Young Ottomans, or lapse backward, to reject not only Europe's post-Enlightenment moral phi-losophies, but philosophy in general. Like medieval Muslim thinkers, such as al-Ghazali, and contemporary neo-mystical movements like Traditionalism (see Chapter 6), he blamed philosophers, starting with the ancient Greek rationalists, for allegedly futile speculation about God and metaphysical questions.[35] But, unlike Iranian and European neo-mystics, he vehemently rejected Sufism along with Shi'ism and the moral teachings of literary masters like Sa'di, Hafez and Rumi. According to Kasravi, poets and Sufi masters, like philosophers, reached beyond reason to deal in speculation, thus leading people to confusion and idleness.

In the end, Kasravi's critique of Sufism, poetry and philosophy, as well as Europeanism, served the purposes of his "integrative" nationalism. Yet, and despite his extraordinary knowledge of Iranian history, Kasravi's understanding of nationalism and nation formation remained ahistorical. Basically, he believed nations were, or had to be, similar to human families, being organic entities living in time. This was ironic, since Kasravi, like his generation of nationalist thinkers, admitted that his idealized Iranian nation did not in fact exist (see Chapter 3). Kasravi's greatest consternation was that, instead of a cohesive unitary nation, Iran was highly fractured along various regional, ethnic, linguistic and religious lines.[36] Therefore, and despite his fiercely independent judgment, he was often in agreement with the official nationalism of the 1930s, endorsing the political centralization and cultural homogenization of Iran. He thus credited Reza Shah for such accomplishments, occasionally praising him, even during the repressive 1930s:

Certain ignoble individuals still call for European advisors in Iran, claiming we do not have such "men" of our own ... These shameless people lack not only brains but eyes to see the difference between the Iranian armed forces today and twenty years ago ... Is not the great comfort and security of today's Iran, and its strides in foreign affairs, all due to a single celebrated Iranian man's intelligence and capability? How blind-hearted and unfair is he who still complains Iran is lacking in men.[37]

Kasravi's alignment with official nationalism was evident, for example, in his participation in the 1934 millennial celebration of Ferdowsi, whose *Shahnameh* he considered a rare positive example of classical Persian literature because it promoted national pride and resoluteness among Iranians.[38] Moreover, Kasravi's personal crusade of "purifying" modern Persian paralleled and surpassed the project of *Farhangestan,* a government academy created for that purpose during the 1930s.[39] At the same time, he remained fiercely independent, refusing to bend, like Taqizadeh or Fo) rughi, to official diktats and political expediency. For example, while teaching history at Tehran's colleges of theology and officer training during the mid-1930s, he was declined promotion to professorship, due to his refusal to rescind his radical views on poets and poetry.[40] He was also a fanatical believer in the autonomy of "national" languages, although his own studies of Iran's old and new languages showed their porous boundaries and considerable overlaps. As a linguistic nationalist, Kasravi insisted that once a distinct language was formed, it had to be kept "pure," by not mixing with other languages. His reasoning was that open-ended change and diversity in a language endangered the cohesion and unity of its speakers.[41] Curiously, Kasravi's advocacy of the communicative functionality of language was contradicted by his project of interjecting hundreds of neologisms into modern Persian, to the point that his own Persian prose became impossible to read without a vocabulary list attached to his books.

Another feature of Kasravi's linguistic nationalism, once again congruent with official nationalist ideology of the 1920s and 1930s, was his passionate advocacy of Persian as Iran's unifying national language, despite the fact that he was a native Turkish (Azeri) speaker.[42] According to him:

The Turkish language came to Azerbaijan from abroad and was accepted by Azerbaijanis as their literary language ... In the wake of constitutionalism, language became a topic of discussion [in Azerbaijan], some arguing, and many agreeing, that [national] education would make slower progress in Turkish. At the same time, in pursuit of a great Turkish empire, Ottoman Pan-Turkism claimed Azeris as part of the Turkish race ... [Iranian] freedom-lovers then realized that [using] Turkish language would allow foreigners to interfere in Azerbaijan. Those Azerbaijanis who wanted to stay part of Iran ... those who loved both Iran and Azerbaijan ... decided to do their best in spreading the Persian language in Azerbaijan ... This was a decision made by Azerbaijan's own freedom-lovers, not by Tehran or its government.[43]

The above passage shows that Kasravi's nationalism was in line with modern authoritarian conceptions of the nation as a self-contained linguistic, social, political and economic community. Nevertheless, his nationalism differed from prevalent global norms in its rejection of political division and conflict, not only within but also between nations. Like Michelet, Gandhi and other nationalists who romanticized pre-industrial utopias, he imagined the nation mainly as a community of small agricultural producers, with no objective conflict of interest. In Kasravi's political economy, "the source of life is air and land."[44] Tilling the land established ownership of it; therefore, those who performed no personal labor on the land had no legitimate claims of proprietorship to it. The latter category was a small minority in every nation, consisting of those who lived an idle or parasitic life, exploiting the labor of others. In addition to large landowners, this included poets, clerics, fiction-writers and merchants, who profited beyond their own productive labor. Like many contemporary thinkers, Kasravi condemned "money-dominated" economies, without being concerned with capitalism as a distinct socioeconomic system. Money, he argued, had to be a means of exchange, and not of wealth creation.[45] Similar again to nationalist thinkers like Gandhi, he condemned European capitalism for its reliance on large-scale industry and mechanized factory production to increase the exploitation of the masses. This European reality of social conflict, he argued, was reflected in materialist and Social Darwinist philosophies that saw class struggle within, and war among, European nations as inevitable.[46] He thus dismissed modern industrial capitalism in favor of preserving more "natural" pre-industrial agricultural economies:

The hue and cry about industry is nonsense. In fact, in order to find its proper place, industry must be brought down several pegs from its current high position. On the other hand, there is no limit to the progress of agriculture and land cultivation. Had Europeans focused their efforts on agriculture, instead of industrialization, the world would become prosperous and hunger and impoverishment would end ... We wish Iranians deemed agriculture more important than industry.[47]

Finally, Kasravi's views on women and gender were typically patriarchal and congruent with those of secular nationalist and Muslim modernists of his generation. To him, the advocacy of gender equality was among the worst influences of Europeanism.[48] Women, he believed, were to enjoy respect and protection as wives and mothers. These were tasks for which they were created, for women's mental and emotional capacities differed from men's.[49] In a rare endorsement of a contemporary

European political leader, Kasravi cited Hitler's views on women positively, praising the Nazis for retiring millions of women from jobs that were returned to men:

We have explained how, contrary to widespread perceptions, Western women lack true dignity. Instead, they are playthings to men's desires, valued while young and beautiful, but discarded when old. That is why most women are forced to earn a living by taking up men's work ... We say: Women should do only women's work. Those without male bread-winners may need to work. But they should take up professions like sewing or making shirts and stockings. Only if such jobs are impossible to find can women be given male professions. Unless absolutely necessary, allowing women to perform men's work will destroy them, while leaving households and families in disarray. Worse, it will make things more difficult for men.[50]

Like his contemporary Muslim modernists, Kasravi thought women were to be educated, but only to become better mothers and household mangers.[51] He also believed the mixing of genders in public spaces inevitably led to women's corruption. Therefore, women were not to mingle with men and had to appear modestly attired and without physical adornments in public. Kasravi even approved of the *hejab*, in its broader sense of "protective" gender barriers in public space. According to him, the covering of women's faces and their being wrapped in chadors was not prescribed by Islam, since such practices did not exist during the Prophet Mohammad's time. This too was fully in accord with 1930s Iran's state-sponsored "anti-veiling" campaign.[52]

A Divine Intellectual Mandate: Appropriating the Sacred and Approximating Socialism

What shall we do to be saved? In politics, establish a constitutional co-operative system of world government. In economics, find working compromises ... between free enterprise and socialism. In the life of the spirit, put the secular super-structure back onto religious foundations.

Arnold J. Toynbee in 1947.[53]

Kasravi probably never read Toynbee, but his worldview bears a vague resemblance to the British historian's globalist constitutionalism and critical perspective on "Western civilization," as well as his appreciation of Asian civilizations and grounding of politics in spirituality. Moreover, Toynbee, like Kasravi, claimed divine inspiration, placing himself in "a long tradition of God's self-revelation to specially sensitive individuals, ... He never called himself a prophet, and was rather embarrassed when others did so. Yet he never repudiated the title either, and sometimes came close to claiming the role."[54] Kasravi's most controversial innovation, of course, was his advocacy of a new religion beyond Islam. During the 1930s, he wrote as a Muslim modernist, seeking to rationalize Islam by purging it from superstition, sectarianism and clerical abuse. Whether consciously or not, he was following the project of intellectuals like Kazemzadeh who had tried to appropriate the sacred "essence" of religion, as social power, to metaphysically fortify nationalist ideology. This important aspect of Kasravi's intellectual endeavor makes him a direct precursor to mid-century socially conscious Islamic modernists and 1960s and 1970s thinkers like Ali Shariati, who turned Islam into a radical political ideology (see Chapters 5–6). Arguably more consistent than Muslim modernists who followed him, Kasravi, by the early 1940s, went farther, claiming divine "inspiration" as founder of a new Religion of Reason (*din-e kherad*). He now argued that what ordinary Muslims were taught to believe and practice was in fact irreligion (*bidini*). Zoroaster, Moses, Jesus and Mohammad, he claimed, were all divinely "inspired" (*bar-angikhteh*) to lead people in the most "rational" manner conceivable at the time. Thus, what these prophets originally taught had been true religion, whereas what their followers believed and practiced would, in time, turn into the opposite of true religion. Kasravi distinguished between God's "messengers" (*peyghambaran*), who received divine "revelation," and religious reformers who, like Zoroaster, were divinely "inspired" to show truth and fight falsehood.[55] He thus considered himself among religious reformers, divinely "inspired" to discern and propagate divine truth.[56] Such fine distinctions, however, were irrelevant to Kasravi's Muslim detractors, and particularly the clerical establishment, who declared him an unrepentant "apostate," and thus technically deserving of a death sentence (see below).

In a pioneering study, Abrahamian observed that by "religion" (*din*), Kasravi meant "an ideology that effectively integrated the individual into a nation, instilling in him social consciousness, cultural ethos, and values oriented toward the public good." He also noted Kasravi probably borrowed this understanding of religion from his contemporary Turkish nationalist reformer Zia Gokalp, who in turn followed Emile

Durkheim's theory of religion as a cultural force serving social integration and national cohesion.[57] Gokalp's fully fledged ideas, appearing in
What is Turkism (1923), define the nation as a cultural community,
based on a common language and core values. In Goklap's illiberal
collectivist view, the individual had to be totally subordinate to the
national community, a position summed up in his dictum "There is no
individual but nation; there are no rights but duties." According to
Gokalp, while the Turkish nation had a trans-historical existence, the
masses acquired national consciousness by following "elites" (*guzide-
ler*), particularly heroes (*kahraman*) who appear in times of crisis as
champions of national culture.[58] Kasravi, who advocated similar ideas
in the 1920s and 1930s, was certainly familiar with the Ottoman/
Turkish project of reconstructing Islam as a rational religion compatible with science and purged of mythical and supernatural features.
By the early twentieth century, the idea of Islam as a "religion of
reason" had appeared in the Young Turk journal *Ijtihad*, partly in
response to the growing influence of positivist materialism among
modernizing intellectuals. As we saw in Chapter 2, the Young Turk
elite had a complicated "love–hate" attitude toward European civilization, admiring its intellectual and political strength, while condemning
its predatory treatment of the Ottoman Empire.[59]

In addition to Ottoman and Turkish intellectuals, Kasravi appears
to be influenced by global ecumenical religious movements, as well as
the cyclical movements of Islamic renewal and purification, including
Wahhabism, and even by the Babi-Baha'i religious innovations he
vehemently attacked.[60] In the politically charged atmosphere of the
early 1940s, his propagation of religion as nationalist ideology was
challenged by Marxists, as well as by the clerical establishment.
Forced to directly confront questions of class, politics and government, the contradictions of Kasravi's thought became more apparent.
On the one hand, he had been a defender of constitutionalism, i.e.
European-style representative government. On the other, his political
thought remained authoritarian, considering ordinary people in need
of strict moral, and hence political, guidance by a divinely inspired
intellectual elite.[61] Rejecting traditional Islam, he nevertheless
believed in intellectual authority as a scared trust, transferred from
clerics and Sufis to the radical intelligentsia, a mandate claimed also
by Arani and his Marxist followers, and later by Islamic-socialists like
Ali Sharati (see Chapters 5 and 6).

The extent of Kasravi's intellectual authoritarianism varied according to time and circumstances. As an "inspired" leader, he could be extremely rigid and fanatical, calling for violent measures to cleanse social ills and deviations. He rejected freedom of thought and imagination, which, he believed, could lead ordinary people to moral corruption and political confusion. In Platonic fashion, he condemned modern European literature along with classical Persian poetry, because they both gave free reign to imagination and sentiment. Debating Fatemeh Sayyah, a Russian-educated professor of comparative literature at Tehran University, he argued that the nation's moral edification hinged on the study of history, rather than works of fiction. Thus, he equally condemned writers ranging from Alexandre Dumas and Giorgy Zeydan to Anatole France and Leo Tolstoy. Particularly disturbing to him was modern and classical literature's alleged inducement of readers to sexual license. Thus, he angrily declared that Iran's great medieval poet Sa'di deserved a death sentence for preaching homosexual acts. Condemning literature as both the cause and consequence of Europe's moral deprivation, Kasravi predicted a day when works of fiction burnt in puritanical bonfires.[62] His advocacy of book burning brings to mind not only familiar Catholic or Nazi practices, but the less well-known recommendation of *Bayan*, the mid-nineteenth-century Babi scripture.[63]

Kasravi's brief debate with Sayyah in the 1930s, over the social function of literature, is a fascinating faded page in twentieth-century Iranian intellectual history. It shows how Tehran University's first woman professor was a more sophisticated intellectual than the country's leading historian, nationalist thinker and religious reformer (on Sayyah, see also Chapter 5). Responding to Kasravi briefly but cogently, Sayyah argued that literature and the arts should not be dismissed as "lies," just because they are not direct reflections of social reality. She reminded Kasravi that even historiography reconstructs true events from the vantage point of historians. Finally, while agreeing with Kasravi in condemning most modern European fiction as crass entertainment, she defended the morally uplifting value of fiction by writers like Charles Dickens, Victor Hugo and Anatole France, noting also how their work had helped bring about progressive social reform.[64]

Kasravi's crusade of cultural cleansing, however, went beyond the purging of classical and modern literature. His targets included philosophy, agnosticism, Sufism, Shi'ism and Baha'ism, all of which he considered socially harmful and therefore to be eliminated. Those preaching such beliefs had to be harshly dealt with at first, and executed if persistent. In Kasravi's strict disciplinary utopia, everyone had to be morally and physically fit, while all deviant behavior, such as drunkenness, was "sinful" and to be severely punished. People were to be entertained by listening to music and reading history books, while roaming in nature and verdant gardens. The cinema was acceptable only if it showed true-to-life stories.[65] Given his own scrupulous record of service in the judiciary, Kasravi's notion of justice and its administration was extraordinarily exacting. Judgeship was a sacrosanct vocation and judges who took bribes, for example, were to be executed. A vast litany of "criminal" offenses also were to be summarily judged and punished harshly. Modern European ideas of reforming criminals in prison were erroneous because incarceration was a social expense that did not reform, but instead hardened, criminals. Those committing premeditated crimes were to be flogged publicly, to suffer additional psychological reprimand. Not only murderers, but those who betrayed their country, or committed sodomy, deserved the death penalty. Similarly, religious frauds, fiction writers, fortune-tellers and poets who defamed others had to be executed for repeat offenses.[66] In an important way, however, Kasravi's advocacy of morally righteous violence differed from the modernist cult of violence and warfare justified in the name of nation, class or religion. While praising the Constitutional Revolution's popular militias and Reza Shah's militaristic nation building, Kasravi shunned Europe's modern arms race and total warfare, considering them as further proof of "moral corruption." His 1930s writings, for instance, condemned growing militarism in Nazi Germany and other European countries, warning that Europe's arms race, market-dominated culture and industrial competition inevitably led to war.[67]

Fanatical Muslim violence, however, abruptly ended Kasravi's intellectual journey just as he was drawn into the tumultuous ideological and political debates of the post-Reza Shah era. In 1945, about a year before his assassination, he published *Toward Politics*, a small book written in response to the political challenges Iran faced while emerging from Allied occupation. In characteristic style, he offered his own definition of politics:

Politics means the solidarity of a people with other peoples, that is to say how a people can find its way to live and advance among other peoples, interacting with them on the basis of reason and understanding ... Today, politics in Iran means focusing on and finding remedies to the backwardness and problems afflicting its people, so that Iranians can enjoy the comforts of life and make progress, in equal measure to all other people in this world. Finally, caught between two great powers, i.e. Russia and Britain, Iran must act in a way that avoids the enmity of these two governments.[68]

Eschewing idealism, he submitted that Iranian politics was to be understood in terms of two conflicting geo-political tendencies, one pro-British and the other pro-Soviet. With uncharacteristic realpolitik, he argued that Allied-occupied Iran had to find a positive balance between these two powerful tendencies, forging good relations with the Soviet Union and Great Britain, while being independent from both.[69] At the same time, he repeated his trademark belief that without proper "cultural cleansing," Iran's problems could not be solved by adherence to modern ideologies like constitutionalism, fascism, socialism and communism:

As long as ignorance and confusion are not uprooted among the masses, socialism, communism, or similar belief systems, cannot take root among them, even if forcibly imposed. This is proven by the fact that after four decades, Iranian constitutionalism remains rootless.[70]

As with his positive estimation of constitutionalism, Kasravi also showed some receptivity to socialism. In a section titled "Not Far from Socialism," he admitted that, while still refusing to follow European ideologies, his own political ideals were close to socialism: "The founders of socialism were well-meaning men who worked toward the world's betterment ... They were close to us. Fortunately, their efforts bore fruit as today the world is rapidly moving toward socialism." This qualified endorsement of socialism showed Kasravi's alignment with an emergent global drift toward Third World socialism, a path that was different from following the Soviet Union or accepting its official ideology. Kasravi in effect approved of a "peasant socialism," protecting small-property holders from the onslaught of large-scale concentrations of capital. Believing that "property was natural," he argued the state should intervene in the economy to regulate markets and capital formation, not to abolish them.[71]

Kasravi's brutal assassination foreclosed the possibility of new departures in his thought, for example, in confrontation with the ascendance of Marxism during the next few decades. In a glaring case of modern selective remembering, he was canonized as a first-rate historian, while his innovative ideas on nationalism, religious reform and resistance to "Europeanism" were largely glossed over as fanciful curiosities. Relegated to footnotes, he was acknowledged in the margins of intellectual history as a thinker whose innovations helped mid-century Iranian intellectuals transition to Marxism and atheism. This occluded his most important intellectual contribution, namely his anti-clerical "Protestant" reinterpretation of Islam as a nationalist ideology of resistance to Western modernity. Below, we shall see how vehement reactions to Kasravi's "apostasy" and anti-clericalism helped derail attention to the more complex and enduring aspects of his intellectual contribution.

Young Khomeini on Clerical Authority and Modern Government

In 1944, shortly before Kasravi's assassination, Ruhollah Khomeini intervened in the country's intellectual and political debates by publishing *Secrets Exposed* (*Kashf al-Asrar*). This was a polemical response to what he considered frontal attacks on Islam and Shi'i clergy in a 1943 pamphlet titled *Millennial Secrets* (*Asrar-e Hezar Saleh*). Written by a former cleric, Ali-Asghar Hakamizadeh, *Millennial Secrets* articulated a bold anti-clerical position similar to Kasravi's.[72] Khomeni's response, in *Secrets Exposed*, therefore was an important intervention, adding a clerical voice to the intellectual and political cacophony following the fall of Reza Shah's dictatorship. Due to its arcane language and strict juridical style of argumentation, *Secrets Exposed* is a daunting read, which may in part explain why it has received much less attention than Khomeini's other writings and pronouncements.[73] Yet this work merits closer scrutiny as the first systematic clerical response to decades of steadily growing criticism of traditional Shi'ism, culminating in significant curtailments of clerical power under Reza Shah.

Kasravi's radical critique of Shi'ism was part of a broader movement that, particularly during the 1920s and 1930s, proposed a return to the "pure" Islam of the Qur'an and the Prophet. This movement's most prominent voice was Shari'at Sangelaji, who, like Kasravi, appealed to reason in purging Shi'ism of "superstitions" and unverifiable sayings attributed to Shi'i Imams (*ahadith*). In a more cautious manner, Sangelaji also proposed a reform of Shi'i jurisprudence (*fiqh*), which, he argued, like its Sunni counterpart, was constructed largely on dubious *ahadith*. Steering clear of politics and social issues, reformers like Sangelaji were generally in line with the modernization projects of the Reza Shah era, including the state's control of the clerical establishment.[74] Kasravi and his associates, like the author of *Millennial Secrets*, radicalized this secularizing tendency, openly challenging and effectively rejecting Shi'ism, calling clerical authority socially parasitic, politically reactionary and intellectually nonsensical.

Millennial Secrets began by addressing "the leaders of religion," i.e. Shi'i clerics, asserting bluntly: "Ninety-five percent of what you call religion is bewilderment." The author then invited Iran's clerics to a public debate, challenging them to respond to about a dozen questions/objections regarding fundamental Shi'i beliefs and practices. These included the very principle of Shi'i Imamate, i.e. belief in the divinely ordained primacy of Ali and his line as successors to the Prophet; the absolutely binding authority of Shi'i clerics over their followers; the clerical establishment's tolerance of "illegitimate" political rulers; whether Shi'i clerics could rule the people directly; whether society could legislate independent of the shar'ia; and finally the reasons for Iranians turning away from Shi'ism.[75] *Secrets Exposed* thus had challenged the foundational beliefs of Shi'ism, as well as the social power and intellectual authority of its clerical guardians. Picking up the gauntlet, Khomeini took it upon himself to not only respond but to demolish the premises of each and every one of these objections. His self-assured rhetorical offensive amounted to traditional Shi'ism declaring defiance of the intellectual challenges posed by modernity.

Khomeini began by promising that, like his adversaries, he would argue strictly according to reason (*kherad*), which he urged readers to rely upon as their criteria for judgment between the two sides.[76] He proceeded to cite "the great Muslim philosopher" Ibn Sina (Avicenna), who had said "those who believe something without reason are beyond the pale of human nature." Without ever mentioning Kasravi or Hakamizadeh by name, he thus started from presumed common grounds they shared with believing Muslims:

Since these writers' discourse shows they accept God and the Qur'an, while submitting to nothing but reason's dictates, we too debate them according to reason's dictates and Qur'anic verses. Based on these two shared principles, we clarify confusions, proving those accepting God and the Qur'an must also and forever submit to the [Shi'i] *ahadith*.[77]

However, Khomeini's promise to debate wholly within the bounds of reason quickly runs into obstacles, which he bypasses by switching to rhetorical assertions and appeals to Shi'i authority. He concedes, for example, that the foundational Shi'i belief in the Imamate needs to be proven by reason, as it is established neither by the Qur'an nor by the Prophet's sayings. Admittedly too, the great majority of Muslims, who are Sunni, do not share the Shi'i belief in the Imamate. Khomeini's adherence to mutually acceptable reasoning breaks down, however, when he proceeds to "prove" the principle of Shi'i Imamate by citing "authoritative" sayings (*ahadith*) of Shi'i Imams.[78]

It soon becomes apparent that Khomeini's goal, throughout *Secrets Exposed*, is to uphold the Shi'i clergy's traditional claims to intellectual authority and social power. He starts by mocking his opponents as "self-described intellectuals" who reject Shi'i clerical authority while "blindly following ignorant and uncivilized *Wahhabi* camel-herders." At the same time, he accuses the same opponents of being inspired by European ideas. Such intellectuals, he says, claim Muslim clerics, have caused Iran to fall behind Europe, whereas in fact "Europe is closer to savagery than civilization."[79] Interestingly, Khomeini's passing critical references to Europe are mainly political, rather than moral and philosophical, as was the case Kasravi. For example, instead of critiquing Western atheism and "materialism," he denounces Europeans for using Reza Shah to weaken the clergy in order to better control Iran. In sum, *Secrets Exposed* is much more concerned with refuting Iran's anti-clerical intellectuals than critiquing Europe. Conceding a main claim of his opponents, Khomeini admits Iranians have become "infirm" in religion and following the clergy. But he blames this on Reza Shah's policies, implying religious infirmity has been politically imposed on Iranians.[80] Occasionally, Khomeini assumes a rationalist posture, making passing references to different religions and philosophical systems. He briefly mentions, for instance, the beliefs of ancient natural philosophers, Zoroastrians, Manichaeans, pre-Islamic Arabs and Christians, asserting that Islam and the Qur'an reject all of these as unbelief (*shirk*).[81] Calling Christians, or even Zoroastrians, "unbelievers" is contrary to traditional Islamic belief, as well as to views Khomeini himself would express later in life. The anti-Zoroastrianism of *Secrets Exposed* seems to be another defensive reaction to the growing cult of pre-Islamic Iran, and its concomitant elevation of Zoroastrians, under Reza Shah.[82]

Curiously, while branding Christians as unbelievers, Khomeini considered Socrates and Plato to be fellow believers in "divine wisdom" (*hekmat-e elahi*), a doctrine he says was incorporated into Shi'ism via Molla Sadra's teachings in sixteenth-century Iran. He also praises Aristotle, the "First Master," in comparison to whose logic, he asserts in passing, Descartes' "rationalist revolution" appears childish.[83] The arbitrary dismissal of Descartes remains Khomeini's only direct reference to modern philosophy, whose progress beyond Molla Sadra he refuses to acknowledge. *Secrets Exposed* thus remains defiantly self-enclosed within the intellectual ambit of traditional Shi'i juridical thought, although Khomeini's appreciation of Sadra's School of Illumination hints at a deviation from the clerical mainstream.[84]

Thus, in the mid-1940s, Khomeini was adamantly unengaged with modern European thought, whether philosophical, social or political. His basic position simply was that Islam, as defined by Shi'i jurisprudence, offered perfect unalterable answers to all the questions humanity ever faces both in this world and in the hereafter. It is important to emphasize that, in contrast to Khomeini's future mindset, *Secrets Exposed* is largely unconcerned with subjects such as Europe's political or cultural domination of Iran or the exploitation of its people and natural resources. For instance, regarding the British control of Iranian oil, a topic of intense national concern in the 1940s, Khomeini merely says that "foreigners handling oil mines must pay the *khoms* [i.e. a clerical tax]."[85] In fact, *Secrets Exposed* has no more than two pages of sustained commentary on Europe. A short section, titled "A Glance at Europe's Chaotic Life," is a harsher summary of Kasravi's criticism, while prescribing Islam and its unalterable laws as the remedy:

Should today's Europe, idolized by an ignorant lot [of Iranians], be counted among civilized nations? A Europe whose only ideal is bloodlust, mass murder and destruction of countries? ... Europe is about dictatorship and tyranny ... Hitler's conquests are beyond the pale of reason ... Such violent chaos and upheavals would not have occurred had Islamic civilization reached Europe. Where do Europe and its laws stand in relation to rational norms? Contemporary European life is among the worst.[86]

Repeating Kazemzadeh's neo-mystical claims (see Chapter 2), Khomeini argues that contemporary European interest in "spirit science," magnetism and hypnosis proves the failure of materialism:

Magnetism has shaken up the world, materialism is in its last gasps, and science soon will unveil the spirit world and eternal life and their bewildering features, such as the unconscious revelations of those under hypnotic spells, and hundreds of such amazing secrets, thus utterly destroying the foundations of materialism ... [However] what Europe's spirit scientists are boasting about was in fact revealed to the world by the Prophet and Shi'i Imams, thirteen hundred years ago ... Without visible means, Solomon covered the distance an airplane would take two months to fly.[87]

During the 1960s and 1970s Khomeini's topics of interest, as well as his discursive style, would become modernized and hence accessible to wider audiences. Conforming to the Marxist and anti-imperialist nomenclature then prevalent in Iran, Khomeini's new vocabulary would be filled with terms like colonialism (*este'mar*), Zionism (*sahyunizm*) and monarchist despotism (*estebdad-e saltanati*). He also would pay attention to the social question, deploring the chasm separating the country's upper and lower classes.[88] *Secrets Exposed*, however, is largely devoid of such terminology and themes, displaying instead respect for property and social hierarchy. Khomeini states categorically, for example, that "world civilization is founded on the principle of property." Moreover, while expressing sympathy for workers, he is clear that a "factory owner" must be in command of his employees.[89]

Khomeini's radical departure from traditional Shi'i views, on politics and government, was his early 1970s declaration of monarchy's incompatibility with Islam. This clearly was not his view in *Secrets Exposed*, a work often considered in accord with constitutional monarchy. More accurately, *Secrets Exposed* accepts constitutional government *only if* all legislation is vetted by clerical authority. As discussed in Chapter 2, this is the doctrine of Islamic Constitutionalism (*mashrute-ye mashru'e*), to which Khomeini remains as committed in *Secrets Exposed* as he would be in his more innovative 1971 *Islamic Government*. Lingering confusion on the evolution of Khomeini's political thought is related in part to an Orientalist understanding of Shi'ism, which echoes in recent scholarly literature on clerical attitudes toward secular political power. Briefly, in traditional Shi'ism, divine sovereignty is invested in the Prophet and Shi'i Imams, delegated, in their absence, to qualified Shi'i jurists (*mujtahids*). Starting from this premise, scholars like Ann Lambton, Hamed Algar and Said Amir Arjomand have concluded that *in principle* Shi'ism considers all secular authority, including kingship or sultanate, to be illegitimate. This conclusion, however, is at odds with the Shi'i clerical establishment's systematic historical accommodation to caliphs, sultans and shahs. Another line of recent scholarship, however, explains that the "illegitimacy" of secular government in Shi'i doctrine is not absolute, but relative and nuanced. In other words, and rather similar to classical Sunni political theory, traditional Shi'ism accepts secular government, i.e. kingship (sultanate), as both necessary and beneficial, granting it legitimacy to the extent it accords with precepts established by Shi'i jurists.[90] A close reading of *Secrets Exposed* shows its compatibility with this latter position. According to Khomeini:

Jurists (*mojtahedin*) never opposed sovereignty and orderliness in Islamic countries. Even when they consider a government tyrannical (*ja'eraneh*), and its laws contrary to God's commands, they have not and do not oppose it because a decadent government is better than none ... Any rational person agrees that the existence of government and sultanate is positive and beneficial to the people and country. A [political] system constituted according to divine commands and justice would be best. But when this is not accepted, the jurists would never oppose even a semblance of order, or try to destroy the foundations of government. They may have opposed a particular sultan, who acted against the country's interest. But *so far they have not opposed the principle of the sultanate ... All historical records available show jurist support of governments.*[91] [emphasis added]

While this passage admits that, historically, Shi'i jurists have not opposed the principle of monarchy, Khomeini's careful insertion of the qualifier "so far," into the last sentence, anticipates the possibility of a future change in this position. Thus, according to "young" Khomeini, the qualified acceptance of monarchy in Shi'ism is a matter of historical contingency, not a doctrinal principle. Given such distinction, Khomeini's 1971 rejection of monarchy would appear a radical "ideological revolution" in Shi'ism. In other words, in 1971 Khomeini proposed an important change in the *functional form* of government,

without changing his basic view on the *normative content* of government, the latter always requiring Shi'i juridical sanction.[92] This is why
Secrets Exposed could argue that "except for deceptive terminology,
there is no essential difference between constitutionalism and despotism, or democracy and dictatorship."[93] His brief discussion, in *Secrets
Exposed*, of the doctrine of the Guardianship of the Jurist elucidates
this point further:

No one but God has the right to govern others or to legislate; and Reason
requires that God Himself must establish government and legislate for the
people. Such are the laws of Islam ... applicable to all people at all times ...
The Prophet and the Imams govern directly in their own time ... [a point] we
now bypass to discuss the present time ... As to the question of the Jurist's
Guardianship (*velayat-e mujtahid*), this has always been controversial
among the jurists themselves, both as to whether or not in principle they
possess such guardianship, as well as this guardianship's extent and its
application to government ... When we say that at present guardianship
and government belong to the jurists (*foqaha*), this does not mean the jurist
must be king, minister, street sweeper, etc. What we say is this: Just as the
people of a country gather in a constituent assembly to form a government
and change a dynasty ... a similar kind of assembly could be formed of jurists
(*mujtahids*) who are just, cognizant of God's injunctions, free from selfish
temptations, and upholding only God's ordinances and the people's interest,
to choose a just king (*sultan-e 'adel*), who obeys God's commands, avoids
oppression and does not transgress upon people's life, property and honor ...
So, *why should not the country's consultative assembly be formed or supervised by jurists (foqaha), as our [existing] laws also require?*[94] [emphasis
added]

This passage contains the kernel of Khomeini's theory of government,
claiming ultimate juridical "guardianship" of its *normative* content,
a traditional Shi'i demand which he upheld throughout his life. But
Khomeini did propose two important innovations during the 1970s:
The first was his categorical rejection of monarchy (see Chapter 6) and
the second was his proposal that Shi'i jurists expand their "guardianship," beyond a supervisory capacity, to rule directly in an Islamic
Republic. A product of historical contingency, the second proposal
was articulated *only after* the monarchy was overthrown in the
1978–1979 Revolution.

   Last but not least, *Secrets Exposed* is emphatic on the necessity of
systematic state violence to keep society in line with juridical norms.

The full and vigorous application of shari'a punishments, Khomeini argues, is not only religiously mandated, but also beneficial to society in pragmatic ways.[95] Thus, *Secrets Exposed* repeatedly exhorts believers to punish transgressors like the author of *Millennial Secrets*. It urges Muslims to use "an iron fist and cleanse the world of the seed of these vile and ignoble individuals," telling them that "Islamic Law will shed your blood."[96] Without being formal *fatvas* of execution, such exhortations effectively amount to the same thing. Thus, the violent temper and language of *Secrets Exposed* is another feature of Khomeini's discourse that remains constant from the 1940s to the 1970s, something de-emphasized in the immediate pre-revolutionary years, only to be unleashed with full force under the Islamic Republic.

Conquest of Europe via Translation: A Liberal Agenda?

European civilization is a different kind of enemy, armed by different weapons, whose conquest of Iran, I believe, will be our last defeat.

> Shadman, *The Conquest of European Civilization* (1948)

In addition to Khomeini's and Kasravi's decidedly illiberal voices, Iran's mid-century debate on encountering Europe included a "liberal" voice, best articulated in a small book titled *The Conquest of European Civilization* (1948).[97] Strictly speaking, during the first half of the twentieth century, Iranian liberalism, whether in *laissez-faire* and natural rights or in utilitarian welfare state varieties, was practically non-existent. Iran of course was not exceptional, since not only the Middle East and Asia, but most of Europe remained under illiberal regimes until after World War II.[98] Nor was liberal government, based on the parliamentary representation of propertied white male citizens, a defining characteristic of "Western" nation-states. That kind of government had slowly appeared only at the metropolitan centers of the British, Dutch, French and American empires, whose global political rule was blatantly, and often violently, illiberal. As comparative historian of empires, Choi Chatterjee, has observed:

In the British, French, and Dutch empires, the distance between the citizens of the privileged metropole that was *confusedly called a nation state* and the subjects in the colonial periphery or the empire proper was maintained by dubious legal frames as well as large doses of extrajudicial violence ... *The uneasy coexistence of national and imperial forms in the west,* an awkward legal and political arrangement that endured for almost two centuries, has begun to be seriously questioned and challenged by post-colonial scholarship. But history books often contain a double narrative about liberal European nations and illiberal European empires![99] [emphasis added]

In the Iranian case, the legal frame and political culture of a would-be liberal government were rudimentarily introduced during the Constitutional Revolution. However, as we saw in Chapters 2 and 3, this potential, for the gradual institutionalization of liberal government, was subverted by the 1920s intellectual and political turn to authoritarian nationalism and nation-state building. Liberal ideology could not flourish in an environment lacking a free press, political parties, meaningful electoral politics and citizens' rights. As noted in Chapter 2, demanding such liberal institutions was introduced in Iran by social democrats and largely abandoned by nationalists, without a liberal party of any import defending them. Nor did intellectual statesmen, like Hassan Taqizadeh, Mohammad-Ali Forughi, Ali-Asghar Hekmat, Isa Sadiq or Ali-Akbar Siasi, leave behind a record of ideas or practices that might properly be called liberal. A recent political and historiographic tendency seeks to rehabilitate these men as "closet" liberals who were hampered by the illiberal constraints of "traditional" Iranian politics and culture. A pioneer of this apologetic genre calls Amir-Abbas Hoveyda, the last Shah's longest serving and notoriously subservient prime minister, "a liberal at heart who served an illiberal master." Such claims typically cobble together scattered utterances and pieces of writing, trying to attribute liberal "intentions" to men, like Hoveyda, Taqizadeh or Forughi, who willingly served monarchs ruling in blatant violation of Iran's constitution.[100] "The hope and goal of Forughi," according to a similar claim, "was to create suitable conditions for the implementation of modern and liberal principles in Iran, by concentrating his efforts in state reforms from above." The author then cites Forughi's famous *The Path of Philosophy in Europe* (1938–1941) as evidence of his "defense of liberal values."[101] The first compendium of modern European thought in Persian, this work in fact reveals Forughi's dated conservatism, shown in his preference of Montesquieu as master political philosopher.[102] Forughi's conservatism is so thorough that he avoids discussing eighteenth-century materialist *philosophes,* calling them atheists whose ideas "need not occupy our time." Similarly, his coverage of the nineteenth century eliminates thinkers like Marx, referring to socialists as "individuals whose ideas were strange and therefore had no success"[103] (on Foroughi, see also Chapter 5).

Linked to constitutionalism, as it properly should be, Iran's liberal nationalist tradition found institutional expression only in the early 1950s, in a number of small political parties joining Premier Mohammad Mosaddeq's National Front coalition. Apart from their support of constitutional government and oil nationalization, none of these liberal parties had a popular agenda or following. (A possible exception perhaps being the Iran Party, whose moderately socialist agenda was a pale reflection of the communist Tudeh Party's systematic program of social reform. See Chapter 5.) Thus, if a 1940s text like *The Conquest of European Civilization* was a liberal manifesto, it certainly had appeared in an inhospitable political and ideological context. The book's author, Fakhreddin Shadman (1907–1967), could boast of an academic resume more impressive than any contemporary intellectual statesman. Born into an affluent clerical family, he had studied jurisprudence and law in Tehran, prior to completing a doctorate in law at the Sorbonne, and another in political science at London University. After a two-year post-doctorate at Harvard, Shadman returned to Iran, where *The Conquest of European Civilization* was published in 1948. The book's considerable merit was acknowledged by contemporaries including Jalal Al-Ahmad whose *West-struck-ness* admitted Shaman's "precedence" in addressing the problem of cultural confrontation with Europe (see Chapter 5). Shadman's intellectual stature, however, was tarnished due to his close association with the country's conservative political establishment. During his years of sojourn and education abroad, Shadman had worked for the Iranian government commission that negotiated a highly unfavorable agreement with the Anglo-Iranian oil company (see Chapter 3). Later, he held ministerial posts in several cabinets, including the one that was installed in 1953 following Mosaddeq's overthrow by an Anglo-American coup.[104]

Its author's political entanglements notwithstanding, *The Conquest of Western Civilization* defined Iran's encounter with Europe as an existential culture war.[105] Caught in a global battleground of cultures/civilizations, he argued, Iran faced only two options: the dissolution of its distinct cultural existence, or its regeneration via adopting the most vital elements of an incomparably more powerful European civilization. Shadman's model followed the challenge/ response paradigm of civilizational encounters, formulated by European thinkers like Oswald Spengler and Arnold Toynbee. "The star of the West," he lamented, "rose and fell while we [Iranians] were oblivious." But he also echoed Kazemzadeh's and Kasravi's verdicts on Europe civilization being "sick and in deep trouble."[106] Oddly for an academically trained scholar, Shadman neither cited his European sources, nor acknowledged obvious Iranian predecessors like Kasravi.[107] His claim to originality proved successful insofar as intellectual historians have considered Shadman, rather than Kasravi, as "the harbinger of the discourse of *gharbzadegi* [West-struck-ness]."[108]

Using a phraseology Al-Ahmad would reiterate in the opening of *West-struckness*, Shadman's text begins by declaring: "Today, Iranians face a calamity whose like they have never seen, a calamity that would destroy them root and branch, wiping off their name from the book of history."[109] The named "calamity" is Iran's encounter with modern Europe, contextualized by Shadman within a familiar narrative arch of Iranian history, with an additional twist from Toynbee's philosophy of history:

The long life of the Iranian nation includes twenty-five hundred years of recorded history. Never in this entire period, filled with victories and defeats, has Iran been invaded by an enemy as powerful and ruthless as the European civilization ... All enemies who previously overran our country began by shedding our blood, satiating their lust for murder and plunder, but eventually surrendered to us after becoming familiar with our ideas and civilization ... The history of every nation is like the life of an individual. A long lifespan is full of ups and downs, just as a long history involves both victories and defeats. A weak nation succumbs with a few defeats, but we are among the great nations that have survived numerous defeats ... Still, European civilization is a different kind of enemy, armed by different weapons, whose conquest of Iran, I believe, will be our last defeat.[110]

Significantly, Shadman considers Iran's real enemy to be not Europeans but Iranians who want to reshape their country according to shallow and false conceptions of Europe. The term he coins for this new type of Iranian is *fokoli*, derived from the French *faux-col*, i.e. necktie or bowtie, referring to Iranians whose superficial claims to modernity hinge on dress and appearance. In choosing this term, Shadman was probably pandering to Muslim sensibility, since wearing ties could be considered Christian or un-Islamic. The *fokoli*'s major fault, however, was his double immersion in cultural superficiality: incapable of truly becoming European, he also forgot how to be Iranian:

Fokoli is the Iranian nation's basest and worst enemy ... *Fokoli* is the shameless tongue-tied Iranian who knows fragments of a European language, and even less Persian, yet claims to introduce us to a European civilization which he does not understand, in a language he does not know.[111]

In several important ways, Shadman's *fokoli* is the obvious precursor of Al-Ahmad's more famous "West-struck man" (*adam-e gharb-zadeh*) (see Chapter 5). Both are lost and bewildered beings, aliened simultaneously from Iranian and European cultures, thus living a doubly inauthentic life. Moreover, *fokoli,* like Al-Ahmad's "West-struck man," is gender-confused or "effeminate," evident, for instance, in his aspiration to superiority by taking a European spouse. Such an Iranian, says Shadman, "has taken a husband instead of a wife, allowing his own language, politics and children's upbringing to follow the whims of a [European] spouse."[112] (We saw above that marrying a non-Iranian was among the litany of charges Kasravi had leveled against Taqizadeh.) Most importantly, Shadman, like both Al-Ahmad and Kasravi, considers such Iranians to be serving the foreign "conquest" of Iran:

Fokoli is Iran's main enemy because he is the indigenous ally of foreigners, at a time when Iran is being invaded by European civilization ... To hasten our conquest by European civilization, he betrays our language, ideas and positive customs and manners. Unless we fend off European civilization, the Iranian nation will be lost.[113]

In an ironic instance of source attribution, Shadman credits Europeans with the *fokoli*'s discovery:

Fokoli existed in Naser al-Din Shah's time, his description being found in *Religions and Philosophies of Central Asia* by Gobineau, the famous French envoy to Iran's court. Hosein-qoli Aqa, the young Iranian graduate of [the French military academy] St. Cyr, is the enemy of Arabs and enamored with Zoroastrian religion. Seeking to purge Persian from Arabic words, he invents a strange unintelligible language. Gobineau, however, says Hosein-qoli Aqa is not an exception: all Iranians returning from Europe, even those educated there, observe and learn things in a bizarre fashion, contrary to European ways. Their beliefs change fundamentally, but without becoming similar to those of Europeans.[114]

Admittedly, then, Shadman did not invent the *fokoli* prototype, whose cruder versions exist in early twentieth-century Iran's avant-garde literary and artistic experiments. One of the most famous of the latter was a satirical play called *Ja'far Khan Returns from Europe*, the hero of whose title clumsily mimics French manners, having lost his Iranian character and the ability to speak Persian, after a short stay in Paris. As seen in Chapter 1, the first sketches of this personality type, dubbed *alafranga*, had appeared in nineteenth-century modernist Ottoman literature. Referring to pseudo-modernized Turks, recognizable by their superficial imitation of European ways, *alafranga* became a widely known label through the popular novels of Ahmet Midhat (1844–1912), most famously *Felatun Bey and Rakim Efendi* (1875). The foil to *alafranga* was the *alaturka*, whose personality showed a "balanced" combination of European and Ottoman cultures.[115] As Kasravi and Shadman would argue a generation later, Midhat believed "what we call European civilization has bad sides as well as good sides." The Ottomans, he proposed, had to adopt the good side of European civilization, consisting of "modern sciences and industries, as the means of economic and utilitarian pursuits," while preserving their own character, defined by religion and language.[116]

Even closer to Shadman's *fokoli* were the *alafranga* types created by another prolific Turkish writer, Hosein Rahmi (1864–1944). Rahmi's early twentieth-century novels portrayed a modernizing Turkish society caught up in moral bewilderment and value disorientation. His *alafranga* characters "did the most ridiculous things imaginable through thinking that they were in a Europeanized Turkish society which did not really exist." But Rahmi went beyond Midhat to show that *alaturka* attempts at balancing modernity and tradition were equally futile and doomed.[117] This particular Ottoman-Turkish line of criticizing the encounter with Europe is reproduced by Shadman, who probably was not aware of its original source. But Ottoman and Turkish sources had most likely influenced Kasravi's critique of "Europeanism," the uncredited Iranian predecessor of Shadman's critical remarks.

Another lacunae in *The Conquest of European Civilization* is the notion of modernity (*tajaddod*), a subject already debated by at least one generation of Iranian intellectuals. As in Kasravi's case, Shadman's conceptual synonym for modernity is "European civilization," something he understood much better than Kasravi did. *The Conquest of European Civilization* thus cautions Iranians against simplistic judgments of an enormously powerful adversary, defined by its conflicted and paradoxical nature:

European civilization is heir to the civilizations of Greeks, Romans, Iranians, Arabs and every other great nation, being the expression of science, humanities and the arts; It is the reflection of human progress and proof of humanity's power ... No one knows who will be heir to this civilization.

One cannot easily define European civilization. Neither are European authorities themselves clear on this subject ... European civilization is not confined to any specific time or space.[118]

Systematically avoiding the language of colonialism and imperialism, he nevertheless concedes Europe's fundamentally predatory posture toward the rest of the world, including Iran:

European civilization has never aided the progress of others willingly ... its only purpose is selling the machine ... its ultimate goal is mercantile profit-seeking ... If not for their rivalries, Europeans certainly would have barred us from their schools and libraries.[119]

Yet Shadman believed Europeans were neither morally superior nor inferior to others. What made them powerful, and thus worthy of emulation, was their incomparable progress in science and knowledge:

In sum, the European is superior because of his science and not his morality. Human ethics and morality are more or less the same everywhere and at all times. The difference is in knowledge, which is what we must seize. Blind imitation is useless; instead the only thing useful and beneficial to us is the cultivation of an Iran whose pivot is the Persian language ... Without Persian language, Iran cannot conquer European civilization.[120]

According to Shadman, intellectuals like Mohammad-Ali Forughi were exceptional role models showing Iranians how to master both Iranian and European cultures:

The conquest of European civilization must be accomplished by Iranians who know Iran's ancient and modern civilization, as well as Europe's civilization ... Only individuals whose wisdom at least equals Forughi's can conquer European Civilization for Iran . . . Rarely are the likes of Forughi found in Iran.[121]

Shadman's solution to the problem of encounter with Europe, therefore, was a cultural crusade, led by an intellectual elite "armed" with a deep knowledge of Europe, a cultural "weapon" he called "Occidentalism" (*farangshenasi*). The obverse of Orientalism, this was to be an ever-expanding project of Persian-language knowledge production, focused on understanding European civilization. Quite literally, therefore, Shadman advocated a massive and systematic national translation pro-ject as the best method of appropriating European modernity. In a revealing analogy, he likened books, in various European languages, to multitudes of soldiers fighting Europe's global war of cultural dom-inance. Consequently, he argued, translating each of these books into Persian enabled Iran to capture, and enlist in its own service, yet another of Europe's endless millions of cultural soldiers.[122]

The idea of a selective state-sponsored translation project, as an intellectual shortcut to modernity, was not entirely new. Its history went back to the nineteenth century, while a version of it was proposed by Fatemeh Sayyah during the 1930s. Responding to Kasravi's catego-rical rejection of fiction, as yet another morally harmful manifestation of "Europeanism," Sayyah had argued:

Instead of attacking fiction, we should try to help people acquire a deeper appreciation of tasteful European fiction. If the Ministry of Education approves, it might support this endeavor by expediting the translation of masterpieces in European fiction. It is of course imperative to safeguard public morality (*akhalq-e mardom*) from the poisonous effect of nonsensical fiction, which unfortunately is too common in contemporary Europe. It may be beneficial that the Ministry set up a special commission to choose fiction worthy of translation, while banning those whose translation would be harmful.[123]

Going beyond Sayyah's more modest proposals, *The Conquest of European Civilization* elevated the question of translation to the level of a global clash of civilizations, where European modernity threatened to devour the rest of the world's cultures. This was itself a European idea, traceable to Toynbee and Spengler, and further back to Herder[124] (see Chapter 2). To his credit, Shadman was attentive to internal tensions and multiplicity within both European and Iranian civilizational constructs. He was cognizant too of history's weight in shaping civilization and culture, although his nationalism at times tilted toward historical essentialism. Still on the positive side, his belief in the continuity of Iranian history assigned equal worth to its pre- and post-Islamic history. Moreover, despite being an advocate of Persian as national language, he was not a linguistic purist, since he criticized intellectuals, even those like his idol Mohammad-Ali Forughi, who claimed "the problem of Persian language is its being mixed with Arabic."[125]

Conclusion: Modernity, Lost in Translation?

Shadman's call for a deeper appreciation and more balanced judgment of Europe was a corrective to Kasravi's hasty prognosis and extreme remedies. But the weakness of his solution was its reduction of everything to a cultural project whereby Iran's Persian-language high culture would seamlessly assimilate modern European culture via a massive translation project. Thus, while unfairly cursory, Al-Ahmad's comments on *The Conquest of European Civilization* were not entirely off the mark. Banishing Shadman to a footnote in *West-struckness*, Al-Ahamd credits him for searching "prior to these writings, for a remedy to the acute ailment of '*fokoli*-mannerism' (*fokoli-maabi*), proposing the serious teaching of Persian and the translation of Western philosophical, scientific and literary works." He then concludes:

While correctly identifying the malady, Shadman does not have a proper remedy. From 1948 to the present, tens of thousands of European books have been translated into Persian, but we gravitate to *fokoli*-mannerism ever more. This is because *fokoli*-mannerism is itself among the symptom of the greater ailment of West-struckness.[126]

The efficacy of his own "remedy," in *Gharbazdegi*, notwithstanding, Al-Ahmad was correct that "conquering" modernity and reversing European domination required much more than a national translation movement.[127] However, as we shall see in the following chapters, something similar to Shadman's notion of a great translation project was indeed undertaken from the 1940s to the 1970s. But, contrary to what Shadman probably had hoped for, the result was the intellectual hegemony of socialist and Marxist ideology, blended with politicized Islamic modernism and Kasravi-style rejection of "Western" or European norms.

5 | The Mid-century Moment of Socialist Hegemony

The major problem in Iran today, as everywhere else in the world, results from rivalry between two major ideologies ... One of those ideologies, supported by Soviet Russia, promises the hungry peasants and workers of Iran a Utopia under communism. The other, supported by the United States and other Western powers, offers an opportunity for gradual improvement under democracy.

George V. Allen, US ambassador to Iran in 1948.[1]

If the Iranians had to decide between the British and the Russians, they would in my opinion unquestionably choose the Russians.

An American general visiting Iran in 1943.[2]

In the years immediately after World War II, the impact of socialism radically changed intellectual debates on Iran's encounter with European or "Western" modernity. Toward the end of its joint occupation by Anglo-American and Soviet armies, Iran had become an early site of the Cold War, splitting the world along a new "East"/ "West" divide. By the end of the 1940s, the "West" meant any part of the globe allied with the US or under its tutelage, countering a new "East" stretching from central Europe through the Soviet Union to communist China. Thus, during the second half of the century, older notions of the "East/Orient," that it was premodern, stagnant and "traditional," were replaced by images of a rapidly modernizing Eurasia, revitalized under socialism, an originally European ideology of enormous universal reach and appeal. Socialist Eurasia hence offered an alternate conception of modernity, challenging a US-led capitalist "West," widely perceived as heir to European colonialism and imperialism. By the 1950s, socialism was globally on the march, adopted in various forms in a new "Third World," stretching from Egypt to Indonesia across Asia, and southward into a newly independent Africa. Iran also experienced this international "moment" of socialist political, cultural and intellectual hegemony, which peaked between the 1940s and 1970s. This global conjuncture coincided with the peak of Pahlavi-era modernity, whose vulnerable strategic alignment with the "West" was challenged, and eventually battered down, by an opposition culture mixing socialism with nationalism and Islam. This chapter will trace the phenomenal rise of Marxian socialism in post-World War II Iran and its decisive reshaping of the discourse on Iran's encounter with "Western" modernity. It will thus attempt to help fill the gap that the neglect or erasure of socialism and communism has left in the intellectual history of Iranian modernity.

Intellectuals Join, and Exit, the Party of the Masses

[T]he story of Iranian intellectuals in the 1940s and 1950s is largely the story of the Tudeh Party, including those who remained faithful to it, those who led its splinter groups, and founded other left-wing movements, and those who left it quietly and gave up political activism.[3]

In August 1941, a coordinated Anglo-Soviet invasion of Iran toppled Reza Shah's regime, which was accused by the Allies of having drawn too close to Nazi Germany. American armies soon joined the occupation, while Reza Shah was exiled and the fate of his dynasty hung in the balance. A caretaker government, headed by Prime Minister Mohammad-Ali Forughi, had hastily tied Iran to the Allied cause. Forughi had been Reza Shah's first prime minister, helping pave the way for his accession to the throne and serving him dutifully until the dictator forced him into retirement (see Chapter 3). On the verge of abdication, Reza Shah once again called on Forughi to save his dynasty, as well as the social and political order it represented. More importantly, Forughi was Britain's choice, while also acceptable to the Soviets. As far back as 1931, he was identified, by Tehran's British diplomats, as the only politician "on whose support Britain could count."[4] This coincided with the estimation of Forughi by nationalists like Mohammad Mosaddeq, who believed he "accepted whatever was dictated to him."[5] In 1941, Forughi proved such estimations correct by keeping the fallen dictator's regime intact as the head of a provisional government under Allied occupation. His inaugural address to the nation lamented decades of dictatorship, while remaining silent on the responsibility of statesmen like himself and passing the blame to ordinary Iranians:

during the last thirty-five years, you seldom have enjoyed the benefit of real freedom and the rule of law, witnessing instead your national government and the foundations of constitutional regime repeatedly trampled upon. Do you know what caused this? I will explain it to you. The real reason was you did not fully appreciate this benefice, failing to meet its requirements.[6]

Such commentary showed the deep chasm separating establishment intellectuals from ordinary people, whose open rebellion, after Reza Shah's fall, was contained only by foreign occupation armies. Forughi's disregard for his suffering and oppressed countrymen, and his subservience to the Allies, is recorded in another infamous speech, where he claimed foreign armies merely "come and go, without bothering anyone."[7] In fact, the first two years of occupation saw growing discontent, especially among the lower classes, as Iran's vital resources were requisitioned by the Allies, causing near-famine and bread riots in Tehran and other cities.[8] The Allies had imposed order, via Iranian surrogates, in their respective zones of occupation. The British strengthened their ties with the court, clerics, and conservative politicians, while the Americans seized the opportunity to finance and train Iran's armed forces and the police. Together, the British and the Americans had occupied southern and central Iran, while the Soviets held the northern provinces, where they sponsored the newly created Tudeh (Masses) Party.

Launched in 1941, as an anti-fascist, constitutionalist and socialist front supporting the Allies, the Tudeh Party soon was taken over by a staunchly communist leadership. Despite, or because of, its incomparable political and cultural impact, the Tudeh Party chapter remains among the most distorted pages of modern Iranian history. From the outset, nationalist and Cold War historiography converged on depicting the party as an "instrument" of Soviet foreign policy, ignoring or downplaying its unrivalled popularity with both intellectuals and the masses. This rigid ideological stance was challenged only in the early 1980s, when Ervand Abrahamian's *Iran between Two Revolutions* moved the Tudeh Party from the maligned margins of twentieth-century historiography to its center. Abrahamian's meticulous research showed that the party's phenomenal success was due primarily to the appeal of its socialist ideology, popular social reform agenda, and unique organizational ability, while Soviet support and impositions had a secondary and often detrimental effect on the party's political fortunes.[9] Whether more harmful or beneficial, affiliation with the Soviet Union cannot explain why the Tudeh became Iran's most popular and successful political party. To answer this question, historians must revisit the party's performance within its Iranian context, where in slightly over a decade (1941–1953), it became a hegemonic force in political culture, and particularly in intellectual life. Below, we will attempt to engage this question, focusing on the party's intellectual impact.

Under Allied occupation, Soviet support initially benefited the Tudeh Party, as Iranians seemed to prefer the USSR to Britain, while the US remained a relatively unknown third contender. Ironically, Iranian preference for the Soviet Union is documented in confidential British and American intelligence reports. For instance, a 1943 confidential report, by the British military attaché in Tehran, contrasts pro-Soviet with anti-British sentiments, curiously analyzing them in terms of class conflict and Iran's revolutionary potential:

There has been recently a very noticeable change in the sentiments of the Persian people towards Russia ... The generally admirable discipline of Russian troops in Persia, their good behavior towards the people, their professed sympathy with the lower classes, their advertised contentment with their own system, the good relations apparently existing between officers and men and the obviously magnificent morale of the Russian people have greatly affected preconceived ideas of the Soviet system ... An increasingly sympathetic interest is being shown in the principles of the Soviet system ... The less frightful Russia is to masses the more of a bogy does she become to the propertied classes. A situation seems to be developing where the masses may draw closer to Russia and the propertied classes come to be associated more closely than they now are with Great Britain. Indeed, Russia is already beginning to be regarded as the champion of the oppressed and is being looked to by the leaders of the discontented as a possible supporter of a revolution against the present ruling classes.[10]

To many Iranians, the Red Army's presence was tangible proof of Soviet power and accomplishment, especially after 1943, when it turned the tide in the war against Nazi Germany. More importantly, as the above document admits, pro-Soviet sympathies were related to the Red Army representing and supporting what politically appealed to many Iranians. This was the Tudeh Party's program of comprehensive social reforms benefiting the country's middle and lower classes. Announced in February 1942 and expanded a year later, the party's program sought to unite "workers, peasants and women" with "middle-class" intellectuals, artisans, small landowners and low-ranking government employees. It demanded an eight-hour work day, disability insurance, pensions and subsidized housing for workers; the redistribution of state and crown lands to peasants; the purchase of large private estates by the government and their resale to landless peasants on easy terms; establishing rural schools and health clinics; equal political rights and equal pay for women; government support of poor mothers and children; and job security, higher pay and lower taxes for salaried government employees.[11] It is therefore more sensible to see the Tudeh Party's advocacy of this unique social reform program, rather than some foreign conspiracy, as the main reason for its phenomenal intellectual and popular appeal.[12]

Among the least acknowledged contributions of the Tudeh Party is its role in promoting women's equal political, social and economic rights. When the party was first established, its nominal leader, elderly socialist politician and Qajar prince Soleyman Eskandari, had opposed women's membership. Soon, however, this changed as leftist women activists began organizing both within and outside the Tudeh Party. In spring 1943, a small group of women, mostly relatives of communist leaders Iraj Eskandari and Bozorg Alvai (see Chapter 4), launched the Women's Organization (*Tashkilat-e Zanan*), which was affiliated with, but organizationally independent of, the Tudeh Party. Later the same year, this organization was joined by the Women's Party (*Hezb-e Zanan*), also aligned with the Tudeh, to advocate for women's equal rights, including suffrage. The year 1943 marked the emergence of the first systematic campaign demanding women's enfranchisement. This demand had emerged in the wake of cautious debates concerning women's right to work in proto-feminist periodicals like *Women's Voice* (*Zaban Zanan*). But it moved to the forefront of politics when the Tudeh Party and its political allies, mainly the Women's Party, took it up. The Women's Party secretary, Tehran University professor Fatemeh Sayyah (see Chapter 4) then became the movement's most articulate voice, also representing it at international meetings and conferences in Turkey and France.[13] The left officially took the lead in the struggle for women's equal rights when the Tudeh Party's 1944 program demanded the following:

1. Striving to expand and establish women's social rights, including the right to vote in, and to be elected to, in parliamentary, provincial and city council elections.
2. Improving women's material conditions and securing their economic independence.
3. Establishing and expanding institutions supporting poor mothers and children.
4. Equality of spousal rights and reforming marriage and divorce laws.[14]

Thus, according to the most meticulous study of women's movement in the 1940s, "Iran's political left retook the initiative on the women question by championing women's suffrage, challenging other political forces in the country to act."[15] In August 1944, the Tudeh Party's Majles representative, Fereydun Keshavazr, proposed women's suffrage as an amendment to a new bill reforming Iran's electoral laws. But the amendment was removed from the bill, which, despite the intervention of Women's Party on its behalf, was never voted on. Meanwhile, the idea of women's enfranchisement received a major boost when it was implemented, along with land reform, by the leftist autonomous government of Azerbaijan in 1945. Iran's leading intellectual periodical, *Sokhan*, noted women's suffrage in Azerbajan positively, while Fatemeh Sayyah tied it to the left's broader agenda for making Iran a "true democracy." About a year before her untimely death, she wrote:

The government must implement agrarian reform by justly distributing land among farmers. This must be done as rapidly as it is now proceeding in Azerbaijan ... Women's equal rights, and their freedom and progress, are the main objective of our [Women's] party ... [But] our objectives cannot be accomplished unless we have a true democracy in our country.[16]

In the summer of 1946, Premier Ahmad Qavam signed an agreement with the government of Azerbaijan that included the promise of supporting legislation to enfranchise women throughout Iran. In a pseudo leftist posture, Qavam also set up his own "Democrat" Party, modeled after the Tudeh Party, complete with an affiliated labor union (ESKI) and a women's organization. Once the Azerbaijan government was forcibly overthrown, however, Qavam gave up on his promises, while his party and its women's organization quickly fell apart. Among the important points lost in the margins of this period's controversial historiography is the left's pioneering role in advocating women's suffrage, a progressive demand cynically embraced by Qavam's government, later to be adopted by the White Revolution[17] (see below).

Beyond articulating Iran's most comprehensive modern social reform agenda, the Tudeh Party also introduced the theory and practice of modern party politics and trade unionism. By 1946, foreign intelligence reports filed independently by British and American ambassadors were describing the Tudeh Party as "the only coherent political force" and "the only large, well organized, and functioning political machine" in Iran.[18] The Tudeh's exceptional role, as a genuine mass political party, remained unmatched not only in this decade, but throughout the rest of the twentieth century.[19] Within a few years of its formation, the Tudeh-affiliated Central Council of Federated Unions of Iranian Workers and Toilers became the largest and best-organized mass movement of its kind, leading hundreds of thousands of laboring men and women, from oil workers to carpet weavers, in countrywide strikes and political action to improve their working and living conditions.[20]

All of the above leads to the paradoxical conclusion that during the single exceptional decade of functioning constitutionalism, a Stalinist party became Iran's most popular and successful political force. Various studies show that, despite its radical rhetoric, the Tudeh Party in practice avoided the revolutionary road, focusing instead on expanding its political clout in a semi-democratic constitutional regime.[21] Regardless of their factional affiliations, party leaders must have realized their strongest hand could be played in the game of parliamentary politics. Thus, operating legally or semi-legally, the party thrived, steadily increasing its political and cultural impact by joining a small, dedicated core membership to a much larger mass of sympathizers and followers. Reporting on the Tudeh's May Day 1946 parade in Tehran, with about 60,000 participants, the *New York Times*, for example, estimated the party and its allies could win as much as 40 percent of the vote in a fair election.[22] The party's membership and clout continued to grow despite the loss of its powerful Azerbaijan branch during the 1945–1946 crisis, its subsequent internal feuds and party split in 1948; and even under conditions of semi-legality, after it was accused of complicity in a 1949 royal assassination attempt.[23] Estimates of official party membership range from 25,000 to 100,000, while Tudeh-affiliated trade unions reportedly enlisted up to about 300,000 workers.[24] Unprecedented in its own time, this level of active popular support for a semi-legal opposition party remains unsurpassed in Iran.

The Tudeh Party also had an illegal clandestine branch, consisting of several hundred junior military officers and a small "hit squad" that carried out a few political assassinations.[25] Such tactics, however, remained marginal to the party's strategy of legal mass mobilization and participation in parliamentary politics. Ultimately, it was the peaceful legal gains of Iranian communism, rather than its alleged designs on seizing power, that alarmed the country's conservative establishment and their Anglo-American backers. As noted above, the latter concerns are amply documented in foreign intelligence and diplomatic records. For instance, a British intelligence study of the Tudeh's last year of legal activity (1951–1952) reported that the party continued its focus on expanding and organizing its mass base, without any apparent moves toward "seizing power" or coup attempts. It concluded: "a most significant feature of the Tudeh activity is the non-appearance of paramilitary organisation and training."[26] But the party's strategic adaptation to legalism proved a fatal weakness when it failed to resist the extralegal violence of the US-sponsored 1953 military coup. A few years later, party leaders in exile confessed to their own lack of revolutionary initiative during the 1953 confrontation, a self-criticism that led younger militants to break with the party, rejecting its admittedly non-revolutionary character[27] (see Chapter 6). In the end, any broad evaluation of the Tudeh Party's record remains daunting, requiring further study and ultimately involving non-academic, normative criteria. This chapter, however, seeks to go beyond facile judgments toward understanding the intellectual legacy the Tudeh Party bequeathed to Iranian political culture from the 1940s to the 1970s.

First of all, the Tudeh Party's founders showed a keen historical awareness when they claimed to be reviving and leading the popular democratic struggle lost by the generation of the Constitutional Revolution. This was no mere ideological posturing since, in slightly more than a decade, the party impacted Iranian politics more profoundly than had the previous generation of social democrats, socialists and communists combined. It was mainly the Tudeh Party, for example, that shaped Iran's modern political nomenclature by defining and popularizing terms such as revolution (*enqelab*), progressive (*moteraqqi*), intellectual (*roshanfekr*), socialism (*sosyalism*), capitalism (*sarmayeh-dari*), imperialism (*amperyalism*), the people (*mardom/khalq/tudeh*), working class (*tabaqe-ye kargar*), ruling class (*tabaqe-ye hakem*) and class struggle (*mobareze-ye tabaqati*). This nomenclature was then framed within a larger political grammar, or grand narrative, explaining Iran's present-day struggles as a necessary phase in the progressive march of universal history.

The party also propagated a crude but accessible Marxist-Leninist philosophy of history, mainly through journalism and translations of modern fiction, and secondarily via historical or philosophical texts. Readers of the 1952 Persian translation of Jack London's *The Iron Heel*, for instance, were assured of a socialist future in the book's introduction by Anatole France:

> The future is ours. The rule of the powerful will be destroyed as even its zenith of power betrays the sings of decay. It will be destroyed because all class systems are doomed. The system of wage labor will die because it is unjust. At the peak of its power, bloated by pride and egoism, this system will collapse, just as those of slavery and serfdom were destroyed before.[28]

More elaborate versions of this message could be found, for instance, in a contemporary translator's introduction to a collection of articles, by Soviet historians, on Iran's Constitutional Revolution. It proclaimed that historical progress was "inevitably" made by the laboring masses, not by elites or by individuals of genius. The main cause of historical transformation was class struggle, itself rooted in economic developments, primarily the changes in the means and relations of production. Similarly, history writing proper was not the recording of events, but their logical analysis in causal relations. Referring to modern Iranian historians, the anonymous translator cited Kasravi's history of the Constitutional Revolution as the only reliable source because of its attention to the masses. Adding a Leninist corrective, he explained that the defeat narrated by Kasravi was due to the masses' lack of proper revolutionary leadership and organization.[29]

A feature of mid-century translations of historical and philosophical texts was the "slippage" of Marxist and Islamic terminology and discourse into each other. For instance, the 1952 translation of Gregory Plekhnov's *The Role of the Individual in History* used the terms *jabr* and *ekhtiar* for "determinism" and "free will."[30] The conventional meaning of such terms was rooted in medieval

Islamic philosophy and theology. Consequently, the term *jabr*, for example, now stood for the modern concept of "determinism," as defined by historical materialism, while also meaning divinely ordained.[31] Whether intentional or not, this overlap of nomenclature helped pave the way for the discursive and conceptual convergence of Marxism and Islam during the 1960s and 1970s, a process whereby Plekhanov's "Monist" view of history could morph into the "Towhidi" (Unitarian) ideology of the so-called "Islamic Marxists" (see Chapter 6).

More concretely, the Tudeh Party revived and expanded the Constitutional Revolution's suppressed social reform agenda, making it a benchmark for populist and progressive demands under the Pahlavi regime and even during the 1978–1979 revolution. The very title of the White Revolution, the Pahlavi era's signature modernization and reform project, as well as its agenda of land reform, women's enfranchisement, literacy corps, workers' rights and the nationalization of natural resources, were directly borrowed from the Tudeh Party and its splinter factions (see below). As we shall see in Chapter 6, even the party's trademark anti-imperialist rhetoric was copied in official Pahlavi discourse, particularly during the 1970s, when the Shah wanted to convey independence from the US.

Thus, in slightly more than a decade (1941–1953), the Tudeh Party established an extraordinary Marxist intellectual and ideological presence, whose powerful effect lasted in modern Iranian politics and culture almost to the end of the century. In the words of Dariush Homayun, an anti-communist intellectual statesman of the 1970s:

Marxism utterly dominated Iranian political culture during the decades following the Second World War. The attraction of Marxism was not seriously diminished by the fact that the Tudeh Party, as the major representative of Marxism, was branded a Soviet client, something the party never denied. Being a Marxist thus became fashionable and prestigious ... In one generation, hundreds of thousands of Iranians, from half-literate high school and university graduates to high-powered intellectuals, came to believe in Marxism as a scientific worldview, synonymous with science itself, and the only path to a just and equitable society.[32]

Homayun in fact describes the Iranian version of a twentieth-century global phenomenon. Similarly, for instance, the philosopher Benedetto

Croce has explained his own youthful attraction to socialism as typical in turn-of-the-century Italy, where Marxism and intellectualism were synonymous.[33] In a more striking comparison to Italy, by the 1950s, Marxism dominated Iran's intellectual scene precisely as the 1930s Arani Circle had hoped, and in line with the project of Marxist cultural hegemony envisaged by the Italian philosopher Antonio Gramsci. By all accounts, the Tudeh Party quickly recruited, as members or sympathizers, the cream of the country's cultural elite, i.e. school teachers, university professors and students, journalists, writers, translators, artists, government employees and junior army officers. These were precisely the "leading intellectuals" (*monavvar al-fekran-e rahbar*) the *Donya* Circle had predicted would be won over to socialism (see Chapter 4).

The Marxist sweep of the intellectual milieu was showcased during the First Congress of Iranian Writers, hosted in the summer of 1946 at the Iran-Soviet Cultural Society (VOX) and featuring seventy-eight leading writers, poets, translators and academics, the most influential of whom were Tudeh Party members or sympathizers. The congress was convened at the peak of Soviet presence and prestige, a situation that began to change when the Red Army was withdrawn from the country later that summer. The first and only event of its kind, this became an unprecedented occasion for face-to-face debate, on modern literature's relation to politics, between Iran's younger, left-leaning intellectuals and the cultural luminaries of the Reza Shah era. Conference proceedings show the older generation on the defensive, largely deferring to their leftist challengers. The Marxist offensive was led by Ehsan Tabari, a young member of the Arani circle, who sharply criticized Ali-Asghar Hekamt, whose opening remarks attempted to bridge the gap between radical and conservative positions.[34] Hekamt had served as chancellor of Tehran University and minister of culture at the height of Reza Shah's dictatorship, a record of which he would boast later.[35] Yet, in 1946, he welcomed Iran's passing from an "era of dictatorship" to a new age of "democracy," marked by "debating communist beliefs, attention to the economic plight of the working class, attempts at improving the life of toilers and peasants, and cognizance of government corruption." Capitulating further to the left, he regurgitated the arguments of the 1920s literary avant-garde movement, whose members were murdered by the dictatorship he had served (see Chapter 3):

As we said before, changes in political and economic history always necessitate change in literary history … In this new era, poetry often deals with subjects such as critiquing the regime and chaotic political conditions, showcasing social ills and shortcomings, and yearning for economic reforms. This era's numerous and wide circulating newspapers refocused the literati's attention from the individual to society. Poetry is now composed for society, and hence in a popular language and inevitably conforming to popular taste. Thus a new literature and poetry is born.[36]

In closing, the 1946 writers' congress passed a resolution calling for socially and politically committed populist literature, while taking an open pro-Soviet stand. The first point of this document stated:

The congress wishes that Iranian writers and poets follow the traditions of Persian literature in opposing evil and oppression, and promoting justice, righteousness, freedom and awareness in their works, while fighting the vestiges of superstition and fascism, thus serving Iran's progress, as well as global peace, humanitarianism and real democracy.

The second point further emphasized the necessity of social commitment in literature:

The congress wishes that writers and poets turn to the people, and, while avoiding extremism, search for new styles and techniques befitting modern life, thus promoting the kind of constructive scientific literary criticism that is necessary for the creation of great literature.

The resolution's third and fourth points called for stronger literary and cultural ties with the Soviet Union and the establishment of a union of Iranian writers.[37] These latter objectives were not pursued, but the first two goals remained high on the agenda of modern Iranian literary production as it turned toward populism, social criticism and political commitment. Beyond modern prose and poetry, leftist cultural hegemony was evident in the translation of foreign fiction, which, prior to the age of cinema and television, shaped both elite and popular conceptions of the world outside Iran. As seen in the previous chapter, thinkers like Shadman had recognized the significance of translation in shaping a modernist worldview. As if responding to this call, left-leaning and socially conscious intellectuals launched a great translation movement, choosing writers like Jack London, Anatole France, Mark Twain, Gustav Flaubert, Charles Dickens, Romain Rolland, Ignazio Silone, Pearl Buck, Nikos Kazantzakis, John Steinbeck, Maxim Gorky,

Bertold Brecht, Anthon Chekhov, Leo Tolstoy, Nikolay Chernyshevsky, Mikhail Sholokhov, Emil Zola, Jean-Paul Sartre, Andre Gide, Maurice Maeterlinck, Bernard Shaw, Ernest Hemingway and William Faulkner.[38]

Most mid-century translations were from the French, often with uneven and poor quality, yet their cumulative effect on the first generation of an Iranian "reading public" was nothing short of revolutionary. To their readers, they imparted a worldview that was unimaginable within the confines of traditional Persian litera-ture (*adab*). Iran's new reading public thus joined an "intellectual international," moving "to break with national habits of thought that create the illusion of uniqueness and insularity, and above all to erase the boundaries assigned by literary nationalism."[39] Numerous mid-century intellectuals have testified how the Tudeh Party's Marxism shaped this new cosmopolitan worldview. Essayist and literary critic Shahrokh Mesukb, for instance, has written:

In those years, the Tudeh Party was a fertile ground of aspirations to many of our long-suffering country's intellectuals and toilers, who, aghast with social oppression, dedicated their lives to defeating destiny and remaking the world and humanity ... On this path, we found our place in the universal progressive movement of the left. To weak unfortunate people like us, the company of such comrades provided more than assurance in the correctness of our path. It was a new self-chosen identity, empowering the oppressed and making the subjugated stronger than their rulers. To us, therefore, "internationalism" was not the negation of "nationalism" but its empowering ally. This great solidarity helped us endure the drabness of daily life, as when sympathy for the heroes of Spain's civil war, for instance, enlivened our daily existence. We were comrades and companions to Paul Eluard, Louis Aragon, Pablo Neruda and Federico Garcia Lorca; and, like Maurice Thorez, we too were Sons of the People. We anxiously followed the Long March of the Chinese communists, being lost in the jagged path of our own ideals: Toilers striving to stay alive and intellectuals to live in freedom.[40]

Meskub's vivid description captures the emotional, as well as intellec-tual, side of his generation's attraction to Marxism. He goes on to explain how socialism responded even to his generation's metaphysical and religious yearnings by providing a "powerful promise of worldly resurrection and earthly paradise, becoming a panacea to social ills and

comforter of our wounded psyche." Finally, Meskub's sense of historical perspective is shown in his refusal to see communist failures in
terms of intellectual naiveté or pointless sacrifice:

In fact, reducing to mere "mistakes" the failure of this century's greatest and
most painful social and cultural human experiment, in Europe and Asia,
including Iran, while seeing as deception and naiveté the sacrifice of its great
mass of followers, is itself a great naïveté in understanding the history of our
times.[41]

Corresponding to the collectivist frame of its intellectual hegemony, the
Tudeh Party did not produce "master thinkers" dominating their
cohorts as Arani, for instance, had done in his time. The party's chief
theorist, Ehsan Tabari (1917–1989), displayed an encyclopedic command of Soviet Marxism, dutifully conforming to its changes, such as
de-Stalinization, while showing mild appreciation of intellectual trends
like existentialism and Marxist Humanism. Tabari also had a certain
aptitude for Marxist readings of premodern Iranian culture and literature. In the end, however, his Marxism remained pedantic and stale, an
intellectual style he would call "neo- Scholasticism" in forced recanta-
tion written under the Islamic Republic.[42] The party's most intellectually polished and cosmopolitan leader was Iraj Eskandari
(1907–1985), who was nicknamed "the Red Prince." Eskandari came
from the Qajar royal family, studied law in France and was Arani's
closest collaborator in *Donya* (see Chapter 3). He was a Tudeh Party
founder, one of its three cabinet ministers in 1946, and later its general
secretary in exile, where he produced the first (incomplete) Persian
translation of Marx's *Capital*. But his relative independence of mind
showed too late, when his open dissent failed to change the Tudeh
Party's unquestioning support of the Islamic Republic.[43]

A Third Force: Democratic and God-Worshipping Socialism

The Tudeh Party set the tune and style for all political parties in Iran.
Leonard Binder, 1962.[44]

The most independent-minded Tudeh Party intellectual was Khalil
Maleki (1901–1969), a German-educated member of the Arani Circle,
who in 1948 led the party's first major split, and whose subsequent
activities and writings amounted to adapting democratic socialism to

Iranian conditions. Maleki's example shows the broader impact of Marxism in shaping Iranian intellectuals capable of thinking independently of the Tudeh Party and Stalinism. Still, the independent socialist tendency Maleki represents has received scant attention by intellectual historians, even in the rare studies that are not hostile to the left.[45] The rest of this chapter, therefore, will focus on Iran's independent Marxists, tracing their impact on Third Worldist and Islamic socialist intellectual trends, as well as on the "socialist" pretensions of the Shah's White Revolution.

Beginning with Maleki, a striking feature of independent Marxists is their intellectual non-conformity and moral autonomy vis-à-vis both Stalinism and "Western" ideological authority. Incarcerated during the 1930s, as a member of Arani's group, Maleki had stood out for his defiance of prison conditions, courageously enduring physical deprivations and torture. During the 1940s, he was similarly courageous in leading a Tudeh Party faction that was critical of subservience to the Soviet Union. When it became clear that the party and the Soviets did not tolerate serious criticism, Maleki and his followers rejected both, and in 1948 formed the Socialist Society of the Iranian Masses (*Jame'e-ye sosyalistha-ye Tudeh-e Iran*). The ensuing feud with the Tudeh Party led Maleki and his Socialist Society to align with European social democracy and the newly emerging Third World socialist movement. By the early 1950s, they referred to themselves as the "Third Force," i.e. an alternative to both Soviet-style communism and Iran's British and American-backed ruling classes. The political and ideological position of this Third Force was clearly spelled out in declarations such as the following:

The U.S. offers the world its free enterprise capitalism, while the Soviet Union offers state capitalism; we prefer a third choice, namely democratic socialism, which is the embodiment of socialism, and its evolutionary adaptation, in post-war conditions ... Before, during, and immediately after the war, only two real powers, the ruling clique and the Tudeh Party, existed in Iran, while no other power ..., with any coherent belief system, stood up to these representatives of Eastern and Western power blocks. In the aftermath of the war and its imposed anti-fascist imperative, the Tudeh Party persisted in strategic subservience to the Soviet Union during the Cold War, making people disillusioned with both of the above forces, and thus was born a third force ... struggling to uphold national interests.[46]

By this time, Maleki and his Third Force had joined premier Mosaddeq's National Front, strongly supporting his campaign to end British control of the Iranian oil industry. At the same time, Maleki criticized Mosaddeq's "liberalism," meaning his failure to mobilize popular support of social reform beyond oil nationalization. Moreover, he foresaw the "threat" of communism becoming the ultimate Anglo-American excuse to attack and destroy Iran's radical nationalist movement. Thus, about a year before the 1953 CIA-sponsored coup, Maleki warned that Iran's defiance of British imperialism over the oil issue would lead to the installation of "a proto-fascist government to prevent the growing clout of the Tudeh Party."[47] Like European and American social democrats, Maleki at times overestimated the threat of Stalinism. Thus, both before and after 1953, he saw the Soviet Union and the Tudeh Party as Iran's most dangerous enemies, thus considering anti-Americanism a strategic mistake.[48] Despite its "softness" toward American predominance, the Third Force remained dormant after the 1953 coup, becoming active again, as the Socialist League of Iran's National Movement, when political repression eased in the early 1960s. This period saw the peak impact of Maleki's brand of socialism, whose 1960 proposed package of social reforms was basically incorporated into the Shah's White Revolution (see below).

Among the least-studied ideological trends in pre-revolutionary Iran is Islamic socialism, another reaction to the Tudeh Party's far-reaching influence. Academic studies have noted a peculiar 1970s intellectual formation called "Islamic Ideology" by its proponents and "Islamic Marxism" by the Shah's regime. Often associated with Ali Shariati, "Islamic Ideology" in fact had different permutations, converging on the project of turning religion, i.e. Shi'i Islam, into a modern political ideology, capable of mass mobilization in a political party intent on assuming state power. Broadly understood, this particular Iranian phenomenon was a precursor to what, since the 1980s has been called "political Islam" or "Islamism," the significant difference being that the 1960s and 1970s Iranian variant of "Islamic Ideology" was predominantly leftist and often socialist. What is little understood is the precise genealogy of Islamic socialism, particularly its original intellectual articulation by a small mid-century organization called the Movement of God-worshipping Socialists (*Nehzat-e khoda-parastan-e sosyalist*).

The obscured genealogy of Islamic socialism, as we shall see below, is related to the God-worshipping Socialists' conflicted yet intimate intellectual association with both the Tudeh Party and Khalil Maleki's Third Force.

As noted in Chapters 1–2, the encounter of Marxism and Islam in Iran began in the early twentieth century with the ambivalent attitude of social democratic thinkers toward religion in general and Shi'ism in particular. The Tudeh Party deliberately pursued the same line of intellectual ambivalence, carefully avoiding critical engagement with Islam. In fact, the party initially declared adherence to Islam, denying charges of atheism and communism, both of which were against the law. Soon after the party's launch, its organ *Rahbar*, for instance, bluntly posed the question: "What is the Tudeh Party's religion?" To which it emphatically answered: "The Tudeh Party of Iran upholds the religion of Islam and the righteous *shari'a* of Mohammad."[49] Thus, it appeared at first that the Tudeh Party had backtracked on the 1930s *Donya* circle's open advocacy of materialism and implicit atheism. Nevertheless, the party's critical stance toward religion gradually became clear in its publications, including translations of Marxist classics, as well as in its open advocacy of separating religion and politics. On the other side of the religious–secular divide, Shi'i clerics, and politically active Muslim thinkers, continued to reject materialism and atheism, while responding to the challenge of Marxism by adding socialist shades to their modern readings of Islam. As we shall see in the following chapters, the 1940s/1950s Shi'i-Marxist encounter set the trend for intellectual exchanges that during the 1960s and 1970s grew more intense and creative. It is worth emphasizing that the pre-revolutionary encounter of Islam and Marxism remained almost entirely political and ideological, lacking deeper philosophical or epistemological reflection or dialogue on both sides. During the immediate pre-revolutionary decades, Marxists and Muslim political activists generally adopted an instrumentalist attitude to each other, both sides trying to appropriate what was politically expedient in a rival ideology. The deep impact of Marxism on Islamic modernism was widely recognized after the revolution, leading to a massive political and ideological campaign to "purge" the post-revolutionary regime of Marxist influences.[50]

Back in the 1940s, initial Muslim reactions to the Tudeh Party's phenomenal intellectual traction were a mixture of panic and envious hostility. All evidence suggests that the sudden and powerful attraction of Marxism was the major impetus to post-World War II Muslim political activism. In 1941, Tehran's Islamic Center (*Kanun-e Eslami*) was established by Mahmud Taleqani (1910–1979) who, along with Mehdi Bazargan and Yadollah Sahabi, became leaders of the religious nationalist movement of the 1950s and 1960s. According to Taleqani, the greatest challenge facing both Islam and the Iranian people during the 1940s was "the rapid spread of Marxist and materialist principles and the founding of the Tudeh Party." Taleqani further argued that whereas "Iran's rulers" had failed to counter revolutionary new ideas by force and repression, he and his colleagues would succeed by offering an Islamic ideological alternative. Quite fittingly, the main intellectual battleground was Tehran University, then the country's only modern institution of higher learning. According to Bazargan, Islamic political activism began in reaction to the Marxist takeover of Tehran University. A professor of engineering and later a university dean during the 1940s, Bazargan has described the situation vividly:

In those days it was not easy to administer a faculty. More difficult than all educational, technical, administrative, financial, and human problems was the struggle against the Tudeh members. The Tudeh party had made the university its main bastion ... We were besieged from all sides – by students, professors, clerical workers, janitors. The communist students had taken over the university clubs held their meetings in classrooms, ordered employees and workers to strike, and claimed they had a right to interfere with the curriculum ... These were truly dark days.[51]

Bazargan began composing a number of tracts updating Islam "scientifically" and explaining social behavior in terms of spiritual properties of energy and matter in motion. Less idiosyncratic and more influential were Taleqni's works, like *Islam and Ownership* (1956), offering a proto-socialist model of "Islamic economics," using Marxist categories like "capital," "class struggle," and "means of production."[52] More scandalously Marxist-inflected was Taleqani's Qur'anic exegesis, where divine revelation was interpreted as a guideline to Prophet Mohammad for setting world history on an evolutionary path toward a classless society. Taleqani's intellectual intervention was groundbreaking, because he tried to stay within the Shi'i exegetical tradition, while reading the Qur'an in a proto-socialist manner by selectively choosing and expanding on passages seemingly favorable to his interpretation.[53]

The breach with traditional Shi'ism, and clerical authority, came when younger, politicized Muslims openly embraced Marxist interpretations of history, class struggle and revolution. In 1944, small circles of Tehran University and high school students joined together to form the Movement of God-worshipping Socialists, the first Iranian political organization adhering simultaneously to Islam and socialism. The choice of "God-worshiping," instead of "Muslim," in the organization's official title underlined the originality of its ideology, hinting perhaps at its Kasravi-style ecumenical monotheism.[54] During intense debates with Tudeh Party members, the founders of God-worshipping Socialists had accepted the party's social and political program, while rejecting its philosophical materialism. Showing Kasravi's influence, they argued that traditional clerical Islam had, over time, ossified into a bundle of superstitious beliefs and obscurantist rituals. This reactionary Islam was inevitably doomed when challenged by Marxists and other modern materialists. True Islam, however, was a perfect ethical, political and socioeconomic system, a genuine "scientific socialism" first propagated by the Prophet Mohammad. Philosophically, this true Islam was a "Median School," uniquely mediating between idealism and materialism. Simultaneously advocating class struggle and belief in God, true Islam provided for humanity's spiritual, as well as material, needs. In all likelihood influenced by Khalil Maleki's Third Force, God-worshipping Socialists argued that Iran belonged to a "Median Bloc" of countries, standing between capitalist and communist blocs, both of which were "world-mongering colonizers and exploiters."[55]

The God-worshiping Socialists fit a twentieth-century ideological trend that combined Islam with socialism and communism. This trend originated in the aftermath of the Russian Revolution when some Central Asian Muslim modernizers (*Jadids*) joined the Bolsheviks, calling themselves "Muslim National Communists."[56] A somewhat similar attempt at merging Bolshevism with Iranian nationalism and Pan-Islam, under the ill-fated 1920–1921 Soviet Socialist Republic of Iran, ended tragically, leaving behind deep scars of mutual mistrust and acrimony (see Chapter 3). At about the same time, Mustafa Kemal (Ataturk) also was claiming to be a "Muslim communist," proposing an anti-imperialist alliance with the Soviet

Union of Turkey and other Muslim countries (see Chapter 2). Initial enthusiasm for the Russian Revolution spread the idea of merging Marxism and Islamic modernism as far as India, where eminent Muslim modernizer Mohammad Iqbal pondered whether Islam might be considered "Bolshevism with God."[57] More serious than these initial probing encounters were mid-century projects of Islamic socialism in Indonesia, Egypt and India, leaders of the Third World bloc of countries, where the idea of adapting socialism to indigenous culture and religion was prevalent. Indonesian nationalist leader Ahmad Sukarno, for instance, openly admitted to borrowing from communists.[58]

Iran's Muslim socialists, therefore, shared the same sentiments as the Third Worldist radical nationalist, populist and anti-imperialist movements. During the oil nationalization movement of the early 1950s, the God-worshipping Socialist movement first merged with the small social democratic Iran Party and then formed the Iranian People's Party (*Hezb-e mardom-e Iran*), whose basic principles were the following:

First, our association is formed by individuals who share faith in God with a belief in socialism as their common social ideal. Second, unlike organizations with limited objectives, our association upholds a great progressive ideal, formed to ensure the victory of our deprived nation's social and anti-colonial movement. Third, our association is the steadfast defender of the just rights of workers, toilers and peasants, being on principle opposed to all forms of dictatorship, colonialism and exploitation.[59]

As we shall see in Chapter 6, the ideological breakthrough of Islamic socialism shaped the thought of young Ali Shariati who, like his father, was affiliated with the God-worshipping socialists and the Iranian People's Party during the 1950s and early 1960s. Blazing a path that Shariati would follow, God-worshiping Socialist leader Mohammad Nakhshab accepted the dialectical voluntarist aspects of Marxist philosophy, while rejecting its "deterministic" and "materialist" side. In 1952, he wrote:

Communist parties ... explain social transformations in materialist terms, thus ignoring the will of nations and societies in shaping their own destiny, assuming instead that social change is determined by evolution in the means of production ... Marxism, however is wrong ... Arabia's fundamental transformation, due to the birth of Islam, is our great historical example.

Eating dates and riding camels, the Arabs brought Rome and Iran to their knees, while no change occurred in Arabia's means of production ... The French Revolution too was in fact a revolution in thought, not in industry and productivity ... The great October Revolution of 1917 clearly proves our contention as well ... Here too, the people transformed society on their own, without waiting for the means of production to evolve.[60]

Another "missing page" in mid-century Iran's intellectual history, Nakhshab's sparse but cogent writings combine Kasravi's understanding of religion as society's motivational moral philosophy, with Khalil Maleki's Third Worldist democratic socialism. Occasionally backed by an obligatory Qur'anic reference, his discourse is effectively secular, being almost totally oblivious to the clergy and juridical Shi'ism. The materialism he rejects is the Soviet Union's official Stalinist ideology, to which he positively contrasts Lenin's voluntarist Marxism and innovative deviations from historical and economic determinism.[61] At the same time, he is clearly on Maleki's side when it comes to aligning Iran with Third Worldist socialism:

Working from Marxist principles, Tito nevertheless parted ways with Moscow, while India's Nehru led a great social democratic movement relying neither on Moscow, nor on London and Washington. Sukarno followed the same path, as did Nasser who led Arab unity to success on a perilous road, without making concessions to the Eisenhower Doctrine or to Moscow's followers.[62]

In 1952, Nakhshab published a short political dictionary, listing socialist definitions of terms like class struggle, revolution, political party, ideology, democracy, popular sovereignty, imperialism, capitalism, Marxism, scientific and utopian socialism, and communism. Interestingly, he also included the following entry for unnamed advocates of a "White Revolution": "Those who do not believe in revolution, yet want to appear as advocates of total change in status quo, preach a White Revolution, which supposedly accomplishes the true objectives of the masses, peacefully and without violence or bloodshed."[63] Ironically, the term "White Revolution" was adopted as the official title of the Shah's 1963 reform project, whose main principles were copied from the programs of Maleki's Socialist League and Nakhshab's Iranian People's Party.

The Shah's Counterfeit Socialism: Toward a White Revolution (1953–1963)[64]

The socialism of my White Revolution is ... a new original socialism.

The Shah.[65]

If they wanted revolution, they'd get it, he [The Shah] used to say in those days, but they'd get it from me.[66]

Revolutionizing the monarch, and the person of the Shah was not unproblematic and indeed would in time generate difficulties ... In short, the White Revolution not only undermined the structural foundations of the Pahlavi monarchy, but also crucially contributed to its ideological destabilization.[67]

In August 1953, a CIA-organized military coup restored the Shah, who had fled the country after a showdown with Premier Mohammad Mosaddeq. While the coup had an Iranian component, blatant foreign involvement in the overthrow of the country's nationalist government left behind a fault-line of political instability beneath a restored Pahlavi monarchy. Following the coup, Mosaddeq's loyal followers and the Tudeh Party were violently repressed. However, radical nationalism and Marxist socialism recoiled underground to challenge a regime sustained via its Cold War alignment with the US.

In addition to the deadweight of a reactionary *ancien regime*, the post-1953 monarchy was burdened by the questionable legitimacy of its own foreign-backed restoration and sustenance. Though ultimately an American "client state," the monarchy was not merely a "puppet," dancing obediently to every American tune.[68] Prior to 1953, the Shah's position, vis-à-vis Britain, then the dominant foreign power in Iran, was quite weak, and even servile. As late as May 1953, for example, the Shah had asked US ambassador Lloyd Henderson whether the British wanted him to stay on the throne, or to leave the country. According to Henderson:

He is reported to be harping on the theme that the British had thrown out the Qajar Dynasty, had brought in his father and had thrown his father out. Now they could keep him in power or remove him in turn as they saw fit. If they desired that he should stay and that the crown should retain the powers given to it by the Constitution he should be informed. If on the other hand they wished him to go he should be told immediately so that he could leave quietly.[69]

Such documents show the Shah's abject servitude toward the British continued into the early 1950s, but the monarchy's post-1953 relations with the US gradually grew more complex. The relationship began with the Shah's total dependence on the US, upon his 1953 restoration, gradually changing to more complicated long-term reliance, marked by occasional serious tensions. As the Shah himself admitted while still in power, during the first post-coup decade, he was in a weak position vis-à-vis the US, thus accepting impositions such as Ali Amini's premiership in the early 1960s. He was also fearful of another America-sponsored coup, this time directed against him.[70] Meanwhile, the Shah was trying to influence US policy, for example, by donating to Richard Nixon's presidential campaign in 1960, a move that would sour his relations with the Kennedy administration. The extent of the Shah's autonomy and agency, vis-à-vis various American administrations, therefore would change in the course of the 1950s to the 1970s. In the long run, US–Iranian relations were not entirely one-sided, being in fact fraught with underlying tensions that eventually culminated in what the Shah saw, with some justification, as his betrayal and abandonment by the American side.[71]

In the aftermath of the 1953 coup, the CIA-installed regime remained preoccupied with uprooting the Tudeh Party, while official propaganda claimed Mosaddeq's removal was necessary to save Iran from falling to communism. This, of course, was the ultimate excuse of American coup-makers, which is often repeated and still persists in historical accounts. As noted above, however, American and British diplomatic and intelligence sources reflect no immediate concern with Tudeh Party takeover plans. Moreover, recent scholarly studies, corroborated by declassified CIA documents, show that a systematic diplomatic and undercover American campaign against Mosaddeq was underway throughout his premiership.[72] As it turned out, the Tudeh Party lacked not only an insurrectionary agenda, but even serious contingency plans for resisting a violent crackdown, thus totally collapsing in the face of crude repressive measures following the coup. Unlike 1930s Spain or 1960s Indonesia, the post-1953 decimation of the Iranian left would cost not hundreds of thousands of lives but dozens of executions and a few thousand jail sentences.

At any rate, although the 1953 coup led to the Tudeh Party's physical destruction, the intellectual sway of socialism and Marxism continued among the post-coup political generation. Having lost a decisive political confrontation, what Antonio Gramsci had called a "War of Manoeuvre," Iranian Marxist and radical nationalists continued waging a "War of Position," resisting and challenging the regime in a protracted battle for hegemony in the cultural arena. From this perspective, the monarchy's late 1970s collapse, in the face of a crushing "legitimacy crisis," was the outcome of a three-decade long struggle for hegemony in political culture (see Chapters 6–7). Here, political culture means at least two things: first, the state's dominant culture and official ideology; second, all aspects of both elite and popular culture that are somehow political. The latter encompass education, entertainment, the arts, literature, social media and broadly shared normative standards of the populace, including religious beliefs. In classical Marxism, political culture was seen as part of society's "superstructure," roughly corresponding to what non-Marxist political theory calls "civil society." Classical Marxism also tended to assign the political and cultural "superstructure" a secondary role, emphasizing instead "the ultimately determining" role of society's material and economic "base," where class struggle, driven by contradictions in the means and relations of production unfolded. Gramsci's contribution to Marxist theory was his focus on the "superstructure" as the primary locus of class domination, affected via both conflict and conciliation. In this sort of "cultural Marxism," social hierarchy ultimately is sustained by the state, but its underlying strength and durability is rooted in the cultural hegemony of dominant classes in "civil society." Thus, in any given society, permanent "culture wars" are waged constantly, via multitudes of scattered daily contestations in social life, cumulatively adding up to decide broader struggles over cultural and political domination.

1950s Iranian political culture was shaped largely by the clash of two grand narratives explaining the events of 1953 and their aftermath. First, there was the monarchist description of the 1953 coup as a "national uprising" (*qiaym-e melli*), saving Iranian nationhood and religion from scheming communists and their misguided nationalist allies.[73] This official version of contemporary history was rejected by a counter-narrative of defiance and dissent, resonating in both elite and popular culture until the monarchy's fall. The counter-culture of dissent was clearly manifest in the literature of shattered idealism of the 1950s and 1960s, which lamented the loss of true belief and was contemptuous of official optimism. Iconic 1950s intellectuals may have been despairing of politics, yet they remained defiant of official culture, as did Sadeq Hedayat, the country's leading modern fiction writer whose brief association with communism ended in deep disillusionment, shortly before his suicide.[74] Meanwhile, the trauma of the 1953 coup, underscored by the constant threat of imprisonment, torture and execution, hung like a dark poisonous cloud over the intellectual horizon of the 1950s.[75]

Less pessimistic dissidents looked beyond 1953 to future political possibilities, expressing their hopes in moderately leftist periodicals that were allowed to publish during the 1950s and into the 1960s. The most prominent of these were *Life's Struggle (Nabard-e zendegi)*, 1955–1956 and *Science and Life (Elm va zendegi)*, 1959–1962, edited by Khalil Maleki; and *Thought and Art (andisheh va honar)*, edited by Naser Vothuqi and published between 1954 and 1973. Vothuqi, like Maleki, was a European-educated ex-communist who had broken with the Tudeh Party, while remaining committed to socialism and critically engaged with Marxism. Catering to the intellectual elite, these periodicals testified to the continued presence of socialist and Marxist thought in post-coup political culture. However, as in similar cases during the Cold War, the socialist left was tolerated as long as it was opposed more to communism than to American involvement in the country's affairs.[76] Meanwhile, left-leaning cultural production continued unabated in the burgeoning field of translation. During the 1950s to the 1970s, translation was dominated by a few publishing houses that were owned and managed, or largely staffed, by leftists and ex-communists. These included Amir Kabir Publishers, NIL Publishers, Franklin Publishers, the Book Translation and Publication Company and the Center for the Intellectual Cultivation of Children and Adolescents. The oldest and largest, Amir Kabir, was owned by Abdol-Rahim Ja'fari (1919–2015), who came from a leftist background and published numerous titles by Iranian and foreign Marxist authors. In the three decades prior to the 1979 Revolution, Amir Kabir became the largest book publisher in the Middle East, turning out 2,700 titles, by 900 authors and translators. Another former communist, Homayun San'atizadeh (1925–2009), became the founding director of the US-sponsored Franklin Book Program in Iran. Responsible for publishing school textbooks, Franklin specialized in high-quality translations, introducing professional editing, with the leading translator, and former Tudeh Party member, Najaf Daryabandari serving as its editor-in-chief.[77] The left's presence could be traced also in *Sokhan* (*The Word*), Iran's leading modernist literary and cultural monthly from 1943 through 1978. *Sokhan*'s general tone, however, was set by its editor Parvzi Natel-Khanlari, sometimes called an Iranian Andre Malraux, i.e. the quintessential former leftist intellectual who had compromised with the establishment. Soon after the 1953 coup, Khanlari joined the circle of Asdollah Alam (1919–1978), then a cabinet minister, who was trusted by the Shah to recruit opposition intellectuals to join the regime. Alam then launched the People's Party (*hezb-e mardom*), relying on intellectual advisors including Khanlari, the ex-communist writer Rasul Parvizi and literary scholar Ehsan Yarshater. When Alam became prime minister in the early 1960s, Khanlari served as minister of education, later being appointed Senator by the Shah.[78]

The scion of a rich and powerful landed family, Alam was a cunning old-school politician who served the Shah as premier and court minister, remaining his closest advisor and confidant into the 1970s. Though not an intellectual by education or temperament, he was the regime's master manipulator of intellectuals, specializing in the recruitment of those from leftist backgrounds. Unlike the Shah, he could appreciate independent thought, hence his capacity for learning from dissenters and luring them into becoming part of the status quo. But even the Shah was borrowing Marxist ideas and rhetoric much earlier than the launch of the White Revolution. As far back as 1949, for instance, and significantly during an official visit to the US, the Shah had argued:

We must strive to provide peasants and other deprived classes with a good life. In Iran, a small minority lives a luxurious life, while the majority is deprived of life's basic necessities, as if that small group does not want the others to count. My real struggle must be against those blocking reforms ... I am not opposed to capitalists or to wealth, but I do oppose capital's concentration in a few hands, blocking its use by others. I don't want a few individuals become rich capitalists at the expense of the majority of Iranians who live in misery and poverty, the former becoming fortunate by destroying others.

The Shah then mentioned land distribution as the pillar of his reform project for Iran. Asked by a reporter whether his idea of land reform came "close to communist principles," he answered it was in fact "moderate and conservative."[79] In the immediate wake of the 1953 coup, the Shah, during a meeting with US ambassador Lloyd

Henderson, again mentioned land reform as a measure to counter communism and move Iran more "towards socialism."[80]

As seen in Chapter 2, comprehensive land reform was first proposed by the (Social) Democrat Party, during the Constitutional Revolution, remaining a core demand of the Iranian left and most systematically advocated by the Tudeh Party. It had become an issue of national concern when Reza Shah's fall led to widespread calls for the return of crown lands he had expropriated, or their distribution to landless peasants. Overlooked in mainstream historiography is the significance of Iran's first actual land reform, carried out in 1946 by the autonomous government of Azerbaijan. Installed under Red Army protection, the leftist government of Azerbaijan, within one year, had implemented important reforms that would be imitated by the White Revolution. In addition to land reform, these included women's enfranchisement and the nationalization of forests and mines.[81] The significance of Azerbaijan's land reform, as a model for the rest of Iran, was noted by contemporary sources, including Hasan Arsanjani (1922–1969), who was to serve as the minister of agriculture responsible for the launch of countrywide land reform under the White Revolution.[82] As with land reform, women's enfranchisement and equal citizenship rights were first proposed by the Democrat Party in the early twentieth century, and revived by the Tudeh Party in mid-century. This demand was advocated by the party-affiliated Women's Organization and the independent Women's Party, both of which were launched in 1943. It also appeared in the Tudeh Party's 1944 program, which asked for women's equal rights to vote for and be elected in legislature, as well as their equal rights in marriage laws.[83]

After 1953, while the Tudeh Party remained illegal, the left's agenda of social reform was rearticulated and expanded upon by the Socialist League, which was allowed a marginal legal presence. The 1960 program of the Socialist League in fact had proposed the essentials of the White Revolution's original six points. These included: first, agrarian reform, backed by rural cooperatives; second, women's "equal political and social rights"; third, the nationalization of large industries, along with oil and natural resources such as forests and water; fourth, the basic protection of Iranian workers and peasants in a "welfare state."[84] Last but not least, the idea of a Literacy Corps, a major plank of the

White Revolution, was first clearly articulated in 1959 by Nasser Pakdaman, a graduate student in Paris affiliated with the Socialist League.[85] Significantly, the 1960 program of the Socialist League was contextualized in a global perspective that would align Iran with Third World "bourgeois nationalist" regimes, on their path of economic development toward socialism, independent of Cold War impositions. It declared:

We adopt freedom, democracy and respect for human values from the legacy of Western civilization, and also from our own national and religious traditions. At the same time, the Soviet Union and similar countries have taught us to strive according to a plan, and with more discipline, in social and political affairs ... [This] is not following Soviet-style communism, but the only way to resist its spread in a country. The main reason for the failure of considerable U.S. assistance to underdeveloped countries is the imposition of Western or American model of social and economic development. But, our model of development and growth must be our own, independent of both the East and the West. To build this model, we must take what we need from both the East and the West, without following either. Therefore, social and economic development must not be separated from the higher goal of establishing a just social order. Economic development must eventually lead to socialism, not to private or state capitalism.[86]

Pushing its flexibility to the limit, the Socialist League foresaw that "parts of a socialist program can be implemented by the ruling regime, even without our coming to power or participating in government."[87] As if obliging this prediction, "the ruling regime" indeed borrowed, and partially implemented, this particular "socialist" program, while also preventing the Socialist League, along with all other political parties, from "participating in government."

In a perceptive study of the White Revolution, Ali Ansari has noted how the Shah fashioned himself as a "revolutionary" monarch by appropriating "the myths of the Left and National Front as a champion of revolutionary nationalism which would assist in legitimizing himself and his dynasty."[88] Ansari points out three crucial features of the White Revolution: first, it functioned as the "legitimating myth" of the Pahlavi monarchy from the early 1960s to its fall in the late 1970s; second, the Shah's growing posture of a philosopher-king, and his taking personal responsibility for the revolution's ideological conception, guidance and implementation, structurally "destabilized" the political system by making it dangerously dependent on a single individual; third, "plagiarizing" nationalist and socialist slogans further destabilized the regime, allowing Marxists and radical nationalists to argue that the Shah's nationalist, revolutionary and populist claims were merely counterfeit copies of their own more authentic projects (these points will be discussed further in Chapters 6–7). Ansari also notes that the idea of a monarchist White Revolution, often credited to the Kennedy administration, was originally conceived by Alam, the regime's shrewdest statesman. Following the Iraqi monarchy's overthrow in 1958, Alam, then leader of the *Mardom* (People) Party, brought up the idea of a "white" revolution during a confidential conversation with British diplomats. In order to pre-empt a similar revolutionary coup in Iran, he argued, the Shah had to lead his own brand of popular revolution:

Asadullah Alam went on to explain that what he had in mind was in fact a *'white revolution'*, which he hoped to bring about under the auspices of the Shah ... Asadullah hoped to prevail upon the Shah to be rid of the present 'establishment', the existing ruling classes must give place to new and younger men. The old gang were not of course to be hurt; this was white not a red revolution; but the Shah must sack them all ... The Mardom Party was to be the instrument of this new order ... The Shah was wary ... He was afraid also that popular and nationalistic policies, however well controlled, might endanger stability.[89]

Borrowing ideas from leftist intellectual advisors, Alam's *Mardom* Party had already incorporated proposal for land reform, women's enfranchisement and workers' private-sharing.[90] With land distribution as its centerpiece, this reform package was already gaining traction in Iran before it was adopted by the Kennedy administration, which then prevailed upon the Shah to endorse it. Thus, land reform began under the US-backed premier Ali Amini (1961–1962), while the White Revolution proper, including its original six points, was launched under Alam's premiership and received the requisite 99 percent approval in a national referendum in January 1963.[91] Meanwhile, a revitalized "Second National Front," including a significant leftist faction, remained divided and uncertain in response to the White Revolution. It was hard to deny that real reforms were underway, since the White Revolution's most important items, i.e. land reform, women's enfranchisement, literacy corps and the nationalization of natural resources, were borrowed from the opposition, and especially from the left. Jalal Al-Ahmad, who was affiliated with the Socialist League, articulated the opposition's frustration:

The regime has stolen these ideas from thinkers like Maleki. If it pretends to distribute land, give workers a share of factory profits, and liberate women, it is because real socialists are barred from government, while their ideas are gurgled incessantly.[92]

The Shah's "stealing" from the left grew more blatant as he assumed the posture of an "anti-feudal" revolutionary monarch, occasionally even declaring himself a socialist.[93] For their part, and without rejecting the content of the White Revolution, leftists and liberal nationalists continued to ask for political participation and the restoration of constitutional government. Their position was summed up in the National Front slogan: "Reforms, Yes; Dictatorship, No!"[94] This led to a breach between the liberal nationalist and leftists and a new clerical-led religious opposition that totally rejected the White Revolution. Thus, the June 1963 uprising, inspired by political neophyte Ayatollah Khomeini, became a turning point in several ways. First, it signaled the arrival of a new Islamic opposition whose ranks and demands overlapped with, but differed from, those of secular nationalists and leftists. Hence, the uprising was contained with relative ease because the secular opposition largely kept away from it. Shielding the Shah from direct responsibility, Premier Alam took full command and managed to put down a few days of street protests, inflicting perhaps hundreds of casualties.[95] Second, and more important, was the Shah's strategic decision on the treatment of secular opposition in the aftermath of the June 1963 uprising. Having crushed a major challenge from the right, the Shah could now reconcile leftists and liberals by allowing them a measure of political participation under a constitutional monarchy. Instead, he chose a different path, making 1963 the effective terminus of constitutional government and all peaceful legal dissent. Consequently, the opposition also began to transform, dividing into two distinct but overlapping branches. First, militant Islamic and secular activists began underground preparations for armed struggle in response to the regime's systematic and violent repression. Second, a broad-based movement of intellectual dissent focused its protracted ideological warfare on the Shah's "pseudo-revolution" in the name of Marxist, national and Islamic authenticity (see Chapters 6–7).

The opposition's last peaceful and legal stand was the 1964–1965 formation of the Third National Front, whose political makeup prefigured the much broader revolutionary coalition that would emerge in 1978. The Third National Front enlisted the Socialist League, the Islamic socialist Iranian People's Party, the secular nationalist Pan-Iranist Party, the religious-nationalist Liberation Movement of Iran and the leftist-dominated Organization of Tehran University Students (OTUS). The regime quickly crushed the Third National Front, jailing Maleki and other leaders of small parties, who asked for no more than the restoration of constitutional government, as Khomeini had done in 1963. The mid-1960s, therefore, marked a threshold, when the regime's violent repression made peaceful constitutional opposition impossible. During his 1965 trial, religious-nationalist leader Mehdi Bazargan warned the regime of the consequences of this new situation: "We are the last" group, he said, "to have struggled politically through the Constitutional means. We expect the judge to convey this point to his superiors." A year earlier, a 1964 resolution passed by the Confederation of Iranian Students/National Union (CISNU) had declared: "The Shah speaks the language of bullets; one must speak to him in his own language." While the regime ignored all such warnings, a younger generation of Muslim and Marxist militants was already preparing for armed struggle underground.[96]

1960s Culture Wars: "West-struck-ness" and "The Services and Betrayal of Intellectuals"

Today, Western civilization is at a stage when its elite look skeptically at all its fundamental values. Western intellectuals are more aware of the Western civilization's immanent decline than we are. This notion has been elaborately discussed in Spengler's great book *The Decline of the West*.

Dariush Ashuri in a 1968 interview in the weekly *Ferdowsi*.[97]

We need our own Eastern culture. The very same that the Indians have preserved and the Japanese have safeguarded, but we have lost it somewhere, and in order to find it, we cannot cling onto history. We have to reconstruct it.

1968 *Ferdowsi* editorial.[98]

Appearing in *Ferdowsi*, a weekly magazine popular with the literati and university students, statements such as those cited above were indicative of the intellectual mood becoming prevalent in 1960s Iran. In a broad sense, the country's intellectuals, including those in the political establishment, were engaged in a collective endeavor to redeem Iran's "cultural authenticity" vis-à-vis "the West." Though intimately linked to its global political and intellectual context, 1960s Iran's critique of the West also had peculiar features. The most famous 1960s manifesto of Iran's defiance of the West is the celebrated and maligned booklet *West-struck-ness,* by leading fiction writer and essayist Jalal Al-Ahmad (1923–1969). Quintessential of his generation, Al-Ahmad 's intellectual qualifications and political legacy have been endlessly debated, scrutinized and criticized. The rest of this chapter, therefore, reconstructs his intellectual and political legacy, whose nuance and complexity, it will be argued, are underappreciated.

Almost upon its 1962 release, Al-Ahmad's *West-struck-ness (Gharbzadegi)* became the most widely noted expression of broad sentiments lamenting Iran's economic, political and cultural subjugation to Euro-American dominance.[99] The book's title has several English translations, such as *Westoxication,* but here it will be rendered "West-struck-ness," which conveys the awkward exactitude of the original Persian neologism. Al-Ahmad borrowed the term *gharb-zadegi* from Ahmad Fardid, who invented it as a literal Persian translation of *dysiplexia,* composed of two Greek words, *dysis,* meaning "the West" and *plexia,* meaning "to be struck by." This term then captured the essence of Fardid's argument concerning the modern world becoming "West-stricken" under the nihilistic technological domination of Euro-American civilization.[100] Fardid, whose ideas will be discussed in Chapter 6, was a French-educated Tehran University professor, who traced his own critique of Western modernity to Martin Heidegger. Recent claims concerning Heidegger's influences on 1960s Iran and particularly on Al-Ahmad's *West-struck-ness,* however, are far-fetched.[101] Although *West-struck-ness* includes a passing reference to contemporary German nihilist thought, there is no evidence of Al-Ahmad ever having read Heidegger.[102]

West-struck-ness is in fact too incoherent to fit a single ideological or philosophical mold. Rather, it corresponds to a particular phase in Al-Ahmad's tumultuous intellectual-cum-political journey. By the time of its publication, Al-Ahmad was Iran's leading fiction writer, whose prose, particularly in essays and semi-autobiographic works like *The School Principle*, had become a widely emulated model of self-expression in modern Persian. Exemplary too were his pioneering translations from the French of modernist writers like Fyodor Dostoyevsky, Albert Camus, Jean-Paul Sartre and Andre Gide.[103] Politically, Al-Ahmad was an ex-communist who sympathized with Khalil Maleki's Socialist League during the 1960s. His intellectual pedagogy had begun with Kasravi, whom Al-Ahmad described as his generation's bridge of transition from religious belief to Marxism. In addition to the Stalinist Marxism of his youth, Al-Ahmad was familiar with French Existentialism, being particularly drawn to notions of intellectual responsibility and moral commitment found in authors like Jean-Paul Sartre and Albert Camus. Toward the end of *West-struck-ness*, for instance, he claimed that Camus' novel *The Plague* was an allegorical critique of *"machinisme"* and modern technology.[104] At any rate, his own "argument," in *West-struck-ness*, was the following:

The main argument of this briefing is that we failed to safeguard our cultural character vis-à-vis the machine and its inexorable onslaught. Instead, we fell apart. We could not come up with a deliberate measured response to this monstrosity of recent centuries, not even as Japan did ... Doubtless, we remain West-struck as long as we are mere consumers, incapable of building the machine. Ironically, we will become machine-struck (*mashin-zadeh*), once we actually build the machine, then we will start crying out against runaway technology and the machine, as the West is doing now.[105]

West-struck-ness lumped together a number of intellectually fashionable, but contradictory, propositions into a simplistic argument. First, it shifted the discourse that was critical of Western modernity from its Marxist focus on colonialism and imperialism toward a critique of Europe's technological domination. Second, it claimed "the West" itself was victimized by a runaway technocratic culture whose universal sway was about to absorb and dissolve all non-Western cultures. Third, facing this apparently inescapable predicament, Al-Ahmad advocated resistance primarily via the upholding of indigenous culture. The fourth, and rather implicit, proposition was that, even if futile, such resistance was the proper moral and intellectual choice, presumably in an existentialist manner.

The phenomenal success of *West-struck-ness* has drawn intellectual historians' attention away from the larger body of anti-imperialist and existentialist texts circulating in 1960s and 1970s Iran, texts that cumulatively formed the proverbial iceberg of which Al-Ahmad's small book was merely the most visible tip. Among such texts were Mehdi Bahar's 1965 *Inheritor of Colonialism* (*Mirath-khar-e este'-mar*), a well-researched Marxist indictment of American neo-colonialism, documenting the crucial role of oil interests in US policy toward Iran. Another example was Ali-Asghar Haj-Seyyed Javadi's *Evaluating Values* (*Arzyabi-e arzeshha*), a collection of articles originally published during the 1960s in the intellectual magazine *Negin* and then reprinted annually throughout the 1970s. Sharing Al-Ahmad's independent socialist background, Haj-Seyed Javadi criticized US neocolonial policy from a Third Worldist perspective, while being attentive, like Al-Ahmad, to the role of culture in anti-imperialist struggles worldwide.[106] There was also Iran's standard-bearer of existentialist Marxism, Mostafa Rahimi, co-translator's Sartre's *What is Literature?* and author of several collections of essays, some dealing with cultural imperialism in more sophisticated ways than Al-Ahmad's in *West-struck-ness*.[107]

A major reason for the success of *West-struck-ness* was Al-Ahmad's incomparable ability to speak as the voice of a trans-historical Iranian Self, rather than as an individual thinker.[108] As Edward Said later would argue, Al-Ahmad equated European colonial and imperial domination with the West's epistemological objectification of the Orient. But he went farther than Said, to speak also for an Islamic Orient, albeit one whose "wholeness" was admittedly illusory, covering up internal decay and fragmentation. The idiosyncrasies of *West-struck-ness* multiplied when Al-Ahmad projected the confrontation of the Iranian Self and its Western nemesis across history.[109]

He then moves from lamenting the Iranian civilization's presumed historical lag, for example in "urbanization," to condemning the "cancerous" urbanization of modern life under Western auspices:

Nowadays, we are bludgeoned into urbanization by the machine, a fast but very belated move, and therefore showing cancerous features. Our cities everywhere are growing like a cancerous tumor. Wow to us if the roots of this tumor reach the countryside, disintegrating it.[110]

If modern urban life was a maligned Western imposition, the ultimate site of resistance could be the countryside, where residues of "uncontaminated" indigenous culture might have survived. It is important to note that Al-Ahmad's turn to the rural population, as the repository of indigenous culture, has political, rather than religious, motivations. In this respect, *Gharb-zadegi* parallels contemporary anti-colonial texts like Frantz Fanon's *The Wretched of the Earth*.[111] Al-Ahmad's next rhetorical move was to foreground Islam as the core of indigenous cultural resistance. His discussion of Islam intertwines traditional Muslim accounts and modern scholarship to present the Islamic conquest of Iran as yet another case of West-struck-ness:

Prior to reaching the developed region between Tigris and Euphrates, Islam was merely Arab ignorance and primitivism, without ever engaging in bloodletting. The Islamic greeting of peace (*salam*) is the most peaceable slogan in any religion. Moreover, before Islam arrived to confront us, we already had invited it … Islam was a response to a centuries-old invitation, crushed when hot lead silenced the cries of [ancient Iranian prophets] Mani and Mazdak. In a slightly more scholarly perspective, the new Islamic call was based on the needs of urban dwellers between Euphrates and Syria, who were exhausted by long wars between Iran and Rome … prepared to support any movement bringing lasting peace to the region … And in the last analysis, is not our attentiveness to Islam also an attention to the West?[112]

The contradictory contentions of *West-struck-ness* did not go unchallenged by contemporary critics. An astute review was penned in 1967 by Dariush Ashuri, a younger intellectual also affiliated with Khalil Maleki's independent socialist movement. In Ashuri's devastating judgment, *West-struck-ness* played havoc with history, making arbitrary and inconsistent assertions, none of which were seriously source-based. Ashuri conceded, however, that *West-struck-ness* had posed a vital question faced by contemporary Iran and many other countries: "Ultimately, does a path toward the making of a new creative culture exist, or must we all dissolve in a 'world culture' imposed by the West? No answers to such questions yet exist."[113] Ashuri's review is proof that 1960s Iranian intellectuals could analyze the challenges of global modernity beyond the rhetoric of *West-struck-ness*. According to him, Al-Ahmad, mistakenly "considers 'the West' an aggregate, coherent and conscious totality, moving historically on a straight line against 'the East,' without any deviation or inconsistency." He then opposes this to an "East" lacking historical awareness and insight.[114] Equally muddled was Al-Ahmad's understanding of technology and "the machine" as the soul of Western civilization:

It is not clear whether his nemesis is the machine and *machinisme,* or how the machine is used. Is he seeking a world culture, or taking flight in religion and national traditions? Are we destitute and West-struck due to the arrival of the machine, or because we still do not have a machine-based economy?[115]

Ashuri also disagreed with Al-Ahmad's claim that contemporary European literary works, such as Albert Camus' *The Plague* or Eugene Ionseco's *Rhinoceros,* were concerned with "the machine."[116] Moreover, Al-Ahmad's praise of the Shi'i clergy, as "the last bastion of resistance to Europeans," and his comments on their role in the Constitutional Revolution, showed a "flight into reaction and tradition."[117] In the end, instead of resisting or opposing "the West," as Al-Ahmad was doing, Ashuri advocated positive but critical engagement with it: "The question is how to utilize humanity's progress on a path toward the public good. There is no returning backwards. Only those forging a path forward serve humanity and are 'committed' to it."[118] His conclusion anticipated an Eastern or "Asian renaissance":

Doubtless, something is developing in the colonized world, especially in Asia. We might call this an Asian Renaissance ... Europe is gradually losing its creativity, already showing signs of civilizational ailment. After five centuries of moving and forging ahead, Europe's bourgeois civilization is nearing the point of decline and despair.[119]

Retrospective judgments of *West-struck-ness* have been affected by the changing historical context of an Iranian revolution, giving rise to a clerically dominated Islamic Republic. Thus, the book is generally seen as an ideological manifesto of the 1978–1979 revolution, advocating the transformation of Shi'ism into an anti-Western revolutionary Islamic ideology. This, for example, was the interpretation of Hamid Dabashi in his pioneering study of Shi'ism as revolutionary "Islamic ideology."[120] Other scholars have disagreed. Negin Nabavi's meticulous study of the Iranian intellectual milieu of the 1960s and 1970s sees *West-struck-ness* as an inconsistent mélange of ideas, concluding that Al-Ahmad had not called for embracing Islam to resist Western domination:

Al-e Ahmad had not defined any course of action. He presented no solution. He did not place much hope in any one aspect of culture that could withstand this Western encroachment. He regarded religion as an element that might have served as a bulwark but that, in its present form, seemed quite ineffectual, having lapsed into old superstitions or, at most, boycotting national television and radio. In fact, he held religious leaders in as much contempt as those Westernized leaders who merely alienated the people.[121]

Nevertheless, estimations of Al-Ahmad as the intellectual harbinger of an anti-Western "Islamic Revolution" persist. Ali Mirsepassi, for example, writes:

Al-e Ahmad's two most important books are the best representations of radical epistemic violence that prophetic intellectuals have inflicted in the Iranian intellectual and social context. *Westoxication* is a totalistic condemnation of modernization in the Iranian context, a radical and intolerant attack on every facet of modern life in contemporary Iran ... His other book, *On the Service and Treason of the Intellectuals*, is an even harsher and more violent critique of modernist intellectuals in Iran.[122]

Mirsepassi misjudges both of these influential books. A collection of essays written during the 1960s, *On the Services and Betrayal of Intellectuals* was Al-Ahmad's last work, showing that his ideas had changed beyond *West-struck-ness*. Curiously, the barely 100-page long *West-struck-ness* continues to overshadow Al-Ahmad's over 400 pages of more nuanced discussion, of intellectuals, religion and politics, in his last book. Even Nabavi and Dabashi remain focused on *West-struck-ness*, allowing *On the Services and Betrayal of Intellectuals* to be continuously misread as a text advocating a return to Islam through "an alliance between intellectuals and the clergy against the Pahlavi regime."[123] The concluding part of this chapter therefore will analyze *On the Services and Betrayal of Intellectuals* as Al-Ahmad's ultimate testimonial, a work showing the broadening of his worldview, something reflected also in his travelogues.

When *West-struck-ness* was published in 1962, Al-Ahmad's fame rested on his short stories, as well as monographs of his travels to the far corners of Iran. Between 1962 and his death in 1969, he traveled and wrote about his visits to France, Switzerland, Germany, Netherland, England, Israel, the US, the Soviet Union and Saudi

Arabia. This new genre of world travelogue shows an Al-Ahmad moving away from the siege mentality of *West-struck-ness* toward
a growing appreciation of the outside world. In a surprising turn, for
example, he was impressed by Israel's exemplary success in turning
religious identity into the foundation of a modern nation-state. He even
went as far as admitting:

Having suffered much at the hands of inauthentic Arabs, my Self is pleased
with Israel's presence in the East. This means the presence of an Israel capable
of shutting down the sheikhdoms' oil pipelines, inspiring cries of justice in
every Bedouin Arab heart, and causing all kinds of headaches to their archaic
lawless governments.[124]

Even more interesting is Al-Ahmad's Hajj travelogue, often considered
another proof of his turn to Islam, but in fact a text that could be read
very differently. Finding little genuine religion in the entire Hajj experience, Al-Ahmad argues Mecca and Medina must be placed under
collective Islamic administration, since "reactionary" Saudi control
had turned the Hajj into nothing more than "mechanized
barbarism."[125] The book's closing remarks clearly contradict the
claims of commentators, like Abbas Milani, who consider Al-Ahmad
a fanatical ideologue incapable of intellectual doubt and self-reflection:

I undertook this journey mostly out of curiosity, just as I stick my head into
any other hole. To have a look, without illusions. And this notebook is the
result. Yet another experience . . . and each experience of this kind . . . leading
to some awakening, or at least some doubt. Thus, with the force of these
experiences, I am breaking down, from under my feet, every stepping stone in
the world of certitude. And what is any life's purpose? It is to doubt the
veracity and authenticity of all those certain truths that inspire illusion,
certitude or action. To lose them one after another. To turn each into
a question mark. There was a time when I imagined the entire world envied
my insights. And now, belonging to one of its corners, I can become a man of
the world by filling my sight with visions from all of its corners . . . And
whether it be confession, blasphemy or protest, in this journey, I have been
searching more for my brother, and all my brothers, than for God, who can
be found anywhere by anyone believing in Him.[126]

Similarly equivocal and self-reflective is Al-Ahmad's *Russian Journey*,
covering his 1964 visit to Moscow, Leningrad, Baku, Tashkent and
Ashkhabad.[127] A notable literary accomplishment, this is another politically ambivalent work that is critical of the Soviet Union, and

particularly its Muslim republics, yet on balance is more positive than Andre Gide's *Return from the USSR*, which Al-Ahmad had translated into Persian.[128] A year later, Al-Ahmad spent two months in the US, invited to Harvard University's annual summer seminar promoting dialogue among international academics, literati and artists. There, he made a summary presentation of *West-struck-ness* as a critique of "neo-colonialism," similar to those advanced by intellectuals like Sartre, Frantz Fanon and Aimé Césaire. "The West," he emphasized, was the industrialized First World, including the Soviet Union, taken to task for its domination and exploitation of the Third World. Significantly, Al-Ahmad's conclusion was to call for a more balanced global culture, rather than advocating for the autonomy of indigenous cultures:

It is often argued that the machine's arrival, and global "standardization," destroys national cultures, leading the world toward uniformity and "conformism." But I have no such worries. What the machine's onslaught destroys would be replaced by the power of a world culture, being a mix of all national cultures. And hence no one can warp himself in excessive nationalism to call humanity back into medieval stagnation.[129]

Nor does Al-Ahmad's Harvard presentation refer to Islam or religion as a cultural resource in resistance to colonialism and imperialism. In fact, Al-Ahmad openly embraces intellectual eclecticism, going as far as declaring: "I am a cosmopolitan in every sense, except when it comes to language." This claim was made in a 1964 interview, where he also refused to be defined by his advocacy of "return to tradition," while reaffirming "lifelong" commitment to what he had learned from Marxism.[130]

In the course of the 1960s, therefore, Al-Ahmad had moved beyond the "excessive nationalism" of *West-struck-ness*, becoming more intellectually cosmopolitan, rather than recoiling into the bosom of Islam. *On the Services and Betrayal of Intellectuals* is a testament to this change. A collection of independent essays, this text is not only larger in scale and scope, but substantially different from *West-struck-ness* in structure, argument, composition, prose and literary style. First, and apparently responding to critics of *West-struck-ness*, Al-Ahmad's essays are more coherent, nuanced and better organized. Second, and again unlike *West-struck-ness*, this work aspires to be a well-researched, almost academic, study. Here, Al-Ahmad cites numerous sources in Persian, French and English, directly quotes long passages, and incorporates translations of relevant short essays, including Antonio Gramsci's "The Formation of Intellectuals." Third, Al-Ahmad's prose is more polished and restrained, displaying less of the aggressive first-person bravura and hyperbolic urgency of *West-struck-ness*. Fourth, he acknowledges indebtedness to several leading intellectuals for feedback on his essays or help with translation.[131]

The title *On the Services and Betrayal of Intellectuals* echoes Julien Benda's famous *The Treason of the Intellectuals*, to which Al-Ahmad adds balance by acknowledging the intellectuals' services along with their alleged betrayals. The title thus captures the book's probing ambivalence toward the social and political role of modern intellectuals. Al-Ahmad begins sensibly with definitions, stating: "to have a clear discussion, we must first agree on terms and their meanings." He then traces the emergence of the Persian neologism *roshanfekr* in relation to its French equivalent *intellectuel*, noting also the relevance to Iran of the Russian notion of the *intelligentsia*. Briefly alluding to its Enlightenment prototypes, like *les eclaires* (the enlightened) and *libre penseur* (free thinker), he concludes that the Persian term *roshanfekr* conveys the original French sense of one who can "think critically" about traditional religious and political authority.[132] Referring to Gramsci's "The Formation of Intellectuals," he argues that human intellectual capacity is a social faculty growing through interaction with the world, via both immediate experience and abstract learning. Still following Gramsci, he argues that intellectuals are made primarily through education and schooling, providing them with broader fields of vision or "world views."[133] Thus, being an intellectual is to be "concerned with the public good, moving beyond the individual self to social concerns."

This means climbing out from the pitfalls of one's own self, home, city, land, language and religion to see the world via the expanse of a singular humanity, encompassing diverse peoples, languages, customs, cultures and religions ... It means assuming no given condition as heavenly-ordained, but to probe instead into its causes. It means that instead of fantasizing about better conditions, one dares to act and change existing conditions, possessing a criteria of judgment based on historical and social comparisons.[134]

This is the Kantian definition of the universal critical thinker, buttressed by the Marxist call for critical thought as guide to action aimed at changing the world. A few pages later, Al-Ahmad restates this basic definition, specifying its application to the Iranian context of monarchist and Islamic authority:

In a broader sense, in the age of intellectualism ... man is forced to act relying only on himself, without any expectation from external sources or the world above. That means being autonomous, free and responsible ... Consequently, intellectualism corresponds to an age, or domain, in which notions such as God's Shadow (*zel-allah*, i.e. king) or God's Sign (*ayatollah*) become meaningless.[135]

Moreover, Al-Ahmad emphatically states that "one who is bound by religious faith cannot be an intellectual."[136] His stringent criterion of intellectualism excludes clerics and military men, since both groups deal in "obedience," (*ta'abod*), the categorical negation of intellectualism.[137] The book's fourth chapter has an extensive discussion of clerics as Iran's "traditional intellectuals," a concept evidently borrowed from Gramsci. Al-Ahmad's concern with the clergy focuses on Ayatollah Khomeini and the anti-regime uprising he inspired in 1963.[138] But Khomeini is mentioned only once, and only where Al-Ahmad is criticizing intellectual "extremism" (*tond-ravi*). He thus places Khomeini next to Kasravi, the Tudeh Party and the National Front, whose "extremism" he criticizes: "As an ayatollah, Khomeini went to such extremes that made his own presence in the country difficult."[139] Clearly therefor, and contrary to Al-Ahmad's detractors, he does not recommend Khomeini as an example for Iranian intellectuals to follow.

Critically reflecting on Iranian intellectuals, Al-Ahmad says they are modern-educated, European-influenced, non-religious and "alienated from their native and traditional environment."[140] With the last point, he returns to *West-struck-ness*, accusing Iranian intellectuals of directing their critical energy against their "native and traditional environment," rather than political regimes sustained by "colonialism." However, instead of advocating return to "native tradition," Al-Ahmad wants Iranian intellectuals to follow global role models, like Franz Fanon and Aimé Césaire, who blend cultural nativism with anti-colonial politics and Third Worldist socialism. Iranian intellectuals, he contends, must also learn from the anti-colonial stance that European public intellectuals, like Jean-Paul Sartre or the British philosopher Bertrand Russell, had adopted.[141]

In the end, while Al-Ahmad does not uncritically embrace indigenous culture or religion, he argues that they could provide intellectuals with the means to resist colonialism and imperialism. The problem is he cannot say exactly how this might be accomplished. Moreover, he could be criticized for failing to anticipate the dangers inherent in neo-traditionalism or Islamist politics, a fault he shares with contemporary Third Worldist thinkers (see Chapter 6 for an Iranian Marxist critique of Islam as political ideology). Still, Al-Ahmad's discussion of Iranian intellectuals finds more nuance as he proceeds:

There are two kinds of Intellectuals. A majority help the ruling system function, providing it with rationalization and intellectual support, and a small minority searching for a way out of this colonial impasse … I consider the first group, i.e. those who are intellectual by profession yet serve the ruling system, to be minimally intellectual, whereas the second group is intellectual par excellence … as the author of these pages, my hope is that Iranian intellectuals move increasingly from minimal to maximal intellectualism.[142]

This differentiation brings Al-Ahmad close to Taqi Arani's contrasting of a small progressive intellectual elite to a majority of "intellectuals by profession," who act as functionaries of the status quo (see Chapter 4). Al-Ahmad, therefore, is cognizant of the distinction between "functionalist" definitions of intellectuals, as society's educators, bureaucrats, literati and clerics, and their "normative" definition as critics of the social order. But, allowing for "degrees" of intellectualism, he relativizes the distinction, placing the two contrasting roles of intellectuals at the opposite poles of a continuum.

Chapter 3, "Birthplaces of Intellectuals," focuses on locating the "native and historical background" of Iranian intellectuals. Citing Frederick Engels' comments on early Christianity, Al-Ahmad claims ancient Iranian prophets, like Zoroaster and Mani, as well as nonconformist Islamic sects, such as early Shi'is, were social protest movements in religious form.[143] In the modern era, he concludes: "intellectuals may appear to be following the same path, when the time of the prophets has passed … They thus carry the same burden, as prophets did, when intelligent thought cannot and need not be presented in metaphysical garb."[144] Once again, modern intellectualism is categorically distinguished from religiosity.

In Chapter 4, "Traditional intellectuals: Clerics and Military Men," Al-Ahmad's evaluation of Muslim clerics, as traditional intellectuals, is summarized in the following, "self-evident" (*badihi*), observations: "First, the clergy deals in obedience ... Second, the clergy defends tradition and opposes all change and progress, hence being called the people's opiate ... Third, the clergy is engaged in a certain kind of educational work."[145] This too cannot be a role model that is recommended to modern intellectuals. However, the chapter ends with Al-Ahmad repeating his admonition of modern intellectuals for opposing religion and the clergy instead of the government. Still, this qualified defense of religious tradition hinges on the argument that, unlike Europe, Iran's less-than-a-century-old modern secular culture is not yet strong enough to challenge the centuries-long power of Islamic culture. In the end, Al-Ahmad wants intellectuals to find ways of reconciling religion to an anti-colonial political agenda, rather than making common cause with traditional clergy.[146]

In Chapter 5, Al-Ahmad boldly questions the taken for granted linkage of Iranian intellectualism to Persian language, noting that "Iranian intellectuals include Turkish speakers from Azerbaijan, Kurdish-speakers from Kurdistan, and Arabic speakers from Khuzistan." He criticizes the "degradation of non-Persians speakers because of the expulsion of their languages from the cultural realm," a situation in which despite "Iran's being a multi-lingual nation, we are left with an inaccurate bourgeois notion of the Iranian intellectual."[147] Referring to the Universal Declaration of Human Rights, he argues: "We have deprived six to seven million people from the most basic of human rights, which is the freedom to use any language they want."[148] His concluding remarks are a challenge to the deeply engrained Persian chauvinism of Iranian intellectuals:

If Azerbaijan were allowed to administer its own cultural affairs, using its own language in education, print and other media, there should be no fear of any potential gravitational pull from across the border. Moreover, our country's intellectualism would be much enriched ... From the conceptual origin of an [Iranian] nation in the constitutional era to the present, Tehran governments have considered Azerbaijan a colony, if not politically and economically, but certainly in a cultural sense. The first negative result of this cultural colonialism is the killing of Turkish culture in Azerbaijan.[149]

Finally, the last chapter of *On the Services and Betrayal of Intellectuals* is arguably the most important, because it draws explicitly on Al-Ahmad's own political experience in order to present the independent socialist leader, Khalil Maleki, as an "ideal type" of modern Iranian intellectual:

So far I have dealt in generalities. In this last chapter, let me be frank and, drawing on memory, speak of my personal experience with contemporary intellectuals … First and foremost, I will speak of my experience with Khalil Maleki, who is not only a teacher to me, and many other contemporary intellectuals, in dealing with social questions, but the most unique example of intellectualism in the past forty years, always present on the scene, and despite apparent defeats, ultimately the real victor.[150]

Al-Ahmad describes his lonely attendance at the 1966 military tribunal of Khalil Maleki and three of his colleagues who were accused of "acting against national security." As the group's leader, Maleki was condemned to three years in prison, while the others received lesser sentences. As seen above, their real charge was participation in the Third National Front, which had joined Maleki's Socialist League to a few small, secular and religious-nationalist, parties. Al-Ahmad then explains why Maleki embodies his ideal-type intellectual: "I consider him as an exemplary intellectual, a remnant of the previous generation, who neither has abased himself by joining governments, nor taken refuge in silence before a horde of thieves." But Al-Ahmad also mentions serious differences with Maleki, whose socialist "orthodoxy" involved an uncritical "persistent defense of European civilization." Related to this difference, adds Al-Ahmad, "is my attention to the clergy, as a source for understanding the political specificity of our society."[151] Thus, while appreciating much in Maleki's socialism, Al-Ahmad rejects its total identification with European cultural models. Returning to the basic Third Worldist premise of *West-struck-ness*, he wants a "native" version of socialism, grounded in Iranian cultural and historical traditions.

Finally, Al-Ahmad uses Maleki's example to draw two important conclusions to the book. First, he argues, Maleki's case shows an intellectual "third path," between the two extremes of pure idealism, leading to defeat and disillusionment, and intellectual non-commitment, effectively meaning political conformism. Clearly, this "third path" is what Al-Ahmad recommends to Iranian intellectuals.

Essentially following the same path, his own politics were those of non-conformist Third World socialist intellectuals, independent from both communist and bourgeois ideologies, and rooted instead in their "native" culture, shaped by the particular contingencies of history, language, religion and ethnicity.[152]

Al-Ahmad's second general comment on Maleki's trial is an astute observation of Iranian politics backsliding into despotism in the aftermath of the White Revolution. Maleki, he notes, was the only Iranian intellectual tried and incarcerated for allegedly "acting against national security," initially alongside Arani's group in the 1930s, and then three decades later in 1966:

This means that from 1933 to 1966, the man has remained intolerable to the state, while threading a logical evolutionary path from that movement to this one in about thirty years. However, if he was first condemned because of communism ... this time the accusation was socialism ... This leads to two conclusions: First, as a political thinker, Maleki exemplifies the transition, during the past three decades, from Stalinist communism to democratic socialism in Iran and the rest of the world ... Second, government intolerance in Iran has grown to the extent that if thirty years ago Stalinist communism set the bar [of intolerance], today even democratic socialism has become intolerable. This means [also] ... that the more reasonable Iranian intellectuals become, the more unreasonable and intolerable becomes the government.[153]

Here, Al-Ahmad perceptively diagnoses an ironic situation, where the Shah's regime grew more intolerant and repressive, while carrying out successful reforms and facing an opposition, including liberal nationalists and the left, as well as Khomeini and his followers, that asked no more than the observance of constitutional government. The next two chapters will show how this crucial moment was decisive to the regime's future, laying the foundations for its demise within about fifteen years.

Conclusion

This chapter began by trying to answer the question of why socialism and Marxism occupied such a prominent place in Iranian political culture from the 1940s to the 1970s. Countering mainstream historiography, it argued that Marxist intellectual hegemony had a positive origin with the Tudeh Party's offering a social program and a worldview that proved exceptionally appealing to the middle-class intelligentsia and urban working classes. Ironically, communists became Iran's most successful political party, as long as a semi-democratic constitutional regime was allowed to function. Second, and again moving to the narrative center what has been at the margins of mainstream historiography, the chapter showed the significance of a democratic socialist left and an Islamic socialist trend, both of which emerged in reaction to the Tudeh Party. Third, it was argued that socialist reform and welfare demands, as originally articulated by the Tudeh Party, also inspired the Pahlavi monarchy's social engineering and reform project of the 1960s and 1970s, when the regime systematically recruited ex-communists and socialists to implement the Shah-People Revolution. The next chapter notes how Marxist, socialist, Third Worldist and Islamic leftist ideologies became hegemonic in the 1960s–1970s university students' and urban guerrillas' opposition, as well as in the academe, fiction writing and translation, journalism, artistic production and popular entertainment. Ending with a specific case study in intellectual history, the chapter revisits the controversial legacy of Jalal Al-Ahmad, concluding that his 1960s essays and travelogues show he was primarily a Third World socialist, rather than an advocate of Islamist and clerical politics.

6 | Revolutionary Monarchy, Political Shi'ism and Islamic Marxism

Mohammad Reza Shah's dictatorship bought into the discourse of "spirituality" in order to fill an ideological void. Despite its economic development plans and dreams of Iran's industrialization – projects requiring proper ideology and propaganda – the regime was fearful of leftist ideologies and obsessed with fantasies of safeguarding "authentic national culture." Thus, in a repressive and suffocating political milieu, it promoted and took refuge in religious and mystical ideologies, unaware that such "philosophical" and "mystical" rhetoric, concerning authentic national culture and familiar Eastern wisdom, eventually would lead to an "Islamic Revolution."

Dariush Ashuri[1]

When Michel Foucault praised the "political spirituality" of Iran's unfolding revolution in 1978, he was repeating his Iranian informants' interpretation of Shi'ism as Iran's expression of cultural revolt against Western modernity.[2] An epistemological circle thus was closed, as postmodern European philosophy borrowed its analysis of a seemingly new kind of revolution from Iranian intellectuals. As seen in previous chapters, the particular critique of modernity Foucault discovered in Tehran in the late 1970s had a complex intellectual genesis and long history of fermentation, reaching its peak in the two prerevolutionary decades. A number of studies have shown how the 1960s and 1970s generation of Iranian intellectuals were preoccupied with constructing an authentically Iranian national culture via a radical critique of "the West." Barely studied or understood, however, is the Pahlavi regime's active participation in anti-Western authenticity politics, a dangerous game that ideologically destabilized the regime and arguably contributed to its downfall. Addressing this lacunae, this chapter briefly sketches the intellectual makeup of major cultural authenticity discourses unfolding in the 1960s and 1970s in Iran, including the regime's authenticity discourse. It begins by tracing attempts at shaping an official national culture, a project that relied

190

significantly on the opposition's discourse of anti-Western native authenticity. The chapter then focuses on two small but influential intellectual circles that developed a conservative counter-modernist project of "returning" to Iranian authenticity via esoteric mystical readings of Shi'i Islam. Finally, we will trace the emergence of "Islamic Marxism" as an influential trend in political culture, as well as an inspiration to armed struggle against the regime during the 1970s.

Pahlavi Cultural Planning and Authenticity Politics: 1960s and 1970s

Until a few years ago, our only hope and desire was to become like the West ... Now, however, while still acknowledging the West's positive qualities, we want to adopt only these qualities and adapt them to Iranian morality, since we must have our own spiritual and philosophical outlook.

The Shah in a 1972 speech[3]

The project of crafting an official national culture had started under Reza Shah, but slackened during the politically contentious 1940s and 1950s. During these decades the Ministry of Culture continued to set national educational guidelines, presiding over school texts, book publication and public libraries. Through a Fine Arts Institute, the ministry also provided some financial support and guidance to arts education and artistic production. By the mid-1960s, in the wake of the White Revolution, a more comprehensive cultural policy agenda gradually emerged. In 1966, the Shah endorsed a national "cultural policy" plan, making the government responsible for issuing "general directives concerning the co-ordination of cultural activities in the public sector." Cultural planning thus became the third tier of a state-sponsored strategy of national development, whose first tier was Iran's five-year economic development plans, complemented by the social engineering project of the White Revolution. Like economic planning and the White Revolution, the 1960s national cultural project was aligned with global trends. Iran's membership in the United Nations, for instance, required the implementation of a national "cultural policy" conforming to UNESCO standards.[4] And as with the White Revolution, the regime's national culture agenda copied the opposition, particularly its discourse of upholding Iranian authenticity vis-à-vis Western intrusions.[5] Official agenda is traceable in documents, such as a booklet written by French-educated sociologist Jamshid Behnam and published by UNESCO, defining the objectives, scope and institutional frame of Iran's national cultural policy. The text's preamble reads:

During the last few decades, the Western technological revolution has aroused a number of different reactions ranging from total imitation (voluntary or imposed by colonizing countries) to total rejection of Western values. Between these two extremes some countries are seeking an intermediate course ... Such is the aim of Iranian cultural policy: to ensure that the country progresses economically and socially but yet does not lose its originality in the face of the uniformity imposed by the values of modern technological civilization.

More specifically, "a further objective of cultural policy is the spread of culture through the establishment of cultural centers and the development of the mass media. In this sphere, the role of the state is considered to be of prime importance." Following UNESCO guidelines, the booklet specified state intervention would not shape the "content" of national culture:

The state ... will encourage the participation of the private sector but will reserve for itself the implementation of a policy concerned with administration and general guidance. This policy will require planning at the level of the five-year plan for economic and social development. But this does not mean that the state will impose any particular concept of culture ... However, the state cannot remain entirely uninvolved in the content of culture ... it is its duty to safeguard the cultural heritage in the face of the increasingly rapid and uniform development of world culture. But we know that the state cannot assume a creative role and become an instrument of cultural production.[6]

This document endorsed recent trends among Asian and African nations toward "abandoning Western models" in order to construct non-elitist national cultures rooted in native traditions. It concluded: "At a time when, in search of new sources of inspiration, the elite of the West looks to the East, has not the moment come for the countries of Asia and Africa to begin to appreciate each other's cultural heritage to their natural benefit?"[7] Thus, official policy was aligned with the opposition's advocacy of cultural authenticity, defending native tradition in defiance of the technological, economic and cultural domination of "the West."

Implementing national cultural policy was the responsibility mainly of the new Ministry of Culture and Art, whose administrative branches covered archaeology, museums and historic monuments, public libraries, cinematographic affairs and artistic activities/education. The Ministry of Culture and Art also supervised a number of parallel cultural institutions, each with its own budget and administration. The most important of these was the High Council of Culture and the Arts (*Shura-ye ali-ye farhang va honar*). Established in 1967, and presided over by the Shah, the Council's specific task was to "supervise the implementation of cultural policy." Its top brass included the ministers of Culture and Art, National Education, Science and Higher Education, Information, Cooperatives and Rural Affairs, and the director of the Iranian National Radio and Television. These were joined by about a dozen leading artists and academic experts, all appointed by royal decree. The Council's official organ, the quarterly *Culture and Life* (*Farhang va zendegi*) was published from 1969 until the outbreak of the revolution in 1978.[8] As noted below, the decade-long run of *Culture and Life* clearly reflects the overlap of official and dissident discourses on Iranian national identity and cultural authenticity.[9] It is important to emphasize that *Culture of Life* was the official version of dissident modernist periodicals in which mostly left-leaning intellectuals circulated their ideas. Another understudied aspect of intellectual history in the 1960s and 1970s, dissident periodicals covered modernist literature and culture, occasionally making social commentary but steering clear of domestic politics. Their forced silence on Iranian politics, however, was somewhat compensated by their wide-ranging attention to contemporary Third Worldist, socialist and Marxist topics, mainly in translation. Notable among such periodicals were *Andishe va honar, Arash, Jahan-e no, Ketab-e hafte, Negin* and *Jong-e Esfahan*.[10] A leading representative of dissident periodicals in the 1960s and 1970s was *Jahan-e no* (*Modern World*),[11] which displayed a mix of intellectual sophistication and broad leftist sympathies. *Jahan-e no* featured translations of works by or articles on Paul Sweezy, Thomas Bottomore, Langston Hughes, Che Guevara, Bertolt Brecht, Maurice Merleau-ponty Isaac Dutcher, Aimé Césaire, Bertrand Russel, Jean-Paul Sartre, Regis Debray, C. Right Mills, Eric Hobsbawm and Henri Lefebvre.[12] Periodicals like *Jahan-e no* show the availability in pre-revolutionary Iran of sophisticated leftist thought from across the globe, which helps explain the leftist intellectual hegemony of the 1960s and 1970s and the monarchy's deference to it.

Structurally, national cultural policy was implemented within three state-controlled frames: the educational system, print and electronic mass media, and a host of new institutions geared specifically to cultural production.[13] In all three frames, official cultural policy borrowed heavily from dissident political culture, particularly leftist discourses. First, throughout the 1960s and 1970s, the government funded, administered and imposed curricular uniformity on a rapidly expanding system of primary, secondary and higher education. However, government control was challenged at the university level, where a culture of intellectual dissent and political opposition prevailed among students and many faculty. Tehran University had been in the forefront of early 1960s opposition, while Iranian universities led the country in political strikes and demonstrations all the way through the 1978–1979 revolution.[14] Moreover, due to the limited enrolment capacity of Iranian universities, during the 1960s half of the country's university student population studied abroad, where it had formed one of the world's largest, best-organized and most effective student opposition movements. At the same time, incorporating the educational system within the unfolding frame of the White Revolution had become a regime priority. Thus, in October 1967, it was announced that Iran would launch an "Administrative and Educational Revolution," as the twelfth plank of what was increasingly referred to as the Shah-People Revolution. Within the next decade, the Educational Revolution significantly expanded state-funded higher education, but it failed to contain student politicization, which intensified during the 1970s, turning university campuses into the main recruiting ground and support base of guerrilla armed struggle.[15]

As well as an increasingly restive university student population, the notable presence of leftist faculty challenged government control of higher education.[16] The left dominated, for example, at Tehran University's Institute for Social Studies and Research, Iran's first modern social science academy. Founded in 1958, it offered a graduate program and sponsored social research projects, while consulting the government on social development programs. The institute's intellectual and political independence was symbolized by its president, Gholam-Hossein Sadaiqi (1905–1991), National Front leader and a founder of Iranian sociology. More important was the institute's directorship by the French-educated sociologist and former communist Ehsan Naraqi (1926–2012). During the 1960s, and supervised by the secret police (SAVAK), Naraqi hired a host of leftist and dissident intellectuals as professors, researchers and translators.[17] In 1969, Naraqi left Iran to work for UNESCO, later returning to serve as director of the Institute for Educational and Scientific Research and Planning. In the 1970s, he became a semi-official intellectual voice of "Return to the Self," publishing a number of books on nativism and cultural authenticity as Iran's defense against Western technological and materialist excesses.[18] Naraqi's recruitment of dissidents to work for the government, however, was part of a grand strategy of harnessing leftist intellectuals through a combination of rewards and punishment. Placing cultural workers on government payroll encouraged political quiescence, while allowing close scrutiny of potentially subversive intellectuals. But this was a game that the other side might also play to its advantage. Trying to circumvent political constraints, leftist and dissident intellectuals could get at least some of their ideas into mainstream culture, while collecting a government salary instead of going to prison. Thus, the apparent paradox that, during the 1970s, prominent writers, translators, poets, artist and filmmakers accepted various degrees of association with a regime whose overthrow they all would support within a few years.[19]

In addition to the educational system, leftists and other dissidents were prominent in the arts and popular entertainment, often working in government-funded bureaus and foundations shaping and guiding cultural policy.[20] The most notable of these were the Cultural Section of the Pahlavi Foundation, the Queen's Special Bureau and the Center for the Intellectual Cultivation of Children and Adolescents. The country's self-appointed high priestess of arts and culture, Queen Farah Diba (Pahlavi) presided over the latter two organizations. Her patronage extended to book publishing, museums, film and theater production, and arts festivals. The Center for the Intellectual Cultivation of Children and Adolescents was established in 1965 to provide institutional support to a younger generation of writers, translators, artists and filmmakers, allowing them considerable creative latitude. The Center's director was Lili Amir Arjomand, an old friend with whom the future queen occasionally had frequented leftist student circles while studying in France. Under Amir Arjomand's management, the Center became another hub of leftist intellectuals in the regime's employ. Its main activity, i.e. book publishing, was supervised by Firuz Shirvanlu (1938–1988), a former Marxist student activist in the UK, who had earlier been condemned to execution for alleged involvement in a royal assassination plot. Pardoned and cleared, Shirvanlu joined the Center for the Intellectual Cultivation of Children and Adolescents, where he hired prominent leftist writers, poets and translators. In 1969, for example, the Center published Marxist writer Samad Behrangi's *Little Black Fish*, a children's fable with a revolutionary message calling for armed struggle. The same year saw the publication of Shirvanlu's own translation of Ernst Fischer's *The Necessity of Art: A Marxist Approach*, a work that went through several printings, becoming the standard text on the subject.[21]

The 1970s signature project of official culture was the Shiraz-Persepolis Festival of Arts. Convened annually for a decade (1967–1977), the festival showcased modernist and classical Iranian and international music, drama, dance and film. The apogee of Queen Farah's cultural patronage, the Shiraz-Persepolis festival was managed by her cousin Reza Qotbi, director of the state-owned National Iranian Radio and Television (NIRT). The festival's mission, according to Qotbi, was to present all the arts "in the context of an encounter between East and West," with a focus on "the best traditional arts of the East, the finest classical traditions of the West, and the avant-garde apropos its place in the world." The country's most talented musicians, dramatists and filmmakers presented their work, including some that were banned from general release, at the Shiraz-Persepolis festival. In keeping with Qotbi's mission statement, traditional Iranian music, popular *ruhozi* theatre, *naqali* oratory, and even *ta'zieh* religious passion plays, were regularly featured. Though catering to the country's artistic and intellectual elite, the festival's performances reached a wide audience, as they were selectively broadcast on national radio and television.

The Queen's promotion of nativism and cultural authenticity was complemented by the monarchy's semi-official Third Worldist posturing and rhetoric. During the 1970s, the National Iranian Radio and Television (NIRT) was the state's most potent means of shaping national culture, with its daily news and entertainment programs reaching millions across the country. The NIRT's general director, Reza Qotbi, and assistant director, Mamhud Jafarian, were former leftists who hired and placed ex-Marxists in sensitive NIRT posts. In the late 1960s, the secret police (SAVAK) had warned the Shah of the NIRT becoming a dangerous leftist haven. Qotbi defended his policy, arguing it was better to lure leftist dissidents into serving the regime than to lose them to various opposition outlets. Apparently, the Shah agreed and ordered the punishment of SAVAK officials who had filed the report against Qotbi.[22] The most prominent ex-Marxist at the NIRT was Parviz Nikkhah, formerly a Maoist student in London who, like Firuz Shirvanlu, was pardoned by the Shah, after being condemned in the 1965 royal assassination plot. Soon hired by the NIRT, Nikkhah joined ex-Tudeh Party member Mahmud Jafarian as chief political commentator and news analyst. Assuming an "anti-imperialist" posture, Nikkhah and Jafarian became top propagandists for strategic policy lines laid down by the Shah.[23] During the 1970s, this official "leftist" rhetoric was discernible in the pages of *Tamasha* (viewing), the NIRT's glossy magazine. Edited by yet another former leftist, Iraj Gorgin, *Tamasha* published quality articles, on contemporary arts and culture, by Iranian and international authors.[24] Its editorials and special columns, however, espoused monarchist propaganda in a pseudo-Marxist language. For example, a special column by ex-Maoist Firuz Fuladi attacked "Stalinist Marxism" and "Third Worldist Socialism," from a monarchist but "anti-imperialist" perspective.[25] Writing on "Systematic Thinking," for the same column, Nikkhah invoked Systems Theory to critique "Marxism and neo-Marxism," as mechanical and deterministic.[26] Meanwhile, he was trying to present the Shah as a globally recognized anti-imperialist leader. On the occasion of the Shah's birthday in 1974, for example, he wrote:

Remembering glories, we celebrate the birthday of an emperor (*shahanshah*), a great man who stands his grounds in Iranian culture to demand more equitable global relations. Recognizing their loftiest ideals in his discourse, hundreds of millions of Asians, and many anti-colonial nations, support him.[27]

Outdoing both of his colleagues, Jafarian's editorials claimed the Shah's leadership had turned Iran into an "extremely leftist" nation, attacked by "Western and Eastern" imperialists:

Both Leftist and Western Worlds consider Third World countries with economic, political and military clout to be on the extreme left. These powerful Third World countries are opposed by a West that tolerates its own communist parties ... Imperialism has both leftist and rightist variants ... Nor should we forget that independent progressive leaders

198 Revolutionary Monarchy, Political Shi'ism and Islamic Marxism

and patriots of the Third World are attacked by both the left and the right. That is because they are the most extreme leftists ... Such has been the situation of the Iranian nation and its leader during the past two decades.[28]

This kind of pseudo-leftist rhetoric extoling the Shah as the revolutionary leader of a powerful Third World nation came into focus in the early 1970s when Iran improved its relations with the Soviet Union, while following the US in warming up to the People's Republic of China. Some Iranian Maoist groups then adopted China's official view of the Shah as an anti-imperialist leader defiant of both superpowers, a claim that was repeated by the regime's "left" propagandists, and increasingly voiced by the Shah himself, who even used it as the ultimate explanation of his downfall.[29] By the mid-1970s, renegade communists and Maoists, like Jafarian and Nikkhah, became even more prominent as chief theorists of the Shah's new single-party Rastakhiz project, providing it with pseudo-Marxist rationalization (see Chapter 7).[30]

Thus, pre-revolutionary Iran's embrace of nativism and cultural authenticity was complemented by the regime's pseudo-leftist Third Worldist political posturing. In both cases, official ideology borrowed, deliberately and substantially, from two rival "counter-cultural" discursive formations. The first of these emphasized Shi'i Islam as the core of modern Iran's national identity, while the second proposed following global models of socialist and Third Worldist modernity. Incapable of articulating a legitimizing ideology of its own the monarchy tried to manipulate and harness both of these ideological formations to its own advantage. This dangerous venture ultimately backfired when, during a moment of crisis in the late 1970s, the left-populist and Shi'i authenticity discourses momentarily converged to provide the opposition with a potent revolutionary ideology of mass mobilization (see Chapter 7).[31]

Traditionalism, Orientalism and Esoteric Shi'ism: In Heidegger's Shadow?

My approach is hermeneutic ... I interpret Heidegger via Islam.

Ahmad Fardid[32]

Corbin's contribution to intellectual and philosophical self-awareness in Iran must never be forgotten.

Seyyed Hossein Nasr[33]

During the 1960s and 1970s, three major discursive formations linked Iranian authenticity to esoteric or unorthodox readings of Shi'ism. Two of these were counter-modernist and politically rightwing, categorically rejecting "Western" modernity, along with democracy, liberalism and Marxism. Below, we will first trace the origins and pre-revolutionary articulation of these two trends, showing how they overlapped with the regime's official authenticity discourse. The third trend, a leftist or Marxist-inflected reading of Shi'ism, which had a crucial role in ideological preparation for the 1978–1979 revolution, will be studied in this chapter's final section.

As noted in Chapter 5, Jalal Al-Ahmad's influential *West-struck-ness* borrowed its title term and key concept (*gharb-zadegi*) from a Persian neologism coined by Ahmad Fardid, Iran's first self-appointed disciple of the German philosopher Martin Heidegger. Although a professor of philosophy at Tehran University, Fardid's academic credentials were dubious. He had spent a few years of graduate study in Paris and Heidelberg, without obtaining a doctoral degree.[34] Returning home, he began teaching at Tehran University, but never published more than a few academically deficient articles in Persian.[35] Admiring followers saw him an "oral philosopher," imparting esoteric wisdom in oral presentations filled with striking neologisms. Making charitable sense of Fardid's ideas, they may be considered a phenomenology of scared Truth and/or Being, manifest in secular time and history via a succession of forms (*soratha*) or names (*asma'*). From this perspective, the eclipse of Truth/Being starts with ancient Greek rationalism and is intensified by Greco-Christian and Islamic scholasticism, secular humanism, and eventually by modern secular ideologies. Perennial Truth/Being is identical with "the East," whereas its long litany of historical "covering names" is equated with "the West." Fardid thus coined the Persian term *gharb-zadegi* to describe the universal demise and concealment of Truth/Being. Moreover, he claimed his schema corresponded to both Heidegger's philosophy and the schools of Islamic mysticism least affected by Greek rationalism. Considering medieval Islamic Illumination (*eshraq*) theosophy "mildly West-struck," he looked farther back to Ibn Arabi and older notions of intuitive (*hozuri/shohudi*) knowledge of divinity. Here, God is the only True Being, whose ultimate presence (*hozur*) is manifest in all other lesser beings, symbolically known to us through a myriad of names (*asma'*).[36]

A synopsis of Fardid's ideas are found in the transcript of his oral response to questions addressed to the country's "intellectuals" in a 1972 issue of *Culture and Life*, the organ of Iran's High Council of Culture and the Arts. Reflecting official attention to debates concerning *West-struck-ness*, the magazine posed questions such as whether the world could be understood in terms of East–West cultural confrontations; if Eastern and Western cultures could be considered spiritual and materialist, respectively; and whether Eastern cultures were beneficial to humanity. Fardid answered these questions by focusing primarily on "the question of Being and the truth of Being." According to him:

Presently, when speaking of the East and the West, we are using only symbols, because the historical referent [*havalat-e tarikhi*] in today's world is the West, while the East is hidden. This means with the arrival of the Greek tradition, the East passes into darkness, no longer being the source of light, while the West becomes everything … According to Heidegger, in each historical era, a certain truth is actualized, which requires the covering of other truths … In other words, in every era, Being has a particular manifestation, with each new manifestation necessarily hiding its own previous features … a new name abrogates an old name; or, in philosophical terms, the new name is equated with "form" and the old one with "matter."

… Modern man reaches a point where he feels endangered. He then says No to this [new] civilization. Yet, merely saying No is not enough; He must also be able to see the hidden light through the veils covering the East. This means passing through the historical darkness of the West toward a future horizon illuminated by the guiding light of the East, without returning to or feeling nostalgic for the past.[37]

Fardid concluded by questioning whether "spirituality" [*ma'naviat*] had any meaning in a contemporary world propelled ever-forward by technological "Eros." Previous modes of human thought, he said, had found spirituality in mysticism [*tasavvof*]. But Westernized modernity made mysticism unavailable:

Today, both "East" and "West" have become meaningless terms, marking mere geographic divisions. Thus, I would replace the East with *valayat*, meaning kindness and affection, equating the West with *velayat*, whose perfect form is "domination." Today's world thus abounds in *velayat*, meaning imperialism.[38]

Their dubious philosophical affinity notwithstanding, Fardid and Heidegger were similar in their attraction to right-wing regimes and politics. During the 1970s, Fardid's lectures, interviews and public debates appeared in government publications and were broadcast on national television. Using these forums, he propounded anti-Western ideas, vehemently attacking liberalism, democracy and Marxism, eventually aligning himself with the politics of the Shah's one-party system[39] (see Chapter 7). Ironically, or perhaps logically, Fardid became more directly political following the monarchy's fall, striving to become the philosophical voice of the postrevolutionary regime. He ran for parliament and tried to participate in drafting the constitution of the Islamic Republic. His obvious entanglements with the old regime, however, precluded his acceptance by the new political establishment. Still, his intellectual impact continued through his disciples and students, most notably Reza Davari-Ardekani, who became the semi-official philosopher of the Islamic Republic.[40]

Davari-Ardekani had followed Fardid since the 1970s, in a circle whose most prominent members included leftist translator and essayist Dariush Ashuri and Tehran University philosophy professor Dariush Shayegan (see below). Ashuri's recognition was due to the essays he wrote in the 1970s on Iran's encounter with the West, as well as a widely noted translation of Nietzsche's *Thus Spoke Zarathustra*.[41] His "archaic-sounding" translation of Nietzsche could be read as another vindication of perennial Iranian wisdom vis-à-vis modern Europe's embrace of value nihilism and God's death. At the same time, Ashuri's attraction to Fardid signaled a certain drift, in the Iranian intellectual milieu, from Marx toward Heidegger and Nietzsche. Later denouncing Fradid as an intellectual fraud, Ashuri has described this period as one of intellectual confusion:

Another reason attracting probing youths, like myself, to Fardid was the general ambiance of an era when radical and revolutionary leftist discourse, fixated on "Eastern" socialism, was being augmented by another discourse attacking Western "materialism," "nihilism," and obsession with science and technology, in the name of Eastern morality, spirituality and mysticism. Eager for "returning to the self" and Eastern Islamic "authenticity," this new front was opened in the first half of the 1960s, via Al-Ahmad's *West-struck-ness* and Ali Sharati's rushed and anxious writings. Influenced too by Third Worldist French intellectualism, it gradually gained ground beyond socio-political language via Fardid's mystic-philosophical jargon. A few years later, this chorus of "Eastern spirituality" was joined by two of [French Orientalist] Henri Corbin's Iranian students, Seyyed Hossein Nasr, and his intransigent Islam, along with Dariush Shayegan, and his mystical tendencies in *Asia Facing the West*; and finally joined by sociologist Ehsan Narqhi and his fashionable essay collection *What Was His Own*.[42]

Ashuri's astute recollection notes another intellectual circle that, along with Fardid's, was defining Iranian authenticity by drawing on European discourses of Eastern spirituality. The second circle was formed by French Orientalist Henri Corbin (1903–1978) and his Iranian associates who, like Fardid, labored to merge esoteric Shi'ism and European counter-modernist philosophy. Europe's foremost authority on Iranian Shi'ism, Corbin was at the center of an intellectual circle that was active in Tehran for almost two decades, from the late 1950s to 1977.[43] Corbin's hermeneutic of "Iranian Islam" involved identification with, including claims of personal conversion to, esoteric mystical Shi'ism.[44] According to an often-repeated anecdote, Corbin had a Sufi-style initiation into Shi'i studies via his teacher Louis Massignon, France's leading expert in Islamic mysticism.[45] Corbin's formative influences also included several years of studying theology and philosophy in Germany, where he witnessed the coming to power of Nazism. Corbin knew Heidegger personally and became his first French translator.[46]

Corbin, of course, minimized his intellectual connection to Heidegger, claiming it was merely an interest in the phenomenological method. But his intellectual linkage to Heidegger is not difficult to find, though not transparent. Heidegger's 1927 *Being and Time* had made true knowledge contingent on the knowing subject's awareness of authentic being/existence.[47] In other words, authentic being was a certain kind of self-recognition, by the knowing subject, achieved by discarding various modes of inauthentic being. Corbin identified this phenomenology with gnostic interpretations of ultimate or divine Being. He then linked this methodology to mystical Islamic notions of *ta'wil* or *kashf al-mahjub*, which involved a similar movement from sense-perceived appearances (*zahir*) to scared inner (*batini*) realms of true meaning. Thus, according to Corbin, the authentic truth of Islam was hidden in esoteric Shi'ism, distinct from both juridical interpretations and the temporal reality of historical Islam.[48] Beyond the phenomenological method, Corbin also shared Heidegger's conservative criticism of modernity. Like many contemporary German thinkers, Heidegger linked modernity to "inauthentic being," "technological frenzy," mankind's state of "fallen-ness" and "the darkening of the world." Corbin too had a damning depiction of modernity, lamenting the loss of truth and authenticity in a modern world darkened by the domination of secular, positivist and technical rationality.[49]

In 1945, Corbin's was stationed in Tehran, following his diplomatic service in Istanbul, where he was dispatched by France's pro-Nazi Vichy government. Officially on a "broadly cultural" mission, he started an "Iran-ology" branch at Tehran's French Institute and began forging ties to the capital's still largely Francophone intellectual elite.[50] Soon, he was at the center of an intellectual-cum-spiritual circle in Tehran. The most extensive account of this circle is by Dariush Shayegan, who joined it in 1959 and later completed a doctoral dissertation under Corbin's supervision. Shayegan credits Corbin with initiating an intellectual movement that bridged the gap between traditional Iran and the modern world.[51] Echoing Taqizadeh's appreciations of Orientalist scholarship (see Chapter 2), Shayagn claimed his generation of Iranians learned the meaning and value of their own spiritual heritage from a European sage:

Thus, Corbin, this pilgrim coming from the West, and using French language, taught us the amazing thought features of our Iranian fore-fathers. This is among the strange paradoxes of our time.[52]

Corbin also linked Iran to the international Eranos circle, a spiritual "meeting place between East and West." Launched in 1933, Eranos meetings brought together, in Ascona Switzerland, leading scholars of religion, spirituality and psychology in annual conferences whose proceedings were published in *Eranos Yearbooks*. From the start, Eranos had politically right-wing leanings, with some of its leading figures, such as Swiss psychologist Carl Gustav Jung (1875–1961) and Romanian scholar of religion Mircea Elidae (1907–1986), having had fascist associations. Moreover, prominent Eranos members shared Corbin's intellectually conservative and metaphysically essentialist assumptions. Jung's psychology explained patterns of human "collective consciousness" in terms of trans-historical archetypes. Similarly, Eliade's enormously influential theory of religion taught that timeless archetypes, symbolically manifest in human language, revealed the common sacred core of all religions. During more than two decades of participation at Eranos, Corbin remained its chief authority on Islam, influencing Eliade and other international scholars of comparative religion such as Huston Smith.[53]

Corbin's most influential collaborator in Iran was the scholar of religion, Seyyed Hossein Nasr. It was Nasr who brought together members of Corbin's circle in Tehran, providing them with institutional, financial and political support, including royal patronage. Moreover, while Corbin's intellectual contribution remained relatively obscure, Nasr's recognition grew, spreading beyond Iran when he became the leader of the internationally active Traditionalist Sufi order. Traditionalism had originated in Europe in the 1930s as yet another movement rejecting Western modernity and advocating a return to the gnostic "Perennial Wisdom" of the East. Traditionalists looked to Asia, where they believed traces of "Perennial Wisdom" had survived in "traditional" Hindu, Buddhist and Muslim religious life. The movement's founder, Rene Guenon (1886–1951), was a French Orientalist who had sought spiritual truth in Hinduism, theosophy and occult sciences, ultimately ending up a Sufi Muslim.[54] Guenon's 1924 *East and West* basically echoed Oswald Spengler's condemnation of nihilistic Western materialism, while his best-known work, *The Crisis of the Modern World* (1927), described modernity as a cosmic "dark age," corresponding to *Kali Yuga*, i.e. the lowest point in Hindu cyclical time.[55] Mircea Eliade too was close to Traditionalism, espousing a "lighter" version of it in his widely influential writings on comparative religion from the 1950s to the 1970s.[56]

Nasr was drawn to Traditionalism while a graduate student of physics in the United States during the 1950s. At the Massachusetts Institute of Technology, he was introduced to Guenon and "Eastern teachings" by the philosopher of science, Giorgio de Santillana.[57] He then immersed himself in the works of Guenon and his Swiss successor Frithjof Schuon (1907–1998), who merged Traditionalism into an Algerian Sufi order, later joining it to the Native American Sioux Nation. By the 1970s, Traditionalism was an American style New Age movement, with branches and splinter factions in Europe and the Middle East.[58] Schuon's erratic leadership led to his replacement by Nasr, who, after the 1979 Iranian Revolution, settled in the United States and reorganized Traditionalism as the order of Alawiya-Maryamiya. While in Iran during the 1960s and 1970s, however,

Nasr cooperated closely with Corbin in a project devoted to studying and publishing material on theosophical and esoteric (*batini*) Sufi trends in Shi'ism. Their cooperation began in 1958, when Nasr returned from his studies in the United States to join a small discussion group meeting in Tehran twice every month. The group's link to main-stream Shi'ism was the cleric Mohammad-Hosein Tabataba'i, an authority on Qur'an commentary and Shi'i theosophy. Tabataba'i's student, Morteza Motahhari, Iran's leading clerical intellectual in the 1970s (see below), was a regular participant in these meetings. Nasr also brought to the circle the young philosophy student and India specialist Dariush Shayegan. The circle's meetings lasted almost two decades, with Corbin regularly participating each fall, when he was in Tehran.[59]

The Nasr–Corbin circle saw Shi'ism as a living spiritual and intellec-tual tradition whose purportedly great relevance to the modern world remained unappreciated. Its members were drawn to esoteric, mystical and theosophical traditions, primarily in Shi'ism, but also in other religions, particularly Christianity and Hinduism. Ostensibly rejecting all modern Western ideologies, Nasr and Corbin were most adamantly opposed to Marxism, an intellectual position aligning them with Iran's political establishment. But the circle's members also had their own ideological and political differences. Motahhari, for example, was neither monarchist nor anti-modernist. In fact, during the 1970s, and under the regime's watchful eyes, he systematically propagated a conservative modernist interpretation of Shi'ism. Motahhari's chief intellectual nemesis was Marxism, which he saw spreading among modern-educated Iranians in various guises, most dangerously in the form of "Islamic Marxism" (see below). In this sense, Motahhari followed his teacher Tabataba'i, whose lectures and teachings, pub-lished as *Origin of Philosophy*, was a defense of Shi'ism against the onslaught of Marxist materialism.[60] While agreeing with Corbin and Nasr in opposition to Marxism, Motahhari and Tabataba'i had clerical training, wrote in Persian and were not exactly in accord with Nasr's Traditionalism or Corbin's esoteric reading of Shi'ism.[61] Corbin, Nasr and Shayegan, on the other hand, had modern academic education, used European languages, and wrote for both Iranian and European readers. In fact, there was a serious linguistic divide within the circle, which Nasr and Shayegan tried to breach by regularly translating for Corbin, Tabataba'i and Motahhari.[62] Nevertheless, the two sides appreciated and complemented each other. The clerics welcomed their Western-educated colleagues' interest in Shi'ism, while Nasr and Shayegan knew their understanding of Shi'ism was appreciated by modern-educated audiences, if endorsed by European scholars like Corbin.[63]

The Nasr–Corbin circle was indirectly sponsored by Iran's political establishment. Corbin's ahistorical metaphysical conception of Iran provided badly needed "depth" to the intellectual vacuity of the monarchist nationalism. Corbin's Iran was "a philosophical object, rather than a geographic or political realm," therefore his "understanding of Iran may be considered the most philosophical and idealist system of Iran-ology in the twentieth century."[64] Among Corbin's promoters was Amir-Abbas Hoveyda, the Francophone prime minister with intellectual pretentions, whose thirteen-year tenure (1965–1977) marked the peak of Pahlavi-era modernity.[65] Nasr's relations with the regime's highest echelons were more direct. Following his tenure as professor and dean at Tehran University, the Shah appointed him, in 1972, as chancellor of Aryamehr Technical University, Iran's most prestigious institution of higher learning. According to Nasr, the Shah supported his vision of reconciling modern science and "traditional knowledge" at the country's flagship technical university. Moreover, Nasr was the director of Queen Farah's Special Bureau, where he advised and encouraged the queen to further promote traditional culture. He was able to secure the queen's direct patronage of the Royal Iranian Academy of Philosophy, founded in 1974 to provide "a truly Iranian space for discussion of philosophy."[66] Corbin, Motahhari and Toshihiko Izutsu, a Japanese scholar of Islam and comparative religion, then joined Nasr as the academy's core faculty, training a number of students who later rose to intellectual and political prominence under the Islamic Republic. Nasr also claims that by the late 1970s he was working on a project to save the embattled Pahlavi regime by changing it into an "Islamic monarchy." With the coming of the revolution, however, he left Iran, his close association with the monarchy making his return impossible.[67]

Despite Nasr's and Corbin's high academic and official profile, it was their student and protégé, Dariush Shayegan, who offered their circle's most intellectually sophisticated take on Iran's encounter with modernity. Shayegan's superior linguistic prowess, as well as his specialization in Indian religions, made him more competent than his teachers at comparing European and Asian cultures and religions. His first major work, *Asia Facing the West* (1977), identified Asian civilizations with "great religions that make up their fundamental essence," offering the promise of "deliverance and redemption," in contrast to a modern Western civilization defined by moral "nihilism."[68] *Asia Facing the West*, however, went beyond Nasr's and Corbin's engagement with modern European thought, directly referring to works in French, German and English by Hegel, Nietzsche, Heidegger, Jose Ortega y Gasset, Nikolai Berdyaev and Michel Foucault.[69] Reviving Fakhreddin Shadman's argument (see Chapter 4), Shayegan in fact parted ways with both Nasr and Corbin by insisting that, without appreciating modernity's tremendous strength, Asian thinkers remained its hapless victims. This was also Ashuri's response to Al-Ahmad (see Chapter 5), where he diagnosed the essence of "West-struck-ness" as ignorance of Europe, its complex history and modernist worldview.[70] The salient contribution of *Asia Facing the West*, however, was its warning about Western nihilism generating dangerous "mutations" in Asian cultures. According to Shayegan, Asian intellectual responses to European modernity had turned proven illusory and hollow, while all projects of return to indigenous culture had failed. He saw contemporary Asian cultures as neither traditional nor modern, but in a confused hybrid state, likely to produce mangled "cultural mutations."[71] Supposedly anti-Western, revolutionary and nativist, Asian ideological responses to modernity, he argued, were cultural dead-ends. They could neither reinvent genuine tradition, nor transcend the confines of Western modernity:

Born of colonialism, the long deprivation of Asia – and Africa or the Third World – could turn distorted and imposed ideologies into revengeful horrific formations, which, like Frankenstein's monster, take revenge on their creator. The monster, however, was Frankenstein's other self, embodying his unconscious and repressed powers. Likewise, these new monsters represent the dark, unconscious, and uncontrollable forces of Western nihilism, invading Asia and the Third World, dressed up as new ideologies and modern "isms."[72]

The most obvious unnamed "ism" of the above passage, of course, was Third Worldist Marxism, a global phenomenon, whose 1970s Iranian variant had indeed produced a "mutated" ideological formation, facetiously labeled "Islamic Marxism." Despite such veiled references to "bastardized" leftist ideologies, Shayegan's concluding chapter, titled "Neo-obscurantism," surprisingly identified neo-traditionalist ideologies as "the greatest danger" facing Iran:

Talking about what we used to be, what we are now, our illumination philosophy, the Satanic West, or of technology as divine affliction, [none of that] will revive illumination, or deliver us from the clutches of technology . . . Instead of curing any ills, this will produce only a new "obscurantism."[73]

In an apparent critique of anti-modernist intellectual projects, such as those of the Nasr–Corbin circle, *Asia Facing the West* warned of a dark nativist horizon descending upon Iran:

The greatest danger threatening us is the recent phenomenon of "neo-obscurantism," which means sinking back into self-righteous all-knowing ignorance, an ignorance born of painful alienation and Orientalized West-struck-ness. We forget the West possesses the world's richest and most diverse and dynamic civilization . . . something that cannot be challenged by fanaticism and a bunch of slogans. We forget too that Westerners have been the keenest critics of their own ways of thinking . . . They taught us how to ask inquiring questions, how to criticize them, and perhaps how to learn from their bitter experience.[74]

In 1976, Shayegan became director of the Foundation for the Study of Cultures, established to promote mutual understanding and critical exchange between Eastern and Western cultures and civilizations. Other members included sociologists Ehsan Naraqi and Jamshid Behnam, National Iranian Radio and Television director Reza Qotbi, and scholar diplomat Majid Rahnema. In 1977, the foundation held an international conference on the question of "whether the impact of Western thought could render a true dialogue of civilizations possible."[75] In addition to Corbin and Izutsu, foreign participants included Roger Garaudy, a French philosopher in transition from communism to Islam, and Christian Jambet, a student of Corbin's and another French ex-Marxist with a new-found appreciation of Islam. The line-up of Iranian and foreign presenters at this conference showcased the ideological convergence of ex-communist and nativist intellectuals with enthusiasts of Iranian authenticity and esoteric Shi'ism. Published conference proceedings prominently display the ideas of Corbin, Shayegan and Naraqi, all critical of "nihilistic" Western modernity and directly referencing Heidegger.[76] Despite his reservations, Shayegan too was now actively contributing to the kind of "mutated" anti-Western rhetoric that within a year would become the dominate discourse of the coming Iranian Revolution.

Shariati's Unfinished Project: Spiritual Socialism as Islamic Ideology

The intellectual and cultural air in which a Muslim of this century breathed was enclosed within the triangle of socialism, existentialism and Islam.[77]

In contrast to the conservatism of Nasr, Shayegan and Motahhari, a more influential intellectual trend, best represented by Ali Shariati (1933–1977), was engaged in a revolutionary reconstruction of Shi'ism via direct engagement with Marxism. Shariati's intellectual contribution remains as controversial today as it was during his lifetime. Arguably, if Al-Ahmad was the quintessential public intellectual of 1960s Iran, Shariati played this role during the 1970s, giving voice to both the ideological innovations and confusions of his time. In retrospect, some scholars consider Shariati a Marxist in Shi'i disguise, while others argue he was an ideologically "amphibious creature," simultaneously both Marxist and Muslim. A recent sympathetic trend is interested in the critical reconstruction of Shariati's intellectual contribution within the context of postrevolutionary reform of Islamic thought in Iran.[78] Official estimations of Shariati, under the Islamic Republic, are also ambivalent, considering him an "eclectic" thinker, praising his devotion to Khomeini and intellectual contribution to the revolution, while rejecting his Marxism and anti-clericalism. A semi-official study, for example, concludes: "Doubtless, Shariati is one of the most complicated subjects in the history of the Islamic Revolution, where judgment is extremely difficult, a problem stemming from the complexity of Shariati's personality." It continues:

Shariati's personality, discourse and practice add up to a bundle of contradictions, which, improperly analyzed, make him appear like both a Westernized modernist and a traditionalist Muslim, a virtual Sunni as well as a dedicated Shi'i. His discourse contains dozens of anti-clerical arguments, as well as an equal number of arguments in favor of the clergy.[79]

As this commentary notes, Shariati's intellectual eclecticism matched a mercurial personality, fluctuating between extreme dejection, and obsession with death and martyrdom, on the one hand, and ecstatic experiences of mystical union with God, on the other.[80] Nor did he develop and present his ideas as carefully constructed scholarly arguments. The bulk of his thirty-six-volume collected works in fact consists of transcriptions of lectures delivered to students and non-academic audiences.[81] Finally, the inherent instability of his thought was compounded by the deliberate ambiguity of his exposition, interjected to evade censure by political and clerical officialdom. The reminder of this chapter critically presents Shariati's intellectual contribution within the broader context of Iran's major ideological currents from the 1950s to the 1970s. The emphasis on his eclecticism and incoherence is not meant to denigrate Shariati, but to explain his powerful contemporary appeal. Countering Shariati's secular and Muslim detractors, his legacy here is considered an unfinished intellectual project whose critical reconstruction remains a formidable challenge to progressive Muslims.

Broadly speaking, Shariati's political thought was rooted in his youthful attraction to Islamic socialism and Kasravi's ideas, defining inspirations he could neither fully credit, nor coherently synthesis. As seen in Chapter 4, Kasravi had condemned Shi'i Imams for their compromise with corrupt rulers and obscurantist practices, such as the dissimulation of true belief (*taqiya*). In addition, he argued, the Safavid Dynasty further corrupted Shi'ism by incorporating clerics into the government and allowing them to collect revenue from believers.[82] Similarly, Shariati vehemently rejected historical, "Safavid," Shi'ism, calling it a "polytheistic religion." Moreover, he refused to condemn Kasravi's anti-clericalism, criticizing only its "improper" manner of presentation. Shariati's clerical opponents therefore were not wrong in considering him a disciple of Kasravi.[83] More perplexing was Shariati's relation to Marxism. His father, who taught him about Kasravi, was involved also with the Movement of God-Worshipping Socialists, an organization Shariati joined as a very young man.[84] In 1954, a twenty-one-year-old Shariati published a series of articles, in Mashhad's daily paper *Khorasan*, on Islam as a "Median School" and "Third Path" between idealism and materialism, capable of bridging the gap between communism and capitalism. As noted above, this was the innovative discourse and nomenclature of the God-Worshipping Socialists. A year later, he repeated the same basic ideas in a pamphlet, titled *The History of the Development of Philosophy*.[85] In 1955, he also published *Abu-Dhar Qifari: God-Worshiping Socialist*, a loose translation of an

Egyptian author's work. As this book's title shows, Shariati had applied the God-Worshipping Socialist label to depict Abu Dhar, one of Prophet Mohammad's companions, as a "perfect human being," because he was an "ultra-socialist" who preached "Islamic communism."[86]

Thus, Shariati's apparent intellectual breakthrough of the 1960s and 1970s was an extension of his 1950s writing and lectures, based primarily on the teachings of God-Worshipping Socialists. From this perspective, Shariati's five years of graduate study in France only enhanced, and provided authoritative European affirmation to, core beliefs he already had formed in Iran. Though hailed as a great teacher and scholar of religion, Shariati's academic training was rather thin, while his intellectual temperament was non-scholarly. The doctorate he received in France was second-class, earned with the lowest possible grade, and based on his translation of a Persian text on the medieval history of the city of Balkh.[87] Uninterested in academic pursuits, his intellectual sources of inspiration in France were figures like Louis Massignon, who had fused Sufism and gnostic Christianity to preach the unity of Abrahamic religions.[88] Equally, if not more important was George Gurvitch, a Sorbonne sociology professor who insisted on supplementing the Marxist notion of class with culturally specific social psychology. Shariati picked up Gurvitch's critique of orthodox Marxism, augmenting it with Franz Fanon's teachings on the contribution of native cultures to anti-colonial struggles and wars of national liberation. Finally, he was interested in Jean-Paul Sartre's existentialist Marxism, though he preferred religious existentialism.[89] In the end, Shariati's engagement with both Marxism and existentialism remained cursory, his lectures and published writings showing familiarity only with secondary literature in both subjects.

In an obvious self-description, Shariati famously had said contemporary Muslim intellectuals were framed "within the triangle of socialism, existentialism and Islam."[90] Still, his own particular rendition of this triangle remained lopsided and unstable, showing problems in handling all of its three sides. First, though obviously influenced by Marxism, Shariati was ultimately a spiritual utopian socialist, rather than an "Islamic Marxist."[91] Second, a strong mystical dimension shows also in his alleged "Protestantism," i.e. personal interpretation of Shi'ism in defiance of clerical authority. Third, Shariati's lectures and writings are inundated with "existential" doubt and anxiety, tempered by "leaps of faith," reminiscent of Soren Kierkegaard's. Also reminiscent of early Sartre, his discourse often conflates authentic being to "witnessing" the Truth, turning the Islamic confession of faith (*shahada*) into commitment to action on behalf of the truth at all costs, including one's martyrdom (also *shahada*).[92]

Upon returning from France in 1964, Shariati was arrested and briefly imprisoned. His reaction to the authorities established a baffling pattern that continued to the end of his life: "In a style that became a hallmark of his written responses to SAVAK's interrogators, Shariati engaged in long-winded, convoluted discourses to confuse and entangle his captors." Basically, he acknowledged the White Revolution's positive results and criticized the opposition's response to them.[93] Though the interrogators were not fooled by Shariati (see below), he was released and allowed to teach, first at a high school and then as history instructor at the University of Mashhad.[94] Following a period of extreme dejection and mental instability, including mystical and suicidal contemplations, he began to thrive in his newfound role of teacher-preacher. Soon, his fame spread as a charismatic professor who ignored academic protocol, boldly discussed politics and boasted of mystical powers.[95] In 1969, he published *Knowing Islam (Eslam-shenasi)*, a work essentially similar to his previous socialist reading of Shi'ism, updated with references to social science methodology and nomenclature he had learned in France. This book's success among young educated Muslims, and its condemnation by both secular leftists and conservative clerics, set the typical pattern of reactions to Shariati's intellectual production. The very same year, a former God-Worshipping Socialist, now turned Marxist, published a book accusing Shariati of being a political reactionary who deliberately confused his readers. Clerical reactions built up too and became steadily more damaging. Labeled a Wahhabi and a "second Kasravi," Shariati was soon condemned by fatwas declaring his views incompatible with Islam and forbidding Muslims from reading his books. Clerical opposition went as far as declaring him "at war with Islam" (*mohareb*), a capital crime, and technically punishable by death in Islamic law.[96]

Shariati's sudden phenomenal impact occurred within a specific institutional context and in the midst of the opposition's drift toward radicalization. The institutional frame was not the academe but a privately funded Tehran lecture house, called Hossienieh Ershad, which was established in 1964 to propagate modernist Shi'ism. The dominant intellectual figure at Ershad was ayatollah Motahhari, a cleric whose recognition and stature had been on the rise since the early 1960s. At the time, the clerical establishment was challenged by the White Revolution, while also facing a crisis caused by the passing of its undisputed conservative leader Ayatollah Boroujerdi. With no clear successor to Boroujedri's leadership, the question of "clerical authority" (*marja'iat*) became a national concern, and was politicized by contenders, like ayatollah Khomeini, who linked it to opposition to the White Revolution. Meanwhile, Motahhari had become the leading voice in an important but less noted debate on the modernization of clerical authority. To remedy the confusion of clashing juridical opinions, he proposed, a council of clerics should formulate authoritative consensus on major issues of public concern.[97] Thus, Motahhari was trying to rationalize and modernize clerical authority, while insisting on its binding sway on all believers, something that "Protestant" Shi'is, like Shariati, would challenge.

It has been argued that, by neglecting clerics like Motahhari, the Shah's regime "lost a chance to ally itself with religious modernists, and thus include religion in the process of modernization." By the second half of the 1960s, however, the regime had in fact forged a tacit alliance with liberal-conservative clerics, including Motahhari, against Marxists, leftist Muslims and radical clerics.[98] It was in this period that Motahhari emerged as Iran's leading clerical public intellectual, teaching at Tehran University and tirelessly lecturing, writing books and publishing articles in popular periodicals. Motahhari's main forum, however, was the Ershad institute, whence he sought to propagate "Islamic ideology" as an alternative to modern ideologies, particularly Marxism. Motahhari himself had declared:

My idea and objective is to fashion this organization into an Islamic research and propaganda institute of the highest quality, responsive to the needs of today's turbulent society. I want this institution to be able to properly present Islamic ideology in the face of other ideologies in today's world.[99]

Thus, during the 1960s and 1970s, it was not only Shi'i radicals, like Shariati, but clerics like Motahhari who were engaged in the project of turning Islam into an "ideology." Initially, Motahhari believed modern-educated intellectuals like Shariati could serve "as a bridge linking

Western and Islamic cultures," if they were kept under the clergy's "strict supervision and control." He therefore agreed to invite Shariati to lecture at the Ershad institute.[100] From a different perspective, the SAVAK also considered Ershad's activities, including Shariati's lectures, to be useful. To secure clearance for his Ershad lectures, Shariati had endured months of SAVAK investigation, including interviews with its chief political operatives like Parviz Thabeti. Trying to appease and confuse them, he wrote detailed descriptions of his beliefs, as well as future projects. Significantly, while emphasizing his opposition to communism and the Tudeh Party, Shariati insisted his commitment to socialism and the "abolition of class discrimination" was in accord with the principles of the Shah-People Revolution. SAVAK officials were not fooled, but allowed him to lecture at Ershad as long as he challenged Marxism and remained loyal to the regime. In the end, Shariati was playing a dangerous "cat and mouse game" with the SAVAK, whereby each side tried to outsmart and use the other. Shariati pretended agreement with the Shah's "revolutionary" posture in order to preach his own interpretation of Shi'ism to the widest audience possible. The regime, on the other hand, tried to harness Shariati for its own purposes, finding him particularly useful in sewing intellectual confusion and escalating discord within the opposition, particularly between clerics and Marxists, as well as within each group.[101]

By 1969, Shariati was a regular lecturer at Ershad, where he quickly surpassed Motahhari as the most popular speaker. In the process, he disappointed and alarmed both Motahhari and the SAVAK by criticizing clerical Islam and arguing that true Shi'ism was an "ideology" more revolutionary than Marxism. In 1971, Motahhari withdrew from Ershad, which was turning into a congregation for Muslim radicals, especially left-leaning university students.[102] Meanwhile, Shariati's lectures were leaning beyond religious and cultural criticism toward the advocacy of revolutionary action, apparently responding to Muslim Mojahedin guerrillas, who sought his endorsement of armed struggle[103] (see below). Between January 1972 and Ershad's closure in November 1972, Shariati delivered his most radical lectures, presenting Shi'ism as a perfect revolutionary "political party" whose "ideology" called for armed insurrection and martyrdom in defiance of oppressive regimes.[104] He was then arrested and imprisoned until 1973, when Tehran's daily press published a series of articles, attributed to him, that rejected armed struggle and called for new conception of Iranian nationalism (see below).

Debating Revolutionary Praxis and Islamic Marxism

Their unwavering will to fight is unbelievable. Even the women fight to their last breath. The men carry cyanide pills, preferring suicide to capture.

The Shah on guerrilla fighters, 1976.[105]

The background to the radicalization of Shariati's discourse was an upsurge in militant and violent opposition in the early 1970s. The new opposition offensive, most prominently a campaign of guerrilla armed struggle, coincided with a political provocation by the regime. This was the extravagant 1971 celebration of 2,500 years of Iranian monarchy, held at Persepolis ruins with international heads of states in tow, and complete with the Shah's bombastic oratory at the tomb of Cyrus, where he declared himself caretaker to Iran's ancient imperial heritage.[106] The year, however, had begun with an outburst of urban guerilla operations in Tehran and a few other cities, a dramatic declaration that radical opposition was not only alive, but on the offensive. At the same time, political protests by university students in Iran and abroad intensified, quickly converging on support for the guerillas. During the same year, the Confederation of Iranian Students, the largest and most effective opposition organization abroad, was declared illegal, which in turn led to its openly calling for the Shah's overthrow. Last but not least, it was also in 1971 that Ayatollah Khomeini, from his exile in Iraq, declared, for the first time, that monarchy was incompatible with Islam.[107] Khomeini's new departure and alignment with the radical opposition was clear in his often-noted June 1971 speech which praised university protests against monarchist celebrations, while admonishing the Shi'i clerical establishment, in both Iran and Iraq, for its "silence" vis-à-vis the regime.[108] Thus, contrary to the argument for the Iranian Revolution being "unthinkable" prior to its occurrence, the upheaval at the end of the 1970s was the culmination of a perceptible upswing in opposition activities throughout that decade.[109]

The most obvious manifestation of radical opposition of course was the urban guerrilla campaign that reached its peak by the mid-1970s. With no more than a few hundred actual members, the

guerrillas managed to politically shake down the regime. Their bold-
ness, determination and self-sacrifice, displayed dramatically in armed
confrontations and in defiance of torture and execution, inspired into
action a vast reservoir of discontent, mainly among university
students.[110] The 1970s guerrilla movement continues to unsettle the
historiography of the Iranian revolution. This is largely because
a clerically dominated Islamic Republic officially distorts prerevolutionary history, when radical opposition was not clerical but largely
secular Marxist or anti-clerical "Islamic-Marxist." However, even
back in the 1970s, the guerrillas posed perplexing challenges, not
only to the regime, but to the entire opposition movement. Guerrilla
theorists, whether Muslim or Marxist, argued that armed action was
the only viable option left after the violent suppression of the legal and
peaceful protests of the early 1960s. Mostly veterans of the 1960s
student opposition, Marxist and Muslim guerrilla theorists also agreed
in blaming Tudeh Party and National Front leaders for their failure to
act in decisive moments of confrontation with the regime, such as in
1953 and 1963. What distinguished the guerrilla generation's worldview was its emphasis on the centrality of "action/practice" (*amal*),
which, it was argued, under a violent dictatorship inevitably meant
revolutionary armed struggle.[111] The guerrillas' commitment to direct
action/praxis, as opposed to defused intellectual and political dissent,
gained them a large following among the revolutionary youth, particularly university and high school students, during the years immediately before and after the 1978–1979 Revolution.[112] Even the
country's dour dean of liberal nationalist historians, Fereydun
Adamiyat, praised the guerrilla movement's penchant for revolutionary praxis, giving it credit for having shaken the 1970s opposition out
of its impasse. He wrote:

There are leftists who launched armed struggle against the Shah's dictatorial
system in the harshest conceivable conditions. Instead of empty talk, they
took to the scene of action, to killing and dying. With unmatched military
prowess, the People's Fada'ian and the People's Mojahedin organizations
dispelled the fear of armed resistance, even if their record also includes
mistakes.[113]

In retrospect, the guerrillas are sometimes seen as impetuous fanatics,
obsessed with a cult of violence and martyrdom. Such interpretations,
however, fail to explain their movement's extraordinary intellectual

appeal and political impact. Nor was the guerrilla movement's intellectual output inferior to that of the opposition's mainstream. Both guerrilla organizations, i.e. the Fada'ian and the Mojahedin, tried to
analyze Iran's socioeconomic conditions and the impact of the White
Revolution, debating also the character of a coming popular revolution. Their literature was also attentive to, and even preoccupied with,
contemporary revolutionary theory and practice in Latin America,
Algeria, Palestine, China and Vietnam. Guerilla theorists thus tried to
justify the necessity of armed struggle in terms of both global revolutionary experiences and specific Iranian conditions. However, it may be
argued that, in addition to its intellectual justifications, the guerrilla call
to action appealed to more compelling moral, psychological and even
religious sentiments. As with its previous generation, Iran's 1960s and
1970s intelligentsia considered itself the nation's moral, intellectual
and political compass and vanguard. Such grand claims, however,
needed actual proof and validation. But Iran's leftist, nationalist and
anti-imperialist movements had been defeated repeatedly and crushed
violently, most recently in the early 1960s. By the 1970s, therefore,
a politically frustrated younger generation saw the litmus test of revolutionary authenticity in bold decisive action, striking back at the
regime with material force. Thus, both Fada'ian and Mojahedin theorists insisted on armed action as a *moral* imperative, requiring "martyrdom" (*shahada*), not only as proof of revolutionary authenticity, but as
redemption for the "sins" of political forefathers whose inaction had
"betrayed" the people's trust. In this sense, Shariati and Muslim
Mojahedin guerrillas were more intellectually consistent, than the
Marxist-Leninist Fada'ian, in admitting the moral and existential
underpinning of their politics.[114]

But the guerrilla initiative was soon contained as the regime imposed
a virtual state of siege, detaining thousands of political prisoners and
killing dozens of guerrillas in shootouts, under torture, or by firing
squads. Meanwhile, the Shah too was awed by the guerrillas' bravery
and determination, baffled by their extraordinary appeal even among
youths close to the royal family.[115] By the second half of the 1970s, and
facing almost total decimation, most surviving Muslim and Marxist
guerrillas had accepted that armed struggle had to be subordinate to
more broad-based mass politics. This had been the view of Fada'ian
leader Bizhan Jazani, often considered the guerrilla movement's most
sophisticated theorist. Most of Jazani's works were produced in prison,

where he survived a few years to reflect on the movements unfolding, before being murdered, along with eight other guerrilla prisoners, by the SAVAK in 1975. One of Jazani's least-noted prison writings is a short 1973 pamphlet entitled *Islamic Marxism or Marxist Islam*. Here, Jazani offered a sharp critique of the Muslim Mojahedin's ideology, including a unique forecast of their fortunes if Islamist forces were to assume leadership of a revolutionary movement.[116] With a frankness uncommon among Iranian Marxists, Jazani began by criticizing historical Islam as a part of society's ideological "superstructure," justifying oppression and exploitation. Moreover, and unlike critics like Kasravi and Shariati, he did not make an exception of an idealized pristine Islam, later degenerating into corruption and decline. Following Kasravi, however, he did criticize particular Shi'i obscurantism and sectarianism within the larger frame of Islam. Finally, he denied the possibility of progressive reform within the Shi'i clerical establishment:

In recent history, and as with other religions, the Shi'i establishment has been a part and an ally of feudalism. It has deployed the principal of *ijtihad* not to make religion more progressive but for making it better serve governments, as well as the domination and exploitation of the toiling masses. Hence, it would be a grave error to restrict our understanding of Islam and Shi'ism merely to the Quran and a few "de-sanitized" texts.[117]

Moreover, Jazani's understanding of Islam foreclosed any possibility of it turning into an anti-colonial or anti-imperialist ideology:

Islam, including its various sects, has no intrinsic anti-colonial character, whereas, like other religions, it has domineering aspirations ... Thus, we reject the claim that Islam is essentially different from Christianity or other religions. It is only the specific conditions of colonized Muslims nations that causes certain clerical factions to move closer to anti-colonial movements.[118]

In the end, Jazani's refusal to concede any progressive potential to organized religion broke with entrenched Marxist, secular liberal, and reformist Muslim assumptions about the instrumental use of Islam for their own purposes, an attitude going back to thinkers like Kermani and Malcom, Constitutional-era social democrats, socialists and the Tudeh Party (see Chapters 1, 2 and 5). Even more poignant was Jazani's warning about the instrumentalist use of Shi'ism as the ideology of revolutionary mass mobilization by contemporary "religious Marxists." He wrote:

Of course, such problems arise if an eclectic trend takes over the revolution- ary movement's leadership, making our society's destiny similar to those of Algeria, Egypt, Iraq or Sukarno's Indonesia ... In sum, religious Marxists misunderstand contemporary society, its balance of forces, and their own base of support. Thus, they will drag the revolution onto a perilous path, endangering the sovereignty of the working class and toilers on the morrow a revolution, whose victory they will prevent.[119]

In fact, Jazani was the unique intellectual who foresaw the destruction of "religious Marxists" by clerical authorities if Islamist forces were to assume leadership of a coming revolution:

The modernized Islam of these religious Marxists has no bearing on the masses, whose backward segments follow the authority of conservative and reactionary circles, rather than religiously modernist intellectuals. Meanwhile, religious Marxists provide religion with more authority by pla- cing their theory and practice under its banner. Their submission to Islam provides religious authorities with the crushing veto power of declaring them heretics (*takfir*), thus decisively impacting their relation with the very masses they hope to mobilize. In other words, these religious revolutionaries place their life and death in the hands of high ranking religious authorities, who would annihilate them as soon as the revolution diverges from their own schemes.[120]

Jazani's astute critique of "religious Marxism," and his prophetic warning against its decisive vulnerability vis-à-vis an inherently con- servative clerical establishment, remained unnoticed and unheeded. Shariati, for example, never considered the possibility of a rightwing variant of Islamist populism or an Islamic state actually negating his own utopian vision of Islam. Such possibilities remained part of the "unthought" in his intellectual project.[121] Still, there is evidence that Shariati too had second thoughts about the project of recasting Shi'ism as revolutionary ideology. Studies of Shariati's life and thought tend to attribute undue coherence to his thinking, considering some of his lectures and writings less "authentic" than others. Arguably, while his body of work includes major tensions and contradictions, what was published after his final release from prison shows a new intellec- tual departure. On the one hand, these last writings return to his earlier arguments against immediate revolutionary action by an intellectual vanguard. More importantly, he attempts a redefinition of Shi'ism, not as revolutionary ideology but as a key dimension of a multi-faceted

Iranian national identity. Both of these views were already present in Shariati's larger body of work, produced prior to his discourse being temporarily swayed by the insurrectionary élan of the Mojahedin.[122]

The controversy over Shariati's last writings continues to the present. From the outset, Shariati supporters refused to accept them as genuine, while his detractors saw them as proof of his ideological capitulation to the regime. Shariati's renunciation of class struggle and revolutionary insurrection, as well as his embrace of nationalism rooted in native culture, of course fitted with the general thrust of the regime's propaganda in the mid-1970s. Moreover, his insistence on the incompatibility of Islam and Marxism appeared to target precisely the regime's main enemy, i.e. "religious Marxists." Finally, Shariati's new discourse appeared to serve SAVAK's strategy of deepening the wedge between Marxist and Muslim factions of the opposition. However, this does not negate the possibility that Shariati had in fact pulled back from the Marxist-inflected revolutionary posture of his Ershad years to a more nuanced version of his original belief in Islamic socialism and cultural nationalism. His clear break with armed struggle may have come in prison and under duress, yet this was a time when most militants engaged in guerrilla warfare were also questioning its value and utility as well. Therefore, it is plausible that, similar to Jazani but from a Muslim perspective, he too had become convinced that Islamic Marxism was not a viable intellectual or political project.[123]

Sharitai's untimely death, at the age of forty-four in 1977, closed the curtain on his intellectual career, precluding any possible reaction he might have had to the revolution dimly appearing on the horizon. As the SAVAK had expected, however, his last writings increased conflict and confusion within the opposition, particularly its Islamic factions.[124] An urgent sense of crisis, for instance, is vividly described in a letter from Motahhari to Khomeini, written shortly after Shariati's death. This text is worth quoting at some length since it reflects the intellectual ambivalence and ideological tensions within the Islamic opposition, about one year before the outbreak of the revolution. Seeking Khomeini's guidance and intervention, Motahhari beings with a list of grave concerns:

Several complex confusing trends recently emerging in Iran require your attention: First, as you are probably well aware, Marxist ideas have made inroads as far as some religious circles, unexpectedly even among certain friends ... Second, the so-called "Mojahedin," who started as a political group, are gradually turning into a religious schism ... The least of their innovations is claiming "self-sufficiency" and rejecting all clerical and religious authority. It is easy to see where this ends up. They profess adherence to Islam, while considering Karl Marx at least as dear and sacred as [the sixth Shi'i] Imam Ja'far Sadeq. This of course pertains to those [Mojahedin] who uphold their original beliefs, and not to those who have changed their ideology [to Marxism].[125]

Another alarming trend, according to Motahhari, was that the Shah's regime, the Marxists, Shariati and the Mojahedin had converged on attacking the clergy. While the regime and the Marxists attacked the clergy in order to destroy religion, he claimed, Shariati and the Mojahedin did this "to appropriate religion, as a popular power, and interpret it for their own purposes."[126] The final dangerous trend was Shariati's "idolization" as the greatest leader of Islam's modernist "Renaissance" and renovation:

Ironically, they want to create a modern Islam with ideas borrowed from Massignon, the French colonial agent in North Africa and chief Christian missionary in Egypt, George Gurvitch, the materialist Jew, Jean-Paul Sartre, the godless existentialist, and Durkheim, the anti-religious sociologist.[127]

Motahhari then asked Khomeini's permission to openly refute Shariati's Marxist-inspired anti-clerical ideas:

The least of this man's sins is his defaming of the clergy. According to him, the clergy's collusion with repressive systems, against the masses, is an established sociological fact. He claims that kings, proprietors and clerics (*malek, malik va molla*), in other words, the Sword, the Gold and the Prayer-bead, have always acted in unison. In hundreds of simple parables, he propagates Marx's famous dictum on the triad of religion, the state and capital, working together against the people, as the three causes of mankind's self-alienation. Shariati, however, substitutes the clergy for religion.[128]

Motahhari invective went as far as attributing Shariati's death in London to divine intervention, mercifully preempting the dangers "his mission abroad had in store for Islam and clergy."[129] He concludes by saying that Sharaiti's works should not be published until they could be "revised and corrected."[130] Ironically, the letter ends with Motahhari's admission of ambivalence, including grudging admiration of Sharati's final publications, i.e. his post-prison articles in the Tehran daily *Kayhan*. He divides these writings into two parts:

The first part consists of good articles against Marxism, with only minor problems in terms of Islamic knowledge. A second set of separately typed articles deals with Iranian nationhood [*melliat*], in fact providing a philosophical foundation for it. Indeed, no one has ever defended Iranian nationhood so well, supporting it by an up-to-date philosophy, worthy of be called "the Philosophy of Resurrection." [*falsafe-ye rastakhiz*]. The gist of these articles, which amount to a book, is the following: Nationhood is defined not by race and blood – a view nowadays rejected – but by culture, which is a product of history and therefore divergent among different nations. It is the culture of each people that makes up its spirit and social character. The real "self" of each people is its culture. People who lacked cultural continuity have perished. But we Iranians have a 2,500-year old culture that defines our existing character, Real Self and Authentic Being. Certain historical events would have alienated us from our Real Self, but we always recovered and returned to our True Self ... He then says Islam is our ideology, not our culture. Islam does not impose cultural uniformity, but recognizes the plurality of cultures ... He claims that our ideology influences our culture and vice versa. Therefore, we are Iranians in a Muslim way, just as our Islam has become Iranian. He thus implicitly denies the existence of a singular Islamic culture ... These articles are quite noteworthy, and certainly written by Shariati himself.[131]

Motahhari thus warned Khomeini about the growing impact of Shariati's Marxist-inflected anti-clericalism, while remaining ambivalent about his project of turning religion into a political ideology serving Iranian nationalism. Though implicit, Motahhari's anxiety seems related to the fact that his own intellectual project of fusing Islam and nationalism also overlaps with those of Shariati and the Shah's regime. His reference to Shartati's project as "the Philosophy of Resurrection" alludes to the political crisis brewing in Iran with the failure of the Shah's new Resurrection Party and its stillborn official "philosophy" (see Chapter 7). Khomeini of course remained prudently silent on Shariati, while defending him indirectly by praising unnamed secular intellectuals who, despite erroneous views, inspired the youth, and especially university students, to join the Islamic opposition.[132]

7 | Conclusion

Aborted Resurrection: An Intellectual Arena Wide Open to Opposition

Whoever is somewhat familiar with Quranic logic can see it is the Quran that makes the prophet be constantly at war against capitalists ... During his lifetime, when he was able to wage war, the prophet's wars were always against the powerful ... These wars pitted the *mostazafin*, i.e. people from the third class, against those in power who wanted to swallow the rights of the poor ... As far as we know their history, previous prophets also came from the poor and the third class, rising up against their sultans.

Ayatollah Khomeini[1]

The above declaration could have come from Ali Shariati and his cohorts on the Islamic left. During the 1970s, however, Khomeini gradually appropriated the Islamic left's rhetoric, blending it with conservative Islamic political thought to forge a new populist discourse. As we saw in Chapters 5 and 6, the project of plagiarizing from the left, to buttress right-wing intellectual hegemony, was already underway during the 1960s and 1970s. This chapter will show how the monarchy's failure at managing this project, during the late 1970s, led to its re-articulation as the revolution's "Islamic Ideology." Thus, the book will conclude by noting how the 1978–1979 revolution's "Islamic Ideology" – summed up in its declaration of intellectual independence, "Neither Eastern, Nor Western" – was both a sharp break with, and a significant continuation of, the political culture of 1970s Iran. The collapse of monarchist modernity, therefore, was the denouement of unresolved intellectual contestations accumulating throughout the twentieth century.

Locating modern revolutions' "intellectual origins" in prerevolutionary political culture has a long pedigree going back to thinkers like Gramsci, Marx and Tocqueville. In part inspired by Gramsci, this book traced the intellectual buildup to the 1978–1979 revolution, focusing not on the moment of sudden political transformation but on long-term contestations whereby moral and intellectual hegemony shifted from one dominant political and cultural bloc to another.[2] Led by Ervand Abrahamian, one school of historiography sees the 1978–1979 revolution, and the Islamic Republic, in terms of continuity with prerevolutionary political culture, noting the indebtedness of "Khomeinism" to socialism and Marxism.[3] On a similar track, this book wrote the socialist and Marxist tradition back into Iranian intellectual history, noting its creative engagement with various strands of nationalist and Islamic thought, while critiquing their shared strengths and weaknesses.

The 1978–1979 revolution, and its "Islamic" trajectory, were neither predetermined nor "unthinkable" *sui generis* "events," impervious to predication and/or post-facto interpretation.[4] While the rumblings of the monarchy's political fault lines were audible throughout the 1970s, the Shah's ultimate fall was the outcome of accumulating contingent crises, each of which could have been handled differently, thus defusing the revolutionary build-up or leading to another kind of political transformation. A different political outcome could have been possible, for instance, had the Shah restored constitutional government in 1977, when the opposition was led by secular liberals, rather than the radical left or Islamists. In this perspective, a revolutionary terminus to the unfolding 1970s political crisis, as well as the revolution's "Islamist" character, were contingent phenomena, appearing increasingly "inevitable" only in 1978.

At the same time, this book has argued the monarchy's fatal political hemorrhage was largely self-inflicted, caused by a succession of serious mistakes that, by the late 1970s, opened the political arena "wide open" to a rapidly radicalizing opposition (see below). Specifically, the chapter will focus on the intellectual underpinnings of the Shah's final strategic blunder, i.e. his 1975 launch of the Resurrection Party, a project meant to overhaul the country's political system beyond the frame of the Shah-People Revolution. Once again borrowing from the playbook of communist and Third World populist regimes, the Shah suddenly dropped all pretense of multi-party constitutional government, declaring Iran a one-party state under his own blatant, but of course benevolent, one-man rule. The ongoing Shah-People Revolution would continue, but according to a new "philosophy" guiding the Resurrection Party. Going beyond capitalist liberal democracy and Marxian socialism, the "Philosophy of Resurrection" (*Falsafe-ye Rastakhiz*) would be monarchist, authentically Iranian and Islamic, and "neither Eastern, nor Western." Conceived as a stabilizing response to escalating economic and political crises in the mid-1970s, including the well-kept secret of the Shah's terminal illness, the Resurrection Party project produced the opposite effect, quickly conceding all political initiative to the opposition. The least-noted feature of the Iranian Revolution is the intellectual overlap between the ill-defined "Philosophy of Resurrection" and the revolution's dominant ideology. This book will conclude on that note of irony.

The Shah as an Intellectual: A Revolutionary Philosopher King?

Who do these intellectuals think they are? A bunch of lazy cowards whose criticisms are merely by our own permission.

The Shah in 1975[5]

By 1978, the Shariati controversy faded into the background as political developments rapidly took new turns. During 1976–1977, the convergence of long-festering economic and political difficulties, as well as uncertainties in relations with the US, had created a multi-pronged political crisis. Unfortunately for the Shah, the plunge into economic and political instability came at the threshold of his promised transition to "Great Civilization," a new era in which Iran was expected to join the ranks of the world's most developed nations.[6] In a broader perspective, the mid-1970s crisis had only exposed the regime's inherent political vulnerability and fragile legitimacy. For about a decade, the apparent success of the Shah-People Revolution had projected the illusion of political stability, coinciding with the 1965–1977 tenure of Amir-Abbas Hoveyda, modern Iran's longest-serving prime minister. But Hoveyda was merely a front man for a pseudo-constitutional political regime, where the Shah made all the important decisions. During these years, however, the autocratic nature of monarchy became more transparent as the Shah increasingly assumed the role of Iran's ideological commander-in-chief. Ironically, as a modern "philosopher king," he had joined the ranks of the very intellectuals he had always despised and feared.

The Shah's mistrust and disdain of intellectuals was barely disguised. Former premier Alam's memoir, for example, notes how the Shah often accused intellectuals of opportunism, claiming they easily betrayed their ideals to join the regime and then cooperated with its intelligence organizations for self-promotion. According to Alam, the Shah appreciated his joking pun on the widely used French loan word *intellectuel*, whose pronunciation (*an-telektuel*) conveys something like "shit-head" in Persian. This in fact had been a self-mocking pun, which Alam had heard from Rasul Parvizi, one of his ex-communist protégés.[7] The prototype of intellectuals mocked by the Shah was Prime Minister Hoveyda, who supposedly had vague leftist associations in his youth, pretended to befriend leftist intellectuals, appreciated French novels and projected a facile cosmopolitanism. Hoveyda's signature image of a pipe-smoking, cane-carrying dandy, with an orchid in his coat-lapel, was routinely ridiculed in the contemporary satirical press.[8] As for the Shah himself, psychological studies have noted his intellectual and emotional insecurity, especially when compared with his father, who was known for decisive forcefulness, and to Premier Mohammad Mosaddeq, who was genuinely popular. The Shah's persistent object of fear and envy, however, remained communist intellectuals, whom he habitually accused of "treason" and "betrayal of the country," particularly when remembering the trauma of his own virtual overthrow in 1953.[9] This exaggerated fear of communism persisted into the 1970s when the Tudeh Party was a politically irrelevant exile group, while Iran's relations with both the Soviet Union and Communist China had become increasingly cordial. Arguably, another reason of the Shah's obsession with leftist intellectuals was his "anxiety of influence," caused by the guilty knowledge that his regime's defining political project, the White Revolution, largely copied their ideas.

Reaching their peak during the 1970s, the Shah's intellectual pretentions are traceable in a number of books published under his name, which, regardless of input by editors and ghost-writers, reflect a rather singular mindset. While not taken seriously at the time or later by intellectual historians, texts like *Mission for my Country* (1961), *The White Revolution* (1966) and *Toward Great Civilization* (1977) are in fact uniquely important due to their "authorship" by the regime's only official ideologue.[10] In terms of broad themes, these texts are attempts at reconciling claims to divine kingship – purportedly rooted in Iranian history and culture – to modern nationalism, democracy, socialism and Islam. But neither the Shah's temperament nor his education prepared him for tackling such intellectual ventures. As his statesmen and courtiers have noted, the Shah was interested and relatively educated in economics and technology, but was neither curious nor knowledgeable about the humanities.[11] This in part explains a royal "division of labor," whereby Queen Farah had assumed the complementary role of Iran's official patron of culture and the arts, presumably more "feminine" subjects (see Chapter 5). But the Shah was not oblivious to debates on Iranian national identity, cultural authenticity and especially intellectual independence from superpower influences. His writings and speeches often emphasized official commitment to "positive nationalism." This meant that, in contrast to the "negatively" defiant nationalism of the Mosaddeq era, monarchist nationalism selectively borrowed political, economic and cultural models from both Eastern and Western blocs. Occasionally, the Shah would criticize the wholesale acceptance of "Western" culture, using terms like *West-struck*, which had found general currency.[12] In a 1972 speech, he said:

Until a few years ago, our only hope and desire was to become like the West. Even I myself, in my first book, *Mission for my Country*, stressed the same idea. Now, however, while still acknowledging the West's positive qualities, we want to adopt only these qualities and adapt them to Iranian morality, since we must have our own spiritual and philosophical outlook.[13]

Given his Swiss education, the Shah had some appreciation of contemporary Francophone political culture. He found appealing, for instance, the idea of "*Negritude*," a mix of indigenous culture, including Islam, with mildly anti-colonialist African socialism. This was advocated by his favorite intellectual-statesman, and rare personal friend, Senegalese poet-president Leopold Sedar Senghor, who coined a similar term, *Iranite,* for the notion of Iranian civilization as a historical bridge linking East and West.[14] The Shah also admired French president Charles de Gaulle's particular balancing of authoritarian nationalism and independence from superpower blocs. The American president closest to him was Richard Nixon, whose personality and political career, like the Shah's, were marked by a combination of hubris and insecurity.[15]

In the end, the Shah's attempt at articulating his own brand of an eclectic neo-monarchist nationalism provided no serious intellectual justification of the regime's legitimacy. This dangerous deficiency of ideological legitimation was compounded by the inherent contradiction of a blatant autocracy pretending to pass for parliamentary democracy. After 1963, constitutional monarchy was clearly a mere façade, while the Shah continued to insist Iran was a multi-party democracy. Thus, his own insincere espousal of commitment to democracy during the 1960s would become a source of embarrassment when he imposed a one-party system in 1975. In his 1966 *Mission for my Country*, for instance, he had written:

If I were a dictator rather than a constitutional monarch, then I might be tempted to sponsor a single dominant party such as Hitler organized or such as you find in communist countries. But as constitutional monarch I can afford to encourage large-scale party activity free from the straight-jacket of one-party rule or the one-party state.[16]

But Iran effectively was a one-party state by the second half of the 1960s, a reality that became *de jure* with the 1975 launch of the Resurrection Party.

De facto one-party rule began in 1965, when the Shah decided the newly formed *Iran-e Novin* (New Iran) party would be the instrument of implementing his White Revolution. Iran-e Novin's single-party mandate was quite clear in royal statements such as the following:

As the leader of the Iranian nation, I certainly endorse the great organization of the Iran-e Novin Party, which, backed by the worker-peasant class, is steered toward its lofty goals by the managerial prowess of intellectuals. From now on, the old worn-out ways of the past are to be discarded. Together, the state and the party must rely on the nation's tremendous power, as well as on my personal support, to do what is in our people's best interest.[17]

Iran-e Novin is thus depicted as a "Leninist" party, whereby the intelligentsia "manages" workers and peasants, mobilizing and leading them toward society's revolutionary transformation, under the Shah's personal command. In fact, Iran-e Novin's top personnel included ex-communists, something that Hoveyda seemed to have been proud of, supposedly having boasted: "I have eight former Tudehis in my cabinet who are my most disciplined ministers."[18]

Nor was Iran-e Novin's pretense of similarity to communist parties a new development. At least one contemporary academic study had noted Iran's "two official parties" of the 1950s were "superficially similar to the Tudeh in organization," because "the Tudeh Party set the tune and style for all political parties in Iran."[19] However, keeping up the pretense of a multi-party system, the Shah allowed a "rival" party to play the role of loyal opposition during Iran-e Novin's decade-long domination of Iranian government. Still, Iran-e Novin's effective single-party rule was in some ways a new political departure. More than anything, the decade from 1965 to 1975 was characterized by elite cynicism and public indifference, born of the fact that the parliamentary system had been turned into a mockery. Another keen commentary on the political culture of the 1960s was recorded in a 1964 dispatch to the State Department by Martin Herz, the political secretary at the US embassy in Tehran. According to Herz, despite the successful launch of the White Revolution, the regime lacked popular support, suffering to its very core from a deep crisis of confidence:

> Evidence of this is to be found at every turn: prominent members of the New Iran party who express the belief, privately and quietly, that their party is a sham and a fraud and that no political party can be expected to do useful work as long as the Shah's heavy hand rests on the decision-making process; hand-picked Majlis members who deplore 'American support' for a regime which they call a travesty of democracy.

Herz's roster of regime discontent included the Shah's "most devoted supporters," "prominent judges," "military officers" and "foreign ministry officials" who were in touch with the Americans:

> These are not members of the opposition. They are members of the Establishment who, even when loyal to the Shah, are suffering from a profound malaise, from lack of conviction in what they are doing, from doubts about whether the regime deserves to endure.

He concluded that "the Shah's regime is a highly unpopular dictatorship," considered so "not only by its opponents, but far more significantly, by its proponents as well."[20]

The same diagnosis of a deep malaise in Iranian politics is found also in the memoirs of Alam, the Shah's court minister and closest confidant during Iran-e Novin's 1965–1969 golden era. Alam's posthumously published memoirs repeatedly record his anxiety and fear concerning the regime's future precisely because of the Shah's one-man style of rule. A 1969 entry, for example, reads:

> Today, I was at the Senate, celebrating the sixty-fourth anniversary of the Constitution's inauguration. But it looked more like a funeral than a celebration. Returning home, I kept thinking how I belonged to a corrupt money-worshiping ruling class, under whose domination Iran has almost no chance of survival.[21]

The same year, Alam, who was the only politician capable of conveying disagreeable opinions to the Shah, warned him:

> The ruling classes ... are above all criticism ... Our Majlis deputies cater to party leaders, instead of the people ... and the entire nation sees through their nonsensical babble. We are surrounded by a pervasive creeping indifference, which grows every day. It is true that the country's progress requires forceful action, but now that things are going our way, it is time for dictatorship to slacken, and for His Majesty's to allow free elections.[22]

As prime minister, Alam had been responsible for violently crushing the 1963 uprising, yet he understood that once firmly in the saddle, it was prudent for the regime to somewhat loosen the political controls. A few years later, he sounded even more alarmed by the drift toward autocracy. Commenting on public apathy, student unrest and guerrilla activity in 1973, he wrote:

> Granted that a few individuals may be tools of our foreign enemies. But this cannot explain the student community's indifference to us. It's hard to believe that the entire nation, men, women and children, have become terrorists ... Our government's indolence is catastrophic ... Its indifference, and occasional transgressions, toward the people is like the behavior of an occupying army toward a defeated nation. On every level, in parliamentary, regional and city councils elections, the government denies the people their freedom, imposing instead its own will and electing its own candidates, as if the electorate has no rights. Being so deaf and dumb to what the nation wants, we should not be surprised by their indifference toward us.[23]

But the Shah refused to pay serious heed to Alam's advice, more or less discarding him, like many others, during the last years of his life.

The "Resurrection of the Iranian Nation" and Its "Philosophical Foundations"[24]

Premier Hoveyda stated that the secret of Iran's economic and social success lay in the fact that it did not follow baseless schools of thought, nor was it inspired by East or West in its revolution – the revolution was inspired by national traditions and the Shah's revolutionary ideals.

   BBC report on Hoveyda's 1970 speech to the Central Committee of the Iran-e Novin Party.[25]

During the early 1970s, with Iran's massive and multiplying oil income at his personal disposal, the Shah's sense of messianic command over Iran's destiny grew more irrational. His self-image as a "philosopher king" was now flaunted on a global scale. Such delusions of grandeur were encouraged by the Nixon administration, giving the Shah uncritical political support and unrestricted access to America's non-nuclear arsenal. The most outstanding display of royal megalomania was the extravagant 1971 celebration of 2,500 years of Iranian monarchy, complete with the Shah's bombastic speech at the tomb of Cyrus, whose legacy of world emporium he promised to revive and uphold. More ominous was his boasting of a new role, as Iran's divinely chosen revolutionary dictator, during interviews with foreign news media. A particularly revealing example was his 1973 conversation with Italian journalist Oriana Fallaci, excerpted below:

The Shah: . . . I believe in God, in the fact of being chosen by God to accomplish a mission. My visions were miracles that saved the country. My reign has saved the country and it's saved it because God was beside me . . .
    Fallaci: . . . [M]any people consider you a dictator . . . would you deny you're a very authoritarian king?
    The Shah: No, I would not deny it. Because in a certain sense I am. But look, to carry out reforms one can't help but be authoritarian . . . I plan on staying there by showing that with force you can do a lot of things, and I will even prove that your socialism is finished . . . I achieve more than the Swedes . . .
    Fallaci: . . . Are you telling me that in a certain sense you're a socialist, and that your socialism is more modern and advanced than the Scandinavian kind?
    The Shah: Of Course. Because that socialism means a system of social security for those who don't work . . . The socialism of my White Revolution, on the other hand, is an incentive to work. It's a new original socialism.[26]

Thus, by the mid-1970s, the Shah was claiming a divine mandate to resurrect Iran's imperial glories, in the form of a modern "Great Civilization," guided by a bizarrely inchoate ideology that was simultaneously monarchist, authentically Iranian, revolutionary, mystically Islamic and superior to both Marxism and bourgeois liberal ideology. Such claims were made in his *Toward the Great Civilization*, which was published one year after the 1975 launch of a single-party regime. The Shah's decision to suddenly declare Iran a one-party state was a surprising move that quickly proved a major disaster. Nor were all of the regime's supporters on board with the Shah's erratic decision. Alam, for example, was opposed to the idea, correctly seeing it as a grave danger to the regime's survival.[27]

The Resurrection Party project was a wrong-headed response to growing economic, political and foreign relations challenges, compounded by the Shah's awareness of his own serious and potentially terminal illness. The economy had spun out of control during the fifth five-year development plan (1973–1978) when Iran's projected oil income suddenly had increased from $20 billion to nearly $100 billion. Beyond the initial euphoria, however, the expenditure of this massive capital inflow quickly an insurmountable obstacle. Between 1970 and 1976, creeping inflation pushed the cost of living up by almost 200 percent, while the state's over-ambitious economic development projects stagnated due to shortages of skilled labor, housing, electricity and transportation infrastructure. By the mid-1970s, Iranian and foreign observers were reporting growing unease in the business community, shown by major capital flight.[28]

The international context, particularly Iran's relations with the US, also played a crucial role in the mid-1970s crisis. The Nixon presidency had been the nadir of the US-Iranian Cold War alliance when the Shah was treated as an American partner and regional ally, rather than a client. The emergence of domestic challenges in Iran coincided with Nixon's fall and the post-Vietnam turn in US foreign policy, with the new Carter Administration perceived to be supportive of the Iranian opposition's call for returning to constitutional government. Meanwhile, the Shah and members of the political establishment were aware of growing domestic discontent, precisely of the kind that Alam had warned about. This was clearly documented in a mid-1970s national survey of popular satisfaction/grievances ordered by the Shah and conducted by a special task force under Hushang Nahavandi, chancellor of Tehran University. According to this survey, most Iranians acknowledged that their living standards had improved, yet they bitterly resented the corruption of "the new ruling class," including the royal family. Political discontent was particularly strong among members of the educated younger generation, who "demanded more freedom of thought and expression." The Shah saw this report, but it was not taken seriously and, like many similar ones, was filed away.[29]

To these domestic and international factors of instability, one must add the Shah's growing concern with his own approaching death. In 1974, two French physicians had diagnosed him with a serious blood disease that was treatable, but eventually would become fatal. For a few years, this secret was known only to a handful of people, including Alam, who suffered from another type of blood disease, and who had brought his French doctors to examine the Shah. The public, of course, was kept in the dark, and even Queen Farah only learned about her husband's illness in 1977. In retrospect, hints of weakening confidence are detectable in the Shah's private conversations and public speeches. As early as 1975, for example, he complained to French President Giscard d'Estaing of not having enough time left for his projects, while his Resurrection Party inaugural speech of the same year included an unprecedented mention of his mortality.[30]

It is not clear exactly how the idea of the Resurrection Party originated, but it had emerged from several sources, all seeking to stabilize and "institutionalize" the regime, with a view to reducing its total dependence on the Shah. Most observers place the idea's gestation period between 1972 and 1974, a time during which the Shah was diagnosed with cancer and therefore presumably was forced to consider the possibility of his own departure from the scene. Ervand Abrahamian was the first scholar to note that the Resurgence Party was an intellectual joint venture of ex-communists and technocrats schooled in American-style modernization theory.[31] Among these technocrats was Gholamreza Afkhami, then a member of a "think tank" formed by "a group of relatively young intellectuals drawn from the universities and mid-level government." According to Afkhami, in 1971–1972, this think tank had produced a draft proposal for the modernization of Iran's political system based on his own doctoral dissertation. Titled "The Resurrection Movement of the Iranian Nation," this proposal aimed to "achieve a nexus between the shah's actual power on one hand and the problems of cultural fragmentation and institutional weakness on the other." Building on the principles of the Shah-People Revolution and Iran's Constitution, the solution would be a broad, consensus-building political movement, not a single party, gradually expanding political participation while leaving the shah in control of the military, foreign policy, oil and national security. Afkhami remembers that the shah considered the project but decided it could not be implemented at the time.[32]

In March 1975, the Shah surprisingly announced the launch of the Iranian Nation's Resurrection Party (*Hezb-e Rastakhiz-e mellat-e Iran*), basing it on three principles: Iran's constitution, the Imperial System (*Nezam-e Shahanshahi*), and the Shah-People Revolution. He had borrowed the new party's name and its national mobilization idea from Afkhami's group, while turning it into a single political party. Officially declaring Iran a one-party state, he said Iranians had three options: join his new party, steer clear of politics, or leave the country. The Resurrection Party's constitution placed "the Imperial System" above all else, defining it as "the secret of the Iranian nation's longevity and the embodiment of its unique cultural, political and social character." As a "divine gift," this Imperial System was "the authentic and natural form of government in the entire span of Iranian history." This type of monarchy being a "spiritual and moral system," the Shah was "the nation's commander, leader, and saviour."[33] Though identified as the regime's foundational feature, the Imperial System remained a nebulous innovation. Monarchy, of course, was a familiar concept, clearly upheld by the 1906 Constitution and more dubiously being the centerpiece of the Shah-People Revolution. But the arbitrary imposition of an ill-defined Imperial System above the constitution obviously violated the latter. Therefore, immediate and persistent objections to the Resurrection Party converged on its blatant violation of Iran's constitutional system. Ironically, even the Shah himself had pointed this out as an objection to the Resurrection project as originally conceived by the Afkhami group in 1972.[34]

The Shah's conception of the Resurrection Party went beyond the Afkhami group's proposal by adopting the organizational structure and nomenclature of communist parties. According to the party's 1975 constitution:

By overthrowing feudalism, granting women political rights, securing workers' rights, founding a robust economic, social and political system, and establishing progressive and just [social] relations, the Shah-People Revolution opened a new era in the country's history ... In Iran's revolutionary society, respect for human dignity has replaced all manifestations and problems of class ... In Iranian society's revolutionary order, the very foundations of man's exploitation by man have been uprooted.[35]

The Resurrection Party's heavy-handed reliance on the language of class struggle and exploitation was more than rhetorical flourish.

The party's organizational and key personnel charts show crucial dependence on former communist intellectuals. Political cadres, for instance, were trained at a special bureau called "the educational center for educators." Prominent political "educators" included Parviz Nikkhah, Kurosh Lasha'i, Firuz Fuldai, Firuz Shirvanlu and Enyatollah Reza. These men, along with Mahmud Ja'farian and Manuchehr Azmun, formed a core group of ex-communists who were already serving the regime in important capacities (see Chapter 6) Lasha'i was an ex-Maoist and protégé of Deputy Court Minister Mohammad Baheri, himself another former Tudeh Party member who became the Resurrection Party's general secretary in 1976. During the 1970s, Lasha'i was involved with charting Iran's "neither Eastern, nor Western" foreign policy, later joining the Resurgence Party's task force for the articulation of a new "dialectical philosophy" for the Shah-People Revolution (see below).[36] Enyatollah Reza was a repentant Tudeh Party leader who had returned from exile in the Soviet Union with a doctorate in philosophy. He had joined the faculty of Pahlavi University after publishing several books criticizing Iranian adaptations of Marxism, particularly its mixture with Islam by thinkers like Shariati. He then became a Resurrection Party theorist, writing numerous articles in the party's theoretical organ, *The Ideas of Resurrection*.[37] Finally, the term "resurrection," and its implied eschatological sense, had a linkage to the Marxist political culture of 1970s Iran. The underground literature of the Marxist Fada'ian organization typically referred to the February 1971 launch of guerrilla armed struggle, in the Siahkal forests of Gilan province, as "the Siahkal Resurrection" (*rastakhiz-e Siahkal*), implying it had resurrected dormant radical opposition to the Shah's regime.[38]

As noted above, instead of stabilizing the political system, the launch of the Resurrection Party unleashed profoundly destabilizing consequences that escalated all the way to the 1978–1979 Revolution. In wake of the Resurrection Party, for instance, the regime began to boldly tamper with the sacred, as the Shah was increasingly and openly referred to as Iran's spiritual, as well as political leader, while it was proposed that a new Religion Corps (*Sepah-e Din*) be added to the ever-expanding roster of the Shah-People Revolution, and the Islamic calendar was changed to a monarchist one. Thus, in 1976, Iranians were hurtled from the year 1355, in the existing solar Islamic calendar, to the year 2535, according to a new officially imposed Imperial Calendar.

This foolhardy stretching of sacred time was accomplished by simply adding the thirty-five years of the Shah's rule to the 2,500 years since Cyrus's founding of the Achaemenid Empire. Such arbitrary religious innovations of the Resurrection Party era had an role in the further mobilization of Islamic and clerical opposition. However, it is important to note that these moves were aimed at appropriating and politicizing Islam, rather than discarding it. In fact, political references to Islam, including the Shah's pretense of religiosity, increased in the second half of the 1970s.[39]

In contrast to the Resurrection Party project's destabilizing effect, a safer path toward political stability would have been moves toward the restoration of constitutional monarchy, an option favored by "old-fashioned" politicians like Alam and demanded by the bulk of the opposition. But the Shah refused to consider this option until it was too late, when the political crisis had spiraled totally out of control in 1978. However, if the Resurrection Party project led to a revolutionary apocalypse, the party's more obscure "Philosophy of Resurrection" was the direct precursor to the revolution's apocalyptic ideology. Officially called the "Philosophy/Ideology of Resurrection" (*falsafe/ ideolozhi-ye Rastakhiz*), this obscure intellectual legacy of the Pahlavi era has an unnoticed linkage to the 1978–1979 Revolution's dominant "Islamic Ideology." Some scholars have noted the Shah's search for an "ideology" as the Shah-People Revolution unfolded into the 1970s. Little to no attention, however, has been paid to the final chapter of this desperate search for monarchist revolutionary ideology in the era of the Resurrection Party.[40] Officially dubbed the "Philosophy of Resurrection," this turned into an ideological "monstrosity," of the kind Dariush Shayegan had described (see Chapter 6): "horrific formations, which, like Frankenstein's monster, take revenge on their creator ... [being] Frankenstein's other self, embodying his unconscious and repressed powers."[41] Pilfering and stitching together vital parts, from Marxist, nationalist, Islamist and nativist ideologies, the monarchy had brought to life an uncontrollable intellectual and political monstrosity. A more successfully managed previous experiment, i.e. the White Revolution, had harnessed the intellectual resources of a multifarious opposition that was itself forcibly buried alive. This time, however, the long "repressed powers" of the monarchy's truly revolutionary "other self" could not be kept at bay. Thus, the Revolution's "Islamic Ideology" breathed new life into the dead body politic the monarchy created. The similarities between monarchist and Islamic revolutionary ideology were like those between a forgery and its true copy. Probing into the monarchy's obscure final intellectual endeavor, therefore, would be a fitting conclusion to this book's journey through modern Iranian intellectual history.

The Philosophy of Resurrection was a project in the making for a number of years. In the fall of 1975, a few months after launching the Resurrection Party, the Shah issued the following directive:

The Esteemed Amir Abbas Hoveyda, General Secretary of the Iranian Nation's Resurrection Party,

Now that the Shah-People Revolution's fourteen principles have borne brilliant results in the social and economic affairs of the Iranian nation, it is time to develop the general philosophy of these principles, as an intellectually comprehensive ideological system, based on a far-sighted dialectical and scientific vision, to declare and clarify the logic of our progress in spiritual life and national culture. We assign the Iranian Nation's Resurrection Party with the task of selecting a group of the most outstanding intellectuals to accomplish this mission, presenting it for our approval, after comprehensive due studies.

The Resurrection Party then commissioned one hundred "outstanding thinkers" to appoint a special ten-member task force responsible for updating the ideology and philosophy of the Shah-People Revolution, in line with the changing conditions of the Resurrection era.[42] The actual task force enlisted about a dozen intellectuals, mostly tied to the rival establishment factions headed by Alam and Hoveyda. On closer inspection, the task force included a bizarre admixture of intellectually and ideologically incompatible individuals. Half of its members, including Mohammad Baheri, Manuchehr Azmun, Enyatollah Reza, Hushang Nahavandi and Kurosh Lasah'i, were former communists. The other half was more incongruent, consisting of the new technocratic prime minster, Jamshid Amuzegar, hypernationalist ideologues Shapur Zandnia and Mohammad-Reza Ameli-Tehrani, Traditionalist Sufi master Seyyed Hossein Nasr and mystical Heideggerian Ahmad Fardid.[43] With one foot planted in each camp, Ehsan Naraqi was another ex-communist who had refashioned himself as Iran's semi-official voice of cultural nativism. In Naraqi's estimation, the Resurgence Party was the political manifestation of indigenous national culture, including its mystical dimensions, thus capable of securing Iran's autonomy from Eastern or Western paradigms:

In sum, the paradigm [*olgu*] of Western Civilization has lost its validity, as we find Western thinkers now becoming curious about new dynamic centers emerging around the world ... The flowering of these potentials, paying attention to the social and civic proclivities of all Iranians – what mystics call appreciating their passion (*eshq*) – this is the expression of an authentic and sensible national culture, making everyone feel at home ... This, in my opinion, is the meaning of the actual participation of the entire nation, and a reflection of Iran's national resurrection.[44]

Despite their ideological divergences, Naraqi and his cohorts managed to present the Shah with a preliminary draft of a text titled *The Dialectical Philosophy of Resurrection*. According to Baheri, who claims to have been this text's main author:

The Shah insisted this philosophy be based on dialectical principles. Therefore a few dialecticians ... joined us for the articulation of the revolution's principles. We must have spent about a thousand hours, working day and night. A very proper text was then produced which presented the dialectic as a divine principle. That was because we did not want to associate the dialectic with materialism. Therefore, all social and natural transformations were called tradition, a divine tradition.[45]

The Shah, however, was not entirely satisfied with this text, and the project itself eventually was abandoned as the country plunged deeper into a prerevolutionary crisis. Facing an impending revolution, the final report of the task force published in mid-1978 admitted to the failure of the entire Resurrection project, including its philosophy:

The Resurrection Party was a particular kind of nation-wide political organization which could have responded to the needs of a transitional period, had it been properly managed ... The most painful point is that the party does not teach the philosophy of Resurrection, political education has no authoritative foundation, while no comprehensive program, based on the revolution's philosophical tenets, is offered ... Despite the best of intentions, the party proved incapable of broadening the revolution's philosophy or offering appealing agendas to the public, thus leaving the intellectual arena of politics wide open to charlatans and the opposition.[46]

Published about six months before the Shah's overthrow, this report concedes the regime's political and ideological bankruptcy, admitting that the failure of the Resurrection Party and its "philosophy" had left the political and intellectual arena "wide open" to the opposition.[47]

Similar admissions of mistakes, including the Shah's own *mea culpa*, pronounced after his overthrow in *Answer to History* (1980), bring us back to the question of whether different strategic choices might have averted the mid-1970s crisis, or prevented its escalation into a revolutionary meltdown. Without recourse to counter-factual history, it is clear that a host of long- and short-term political options were available throughout the 1960s and 1970s. For instance, having contained all political challengers in 1963, the Shah could have restored constitutional monarchy, allowing some meaningful political participation, instead of irrationally imposing his personal dictatorship. Until 1978, the bulk of the opposition, including its leftist wing, was not calling for the monarchy's overthrow. Nor was the opposition mainly Islamic, or led by the clergy, until 1978. The predominantly secular bent of the opposition was clear in the 1976–1977 liberal-democratic protests of National Front politicians, lawyers, and human rights activists, as well as leftist-dominated events such as the celebrated ten nights of lectures and poetry reading at Tehran's Goethe Institute.[48] In response to these events, and presumably to placate the Carter administration as well, the regime began to allow more freedom of expression, while curbing the worst excess of political repression. The new official policy of "opening up the political space" (*faza-ye baz-e sisai*), however, did not mean real power-sharing, since the Shah remained in total control. According to an intellectual insider: "He was attempting to take over the idea of 'democratization' launched by the opposition, just as in 1960 he had appropriated the reforms advocated by the revolutionaries of that time."[49] This time around, such pretentions would not work.

The Shah's last major address to the nation, delivered in early November 1978, was an overdue admission of political culpability, based on a text once again concocted jointly by his ex-leftist and right-wing intellectual cronies. Reportedly composed by Reza Qotbi and Seyyed Hossein Nasr, the speech totally discarded the ideas and language of the Resurrection era and the Shah-People Revolution. Instead, the Shah now acknowledged hearing "the message of the People's Revolution," pleaded forgiveness for his own despotic, oppressive and corrupt rule and promised to restore constitutional government:

Dear people of Iran, while the political space opened in the last two years, you rose up against oppression and corruption. As the king, and also an Iranian, I can only approve of the Iranian people's revolution.

... I know that, in the name of preventing chaos, the past mistakes, oppression and repression may return. I know some may feel the danger that, in the name of the country's interests and progress, the unholy alliance of political and financial corruption may be re-imposed. But, as your king ... I promise that past mistakes, lawlessness, oppression and corruption, would not return, but instead [you] receive full recompense. I promise that once order is restored, a popular government would be quickly formed to safeguard basic liberties and hold free elections, so that the Fundamental Law, purchased with blood during the Constitutional Revolution, be fully implemented. I too heard the message of the people's revolution ... I promise Iran's future government would be based on the constitution, social justice and popular sovereignty, and be far from despotism, oppression and corruption.[50]

But this final promise of ending decades of Pahlavi autocracy had come too late, when the dictator was obviously broken and defeated. The revolutionary potential he had tried to harness now surged beyond the Shah's control, quickly culminating in his overthrow.

Epilogue

This book concludes at the threshold of the 1978–1979 Revolution, whose intellectual and ideological continuity with Pahlavi-era modernity has been suggested throughout its chapters. Despite its dominant "Islamic" discourse and fierce assertion of native authenticity, the Revolution was as deeply "Eastern and Western" as a century of Iranian modernity had been. Khomeini, like the Shah, appropriated the modern concept of revolution, foregrounding its populist and anti-imperialist aspects, while assimilating everything to the language of Islam. Khomeini's revolutionary interpretation of Islam drew on an intellectual project with at least three decades of history articulated in part by thinkers like Ali Shariati and organizations such as the People's Mojahedin and the God-worshipping Socialists. However, the larger project of accommodating nationalism, constitutionalism and socialism to Islam had begun earlier, around the turn of the twentieth century. Given his earlier political views, Khomeini made an intellectual breakthrough when, in the 1970s, he joined the radical opposition to reject the monarchy. Moreover, his early 1970s nebulous proposal of an "Islamic government" took concrete shape only when he embraced another modern concept, namely that of a "republic," when the monarchy's collapse became evident in late 1978. Still, what remained ambiguous, and led to bloody post-revolutionary contestations, was the question of where political authority ultimately resided. Often implicit in the intellectual debates surveyed throughout this book, the question of modern political authority's grounding nevertheless remained inadequately addressed by nationalist, Marxist or Islamic ideological trends.

The Iranian Revolution not only shattered the monarchy as a political system but radically questioned the entire culture of Iranian modernity. This cultural edifice, the Islamic Republic would claim, was something alien and inauthentic, forcibly imposed on Iran by about half a century of illegitimate Pahlavi political authority.

242   Epilogue

Primarily attuned to culture, the revolution would now reverse the process, deploying its political authority to forcibly reconstitute Iranian modernity, or, as observers like Michel Foucault had hoped, initiate a postmodern Iran guided by "spiritual politics." This book, however, has shown that what Foucault took for "spiritual politics," as well as the revolution's discourse of return to nativist spirituality and authentic national culture, were intellectual artifacts of Iranian modernity. As all post-revolutionary regimes do, the Islamic Republic constituted a new political authority, but inevitably it did so by using cultural building blocks and foundations that were already in place. Addressed implicitly in this book, it was indeed the question of political authority, its social grounding and cultural legitimacy which had posed the thorniest challenge to the intellectual debates of Iranian modernity.

We saw in previous chapters that by the late twentieth century at least three generations of Iranian intellectuals had been engaged with modern global ideologies, debating the nation, revolution, the people, imperialism, class and gender. Despite considerable accomplishments, however, their collective endeavors fell short when it came to the question of political authority. During the 1978–1979 Revolution, a left-liberal minority proposed a democratic model of governance within the existing frame of constitutional government. But, as several chapters of this book argued in detail, the Pahlavi state, and the intellectuals serving it in various capacities, systematically subverted Iran's constitutional tradition and hence the potential for democratic politics.

While historians might generally concur with some of the above conclusions, the present book arrived at them via the uncommon route of tracing the genealogy and inherent antinomies of modern Iran's political culture within global intellectual trends and ideologies. Chapter 1 introduced the book's overall argument about the global, rather than "Western" character of modern Iran by focusing on the intellectual impact of Ottoman and Russian constitutionalism and revolutionary modernity. Critiquing historiographical debates on Iran's transition to modernity, particularly the 1906–1911 Constitutional Revolution, this chapter also introduced the book's argument on the significance of socialism as the second (next to nationalism) most important intellectual project of Iranian modernity. Chapters 2 and 3 located the 1920s launch of Iranian nationalism and nation-state building within a particular intellectual matrix shaped by World War I and the Russian Revolution. Thus, in terms of intellectual moorings, Reza Shah's dictatorship in Iran epitomized the global triumph of authoritarian nation-state building over contending Bolshevik and/or liberal-democratic models. Chapters 4 and 5 covered intellectual departures in the mid-twentieth century, when political authority once again became contestable with the collapse of Reza Shah's regime during World War II. Among such departures, Ahmad Kasravi's articulation of nationalism as a secular religion was identified as the harbinger of the coming convergence between nationalism, Islamism and populist socialism, whereby political authority is metaphysically mandated to an intellectual elite. More significant in the long run was the intellectual impact of socialism in its various Soviet-style, democratic and Islamic versions. While Chapter 4 had traced the intellectual formation of an Iranian brand of Marxism during the 1930s, Chapter 5 focused on the 1940s and 1950s, when Marxism-Leninism, social democracy and Islamic socialism emerged to collectively play a hegemonic role in intellectual life and political culture. Combing through untapped primary sources, the intellectual imprint of socialism was deciphered in the White Revolution, the Pahlavi monarchy's signature reform and modernization project. The chapter then revisited the political legacy of 1960s Iran's quintessential public intellectual Jalal Al-Ahmad, whose last works, it concluded, show greater commitment to socialist universalism than to Islamism or cultural nativism.

The book's last two chapters delineated and analyzed the complex intellectual contestations of Pahlavi-era "high modernity" during the 1960s and 1970s. Chapter 6 focused on three sites of intellectual production to show that the broad ideological drift toward "spiritual politics," nativism and "Return to the Self" was well underway during the pre-revolutionary decades. The first and least studied of these sites was that of official political culture, directed through national cultural planning via state-sponsored public education, government-owned or controlled print and electronic media, and state patronage of the arts and popular entertainment. A second site of intellectual production sought to anchor Iranian national identity in Shi'i metaphysics, Orientalist notions of "Eastern" perennial wisdom, and Traditionalist theosophy, all joined in opposition to the sway of modern secular ideologies, particularly Marxism. Backed by the Pahlavi state, this proto-religious conservative nationalism dominated Iran's

Royal Academy of Philosophy, also enlisting the country's leading clerical intellectual, and Khomeini confidant, Ayatollah Moretza Motahhari. The third and most innovative and dynamic intellectual trend was left-leaning Islam, particularly the so-called "Islamic Marxism" of Ali Shariati and the People's Mojahedin organization, which animated radical Islamic opposition during the 1970s. The chapter argues that the monarchy's nativist and pseudo-leftist cultural politics, as well as both rightist and leftist political Shi'ism, were reactions to the hegemony of leftist and Third Worldist ideologies among the country's cultural workers and their main audience of a burgeoning university student population.

Chapter 7 concludes the book by analyzing the intellectual premises of the political blunders that undermined the monarchy's legitimacy during the second half of the 1970s. Building on the book's broad survey of modern Iranian intellectual contestations, this chapter also points out the revolution's ideological indebtedness to Pahlavi modernity and particularly to the creative intellectual fermentation of the immediate pre-revolutionary decades. Assuming the role of Iran's intellectual commander-in-chief, the Shah sank the ship of the state by launching the Resurrection Party and its bizarre revolutionary philosophy in the midst of a deep mid-1970s political crisis. The pseudo-revolutionary philosophy of the Shah's new party sought a grand synthesis of the various ideological items his regime had copied from leftist, nativists and Islamist intellectuals throughout the 1960s and 1970s. This was a desperate attempt to salvage the monarchy's shaky political authority by enlisting the rhetoric of radical revolution, welfare state, anti-imperialism, esoteric and mystical Shi'ism, and Iranian authenticity. Ironically, the ideological recipe worked too well, with all of its ingredients perfectly coming together, but this time producing a real revolutionary outburst that brought an end to the monarchy.

Notes

Introduction: Intellectual Constructions of Iranian Modernity

1. The predominance of Cultural History, since the mid-1990s, is based on data published by the American Historical Association. See Lynn Hunt, *Writing History in the Global Era* (New York and London: W.W. Norton & Company 2014), p. 31.

2. Israel Gershoni and Amy Singer, "Introduction: Intellectual History in Middle Eastern Studies" in *Comparative Studies of South Asia, Africa and the Middle East*, vol. 28, no. 3 (2008), pp. 383–389, quoted on pp. 383–384. This is the guest editors' introduction to the journal's special issue on Intellectual History in Middle Eastern Studies. The field's "ghettoization," along national and regional lines, is evident in the fact that all four articles in this issue deal with Arab countries, while Iran and Turkey are not covered.

3. Janet Afary and Kevin B. Anderson, *Foucault and the Iranian Revolution: Gender and the Seduction of Islamism* (Chicago: Chicago University Press, 2005).

4. Said Amir Arjomand, "Ideological revolution in Shi'ism" in Said Amir Arjomand ed. *Authority and Political Culture in Shi'ism* (Albany: State University of New York Press, 1988): pp. 178–209.

5. Hamid Enayat, *Modern Islamic Political Thought* (Austin, TX: University of Texas Press, 1982) and Shahrough Akhavi, *Religion and Politics in Contemporary Iran: Clergy-state Relations in the Pahlavi Period* (Albany: State University of New York Press, 1980). Both books focused on Shi'i doctrine, institutions and clergy-state relations. The same focus continues in recent works, for example, Behrooz Moazami, *State, Religion, and Revolution in Iran, 1796 to the Present* (New York: Palgrave Macmillan, 2013).

6. Published a few years after the revolution, Ervand Abrahamian's *Iran between Two Revolutions* (Princeton, NJ: Princeton University Press, 1982), was the first scholarly work giving the left a prominent place in modern Iranian history. This was followed by Abrahamian's *The Iranian Mojahedin* (New Haven CT: Yale University Press, 1989) and *Khomeinism:*

Essays on the Islamic Republic (Berkeley, CA: University of California Press, 1993). Serious recognition, along with condemnation, of the left's impact on the revolution began with Sadeq Ziabaklam, *Moqaddamehi bar enqelab-e Eslami* (Tehran, n.d.).

7. Hamid Dabashi, *Theology of Discontent: The Ideological Foundations of the Islamic Revolution in Iran* (New York: New York University Press, 1993), p. 5.

8. Mehrzad Boroujerdi's *Iranian Intellectuals and the West: The Tormented Triumph of Nativism* (Syracuse, NY: Syracuse University Press, 1996), p. xv.

9. Negin Nabavi, *Intellectuals and the State in Iran: Politics, Discourse and the Dilemma of Authenticity* (Gainesville, FL: University of Florida Press, 2003). At about the same time, Farzin Vahdat's *God and Juggernaut: Iran's Intellectual Encounter with Modernity* (2002). Ali Gheissari, *Iranian Intellectuals in the 20th Century* (Austin, TX: University of Texas Press, 1998); Ali Mirsepassi, *Intellectual Discourse and the Politics of Modernization: Negotiating Modernity in Iran* (Cambridge, MA: Cambridge University Press, 2000); Mohammad Tavakoli-Targhi, *Refashioning Iran: Orientalism, Occidentalism and Historiography* (New York: Palgrave, 2001). For an outstanding study of modernity in Persian and published in Iran see Shahrokh Haghighi, *Gozar az moderniteh? Nicheh, Fuko, liotar, derida (Beyond Modernity? Nietzsche, Foucault, Lyotard, Derrida)* (Tehran: Agah, 2001). For a discussion of this and related works in Persian see Afshin Matin-asgari, "Iranian Postmodernity: The Rhetoric of Irrationality?" *Critique*, vol. 13, no. 1 (spring 2004): pp. 113–123.

10. Among Dabashi's prolific output, *Shi'ism: A Religion of Protest* (Cambridge, MA: Harvard University Press, 2011), *A People Interrupted* (New York: New Press, 2007) and *Literary Humanisms* (Cambridge, MA: Harvard University Press, 2012) are more directly related to intellectual history.

11. Ali Mirsepassi, *Political Islam, Iran and the Enlightenment* (New York: Cambridge University Press, 2011), pp. 4–5.

12. Ali Mirsepassi, *Transnationalism in Iranian Political Thought: The Life and Times of Ahmad Fardid* (New York: Cambridge University Press, 2017). See my review of this book in *The American Historical Review*, vol. 123, no. 2 (April 2018): 668–69.

13. In English, this famous phrase often appears as "Neither East, Nor West"; see, for example, Nikki R. Keddie and Mark J. Gasiorowski, eds., *Neither East, Nor West: Iran, the Soviet Union, and the United States* (New Haven, CT: Yale University Press, 1990) and Christiane Bird: *Neither East, Nor West: One Woman's Journey through the*

Islamic Republic of Iran (New York: Pocket Books, 2001). In the original Persian, however, the adjectives *sharqi va gharbi*, literally "Eastern and Western," are used. For example, a 1974 collection of essays by Iran's leading historian, Abdol-Hosein Zarrinkub was titled *Nah sharqi, nah Gharbi, ensani* (Neither Eastern, Nor Western: Humanist), referring to a famous Qur'anic phrase in Surah 24 (Light) verse 35. See pp. 27–39.

14. On Modernity conceptualized in terms of antinomies see Vasant Kaiwar and Sucheta Mazumdar, eds. *Antinomies of Modernity: Essays on Race, Orient, Nation* (Durham and London: Duke University Press, 2003). Kaiwar and Mazumadr adapt the concept of "antinomy" from Frederick Jameson, *Postmodernism, or, The Cultural Logic of Late Capitalism* (Durham, NC: Duke University Press, 1991) and Marshall Berman, *All that Is Solid Melts into the Air: The Experience of Modernity* (New York: Simon and Shuster, 1982). I have applied this concept to Iran, in Afshin Matin-asgari, "Iranian Modernity in Global Perspective: Nationalist, Marxist and Authenticity Discourses" in Sucheta Mazumdar, Vasant Kaiwar and Thierry Labiaca, eds. *From Orientalism to Postcolonialism: Asia, Europe and the Lineage of Difference* (London and New York: Routledge, 2009): pp. 129–153.

15. For a fairly recent historians' debate on modernity see "Introduction," *American Historical Review*, vol. 116, no. 3 (June 2011): pp. 631–637. Dipesh Chakrabarty, "The Muddle of Modernity," ibid., pp. 663–675. For an impassioned defense of modernity, as a culture of "self-reflection," see Richard Wolin, "Modernity: The Peregrinations of a Contested Historiographic Concept," in ibid., pp. 741–751. This debate's most stringent critic of modernity is medievalist historian Carol Symes. See her "When We Talk about Modernity," ibid., pp. 715–726.

16. See Afshin Matin-asgari's review of Kamran Matin, *Recasting Iranian Modernity* (London and New York: Routledge, 2013), in *Middle East Journal*, vol. 51, no. 4 (2015): pp. 680–685. Sanjay Subrahmanyam, "Connected Histories: Notes toward a Reconfiguration of Early Modern Eurasia" in *Modern Asian Studies*, vol. 3, no. 3 (July 1997): pp. 735–762; quoted on p. 745.

17. Ninan Smart, *Worldviews: Crosscultural Explorations of Human Beliefs* (New York: Charles Scribner's Sons, 1983), introduction. See also James W. Lane Meta-Religion: *Religion and* Power in World History (Oakland, CA: The University of California Press, 2014).

18. See Marx's "Toward the Critique of Hegel's Philosophy of Right" in Lewis S. Feuer, *Marx & Engels: Basic Writings in on Politics & Philosophy* (New York: Anchor Books, 1959), pp. 262–263; and Friedrich Engels, "On the History of Early Christianity," in ibid.,

pp. 168–194 and also Frederick Engels, *The Peasant War in Germany* (Moscow: Foreign Languages Publishing House, 1934).

19. See Afshin Matin-asgari, "The Impact of Imperial Russia and the Soviet Union on Qajar and Pahlavi Iran: Notes toward a Revisionist Historiography," in Stephanie Cronin, ed. *Iranian-Russian Encounters: Empires and Revolutions since 1800* (London and New York: Routledge, 2012), pp. 11–46. For a recent appreciation of Russian and Soviet impact on modern Iranian history see the essays in Rudi Matthee and Elena Andreeva, eds. *Russians in Iran: Diplomacy and Power in Iran in the Qajar Era and beyond* (London and New York: I. B. Tauris, 2018).

20. Marshall G.S. Hodgson, *The Venture of Islam* (Chicago, IL: The University of Chicago Press, 1974) recognized this in its designation of Islam as the most productive synthesis of Irano-Semitic civilizations. See Abbas Amanat and Farzin Vejdani, eds., *Facing Others: Iranian Identity Boundaries and Modern Political Cultures* (London and New York: Routledge, 2012). Clive Irving, *Crossroad of Civilization; 3000 years of Persian History* (London: Weidenfeld and Nicolson, 1979). Michael Axworthy, *A History of Iran: Empire of the Mind* (New York: Basic Books, 2008). On Iran as cultural bridge between civilizations see, for example, Dariush Shayegan, *Asia dar barabar-e gharb* (Tehran, 1977), pp. 186–187.

21. The chapter on the Constitutional Revolution, in Ervand Abrahamian's classic *Iran between Two Revolutions* (Princeton, NJ: Princeton University Press, 1982), opens with a section entitled "The Impact of the West." See pp. 50–52.

Lineages of Authoritarian Modernity: The Russo-Ottoman Model

1. Hassan Taqizadeh, *Khatabe-ye aqa-ye seyyed Hassan Taqizadeh* (Tehran, 1959), p. 18.

2. Edward Granville Browne, *The Persian Revolution of 1906–1909* (Washington, DC: Mage, 2006), p. xix.

3. Opening with a section titled "the Impact of the West," the chapter on the Iranian Constitutional Revolution, in Ervand Abrahamian's *Iran between Two Revolutions* (Princeton, NJ: Princeton University Press, 1982), mentions the precedence of Ottoman constitutionalism in passing. Ibid., pp. 50–52.

4. Afshin Marashi, "Paradigms of Iranian Nationalism: History, Theory and Historiography" in Kamran Scot Aghaie and Afshin Marashi eds., *Rethinking Iranian Nationalism and Modernity* (Austin, TX: University of Texas Press, 2014), pp. 3–24; quoted on p. 12.

5. Gherardo Gnoli, *The Idea of Iran: An Essay on Its Origin* (Rome: 1989), especially "conclusion." See also James W. Laine, *Meta-Religion: Religion and Power in World History* (Oakland, CA: The University of California Press, 2014). On Qajar political and territorial references to "Iran" see Mohammad Tavakoli-Targhi, "Historiography and Crafting Iranian National Identity," in Touraj Atabaki ed. *Iran in the 20th Century: Historiography and Political Culture* (London and New York: I. B. Tauris, 2009), pp. 5–22.

6. Afshin Matin-Asgari, "The Academic Debate on Iranian Identity," in Abbas Amanat and Farzin Vejdani, eds. *Facing Others: Iranian Identity Boundaries and Modern Political Cultures* (London and New York: Routledge, 2012), pp. 171–190. For broad comparisons of empires in world history see Walter Scheidel, ed. *Rome and China: Comparative Perspectives on Ancient World Empires* (Oxford and New York: Oxford University Press, 2009). See also, Beate Dignas and Engelbert Winter, *Rome and Persia in Late Antiquity: Neighbors and Rivals* (New York: Cambridge University Press, 2007). On new comparative studies of empires see, for example, Kimberly Kagan, ed. *The Imperial Moment* (Cambridge, MA and London: Harvard University Press, 2010).

7. Marshall G. S. Hodgson, *The Venture of Islam: Conscience and History in a World Civilization* (Chicago, IL: Chicago University Press, 1974), vol. I, introduction.

8. Clive Irving, *Crossroads of Civilizations: 3000 Years of Persian History* (London: Weidenfeld and Nicolson, 1979).

9. Parvaneh Pourshariati, *Decline and Fall of the Sasanian Empire: The Sasanian-Parthian Confederacy and the Arab Conquest of Iran* (London: I. B. Tauris, 2008).

10. Mohamad Tavakoli-Targhi, *Refashioning Iran*, pp. 80–84. Firoozeh Kashani-Sabet, "Fragile Frontiers: The Diminishing Domains of Qajar Iran." in *International Journal of Middle East Studies*, vol. 29 (1997): pp. 205–234; Mustafa Vaziri, *Iran as Imagined Nation* (New York: Paragon House, 1993), pp. 106–109, 121. Vaziri's book radically rejected assumptions of continuity in Iranian history, while overstating its case for the "borrowed" and "constructed" nature of modern Iranian nationalism. See Afshin Matin-Asgari's review of this book in *Iranian Studies*, vol. 28, nos. 3–5 (1995): pp. 260–263.

11. Quoted in Ann K. S. Lambton, *Qajar Persia: Eleven Studies* (Austin, TX: University of Texas Press, 1987), p. 319.

12. Jack P. Greene, "State Formation, Resistance, and the Creation of Revolutionary Traditions in the Early Modern Era," in Michael A. Morrison and Melinda Zook, eds. *Revolutionary Currents: Nation*

Building in the Transatlantic World (New York: Rowman and Littlefield, 2004), p. 3.

13. Jane Burbank and Frederik Copper, *Empires in World History: Power and the Politics of Difference* (Princeton, NJ: Princeton University Press, 2010).

14. Tapper, *Frontier Nomads of Iran: A Political and Social History of the Shahsevan* (New York: Cambridge University Press, 1997), pp. 101–112 and conclusion.

15. David Wasserstein, *The Rise and Fall of the Party-kings: Politics and Society in Islamic Spain 1002–1086* (Princeton, NJ: Princeton University Press, 1985), especially chapter 4. For a sophisticated overview of the historians' debate on the applicability of the concept of feudalism outside of Europe, including Iran, see Abbas Vali, *Pre-capitalist Iran: A Theoretical History* (New York: New York University Press, 1993), chapter 6.

16. Mary Elaine Hegland, *Days of Revolution: Political Unrest in an Iranian Village* (Stanford: Stanford University Press, 2014), especially her summary of the *taifeh* system in her introduction, pp. 8–18. For a brief discussion of *taifeh* see Gene R. Garthwaite, "Khan and Kings: The Dialectics of Power in Bakhtiyari History" in Michael E. Bonine and Nikki R. Keddie, eds. *Continuity and Change in Modern Iran* (New York: State University of New York Press, 1988), pp. 129–142, and Garthwaite, *Khans and Shahs: A Documentary Analysis of the Bakhtiyari in Iran* (New York: Cambridge University Press, 1983).

17. By the nineteenth century, the Iranian system of parceling out land assignments was called *Tuyul-dari*, a practice that the 1906 Constitution abolished. Janet Afary, *The Iranian Constitutional Revolution, 1906–1911: Grassroots Democracy, Social Democracy and the Origins of Feminism* (New York: Columbia University Press, 1996), p. 70.

18. Ann K. S. Lambton, *Qajar Persia: Eleven Studies* (Austin, TX: University of Texas Press, 1988), pp. x–xi.

19. For a comparable critique of Orientalist notions of "royal absolutism" and its presumed impact on retarding the development private property in Ottoman history, see Suraiya Faroqhi, *The Ottoman Empire and the World around It* (New York: I. B. Tauris 2004), introduction.

20. Anne Lambton quoted in Vali, *Pre-capitalist Iran*, p. 145.

21. Faroqhi, *The Ottoman Empire and the World around It*.

22. See Farzin Vejdani, *Making History in Iran: Education, Nationalism and Print Culture* (Stanford, CA: Stanford University Press, 2015), pp. 117–144, and Vanessa Martin, *The Qajar Pact: Bargaining, Protest and the State in Nineteenth-century Persia* (New York: I. B. Tauris, 2005).

23. Arash Khazeni, *Tribes and Empire on the Margins of Nineteenth-century Iran* (Seattle: University of Washington Press, 2009), quoted on p. 193, emphasis added.
24. Lambton, *Qajar Persia*, p. 279.
25. Mikhail Hanna, *Politics and Revelation: Mawardi and After* (Edinburgh: Edinburgh University Press, 1995). According to Ibn Khaldun's *Muqaddama*, after the tenth century, the Muslim world entered a new historical phase involving the decline of the ulema and the rise of the Sultanate based on secular "superiority and force." The sultan's kingly authority derived not from the sharia, but from "the nature of society and human existence." Quoted in Stephan Frederic Dale, *The Orange Tree of Marrakesh: Ibn Khaldun and the Science of Man* (Cambridge, MA: Harvard University Press, 2015), p. 213.
26. Crone, *God's Rule: Government in Islam* (New York: Columbia University Press, 2004), Epilogue and pp. 306, 394. See also, Crone, *Roman, Provincial and Islamic Law: The Origins of the Islamic Patronate* (New York: Cambridge University Press, 1987), conclusion. For a recent unconventional view on the origins of Islam see Karl-Heinz Ohlig, *Early Islam: A Critical Reconstruction Based on Contemporary Sources* (New York: Prometheus Books, 2013). This book's sweeping assertions, however, are mostly unconvincing.
27. Sami Zubaida, *Law and Power in the Islamic World* (New York: I. B. Tauris, 2005). On the secular features of Medieval Islamic polities see also Neguin Yavari, *Advice for the Sultan: Prophetic Vices and Secular Politics in Medieval Islam* (London: Hurst & Company, 2014).
28. According to recent studies, the Safavid Empire occupied a "middle ground" position between royal absolutism and total decentralization. See Rudi Matthee, Persia in Crisis: *Safavid Decline* and *the Fall of Isfahan* (London and New York: I. B. Tauris, 2012), p. xxxi. Also, Matthee, "Was Safavid Iran an Empire" in *Journal of the Economic and Social History of the Orient*, vol. 53, no. 1/2 (2010): pp. 233–265. For a new critical study of the rise of Shi'i establishment under the Safavids see Ali Rahnema, *Superstition as Ideology in Iranian Politics: From Majlesi to Ahmadinejad* (New York: Cambridge University Press, 2011).
29. Hamid Algar, *Religion and State in Iran, 1785–1906: The Role of the Ulema in the Qajar Period* (Berkeley, CA: University of California Press, 1969), especially the section on "Doctrinal Reassertion," pp. 33–44 and chapter III. See also Vanessa Martin, *Islam and Modernism: The Iranian Revolution of 1906* (London: I. B. Tauris, 1989), pp. 19–22. On high clerical support for Safavi shahs see Rahnema, *Superstition as Ideology in Iranian Politics*.
30. Algar, *Religion and State in Iran*, conclusion, pp. 257–260.

31. Lambton's analysis of the clergy's relation to social groups tends their strong ties to "townspeople." She mentions that peasants also had great respect for the ulema, although many mullahs were "charlatans" who went around the countryside collecting dues at harvest time. She admits that tribal people had less contact with ulema, although dervishes may have gone around among them. Lambton, *Qajar Persia*, 283.

32. Eric J. Hooglund, *Land and Revolution in Iran: 1960–1980* (Austin, TX: University of Texas Press, 1982), pp. 29–30.

33. Ernst Gellner, *Post-modernism, Reason and Religion* (New York: Routledge, 1982).

34. Taqizadeh in *Zendegi-ye Tufani*, quoted in Fariba Zariebaf, "From Istanbul to Tabriz: Modernity and Constitutionalism in the Ottoman Empire and Iran" in *Comparative Studies of South Asia, Africa and the Middle East*, vol. 28, no. 1 (2008): pp. 154–169, p. 156. On Taqizadeh, see also Manucher Bakhtiar, *Nehzat-e mashruteh va Naqsh-e taqizadeh* (Toronto: Pegah Publications, 2015). Though not a scholarly study, this two-volume work is a large compilation of primary and secondary sources.

35. Houri Berberian, "Nest of Revolution: The Caucasus, Iran, and Armenians" in Rudi Matthee and Elena Andreeva, eds. Russians in Iran: Diplomacy and Power in Iran in the Qajar *Era* and *beyond* (London and New York: I. B. Tauris, 2018): pp. 95–121. Quoted on p. 96.

36. Atabaki, "Constitutionalism in Iran and Its Asian Interdependencies," in *Comparative Studies of South Asia, Africa and the Middle East*, vol. 28, no. 1 (2008): pp. 142–153. Atabaki follows Dipesh Chakrabarty, *Provincializing Europe: Postcolonial Thought and Historical Difference* (Princeton, NJ: Princeton University Press, 2000).

37. Kamran Matin, *Recasting Iranian Modernity* (London and New York: Routledge, 2013), pp. 15–18. Matin revamps Trotsky's "Uneven and Combined Development" model into a grand theory of world history and international relations, where both spatial and temporal notions of totality, whether social, national or global, are shifting amalgams of variable parts, perpetually recombining, at all levels, to produce non-linear open-ended historical trajectories. See Afshin Matin-Asgari's review of *Recasting Iranian Modernity, Middle East Journal*, vol. 51, no. 4 (2015): pp. 680–685.

38. Nikki R. Keddie, *Modern Iran: Roots and Results of Revolution* (New Haven, CT: Yale University Press, 2003), pp. 66–67. Keddie has noted this point in her earlier works. Similar comparisons of Japan and Turkey go back to at least the 1960s. See, for example, Robert E. Ward and Dankwart A. Rostow, eds. *Political Modernization in Japan and*

Turkey (Princeton, NJ: Princeton University Press, 1964). See also Anja
Pistor Hatam, "Progress and Civilization in Nineteenth-century Japan:
The Far Eastern State as a Model for Modernization," in *Iranian
Studies*, vol. 29 (1996): pp. 111–127. I am grateful to Rudi Matthee
for recommending this last source.

39. Similar reactions, by Turkish, Egyptian, Indian and Chinese
intellectuals, to Japan's victory over Russia are noted and compared in
Cemil Aydin, *The Politics of Anti-Westernism in Asia: Visions of World
Order in Pan-Islamic and Pan-Asian Thought* (New York: Columbia
University Press, 2007), chapter 4. See also Pankaj Mishra, *From the
Ruins of Empire: The Intellectuals Who Remade Asia* (New York:
Farrar, Straus and Giroux, 2012), pp. 1–6. For an informed brief
reflection on the complexity of Japanese modernity see Carol Gluck,
"The End of Elsewhere: Writing Modernity Now" in *American
Historical Review*, vol. 116, no. 3 (June 2011): pp. 676–687.

40. Aydin, *The Politics of Anti-Westernism in Asia*. Constitutional Japan's
victory over absolutist Russia was much discussed and hailed in Young
Turk publications. See Sohrabi, *Revolution and Constitutionalism in the
Ottoman Empire and Iran* (New York: Cambridge University Press,
2011), pp. 75–78. See also Sohrabi's "Global Waves, Local Actors:
What the Young Turks Knew about Other Revolutions and Why It
Mattered" in *Comparative Studies in Society and History*, vol. 44, no.
1 (January 2002): pp. 45–79, noting great Young Turk enthusiasm for
Japan's victory over Russia being linked to Japan's constitutional
tradition,
pp. 53–57.

41. Mohammad Tavakoli-Targhi, "Historiography and Crafting Iranian
National Identity," and *Refashioning Iran*.

42. For studies of "Eastern" or Asian influences on Iranian modernity see
Monica M. Ringer, *Pious Citizens: Reforming Zoroastrianism in India
and Iran* (Syracuse, NY: Syracuse University Press, 2011) and Afshin
Marashi, "Imagining Hafiz: Rabindranath Tagore in Iran, 1932" in the
Journal of Persianate Studies vol. 3, no. 1 (June 2010): pp. 46–77. Both
studies show India's impact on Iranian modernity, whether via the Parsi
community or through intellectuals like Tagore, were rather marginal.

43. Firoozeh Kashani-Sabet, *Frontier Fictions: Shaping the Iranian Nation,
1804–1946* (Princeton, NJ: Princeton University Press, 1999).

44. Ali Gheissari, "Iran's Dialectic of the Enlightenment: Constitutional
Experience, Transregional Connections, and Conflicting Narratives of
Modernity" in Ali M. Ansari ed., *Iran's Constitutional Revolution of
1906: Narratives of the Enlightenment* (London: Gingko Library, 2016):
pp. 15–47. Recognizing Iran's "conflicting narratives of modernity,"

Gheissari traces their departure "routes," from Europe's Enlightenment to Iran, in India, the Caucasus, Istanbul and Ottoman Iraq. However, he does not emphasize the impact of Ottoman and Russian intellectual paradigms, nor does he discuss any decisive influence of Ottoman constitutionalism on its Iranian counterpart.

45. Fariba Zarinebaf, "From Istanbul to Tabriz: Modernity and Constitutionalism in the Ottoman Empire and Iran," p. 169.

46. As Rudi Matthee has pointed out to me, this is not the case in German. He cites, for example, Anja Pistor-Hatam, *Nachrichtenblatt, Informationsbörse und Diskussionsforum: Ahtar-e Estānbūl (1876–1896) – Anstöße zur frühen persischen Moderne* (Münster, 1999).

47. Zarinebaf, ibid., p. 155.

48. Said Amir Arjomand's *The Turban for the Crown: The Islamic Revolution in Iran* (New York: Oxford University Press, 1988) and his "Ideological Revolution in Shi'ism" in Arjomand ed. *Authority and Political Culture in Shi'ism*: (Albany: State University of New York, 1988), pp. 178–209. Nor does Arjomand's *Shadow of God and the Hidden Imam* (Chicago and London: University of Chicago Press, 1984) discuss the Ottoman impact on Iranian constitutionalism or the modernization of Shi'i thought. See also Vanessa Martin, *Islam and Modernism: The Iranian revolution of 1906* (London: I. B. Tauris, 1989). As in theses earlier works, the Ottoman impact on Iranian constitutionalist thought is absent in recent studies of Iranian constitutionalism and nationalism. Among the latter, see Kamran Scot Aghaie and Afshin Marashi, eds. *Modern Iranian Nationalism* and Touraj Atabaki ed. *Iran in the 20th Century: Historiography and Political Culture.* Houchang Chehabi and Vanessa Martin eds. *Iran's Constitutional Revolution: Popular Politics, Cultural Transformations, and Transnational Connections* (London and New York: I. B. Tauris, 2010), has a whole section on "transnational perspectives," analyzing the revolution's early twentieth-century unfolding, within a global perspective. But none of these chapters focus on the early impact of Young Ottoman thought on Iranian constitutionalism. The only chapter whose title suggests such a focus gets to the topic only on its very last page. See Charles Kurzman, "*Mashrutiyat, Mesrutiyet,* and Beyond: Intellectuals and the Constitutional Revolutions of 1905–12," pp. 277–290. Touraj Atabaki's comparative study of Turkish and Iranian nationalism focuses on close parallels, going back to the Ottoman and Qajar periods. See Touraj Atabaki and Eric J. Zurcehr, *Men of Order: Authoritarian Modernization under Ataturk and Reza Shah* (New York: I. B. Tauris, 2004). Atabaki notes how the discourse of Ottoman reform in the early nineteenth century had introduced concepts like

constitutionalism (*mashrutiyat*) and republicanism (*jumhuriyat*), with imprecise meanings, pp. 46–47. Nader Sohrabi *Revolution and Constitutionalism in the Ottoman Empire and Iran* notes intellectual connections of emerging Iranian and Ottoman-Turkish nationalism in passing, focusing primarily on comparing the political process of Young Turk and Iranian Constitutional Revolutions. Qajar historian, Abbas Amanat's *Encyclopedia Iranica* entry on the intellectual background of the Constitutional Revolution mentions the precedence of Ottoman constitutionalism. "Like some other key terms of the period, *masruta* can be traced to the Young Ottomans. Nameq Kemal had referred to constitutional government as *dawlat-e masruta* and a representational system under the auspices of Islam." Amanat, "Constitutional Revolution I. Intellectual Background," p. 170. www.Iraniaonline.org.

49. For an alternative to nationalist paradigms, emphasizing modernity's global context, see Kamran Matin, *Recasting Iranian Modernity*.

50. Hasan Taqizadeh, *Khatebe-ye aqa-ye seyyed Hasan Taqizadeh*, p. 18.

51. Fereydun Adamiyat, *Andisheh-ha-ye Mirza Aqa Khan Kermani* (Tehran: Payam, 1967), pp. 250–251.

52. Ibid., pp. 246–247.

53. Nader Sohrabi, *Revolution and Constitutionalism in the Ottoman Empire and Iran* notes how Qajar reforms largely followed the example of Ottoman modernization and constitutionalism, though the bulk of his book compares the "Young Turk Revolution" to Iran's Constitutional Revolution, i.e. events that were less similar or inter-related. See also Sohrabi, "Historicizing Revolution: Constitutional Revolutions in the Ottoman Empire, Iran, and Russia, 1905–1908," *American Journal of Sociology*, vol. 100, no. 6 (May 1995): pp. 1383–1447. This long and fairly comprehensive study focuses on the process and unfolding of these three revolutions, and not on their backgrounds. It has virtually nothing on the discourse of Islamic constitutionalism. "Here I am not concerned with the institutional history of constitutionalism" p. 1384. Sohrabi's "Global Waves, Local Actors: What the Young Turks Knew about Other Revolutions and Why It Mattered" in *Comparative Studies in Society and History*, vol. 44, no. 1(2002): pp. 45–79, notes that "the Young Turk Revolution of 1908 noted Islamic constitutionalism after seeing how, in the Iranian's case of 1906 revolution, it helped with popular mobilization. Thus they drew 'on the language of Islam and the 'invented' constitutional 'tradition' of Islam." Ibid., p. 46.

54. For a brief but fascinating study of this intellectual network see Touraj Atabaki, "Constitutionalism in Iran and Its Asian Dependencies" in *Comparative Studies of South Asia, Africa and the Middle East*, vol. 28,

no.1 (2008): pp. 142–153. See also Gheissari, "Iran's Dialectic of the Enlightenment: Constitutional Experience, Transregional Connections, and Conflicting Narratives of Modernity."

55. On Russia as the Ottomans' chief adversary as well as modernization model see M. Sukru Hanioglu, *A Brief History of the Late Ottoman Empire* (Princeton, NJ: Princeton University Press, 2010), pp. 42–44 and Karen Barkey, *Empire of Difference: The Ottomans in Comparative Perspective* (New York: Cambridge University Press, 2008), pp. 268–269.

56. Mirza Saleh Shirazi, *Gozaresh-e safar-e Mirza Saleh-e Shirazi* (Tehran, 1983), quoted on pp. 131, 138. For a fascinating new study of Mirza Saleh and a few other Iranian travelers in early-nineteenth-century England see Nile Green, *The Love of Strangers: What Six Muslim Students Learned in Jane Austen's London* (Princeton and Oxford: Princeton University Press, 2016).

57. Ottoman fascination with modern technology, especially its military application, had begun with figures like Ibrahim Muteferrika, a mid-level administrator who, in 1727 obtained clerical approval for introducing the printing press into the empire. In 1731, Muteferrika published a treatise on how to make the Ottoman government as strong as its European rivals. While it mentioned European political systems, the book's basic recommendation was to combine military modernization with an innate Ottoman proclivity for orderliness. Nizai Berkes, *The Development of Secularism in Turkey* (Montreal: McGill University Press, 1964), pp. 36–45.

58. A translation movement started with selections from authors like Voltaire, Montesquieu and Fenelon, often read as advocates of enlightened despotism. It was soon complemented by interest in popular French novelists, especially Victor Hugh, Alexander Duma, Moliere, and Jules Vernes. Berkes, *The Development of Secularism in Turkey*, pp. 175, 199–200, 278.

59. Sukru Haniuglu, *Ataturk: An Intellectual Biography* (Princeton, NJ: Princeton University Press, 2011), pp. 33–35.

60. Berkes, *The Development of Secularism in Turkey*, pp. 203, 205–206. Hanioglu agrees with Berkes, adding that some kind of representative government had gradually emerged in various semi-independent parts of Ottoman Empire during the nineteenth century, including Serbia (1805), Rumania (1866), Mount Lebanon (1864), Egypt (1866) and in Tunis, which in 1861, became the first Muslim country with a constitution, while still part of Ottoman Empire. Ottoman constitutionalists would argue: "Montenegro, Serbia, and Egypt each have [representative] councils ... Are we at a lower level of culture than even the savages of

Montenegro?" Or: "Even Greece has a [constitution] and parliament." Hanioglu, *A Brief History of the Late Ottoman Empire*, pp. 113–114.

61. Berkes, *The Development of Secularism in Turkey*, pp. 209–218; quoted on p. 218.

62. The assimilation of Shi'ism to constitutionalism by Iranian clerics, such as Na'ini, followed Ottoman Sunni precedent argued in texts such as the 1876 *Principles of Constitutionalism (usul-u mesruta)*. According to this book, constitutional governments were based on fundamental laws. But the Ottoman Empire was an Islamic state whose fundamental law was the shari'a. Unfortunately, the book argued, the non-observance of the shari'a had turned the Ottoman state into an absolute monarchy, which obviously was contrary to Islam. The solution therefore was to restore the shari'a as Ottoman fundamental law, implemented through an assembly representing the Islamic umma. This assembly would not legislate, but supervise the implementation of shari'a-based laws by an imperial administration headed by the Sultan-Caliph. Such a regime was fully compatible with the Ottoman-Islamic tradition and not an imitation of European political systems. Berkes, ibid., 240–241.

63. For a good discussion of the Ottoman Constitution's adaptation to Islam see Hanioglu, *A Brief History of the Late Ottoman Empire*, pp. 114–121.

64. Berkes, *The Development of Secularism in Turkey*, pp. 244–247.

65. Ibid., 232.

66. Hanioglu, *A Brief History of the Late Ottoman Empire*, p. 117.

67. Berkes, *The Development of Secularism in Turkey*, pp. 233–234.

68. Ibid., pp. 217, 228 and 233–234, 261.

69. Mohammad-Amin Rasulzadeh, *Gozaresh-ha'i az enqelab-e mashrutiyat-e Iran* (Tehran: Shirazeh, 2016), Rahim Ra'isnia, trans. p. 57.

70. "Iranian enlightenment" is the title of a chapter in Ali M. Ansari, *The Politics of Nationalism in Modern Iran* (Cambridge: Cambridge University Press, 2012). Ahmad Kasravi's *Tarikh-e mashrute-ye Iran* (Tehran, 1940) begins with a chapter titled: "How the Iranians awakened"; Mohammad Nazem al-Islam's Kermani, *Tarikh-e bidari-ye Iranian* [The History of Iranian Awakening] (Tehran, 1910). Fereydun Adamiyat, *Ideolozhi-ye nehzat-e mashrutiat-e Iran* (Tehran: Payam, 1974). See also Maryam B. Sanjabi, "Rereading the Enlightenment: Akhundzada and His Voltaire," in *Iranian Studies*, vol. 28, nos. 1–2 (1995): pp. 39–60.

71. Fereydun Adamiyat, quoted in Lotfollah Ajudani, *Roshanfekran-e Iran dar asr-e mashrutiyat* (Tehran: Akhtaran, 2008), p. 27.

72. Mehrdad Kia, "Pan-Islamism in Late Nineteenth-century Iran" in *Middle Eastern Studies*, vol. 32, no. 1 (January 1996): pp. 30–52, p. 33.
73. Ibid., pp. 39–48.
74. Abbas Amanat, "Memory and Amnesia in the Historiography of the Constitutional Revolution" in Touraj Atabaki ed. *Iran in the 20th Century*, pp. 23–54; quoted on pp. 31–32.
75. Zarinehbaf, "*Az estanbul ta Tabriz*" in *Iran Nameh*, vol. XXIII, nos. 3–4 (Fall–Winter 2007): pp. 305–332.
76. Quoted in Ajudani, *Roshanfekran-e Iran*, p. 51.
77. Nader Sohrabi, *Revolution and Constitutionalism in the Ottoman Empire and Iran*, pp. 302–303.
78. Quoted in Ajudani, *Roshanfekran-e Iran*, pp. 42, 43.
79. James D. Clark, *Provincial Concerns: A History of the Iranian Province of Azerbaijan, 1848–1906* (Costa Mesa, CA: Mazda, 2006), pp. 133–138. By the late nineteenth century, 1888, there was a large Iranian Azeri merchant community in Istanbul, whose Iranian residents were estimated at about 16,000. There were about 10,000 Iranians in Anatolia. Many of these Iranians had become Ottoman subjects and some joined political parties such as the C. U. P. See Farbiba Zarinebaf, "The Iranian (Azeri) Merchant Community in the Ottoman Empire and the Constitutional Revolution" in *Les Iraniens d'Istanbul*, pp. 203–212. Also, Khan Malek Sasani, *Yadbudha-ye sefarat-e Estanbul* (Tehran, 1966): pp. 94–100.
80. Ali Kalirad, *Az jame-ye Irani ta mihan-e Turki*, p. 76.
81. Hasan Taqizadeh, *Khatabe*, p. 45. According to Taqizadeh, during the 1906 convening of Iran's first Majlis, the shah claimed the Majlis was officially "*adalat-kahneh*" and the new government was "*mashru'eh*" (*shar'i*), and not *mashruteh* (constitutional). Mashhadi Baqer, a representative of shop-keepers (*baqal*), objected strongly to accepting anything other than *mashruteh*. Moreover, Taqizadeh cites a Tabriz mujtahid, Aqa Mirza Sadeq, who recommended the adoption in Persian of the French/English term "constitution," which had a direct and unambiguous reference to its original European context, whereas the adoption of the Arabic term *mashruteh* would pass the authority of interpretation to the ulema, who would then turn it into a form of government contingent on their own approval and the lack of freedom to choose. Ibid., pp. 53–54.
82. The most famous associates of Sa'adat were Ali-Akbar Dehkhoda, Yahya Dowlatabadi, Ahamd Aqaoglu and Hossein Kazemzadeh. See Taqizadeh, *Khatabe*, p. 100. Nader Entekhabi, *Nasionlaism va tajaddod dar Iran va Torkieh* (Tehran: Negareh, 2011), pp. 208–211. See also John Gurney, "E. G. Browne and the Iranian Community in

Istanbul," in Thierry Zarcone and Fariba Zarinebafe, eds. *Les Iraniens d'Istanbul* (Istanbul and Tehran, 1993), pp. 149–175, and Thierry Zarcone, "*Ali Akbar Dihkhuda et le journal Surush d'Istanbul* (Juin-November 1909)" in *Les Iraniens d'Istanbul*, pp. 243–251; and Farbiba Zrinebaf, "The Iranian (Azeri) Merchant Community in the Ottoman Empire and the Constitutional Revolution" in *Les Iraniens d'Istanbul*, pp. 203–212.

83. Azeri intellectuals, including Taqizadeh, Hosein Kazemzadeh (Iranshar), Rezazadeh Shafaq, Ja'far Pishevari, Taqi Arani, Ahmad Kasravi, were leading figures in the first generation of Iranian nationalist and Marxist thinkers. Moreover, the entire leadership of the Communist Party of Iran (1920s–1930s) was formed by Azeri intellectuals. See Kaveh Bayat, *Panturkism va Iran* (Tehran, 2008), p. 114. On Azeri domination of the Communist Party see Abrahamian, *Iran between Two Revolutions*, pp. 132–133.

84. Holland Shissler's "Afterword" to Ahmet Midhat, *Felatun Bey and Rakim Efendi*, trans. Meliheh Levi and Monica M. Ringer (New York: Syracuse University Press, 2016), pp. 149–159. On alafranga versus alaturka see also See Aydin, *The Politics of Anti-Westernism in Asia: Visions of World Order in Pan-Islamic and Pan-Asian Thought*, pp. 42–43 and Hanioglu, *Ataturk*, pp. 12–19.

85. On Belinski and Herzen see Philip Pomper, *The Russian Revolutionary Intelligentsia* (New York: Crowell, 1970), pp. 44–49 and Nicolas Berdyaev, *The Russian Idea* (Boston: Beacon Press, 1962). On the relation of militaristic and technological modernization to long term patterns of "siege mentality" in Russian, including Soviet, history see Arnold J. Toynbee and G. R. Urban, *Toynbee on Toynbee* (New York: Oxford University Press, 1974), pp. 72–76.

86. Isaiah Berlin, *Russian Thinkers* (New York: The Viking Press, 1978), 117.

87. Hamid Dabashi, "The Poetics of Politics: Commitment in Modern Persian Literature," in *Iranian Studies*, vol. 18, nos. 2–4 (1985): pp. 147–188, 155. Historian Mangol Bayat reproduces Berlin's passage verbatim to explain Iran's modern revolutionary messianic movements. Nineteenth-century Iranian reformers, she writes, "thought of themselves as united by something more than mere interest in ideas; they conceived themselves as being a dedicated, special class of Perfect Men, devoted to spreading a new revelation ... Their thought, in spirit if not in content, represented a secularized form of the quest for the True Prophet." Mangol Bayat's *Mysticism and Dissent: Socioreligious Thought in Qajar Iran* (Syracuse, NY: Syracuse University Press, 1982), p. 175.

88. Memoirs of Etemad al-Saltaneh, quoted in Fereydun Adamiyat, *Feker-e azadi va moqaddameh-e nehzat mashrutiyat-e Iran* (Tehran: Payam, 1961), p. 8.

89. See Amanat, "Memory and Amnesia in the Historiography of the Constitutional Revolution." On the longer history of Iran's messianic religious movements see Abbas Amanat, *Apocalyptic Islam and Iranian Shi'ism* (London and New York: I. B. Tauris, 2009). See also Mangol Bayat, "The *Rowshanfekr* in the Constitutional Period: An Overview" in Chehabi and Martin, eds. *Iran's Constitutional Revolution: Popular Politics, Cultural Transformations, and Transnational Connections* (London and New York: I. B. Tauris, 2010): pp. 165–191. As both historians show the boundaries between "free thinkers," secular radicals, and the religious heterodoxy were rather blurry. Significantly, and unlike Baha'is, the followers of Sobh-e Azal did not develop an established religious doctrine or organization. Therefore labels like "Azali" or "Babi" do not signify clear ideological or doctrinal orientation. On the significance of Babi participation in the Constitutional movement see also Seyyed Meqdad Nabavi-Tabrizi, *Tarkih-e Maktum* (Tehran: Shirazeh, 2014). This source emphasizes Babi presence in the constitutional movement's intellectual leadership, without addressing the problem of what Babism meant religiously.

90. Zarinebafe, *Les Iraniens d'Istanbul*, p. 155.

91. Rasulzadeh, *Gozaresh-ha'i az enqelab-e mashrutiyat-e Iran*, pp. 36–49.

92. Ibid., p. 57.

93. Ibid., p. 219.

94. Hasan Taqizadeh, *Zendegi-e Tufani* (Tehran, 1993), pp. 465–468.

95. For a brief biography of Aqaoglu, see Entekhabi, *Nasionalism va tajaddod*, pp. 222–223. Aqaoglu later helped draft the 1924 Constitution of Turkish Republic. He taught law at Ankara University and served as a member of the Turkish parliament, but was removed from both positions and marginalized after his 1930 joining of a new liberal party Ataturk allowed to function briefly for three months. See ibid. The most comprehensive study of Aqaoglu in Persian is Ali Kalirad, *Az jame'-ye Irani ta mihan-e Turki* (Tehran: Shirazeh, 2014).

96. This is noted recently in Iran, for example in Kalirad, *Az jame-ye Irani ta mihan-e Turki*, pp. 46–48, 52–54, 70–72.

97. Holland Ada Shissler, *Between Two Empires: Ahmed Agaoglu and the New Turkey* (New York: I. B. Tauris, 2003), pp. 82–87.

98. Ibid., p. 47.

99. Kia, "Pan-Islamism in Late Nineteenth-century Iran," in p. 36.

100. *Qanun*, no. 9, 1890; quoted in Abbas Amanat, "Constitutional Revolution I. Intellectual Background," p. 164. www.Iraniaonline.org.
101. *Qanun*, no. 12 in Ajudani, *Roshanfekran-e Iran dar asr-e mashrutiyat*, p. 57.
102. Adamiyat, *Feker-e azadi*, p. 58, quoted in Hamid Algar, *Religion and State in Iran*, p. 170.
103. Kia, "Pan-Islamism in Late Nineteenth-century Iran," pp. 37–38.
104. The date is not precise. Adamiayt, *Ideolozhi-ye nehzat-e mashrutiyat-e Iran*, p. 30.
105. Ibid.
106. Ibid., p. 32.
107. On dissimulation *(taqiya)* in the historiography of Constitutional Revolution see Amanat "Memory and Amnesia in the Historiography of the Constitutional Revolution," p. 23. Also, Bayat, *Mysticism and Dissent*, p. 172.
108. Mashallah Ajudani, *Mashrute-ye Irani* (Tehran: Akhtaran, 2004), p. 424. See also the conclusion. Historians of the Constitutional Revolution, however, differ on their estimation of this kind of dissimulation. Mansureh Ettehadieh, for example, considers the pretense of social democracy's compatibility to Islam as dictated by expediency. See Ettehadieh, *Peydayesh va tahavvol-e ahzab-e sisasi-ye mashrutiat* (Tehran: Siamak, 2002), pp. 118–124. Khosrow Shakeri, on the other hand, sees this tactic of social democrats as harmful. Shakeri, *Pishineha-ye eqtesadi-ejetma'i-ye jonbesh-e mashrutiat va enkeshaf-e sosial demokrasi* (Tehran: Akhtaran, 1995), pp. 214–219.
109. Sohrabi argues that about a century of intellectual and institutional modernization eventually clarified the "semantic ambiguity" of Ottoman Islamic constitutionalism. Sohrabi, *Revolution and Constitutionalism in the Ottoman Empire and Iran*, pp. 44–45. See also Ami Ayalon, *Language of Change in the Arab Middle East: The Evolution of Modern Arabic Political Discourse* (New York: Oxford University Press, 1987).
110. This absence continues in a recent study of Khorasani's life and ideas. Mateo Frazaneh, *The Iranian Constitutional Revolution and the Clerical Leadership of Khurasani* (Syracuse, NY: Syracuse University Press, 2015).
111. Vanessa Martin, *Islam and Modernism: The Iranian Revolution of 1906*, pp. 65–66. On page 30: "He was one of the first *mujtahids* to turn to Western political thought for solution." Ibid.
112. Ibid., pp. 180, 183–185.
113. Sohrabi, *Revolution and Constitutionalism in the Ottoman Empire and Iran*, p. 399.

114. Mohammad Mehdi Khalaji, "*Naqd-e daruni-ye ruhaniyat: gozaresh-e resalehi dar sekularizm*" in *Iran Nameh*, vol. XXI, no. 4 (Winter 2004): pp. 489–512.

115. Ibid., 493–495. Zanjani concludes: "The more I probed into the foundations of Islam and the truth of its ordinances, the more clearly I saw nothing left of religion but a name serving some to enjoy the good life, enrich themselves, and heap various impositions on ignorant masses," pp. 496–497.

116. See Chapter 9, "Constitutionalism according to Clerics" in Adamiyat, *Ideolozhi-ye nehzat-e mashrutiat-e Iran*, pp. 226–227. Janet Afary, *The Iranian Constitutional Revolution, 1906–1911: Grassroots Democracy, Social Democracy and the Origins of Feminism* (New York: Columbia University Press, 1996), p. 23. Sohrabi, *Revolution and Constitutionalism in the Ottoman Empire and Iran*, mentions Caucasian revolutionaries in passing, p. 404.

117. According to Amanat, Browne wrote the Constitutional Revolution's "master narrative." Amanat, "Memory and Amnesia in the Historiography of the Constitutional Revolution," p. 24.

118. In a letter to Taqizadeh, dated January 28, 1910, Browne mentions having recently received and read parts of *Tarikh-i bidari*, which he calls "really a very good and useful book." Abbas Zaryab and Iraj Afshar, *Nameha-ye Taqizadeh* (Tehran, 1354), p. 30.

119. On the activities of the "Persia Committee" see *Nameha-ye Taqizadeh*, pp. 23, 43–44, 49.

120. Browne, *The Persian Revolution*, preface, p. xiii.

121. Ali Ansari, *The Politics of Nationalism in Modern Iran* (London: Cambridge University Press, 2012), p. 52. Ansari also finds, in the 1906 Iranian constitution, allusions to "the U. S. declaration of independence." Ibid.

122. Amanat, "Memory and Amnesia in the Historiography of the Constitutional Revolution," pp. 41–42.

123. Afary, *The Iranian Constitutional Revolution*, p. 229 and Browne, *The Persian Revolution*, p. 339.

124. This is attributed to an unnamed contemporary source. Browne, *The Persian Revolution*, p. 23.

125. Browne, *The Persian Revolution*, p. 123.

126. Afary also notes deliberate erasure and distortion of Constitutional Revolution, including by Taqizadeh, in her last chapter, *The Iranian Constitutional Revolution*, pp. 341–342.

127. Taqizadeh, *Zendegi-e Tufani*, pp. 452–454.

128. Amanat, "Memory and Amnesia in the Historiography of the Constitutional Revolution," p. 52.

129. Nikki R. Keddie, *Religion and Rebellion in Iran: The Tobacco Protest of 1891–92* (London: Frank Cass, 1966), p. 15, quoted in Afary, *The Iranian Constitutional Revolution*, p. 28. On the origins of the "paradox" of ulema leadership of the Constitutional Revolution and of the ulema-state conflict in Iranian history, see Ann K. S. Lambton, "Quis Custodiet Custodes: Some Reflections on the Persian Theory of Government," in *Studia Islamica*, vol. 5 (1956): pp. 125–148; and (1965): pp. 125–146; and "The Persian Ulema and Constitutional Reform" in T. Fahd, ed. *Le Shi'ism imamate* (Paris, 1970), pp. 245–269; and The Persian Constitutional Revolution of 1905–06," in P. J. Vatikiotis, ed. *Revolutions in the Middle East* (London, 1972). Lambton's writings on the subject are gathered in her *Qajar Persia: Eleven Studies* (Austin, TX: University of Texas Press, 1988), chapters 8–11. See also Nikki R. Keddie, "Religion and Irreligion in Early Iranian Nationalism," in *Comparative Studies in Society and History*, vol. 4 (1962): pp. 266–295; and *Religion and Rebellion in Iran*; and *Iran: Religion, Politics and Society* (London, 1980). For a good overview of this topic see Shaul Bakhash, "Iran" in *American Historical Review*, vol. 5 (1991): pp. 1479–1496.

130. Keddie mentions Taqizadeh, among the sources she had "conversations and correspondence" with, for example in the preface to her *An Islamic Response to Imperialism: Political and Religious Writings of Sayyid Jamal ad-Din "al-Afghani"* (Berkeley, CA: University of California Press, 1983), p. xii. This book was first published in 1968.

131. Almost immediately, the Browne "paradox" echoed in another highly influential contemporary source, W. Morgan Shuster's *The Strangling Persia* (New York: The Century Company, 1912). See Shuster's remarks, for example, on p. 192. Shuster also reports a bread riot, which he portrays as a revolutionary demonstration by women. He also writes of "secret societies" without source verification; pp. 192–193.

The Berlin Circle: Crafting the Worldview of Iranian Nationalism

* A version of this chapter appeared in Kamran Scot Aghaie and Afshin Marashi, *Rethinking Iranian Nationalism and Modernity* (Austin, TX: University of Texas Press, 2014). This chapter is expanded with new material from primary and secondary sources, adding also new arguments and analysis.

1. Afshin Marashi, *Nationalizing Iran: Culture, Power and the State* (Seattle and London: The University of Washington Press, 2008), p. 53. See also Stephanie Cronin, *Soldiers, Shahs and Subalterns in Iran: Opposition,*

Protest and Revolt, 1921–1941 (New York: Palgrave Macmillan, 2010), pp. 4–5 on what she calls the "catastrophic perspective" on the World War I historiography. The label "period of disintegration" is used in Oliver Bast, "Disintegrating the 'Discourse of Disintegration': Some Reflections on the Historiography of the Late Qajar Period and Iranian *Cultural Memory*" in Touraj Atabaki ed. *Iran in the 20th Century: Historiography and Political Culture* (London and New York: I. B. Tauris, 2009), pp. 55–68. Especially pp. 61–65.

2. Touraj Atabaki, ed. *Iran and the First World War: Battleground of the Great Powers* (London: I. B. Tauris: 2006); Mohammad Gholi Majd, *The Great Famine and Genocide in Persia, 1917–1919* (Lanham, MD: University Press of America, 2003); and Mohammad Gholi Majd, *Persia in World War I and Its Conquest by Great Britain* (Lanham, MD: University Press of America, 2003). On the strengths and weakness of Majd's historiography see Stephanie Cronin's review of *Persia in World War I and Its Conquest by Great Britain*, *Iranian Studies*, vol. 37, no. 4 (December 2004): pp. 721–723.

3. Abbas Amanat, "Memory and Amnesia in the Historiography of the Constitutional Revolution" in Touraj Atabaki ed. *Iran in the 20th Century: Historiography and Political Culture* (London and New York: I. B. Tauris, 2009), p. 25.

4. Marashi, *Nationalizing Iran*, p. 53.

5. Half a century later, Taqizadeh still argued that, excepting outlawed communist organizations, Social Democrats and Social Conservatives were the only examples in Iran of "national political parties in a strict Western sense." Hasan Taqizadeh, *Khatabe-ye aqa-ye Seyyed Hsan Taqizadeh* (Tehran, 1959), pp. 116–117.

6. Jamshid Behnam, "Taqizadeh va mas'ale-ye tajddod," *Iran Nameh*, vol. xxi, nos. 1–2 (spring–summer 2003): pp. 77–89. Quoted on p. 79.

7. For a brief description of these two parties and their formation, see Mohammad-Taqi Bahar, *Tarikh-e mokhtasar-e ahzab-e sisai-e Iran* (Tehran, 1978), pp. 8–10. See also Khosrow Shakeri, *Pishineha-ye eqtesadi-ejetma'i-ye jonbesh-e mashrutiayt va enkeshaf-e sosial demokrasi* (Tehran, 1995), pp. 265–269; and Mansureh Ettehaddieh, *Peydayesh va tahavvol-e ahzab-e siasi-ye mashrutiyat* (Tehran, 1992), pp. 309–347. Ettehadieh notes how Social Moderates appealed to the evolutionary socialism of Edward Bernstein, pp. 346–347. Eric Hooglund notes Democrats of Second Majles were the first party proposing land reform in Iran. See his *Land and Revolution in Iran, 1960–1980* (Austin, TX: University of Texas Press, 1982), pp. 37–38.

8. Ettehadieh, *Peydayesh va tahavvol-e ahzab-e siasi-ye mashrutiyat*, p. 311.

9. Janet Afary, *The Iranian Constitutional Revolution, 1906–1911: Grassroots Democracy, Social Democracy and the Origins of Feminism* (New York: Columbia University Press, 1996), pp. 242–247.

10. Marashi, *Nationalizing Iran,* p. 49.

11. Nancy Bisaha, *Creating East and West: Renaissance Humanists and the Ottoman Turks* (Philadelphia: University of Pen Press, 2004), Epilogue, especially p. 183. See also Walter D. Mingolo, *The Darker Side of the Renaissance: Literacy, Territoriality and Colonization* (Ann Arbor: University of Michigan, 1994). Edward Said, *Orientalism* (New York: Vantage Books, 1979).

12. Nina Berman, *German Literature on the Middle East* (Ann Arbor, MI: The University of Michigan Press, 2011), chapters 1–2.

13. Suzanne Marchand, *German Orientalism in the Age of Empire: Religion, Race and Scholarship* (New York: Cambridge University Press, 2009). Late Nineteenth-century German "Islamic studies" was a departure from older patterns of German philological and philosophical interest in Oriental texts toward more systematic scholarly interest in contemporary Asia and the Middle East, coinciding with Imperial Germany's geopolitical and potentially colonial interests. See Ursula Wokoeck, *German Orientalism: The Study of the Middle East and Islam from 1899 to 1945* (London & New York: Routledge, 2009), pp. 90–91, 164–167.

14. Norbert Elias, *The Civilizing Process* (New York: Urizen Books, 1978), Edmond Jeffcott, trans., vol. I, p. 5. Todd Curtis Kontje, *German Orientalisms* (Ann Arbor, MI: The University of Michigan Press, 2004), p. 7.

15. Herder condemned ancient Roman and modern European empire-builders, the latter referring particularly to the French, whose universal notions of civilization seeks to dissolve the distinction and autonomy of distinct cultures, such as that of the Germans. Based on such views, Herder, along with major Enlightenment figures like Kant and Diderot, may be seen as "anti-imperialists" since they opposed Europe's empire-builders and their domination of non-European peoples and cultures. See Sankar Muthu, *Enlightenment against Empire* (Princeton, NJ: Princeton University Press, 2003), conclusion.

16. Michael C. Carhart, *The Science of Culture in Enlightenment Germany* (Cambridge, MA and London: Harvard University Press, 2007) and particularly the section on Herder in Chapter 2. Patrick Geary, *Before France and Germany: The Creation and Transformation of the Merovingian World* (New York: Oxford University Press, 1988), p. 42. On early Germans, see Chapter II.

17. Kontje, *German Orientalisms,* p. 35.

18. Kontje, *German Orientalisms*, pp. 64–77, 82–83, 121. See also Rudi Matthee, "The Imaginary Realm: Europe's Enlightenment Image of Early Modern Iran," in *Comparative Studies of South Asia, Africa and the Middle East*, vol. 30, no. 3 (2010): pp. 449–462, quoted on p. 457.

19. Raymond Schwab, *Oriental Renaissance: Europe's Rediscovery of India and the East, 1680–1880* (New York: Columbia University Press, 1984), Gene Patterson-Black and Victor Reinking trans. See Chapter 1.

20. Schwab, *Oriental Renaissance*, pp. 427–429, quoted on p. 427.

21. Schwab, *Oriental Renaissance*, pp. 435–437; Ali M. Ansari, *The Politics of Nationalism in Modern Iran* (Cambridge: Cambridge University Press, 2012), introduction, pp. 12–14.

22. Marashi, *Nationalizing Iran*, p. 53.

23. Kontje, *German Orientalisms*, pp. 108–109. Stefan Arvidsson, *Aryan Idols: Indo-European Mythology as Ideology and Science* Sonia Wichmann, trans. (Chicago, IL: The University of Chicago Press, 2006). Matthee, "The Imaginary Realm: Europe's Enlightenment Image of Early Modern Iran," p. 459.

24. Kemal H. Karapat, *The Politicization of Islam: Reconstructing Identity, State, Faith, and Community in the Late Ottoman State* (Oxford and New York: Oxford University Press, 2001), p. 121.

25. Baqer Aqeli, *Ruzshomar-e tarikh-e Iran: Az mashruteh ta enqelab-e eslami* (Tehran, 1990), vol. 1, pp. 79–81. On pro-German sympathies among Iran's nationalist elite, especially influential literary figures, see Yahya Ariyanpur, *Az Saba ta Nima*, vol. 2 (Tehran, 2002), pp. 319–329. See also Khan-Malek Sasani, *Yadbudha-ye sefarat-e Estanbul* (Tehran, 1966), pp. 27–37. According to one source, the alternate "national government" (*dowlat-e melli*) was able to mobilize up to 10,000 armed men. Abbas Khaksar, *Ta'amoli dar enqelab-e mashrute-ye Iran* (Tehran, 2015), p. 108. See also pp. 93–107.

26. Members also included Esmail Amirkhizi (social democrat), Mahmud Ashrafzadeh, Abolhasan Alavi, Ebrahim Alizadeh, Habibollah Sheybani (social democrat gendarmerie officer), Soleiman Meykadeh (former minister), Hasan Kazazi (social democrat) and Mahmud Ghanizadeh (social democrat poet). Iraj Afshar, ed. *Zendegi-e tufani: khaterat-e seyyed Hasan Taqizadeh* (Tehran, 1993), pp. 181–185 and 479–484. On the links between the Iranian and Indian committees see Mohammd-baqer Nozar, "*Naqsh-e komite-ye melliyun-e hendi dar sheklgiri-ye komite-ye melliyun-e Irani dar Berlin*," *Faslnameh motaleta-e tarikhi* vol. 6, no. 23 (winter 2009), pp. 47–59. See also, Isle Itscherenska, "*Taqizadeh dar Alman-e Qeysari*," *Iran Nameh*, vol. xxi, nos. 1–2 (spring–summer 2003). This is a Persian translation of a German article using German government archival material.

27. Itscherenska, *"Taqizdaeh dar alman-e Qeysari,"* pp. 185–186.
28. Jamshid Behnam, *Berlaniha* (Tehran: Farzan, 2000), p. 61.
29. On this generation, Behnam writes:

> Most of the first generation stayed social democrats committed to Enlightenment ideas. They had come to Berlin as nationalist and constitutionalist followers of a Social Democratic party. Their cooperation with Germans was for the cause of Iranian freedom and not German expansionism.
>
> *Berlaniha*, p. 61.

30. *Kaveh*, vol. 1, no. 1, pp. 1–5. All references to *Kaveh* are from its complete series reprinted by *Nashr-e vis* (Tehran, n.d.).
31. *Kaveh*, vol. 1, no. 2, p. 3 and quoted on p. 8.
32. *Kaveh*, vol. 1, no.1, p. 4. Mohammad-Ali Foroughi had already proposed adopting the banner of Kaveh as the national flag of Iran. See Tavakoli-Targhi, "Historiography" in Touraj Atabaki ed. *Iran in the 20th Century*, p. 11. Ahmad Kasravi, *Tarikhche-ye shir va khorshid* (Tehran, n.d.) traces the origin of the Lion-Sun combination to a flag belonging to the Seljuks of Rum, adopted by the Safavids and later by the Qajars, who added a sword.
33. On Taqizadeh's collusion with the political mission of Mann and Beck in *Kaveh,* see Isle Itscherenska, *"Taqizdaeh dar alman-e Qeysari."*
34. *Kaveh*, vol. 1, no. 25, pp. 12–14. Marashi cites some of these passages in more condensed translation and identifies Taqizadeh as the author. See *Nationalizing Iran*, p. 81. Interestingly, Taqizadeh thought very differently when it came to Turkish nationalism and pan-Turkism. He wrote:

> Those who know about the strange notion of Pan-Turkism or Pan-Turanism . . . may not be aware that the strange ludicrous idea of reviving Chengiz Khan's empire, exonerating the Mongols from all blemish, and exaggerating the Turks' historical glories . . . mostly originated in a fiction-like book, written by a French Jew and translated into Turkish during the early years of the Ottoman Constitutional Revolution . . . The wretched Ottoman public, and their shallow vainglorious elite, trusted Mr. Leon Cahun as a great European scholar and philosopher, seizing his every word and swallowing his exaggerated arguments. Thus, belief in a great Turanian race was scientifically established, as it was supposedly "attested to by Europeans, particularly by the famous Cahun," and also because it agreed with their own [Turkish] egoism. This belief then spread like cholera, affecting the Caucasus and Turkistan. From an article Taqizadeh wrote in the 1920s, quoted in Kaveh Bayat, *Pan Tutkism va Iran* (Tehran: Shirazeh, 2008), pp. 8–9.

35. He is also quite cynical toward European imperialism and modern politics in general. See Iraj Afshar, ed. *Nameha-ye Qazvini beh Taqizadeh* (Tehran, 1973), pp. 174–176. On Qazvini's critique of Orientalism see also Farzin Vejdani, *Making History in Iran: Education, Nationalism and Print Culture* (Stanford, CA: Stanford University Press, 2015), pp. 155–156.
36. *Nameha-ye Qazvini*, p. 106.
37. Ibid., pp. 103–108.
38. *Kaveh*, vol. 1, no. 22, pp. 1–2.
39. Vahidolmolk Sheybani, *Khaterat-e mohajerat: Az dowlat-e moqvemat-e Kermanshah ta komite-ye melliyun-e Berlan* (Tehran: Shirazeh, 1999), Kaveh Bayat and Iraj Afshar, eds., pp. 293, 725. The full text of this resolution is in *Kaveh*, vol. 1, no. 22, pp. 2–5. A slightly different version is given in Sheybani, pp. 727–737. Technically, Sheybani and Taqizadeh represented "various Iranian political parties," rather than Iranian socialists. This was due to the fact that, during the war, the Democrat and Social Moderate parties had dissolved themselves into a nationalist coalition of various parties. Sheybani, *Khaterat-e mohajerat*, pp. 710–713. Consequently, the above resolution reflected a blend of socialist and nationalist ideas. For example, it blamed "capitalists from the banks of Thames and Neva rivers" for encroaching upon the independence of an "Iranian nation sustaining an undeniably pure and indivisible nationality in its ancestral land, ever since the time of Cyrus and Zoroaster," pp. 727, 733. It also claimed that "Iran produced Zoroaster, who, centuries before Christ, considered labor and land cultivation among religion virtues." p. 733.
40. Sheybani, *Khaterat-e mohajerat*, pp. 324–326, 337–338, 369–370.
41. On the Brest-Litovsk treaty, see Sean McMeekin, *The Ottoman Endgame: War Revolution and the Making of the Modern Middle East, 1908–1923* (New York: Penguin Press, 2015), Chapter 16, "Brest-Litovsk: The Poisoned Chalice." Article VII of the Brest-Litovsk peace treaty specifically committed the Bolshevik regime and Imperial Germany to recognize Iran's political sovereignty and territorial integrity: "In view of the fact that Persia and Afghanistan are free and independent states, the contracting parties obligate themselves to respect the political and economic independence and the territorial integrity of these states." See the Treaty of Brest-Litovsk, March 3, 1918 in www.firstworldwar.com/source/brestlitovsk.htm. Accessed April 16, 2013. According to Sheybani, *Khaterat-e mohajerat*, Iranian nationalists and democrats (*"mellion va azdaikhahan"*) were enthusiastic and thankful about Brest-Litovsk, pp. 468–470. The Iranian government's request to

send an official delegation to Brest-Litovsk was turned down because Iran was not a belligerent. Instead, the Ottomans promised to represent Iran. Ibid., pp. 474–476. This was followed by a major change in British attitude toward promising to respect Iran's independence. Ibid., p. 484.

42. *Kaveh*, vol. 1, no. 24, January 1918. This was further emphasized in vol. 1, no. 25.

43. Oliver Bast, "Duping the British and Outwitting the Russians? Iran's Foreign Policy, the 'Bolshevik threat' and the Genesis of the Soviet-Iranian Treaty of 1921" in Stephanie Cronin, ed. *Iranian Russian Encounters: Empires and Revolutions since 1800* (London and New York: Routledge, 2013), pp. 261–297.

44. *Kaveh*, vol. 2, no. 8, published the entire text of the 1921 Iran-Soviet Treaty, contrasting it to 1828 Qajar-Tsarist Turkamanchai treaty as a highly positive change.

45. According to a 1970 government-published fifth-grade social studies textbook: "Lenin, the leader of the Russian Revolution, nullified the oppressive privileges that tsars had obtained in Iran." Quoted in Mostafa Sho'aian, *Negahi be ravabet-e Shuravi va jonbesh-e enqelabi-ye jangal* (Florence: Mazdak Publishers, 1976), p. 6.

46. Hassan Taqizadeh, *Khatabe-ye Aqa-ye Seyyed Hasan Taqizadeh* (Tehran, 1959), p. 67.

47. On the significance of Brest-Litovsk and its subsequent Bolshevik support of Turkey's war of independence, see Michael A. Reynolds, *Shattering Empires: The Clash and Collapse of the Ottoman and Russian Empires, 1908–1918* (New York: Cambridge University Press, 2011), pp. 170–178 and 255–261. See also Sina Aksin, *Turkey: From Empire to Revolutionary Republic* (New York: New York University Press, 2007), pp. 164–165; and also McMeekin, *The Ottoman Endgame*, chapter 16 and pp. 464–465.

48. Sukru Hanioglu, *Ataturk: An Intellectual Biography* (Princeton, NJ: Princeton University Press, 2011), pp. 105–106. Kemalist flirtation with Bolshevism was brief and cynical, since the Ankara regime quickly murdered the leaders of an indigenous communist organization, replacing it with its own "communist" party. Kemal told Soviet officials that "in Turkey even communism is our business." Subsequently, he banned the advocacy of socialism, throwing many Turkish socialists and communists into prison. Early Kemalist Turkey's relations with the Soviet Union, however, remained positive on pragmatic grounds, both sides needing each other in the face of common Western European adversaries. Ibid., pp. 107–108. On a more genuine contemporary attempt at mixing Islam and communism, see Alexandre Bennigsen and S. Enders Wimbush, *Muslim National*

Communism in the Soviet Union (Chicago, IL: The University of Chicago Press, 1979).

49. Behnam, *Berlaniha*, p. 52.
50. Sheybani, *Khaterat-e mohajerat*, p. 650.
51. *Kaveh*, vol. 1, no. 34.
52. For example, a lengthy two-issue 1920 article, entitled "Bolshevism in Ancient Iran," depicted the sixth-century Iranian prophet Mazdak as a socialist, citing Theodore Noldeke's judgment, as well as Ferdowsi's sympathetic references to Mazdak and his ideas. *Kaveh*, vol. 2, nos. 3, and 4/5. Another article was devoted to Karl Marx, who was described as "undoubtedly a genius of world historical fame" and "a great leader to a large portion of humanity." *Kaveh*, vol. 2, no. 7.
53. *Kaveh*, vol. 2, no. 1, p. 2.
54. Taqizadeh, *Khatabeh*, p. 28.
55. Ibid., p. 30.
56. Nizai Berkes, *The Development of Secularism in Turkey* (Montreal: McGill University Press, 1964), pp. 357–358.
57. Behnam, *Berlaniha*, p. 56.
58. Iraj Afshar, ed. *Nameha-ye Qazvini be Taqizadeh* (Tehran, 1973), pp. 19–20.
59. Vejdani, *Making History in Iran*, p. 40. See also, Mohammad Tavakoli-Targhi, "*Tajaddod-e ekhtera'i, tamaddon-e ariati va enqelab-e ruhani,*" *Iran Nameh*, vol. XX, nos. 1–2 (spring–summer 2012): pp. 195–235, especially pp. 200–201.
60. Farzin Vejdani, "Purveyors of the Past: Iranian Historians and National Historiography, 1900–1940" (Ph.D. diss., Yale University, 2009), pp. 161–163, 169.
61. Quoted in ibid., pp. 178–179.
62. The 1919 Anglo-Persian agreement stipulated the following points: first, Great Britain would reiterate its previous commitments, "respecting Iran's independence and integrity," (a promise flagrantly contradicted by the British occupation of the country!); Second, the Iranian government would hire British advisors; third, Iranian armed forces would be unified and centralized under British supervision; fourth, the above projects would be financed by a British loan; fifth, Iran's transportation system, specifically via a railroad, would be improved; and, sixth, the British loan would be paid back via revenues of joint Anglo-Persian control of Iran's customs taxes. See the treaty's text in Baqer Aqeli, *Ruzshomar-e tarikh-e Iran: Az mashruteh ta enqelab-e Eslami* (Tehran, 1990), vol. 1, pp. 270–280 and Kaveh Bayat and Reza Azari-Shahrezai,

Amal-e Iranian: Az konfrans-e solh-e Paris ta qarardad-e 1919 Iran va Engelis (Tehran: Shirazeh, 2013), p. 445. See also the preface, especially pp. 17–21.

63. Quoted in Ali-Asghar Haqdar, *Mohammad-Ali Forughi va sakhtarha-ye novin-e madani* (Tehran, 2005), p. 160. On support for the 1919 agreement, among the Iranian elite including Mohamad-Taqi Bahar, see Bayat and Azari-Shahrezai, *Amal-e Iranian*. An article in *Iran* newspaper was quite explicit: "If Iran must rely on a foreign government, that can only be Great Britain," ibid., p. 494.

64. Quoted in Behnam, *Berlaniha*, p. 54.

65. See Erez Manela, *The Wilsonian Moment: Self-determination and the International Origins of Anticolonial Nationalism* (Oxford and New York: Oxford University Press, 2007), especially the conclusion, pp. 219–225.

66. *Kaveh*, vol. 2, no. 3, p. 3.

67. Ibid.

68. Ibid.

69. Ibid., pp. 2–3.

70. Ansari, *The Politics of Nationalism in Modern Iran*, p. 65. Ansari sees *Kaveh*'s 1921 position as a marking "a significant shift" on Taqizdeh's part "from the 'constitutional republican' to the revolutionary social democrat." Yet, in a footnote on the following page, he admits *Kaveh*'s 1921 advocacy of "enlightened despotism." The lack of attention to the nuances of *Kaveh*'s ideological evolution underlines the difficulty in explaining why intellectuals like Taqizadeh supported the rise of Reza Khan, whose dictatorial ambitions were quite obvious. See ibid., pp. 66–67. Abbas Milani, on the other hand, totally overlooks the socialist tendency of *Kaveh*'s first series, as well as the retreat from constitutionalism in *Kaveh*'s second series. See Milani, "*Majalle-ye Kaveh va mas'ale-ye tajaddod*" in *Iranshenasi*, vol. ii, no. 3 (Autumn 1990): pp. 504–519.

71. *Kaveh*, vol. 2, no. 9, p. 3.

72. Ibid.

73. Ibid., p. 4.

74. A new translation movement from original Greek sources will help Iranians compensate on what they have missed. *Kaveh*, vol. 2, no. 10.

75. *Iranshahr*, October 1924, nos. 1–2; quoted in Amir-Hushang Keshavarz, *Do maqale az Hosein Kazemzadeh Iranshahr* (n.p., 1991) p. 24.

76. Tavakoli-Targhi, "*Tajaddod-e ekhtera'i*," notes *Iranshahr*'s important contribution to the critique of European civilization and advocacy of a "spiritual revolution."

77. Said Amir Arjomand, "*A la recherche de la conscience collective*: Durkheim's Ideological Impact in Turkey and Iran" in *The American Sociologist*, vol. 17, no. 2 (May 1982): pp. 94–102.
78. Behnam notes two main tendencies in *Iranshahr*. First, belief in an Iranian "national spirit" surviving from ancient times and, second, a certain mystical-philosophical, or rather theosophical, tendency. He denies such tendencies were related to racist nationalism then on the rise in Germany. *Berlaniha*, pp. 89–90. Tavakoli-Targhi's more perceptive analysis notes Kazemzadeh's positive estimation of Ottoman and Republican Turkish models of subordinating religion to the state, but not the impact on *Iranshahr* of Weimar counter-modernity. Tavakoli-Targhi sees Kazemzadeh to be following Kant, a more unlikely and remote German connection. See "*Tajaddod-e ekhtera'i*," pp. 211–213.
79. Almost unanimously, German university professors supported their nation's war effort ... They wrote of a profound struggle between German "culture" and Western "civilization." They castigated Western commercialism, rationalism, and utilitarian individualism, as against the uniqueness of Germany's cultural traditions, political institutions, and sense of "community." Invoking "the idea of 1914," they envisaged a German alternative to the opposition between unfettered capitalism and radical socialism, a system in which both capital and labor were organized to serve the larger objectives of the nation ... It became painfully obvious during the war that the rhetoric of the national cause represented an exclusionary tactic, a right-wing attack upon liberal reformers and Social Democrats.
   Fritz Ringer, *Max Weber: An Intellectual Biography* (Chicago and London: The University of Chicago Press, 2004), pp. 14–15.
80. Kontje, *German Orientalisms*, pp. 140, 143–144.
81. Arthur Herman, *The Idea of Decline in Western History* (New York: The Free Press, 1997). Although the first volume of *The Decline of the West* appeared in 1918, Spengler had finished its first draft in 1914, before the Great War, pp. 241–242. A study more sympathetic to Spengler is John Farrenkopf, *Prophet of Decline: Spengler on World History and Politics* (Baton Rouge, LA: Louisiana State University Press, 2001), pp. 20–21.
82. Farrenkopf, *Prophet of Decline*, pp. 28–30, 40–41. Herman, *The Idea of Decline*, p. 240.
83. Mikhail Agursky, *The Third Rome: National Bolshevism in the USSR* (Boulder and London: Westview Press, 1987), p. 229. Lenin wrote:

   The old bourgeois and imperialist Europe, which was accustomed to look upon itself as the centre of the Universe, rotted and burst like a putrid ulcer in the first imperialist holocaust. No matter how the Spenglers and all the enlightened philistines, who are capable of admiring (or even studying) Spengler, lament it, this decline of the old Europe is but an episode in the history of the downfall of the world bourgeois, oversatiated by imperialist rapine and the oppression of the majority of the world's population.

Quoted in ibid., p. 295.

84. Farrenkopf, *Prophet of Decline*, pp. 50–51. Herman, *The Idea of Decline*, pp. 236–240.
85. Robert O. Paxton, *The Anatomy of Fascism* (New York: Alfred A. Knopf, 2004), p. 38.
86. The terms "civilization" and "the West" were prominent in seminal titles such as Freud's *Civilization and Its Discontents* (1930). Toynbee, whose sweeping conception of world of history was influenced by Spengler, used the terms "Western" and "Civilization" as early as 1923 in his *The Western Question in Greece and Turkey: A Study in the Contact of Civilizations* (1923), and more famously in his *Civilization on Trial* (1948). See William H. McNeill, *Arnold Toynbee: A life* (New York and Oxford: Oxford University Press, 1989), pp. 98–101, Weber's pessimism about the "bureaucratization" of modern society is well known. See, for example, Reinhard Bendix, *Max Weber: An Intellectual Portrait* (New York: Anchor Books, 1962), Chapter XIV; Fritz Ringer, *Max Weber*, pp. 220–224. Weber, however, was not impressed by *The Decline of the West*. See Herman, *The Idea of Decline*, p. 246.
87. In 1926, for example, American Protestant missionary Basil Matthews published *Young Islam on Trek: A Study on the Clash of Civilizations*. Rejecting the view that the modern West could show Muslims "a new order of life," Matthews wrote:

Western civilization can never lead them to that goal. Obsessed by material wealth, obese with an industrial plethora, drunk with the miracles of its scientific advances, blind to the riches of the world of the spirit, and deafened to the inner Voice by the outer clamor, Western civilization may destroy the old Islam, but it cannot fulfill the new.
Quoted in Richard W. Bulliet, *The Case for Islamo-Christian Civilization* (New York: Columbia University Press, 2004), pp. 2–3.

88. Roger Griffin, *Modernism and Fascism: The sense of Beginning under Hitler and Mussolini* (New York: Palgrave, 2007), defines fascism as a radical modernist political and cultural response to the early twentieth-century perception of the decline and decadence of the West. See also Paxton, *The Anatomy of Fascism*, especially chapters 1–2.

89. According to Spengler, it was "imperative to free German socialism from Marx." Spengler in *Prussianism and Socialism*, quoted in Farrenkopf, *Prophet of Decline*, p. 23. More accurately, and similar to Italian and French fascists, Spengler and his German cohorts, like Ernst Junger, blended elements of radical rightist and leftist ideologies. Junger's influential book *The Worker* (1932) advocated a proto-fascist political regime led by a worker-soldier-scholar elite. On the blending of right-wing and left-wing elements in European, and specially French, fascism see Zeev Sternhell, *Neither Right nor Left: Fascist Ideology in France* (Berkeley, Los Angeles and London: University of California Press, 1986).

90. Paxton, *The Anatomy of Fascism*, pp. 27–28.

91. Despite Nazi enthusiasm for his work, Spengler refused to endorse National Socialism, considering Hitler not perfectly fitting the Nietzschean profile of his "heroic" German savior. Herman, *The Idea of Decline*, pp. 246–254. Spengler's reservations about Hitler therefore appear more genuine than those by thinkers like Heidegger, who expressed them only after National Socialism was defeated. See Tom Rockmore, *Heidegger and French Philosophy: Humanism, Antihumanism and Being* (London and New York: Routledge, 1995), pp. 149–150.

92. Rejecting both Natural Rights and Social Contract theories of the state, Schmitt went back to thinkers like Hobbes to argue that rights and political sovereignty were created by the state, which could therefore reconstitute or nullify them. Schmitt, *The Concept of the Political* (New Brunswick, NJ: Rutgers University Press, 1976), George Schwab trans. See also Joseph W. Bendersky, *Carl Schmitt: Theorist of the Rich* (Princeton, NJ: Princeton University Press, 1983). Like his generation of conservative German thinkers, Schmitt's actual point of reference was the Imperial Reich, where ultimate sovereignty resided in the "decisions" of the emperor, backed by a military-bureaucratic elite. Bendersky, p. 16.

93. Quoted in Bendersky, *Carl Schmitt*, p. 18.

94. These terms appear in Heidegger's *What Is Metaphysics*. Julian Young, *Heidegger, Philosophy, Nazism* (New York: Cambridge University Press, 1997), p. 33.

95. Serif Mardin, *Religion and Social Change in Modern Turkey: The Case of Bedizzaman Said Nursi* (New York: State University of New York, 1989), p. 125.

96. Cemil Aydin, *The Politics of Anti-Westernism in Asia, Visions of World order in Pan-Islamic and Pan-Asian Thought* (New York: Columbia University Press, 2007), pp. 97–106.

97. Also included were Hosein Nafisi and Ahmad Farhad. Behnam, *Berlaniha*, pp. 89–91.
98. *Iranshahr*, vol. 1, no. 1, pp. 1–2.
99. "Today, while Eastern countries need to adopt the complex and multifaceted aspects of Western civilization, we think it's necessary that individuals who know the conditions of Western countries and their civilization, having learned of these while traveling or studying abroad, or learning of Western nations." *Iranshahr*, vol. 1, no. 1, pp. 13–14.
100. Ibid., p. 36.
101. "Thus it is certain that science alone cannot save us from the vortex of misfortune. What is needed is morality and more morality." Ibid., p. 37.
102. *Iranshahr*, vol. 2, no. 1, p. 3.
103. "Acting with the power of a new religion, the Bolshevik or communist creed is merely a reaction to capitalism. The fire it ignited in the hearts of European masses will burn down everything, replacing all other motivations, until it too is replaced by another ideal." *Iranshahr*, vol. 1, no. 2, p. 72.
104. *Iranshahr*, vol. 2, no. 10. In another issue, he declares: "Wow to us and our future if the civilization we are trying to bring to Iran, at bayonet point and purchased with the blood of our youth, is one whose fruit we see in the West." *Iranshahr*, vol. 2, no. 8, April 1924.
105. *Iranshahr,* vol. 2, no. 2, October 1923.
106. *Iranshahr*, vol. 2, nos. 1–2, October 1924.
107. "Republicanism and Social Revolution" in *Iranshahr*, vol. 2, nos. 5–6, February 1924.
108. *Iranshahr*, vol. 1, no. 11, April 1923.
109. Ibid.
110. *Iranshahr*, vol. 2, nos. 5–6, 15 February 1924.
111. *Iranshahr*, vol. 2, no. 3, November 1923, no. 3, p. 139.
112. A 1925 article in *Iranshahr* argued Kazemzadeh's "religious revolution" could be accomplished only if leaders like Luther or Calvin launched "a bloody revolution beginning and ending with the murdering of all clerics." Tavakoli-Targhi, *"Tajaddod-e ekhtera'i,"* p. 207.
113. *Iranshahr*, vol. 2, nos. 11–12, "Woman and Marriage," cited in Behnam, *Berlaniha*, p. 179.
114. Tenshin quoted in Aydin, *The Politics of Anti-Westernism in Asia*, p. 58.
115. This movement was launched at the first meeting of the Parliament of the World's Religions in Chicago in 1893. In addition to Christian denominations, Hinduism, Buddhism and Islam, this meeting included

representatives from new religious and spiritual movements such as Spiritualism, Christian Science and the Baha'i Faith. See www.parlai mentofreligions.org.

116. *Iranshahr*, vol. 2, no. 10, June 1924.
117. Quoted in Behnam, *Berlaniha*, p. 174.
118. Aydin, *The Politics of Anti-Westernism in Asia,* pp. 58–59.
119. Steven M. Wasserstrom, *Religion after Religion: Gershom Scholem and Mircea Eliade, and Henry Corbin at Eranos* (Princeton, NJ: Princeton University Press, 1999).
120. Monica M. Ringer, *Pious Citizens: Reforming Zoroastrianism in India and Iran* (Syracuse, NY: Syracuse University Press, 2001), chapter 6.
121. Reza Bigdlu, *Bastangarai dar tarikh-e mo'aser-e Iran* (Tehran, 2001), p. 198.
122. Afshin Marashi, "Imagining Hafez: Rabindranath Tagore in Iran, 1932," in *Journal of Persianate Studies*, vol. 3 (2010): pp. 46–77.
123. Behnam, *Berlaniha,* pp. 33–36, 104, 131. In 1930, while still in Berlin, Kazemzadeh wrote a small book, titled *Spiritual Therapy for Individuals and Society,* focused more specifically on the theosophical themes he had developed in *Iranshahr*. See Hosein Kazemzadeh Iranshahr, *Tadavi-e ruhi baray-e afrad va jame'eh* (Tehran: Eqbal, 1978).
124. *Name-ye Farangestan*, no. 1. Quoted in Nader Entekhabi, *Nasionlaism va tajaddod dar Iran va Torkieh* (Tehran: Negare-ye aftab, 2011), p. 177.
125. Ibid. Ahmad Farhad, in *Name-ye Farangestan*, no. 5, quoted in Entekhabi, p. 181.
126. Moshfeq-Kazemi, *Name-ye Farangestan*, no. 1. Quoted in Entekhabi, *Nasionlaism va tajaddod*, p. 179.
127. *Name-ye Farangestan*, no. 5. Quoted in Entekhabi, *Nasionlaism va tajaddod*, p. 178.
128. Entekhabi, *Nasionlaism va tajaddod*, pp. 182–188. See also Tavakoli-Targhi, "*Tajaddod-e ekhtera'i.*"
129. Advocating voting rights for elite women followed Mussolini's 1919 fascist program that proposed women's enfranchisement. Paxton, *The Anatomy of Fascism*, p. 5.
130. Moshfeq-Kazemi, *Ruzgar va andisheha* (Tehran, 1971) vol. 1, pp. 180–182.
131. Ibid., pp. 173, 176.
132. Ibid., p. 242; quoted on p. 270.
133. Ibid., p. 29.

Subverting Constitutionalism: Intellectuals as Instruments of Modern Dictatorship

1. From Mohammad-Ali Foroughi's notes taken while attending the Versailles peace conference. Quoted in Iraj Parsinejad, "*Yaddashtha-ye yek Irani-ye motemadden-e ba-ma'rafat*," *Bokhara*, no. 108 (October–November): pp. 463–493, quoted on p. 471.
2. Kaveh Bayat, "*Andishe-ye siasi-ye Davar va ta'sis-e dowlat-e modern dar Iran*," *Goft-o-gu*, no. 2 (1993): pp. 116–133. Davar quoted on p. 125.
3. Homa Katouzian, preface to the special issue on Seyyed Hasan Taqizadeh, *Iran Nameh*, vol. XXI, nos. 1–2 (spring–summer 2003): p. 3.
4. For a critique of the "catastrophic perspective" see Stephanie Cronin, *Soldiers, Shahs and Subalterns in Iran: Opposition, Protest and Revolt, 1921–1941* (New York: Palgrave Macmillan, 2010), pp. 4–5. According to historian Kaveh Bayat, the paradigmatic text of "the Pahlavi school of historiography," was Said Nafisi's *Pishraftha-ye Iran dar dore-ye Pahlavi* (Tehran, 1933), which juxtaposed the Qajar "period of utter anarchy and chaos" to the Pahlavi era's two main accomplishments of "political independence and internal security." See Kaveh Bayat, "The Pahlavi School of Historiography on the Pahlavi Era" in Touraj Atabaki (ed.) *Iran in the 20th Century: Historiography and Political Culture* (London and New York: I. B. Tauris, 2009), pp. 113–120. Cited on p. 114.
5. Homa Katouzian, for example, has explained the rise of Reza Shah according to a trans-historical model of Iranian government and society, permanently trapped in a "dialectical" oscillation between "chaos" and "arbitrary rule." This model is basically the old Orientalist paradigm of Asiatic Despotism. See Katouzian, *State and Society in Iran: The Eclipse of the Qajars and the Emergence of the Pahlavis* (London and New York: I. B. Tauris, 2006), as well as his *Iranian History and Politics: The Dialectic of State and Society* (London and New York: Routledge Curzon, 2003). This claim is repeated in Katouzian's chapter in Touraj Atabaki and Eric J. Zurcher, *Men of Order: Authoritarian Modernization under Ataturk and Reza Shah* (New York: I. B. Tauris, 2004). His reference to "arbitrary rule-chaos-arbitrary rule" is on p. 14. Explanations of the rise of Reza Khan as a British conspiracy are part of the official historiography of the Islamic Republic. For its academic variants see Mohammad Gholi Majd, *Persia in World War I and Its Conquest by Great Britain* (Lanham, MD: University Press of America, 2003), reviewed by Cronin in *Iranian Studies*, vol. 37, no. 4 (December 2004): pp. 721–723.

6. Homa Katouzian, "*Seyyed Hasan Taqiadeh: seh zendegi dar yek 'omr*," *Iran Nameh* vol. XXI, nos. 1–2 (spring–summer 2003): pp. 7–48; quoted on p. 17.

7. See, for example, Cronin, *Soldiers, Shahs and Subalterns in Iran*, especially chapter 1.

8. Taqizadeh in Iraj Afshar, ed. *Zendegi-ye tufani: khaterat-e seyyed Hasan Taqizadeh* (Tehran, 1993), p. 233.

9. *Salname-ye Pars* (Tehran: The Organization of Iranian Ministries, 1927–1928), p. 38.

10. *Kaveh*, vol. 2, no. 9, p. 3.

11. Afshar, *Zendegi-e tufani*, pp. 198–199.

12. Katouzian, "*Seyyed Hasan Taqizadeh*," quoted on p. 19. For Taqizadeh's speech, as well as those by Mosaddeq and Yahya Dowlatabadi, against the transfer of monarchy to Reza Khan, see Hosein Maki, ed. *Doktor Mosaddeq va notqha-ye tarikhi-ye o* (Tehran, 1985), pp. 128–157. Davar's response is also include there.

13. Mosaddeq's 1945 Majles speech, quoted in *Iran Nameh*, vol. XXI, nos. 1–2 (spring–summer 2003): p. 165.

14. "I had absolutely no involvement in this affair, except for putting my signature to it … Shortcoming or mistakes in this affair must be blamed on the actor, not on the instrument of action." Taqizadeh on his role in the 1933 renewal of the Anglo-Iranian oil agreement. See the text of Taqizadeh's speech defending himself in the Majles after Reza Shah's fall. Baqer Aqeli, *Ruzshomar-e tarikh-e Iran: Az mashruteh ta enqelab-e Eslami* (Tehran, 1990), vol. 1, pp. 444–449, quoted on p. 448.

15. For the exchange with Mosaddeq see ibid. pp. 165–170.

16. According to Jamalzadeh, in a 1955 private correspondence, Taqizadeh bitterly complained of his "tormented conscience" causing him sleepless nights. He wrote:

   It is to you, and only you, that I finally make this shameful confession about being occupied by constant and incessant torment …

   I prefer any less-paying occupation that might be far from politics and governmental affairs, swearing to God that what I say is but a small fraction of the truth burdening my conscience.
   Quoted in Hasan Shayegan, *Eqbal va tarikhnegari* (Tehran, 2004), p. 146.

17. Quoted in Katouzian, "*Seyyed Hasan Taqizadeh*," p. 41. Katouzian's sympathetic estimation of Taqizadeh's intellectual and political career is shared by other contributors to this special collection. For instance, Jamshid Behnam's "*Taqizadeh va mas'ale-ye tajaddod*," ibid., pp. 77–89, concludes that Taqizadeh must be considered the first Iranian

intellectual who understood the "essence of modernity," p. 86. See also the article by Bastani-Parizi who argues Taqizadeh's destruction of his personal notes and documents conforms to a long-standing patterns of Iranian intellectual dissimulation. Ibid., *"atash dar zir-e panjereh,"* pp. 113–140.

18. Mojtaba Minovi, *Naqd-e hal* (Tehran, 1980), pp. 498–506. Minovi, who was introduced to this circle by his teacher Mohamad Eqbal-Ashtiani, also mentions studying Pahlavi with Orientalist scholar Ernst Herzfeld along with Mohammad-Taqi Bahar, Rashid Jasami, Ahmad Kasravi and Taqizadeh. Ibid., p. 506.

19. The 1921 program of Young Iran Society is listed in Shahrokh Meskub, *Dastan-e adabiyat va sargozasht-e ejtema'* (Tehran, 1994), p. 30.

20. Originally told by Siasi in his memoir, this story is cited in many sources, for example in Meskub, *Dastan-e adabiyat*, pp. 37–38. See Siasi, *Yek zendegi-ye sisai* (Tehran: Thaleth, 1994), pp. 96–99. Siasi claims that although Reza Shah implemented Young Iran's program, the circle's members did not approve of his dictatorial ways. Ibid., p. 129.

21. Jamshid Behnam, *Berlaniha* (Tehran, 2000), p. 125. As we saw in Chapter 2, Moshfeq-Kazemi returned to Tehran in 1926, joined the Young Iran Party and wrote for its organ *Iran-e javan*.

22. Mahmud Afshar in *Ayandeh,* no. 1, quoted in Nader Entekhabi, *Nasionlaism va tajaddod dar Iran va Torkieh* (Tehran, 2011), p. 42.

23. Siasi quoted in Atabaki and Zurcher, *Men of Order*, pp. 226–227.

24. Afsahr in *Ayandeh*, quoted in Entekhabi, *Nasionlaism va tajaddod*, p. 43. Using "Pan-Turkist" as his model, Afshar is said to have coined the Persian term "Pan-Iranist" to describe the "cultural unity" of "all Iranians," including those in Afghanistan, India, Tajikistan and Pakistan. Ibid., pp. 243–244. See also *"Hezb-e Iranian"* in *Tarikh-e Mo'aser Iran*, vol. 14, nos. 53–54 (spring–summer 2010): pp. 225–276.

25. Reza Ziba-Ebrahimi, "Self-Orientalization and Dislocation: The Uses and Abuses of the 'Aryan' Discourse in Iran," in *Iranian Studies*, no. 24 (June 2011): pp. 445–472, especially pp. 450–455. A more extensive discussion of Aryan racial discourse impacting Iranian nationalism is found in Zia-Ebrahimi, *The Emergence of Iranian Nationalism: Race and the Politics of Dislocation* (New York: Columbia University Press, 2016). On Abbas Eqbal-Ashtiani see Farzin Vejdani, *Making History in Iran: Education, Nationalism and Print Culture* (Stanford, CA: Stanford University Press, 2015), pp. 290–291.

26. See the text of Forughi's speech in *Khaterat-e Nasrollah Entezam* (Tehran, 1378), pp. 221–225, quoted on p. 223.

27. Ibid., p. 26.

28. Atabaki and Zurcher, *Men of Order*, p. 82.

29. Kaveh Bayat, *"Andishe-ye siasi-ye Davar,"* p. 126.

30. Quoted in Bayat, *"Andishe-ye siasi-ye Davar,"* pp. 121–122.

31. Davar, quoted in ibid., pp. 125, 130.

32. He feared for his life, already warned by Reza Shah that he might be annihilated. Afsahr, *Zendegi-e Tufani*, p. 233.

33. Vejdani, *Making History in Iran*, p. 145.

34. Hamaid Dabashi, *The World of Persian Literary Humanism* (Cambridge, MA: Harvard University Press, 2012), Introduction, pp. 34–35. While its modern coinage goes back to the nineteenth century, the term "humanism" is rooted in the Latin *humanitas,* which Roman writers, like Cicero, used to convey their appreciation of humanity's common cultural heritage, as well as its refined expression in Latin literature. A Hellenistic legacy, the *humanitas* tradition was absorbed into the classical Islamic cultural synthesis of the Abbasid era, producing a discourse called *adab,* concerned with humanity's moral perfection and articulated in Arabic and Persian masterworks of literature, history and governance.

35. See Dabashi, *The World of Persian Literary Humanism*, conclusion.

36. Vejdani, *Making History in Iran*, pp. 145–152. See Pascale Casanova, *A World Republic of Letters* (Cambridge, MA: Harvard University Press, 2004), trans. M. B. DeBevoise and Dena Goodman, *The Republic of Letters: A Cultural History of the French Enlightenment* (Ithaca, NY: Cornell University Press, 1994).

37. Quoted in Nizai Berkes, *The Development of Secularism in Turkey* (Montreal: McGill University Press, 1964), p. 296. On the clash of "new" and "old" literature in the late Ottoman era, see also Kemal H. Karapat, *The Politicization of Islam: Reconstructing Identity, State, Faith, and Community in the Late Ottoman State* (Oxford and New York: Oxford University Press, 2001), pp. 361–363.

38. Berkes, *The Development of Secularism in Turkey*, pp. 298–299.

39. Holland Ada Shissler, *Between Two Empires: Ahmed Agaoglu and the New Turkey* (New York: I. B. Tauris, 2003), pp. 219–221, quoted on p. 221.

40. Kermani quoted in Ahmad Karimi-Hakkak, *Recasting Persian Poetry: Scenarios of Poetic Modernity in Iran* (Salt Lake City, UT: University of Utah Press, 1995), pp. 42 and 43.

41. Ibid., p. 63.

42. Sohrab Yazdani, *Sur-e Esrafil: Name-ye azadi* (Tehran: Ney, 2007), pp. 184–187.

43. Ibid., pp. 138, 148–150.

44. Ibid., chapter 6. *Sure-Esrafil*'s link to the Tiflis-based Turkish paper Molla Naser-al Din is noted by Ahmad Kasravi, cited in Yahya

Aryanpur, *Az Saba ta Nima* (Tehran, 1971), p. 78. On the pioneering role of papers like *Sure-e Esrafil* in the broad literary transition to simplified modern Persian, see Afshin Marashi, "Print Culture and Its Publics: A Social History of Bookstores in Tehran, 1900–1950," in *International Journal of Middle East Studies*, vol. 47 (2015): pp. 89–108, pp. 94–95. See Ali-Akbar Dehkhoda, *Charand-o-Parand: Revolutionary Satire from Iran, 1907–1909* (New Haven and London: Yale University Press, 2016), translated and with an introduction and notes by Janet Afary and John R. Perry.

45. Aryanpur, *Az Saba ta Nima* (Tehran, 1971), pp. 86–92.
46. Bahar, *Daneshkadeh*, no. 1. 1918, quoted in Ariaynpur, *Az Saba ta Nima*, p. 436.
47. Bahar in *Nobahar*. Quoted in Aryanpur, *Az Saba ta Nima*, p. 443.
48. Quoted in Aryanpur, *Az Saba ta Nima*, vol. 2, p. 440. See also Mohammad-Ali Sepanlu, *Bahar* (Tehran, 1995), pp. 26–31.
49. Aryanpur, *Az Saba ta Nima*, vol. 2, p. 444.
50. Ibid., p. 446
51. Ibid., pp. 447–449.
52. Ibid., p. 450.
53. Ibid., pp. 450–451.
54. Ibid., p. 451.
55. Seyyed Hadi Khosro-Shahi, *Nehzat-e Aziadistan va Sheykh Mohammad Khiabai* (Tehran: Markaz-e asnad-e enqelab-e eslami, 2010), pp. 141–153. For Khiabani's 1920 speeches in *Tajaddod*, showing commitment to Iranian nationalism and constitutional government, see ibid. pp. 252–362.
56. Quoted in Karimi-Hakkak, *Recasting Persian Poetry*, p. 218. I have changed the translation slightly. For a good discussion of the modernist literary avant-garde's politics, including translations of long passages of Eshqi's poetry, see Homa Katouzian, "Private Parts and Public Discourses in Modern Iran" in *Comparative Studies of South Asia*, vol. 28. no. 2 (2008): pp. 283–290.
57. Aqeli, *Ruzshomar-e tarikh-e Iran*, pp. 135, 141. Cronin, *Soldiers, Shahs and Subalterns in Iran*, p. 145. For a study of Eshqi, as an anarchist, see Mohammad Qa'ed, *Mirzadeh Eshqi* (Tehran, 1998).
58. On the murder of Turkish communists see Sukru Hanioglu, *Ataturk: An Intellectual Biography* (Princeton, NJ: Princeton University Press, 2011), p. 108.
59. Sohrab Yazdani, *Mojahedan-e Mashruteh* (Tehran, 2011), pp. 82–85.
60. According to Taqizadeh, 3,200 out of the total 4,200 ballots cast in Tabriz for the Second Majles elections were for the Democrat Party. See Afshar, *Zendegi-ye tufani*, p. 348.

282	Notes to Pages 96–100

61. Fereydun Adamiayt, *Ideolozhi-ye nehzat-e mashrutiyat-e Iran* (Tehran, 1974), pp. 285–306.

62. The most comprehensive English language study of the 1920–1921 Gilan revolution is Cosroe Chaqueri, *The Soviet Socialist Republic of Iran, 1920–1921: Birth of the Trauma* (Pittsburgh and London: University of Pittsburgh Press, 1995).

63. Norman's September 1920 "monthly summary" (FO 371/4910) is quoted in Chaqueri, *The Soviet Socialist Republic of Iran*, p. 261. Norman wrote that in addition to the capital, Azerbaijan, Gilan and Mazandaran were on the verge of falling to Bolshevism. Ibid.

64. Chaqueri's *The Soviet Socialist Republic of Iran* is an example of leftist historiography blaming the failure of Gilan's revolution more on the Bolsheviks than on Iranians revolutionaries.

65. Ervand Abrahamian, *Iran between Two Revolutions* (Princeton, NJ: Princeton University Press, 1983), pp. 126–130.

66. Rahim Ra'isnia, *Akharin sangar-e azadi: Majmo'e-ye maqalat-e Mir-Jafar Pishevari dar ruzname-ye Haqiqat, organ-e ettehadiy-ye omomi-ye kargaran-e Iran: 1300–1301* (Tehran, 1998).

67. Atabaki and Zurcher, *Men of Order*, pp. 306–307.

68. Baqer Momeni, *Donya-ye Arani* (Tehran: Akhtaran, 2005), p. 100.

69. Khosrow Shakeri, *Taqi Arani dar Ayene-ye tarikh* (Tehran: Akhtaran, 2008), p. 28.

70. For example, a 1924 article by Arani gave a technical explanation of electro-magnetic waves and their practical application in electrical trains. See Taqi Arani "The Solution to a scientific puzzle," in *Iranshahr*, June 20, 1924.

71. Shakeri, *Taqi Arani dar Ayene-ye tarikh*, pp. 329–330.

72. Some of these were small books and pamphlets he had published in Germany during the 1920s, while others, including *The Principles of the Science of Psychology* (1932) and a pamphlet entitled *Mysticism and Materialist Principles* (1934) were written in Iran. Momeni, *Donya-ye Arani*, p. 102.

73. Ibid., pp. 157–160.

74. Claiming the Arani circle as its immediate predecessor, the Tudeh Party adopted the *Donya* as the title of its main theoretical journal, depicting Arani as a full-fledged Stalinist. Meanwhile, it chose to its central committee Abdolsamad Kambakhsh, who was linked to the Soviet NKVD but had cooperated with the Iranian police to implicate Arani's circle as communists, passing the blame to Arani. Momeni, *Donya-ye Arani*, pp. 63–67. Shakeri, *Taqi Arani dar Ayene-ye tarikh*, p. 186.

75. The names and sentences of Arani's group are listed in an Iranian Ministry of Justice document (no. 22539), dated February 20, 1939. Accessed at the Iranian National Archives Organization, Tehran, Iran.

76. Taqi Arani, *Defa'iyat-e doktor Arani* (n.p., n.d.), pp. 3, 6.

77. Shakeri, *Taqi Arani dar Ayene-ye tarikh*, pp. 31–33.

78. On *Kadro* see Hanioglu, *Ataturk*, pp. 188–190.

79. Momeni, *Donya-ye Arani*, p. 13.

80. Ibid., pp. 1–2.

81. Ibid., p. 17.

82. Momeni, *Donya-ye Arani*, pp. 9–10, 14–15. My interpretation of Gramsci is based on studies such as John M. Cammett, *Antonio Gramsci and the Origins of Italian Communism* (Stanford, CA: Stanford University Press, 1967) and Perry Anderson *The Antinomies of Antonio Gramsci* (London and New York: Verso, 2017).

83. Qasem Ghani, "*Eslah-e nezhad*," *Yadegar*, no. 8 (March–April 1945), pp. 8–26; quoted on p. 8. Ghani's ideas are expanded in a second article that cites statistics on 1920s US forced sterilization of people with racial "impurities and defects." See *Yadegar*, no. 9 (April–May 1945): pp. 12–27.

84. Cyrus Schayegh, *Who Is Knowledgeable Is Strong: Science, Class, and the Formation of Modern Iranian Society, 1900–1950* (Berekley, CA: University of California Press, 2009), pp. 36–39. Similarly, Schayegh misses Kasravi's intervention and objection to attempts, such as Arani's, linking modern science to materialism and/or to moral guidelines for social betterment.

85. *Donya*, no. 1; quoted in Momeni, *Donya-ye Arani*, p. 247.

86. Momeni, *Donya-ye Arani*, pp. 256–257.

87. Fatemeh Sayyah, "*Tahqiq-e mokhtasar dar ahval va zendegi-ye Ferdowsi*," a presentation at the millennial celebration of Ferdowsi's birth, reproduced in Mohammad Golbon, *Naqd va siahat: Doktor Fatemeh Sayyah* (Tehran, 2004), pp. 73–92; especially p. 78.

88. Taqi Arani, *Defa'iyat-e doktor Arani* (n.p., n.d.), p. 3.

89. It used the older term "*monavvar al-fekr*," rather than "*roshanfekr*," for intellectuals. *Donya*, no. 6, quoted in Momeni, *Donya-ye Arani*, pp. 268–269.

90. Karl Mannheim's *Ideology and Utopia* was first published in German in 1929, while Gramsci wrote on intellectuals during the late 1920s and early 1930s. However, there is no evidence Arani had read either thinker. For Mannheim's classic definition of intellectuals see *Ideology and Utopia* (New York, 1936), for example, pp. 10–11. See also Antonio Gramsci, *The Modern Prince and Other Writings* (New York:

International Publishers, 1978), particularly "The Formation of Intellectuals," pp. 118–125.

91. Momeni, *Donya-ye Arani*, pp. 271, 274.
92. Ibid., p. 275.
93. Ibid., p. 274.
94. Ibid., p. 278.
95. Ibid., p. 279.
96. Quoted in Hamid Ahmadi, *Tarikhche-ye ferqe-ye jomhuri-ye enqelabi-ye Iran va goruh-e Arani* (Tehran, 2000), p. 192
97. Quoted in Hamid Dabashi, *Theology of Discontent: The Ideological Foundations of the Islamic Revolution in Iran* (New York: New York University Press, 1993). p. 283. See also ibid., pp. 278–284.
98. Ahmadi, *Arani*, pp. 186–187. Ahmadi also quotes Kasravi writing about his friendship with Arani and how despite their differences, they shared "the same ideals." Ibid., p. 192.
99. Moretza Motahhari, *Elal-e garayesh be maddigari* (Tehran, 1999), pp. 10–11.

Intellectual Missing Links: Criticizing Europeanism and Translating Modernity

1. *Peyman*, p. 268. *Peyman* [The Pact] was a monthly periodical Kasravi published in ninety-nine issues starting in 1933 and ending in 1942. The reference in this chapter are to Ahmad Kasravi, *Peyman* (Tehran, 2002), which is a selection of *Peyman*'s articles arranged by topic, but without exact publication dates.
2. Khomeini quoted in Lloyd Ridgeon, "Ahamd Kasravi's Criticism of Edward Granville Browne," in *Iran*, vol. 42 (2004): pp. 219–233; quoted on p. 219.
3. Quoted in Mohammad Amini, ed. *Zendegi va zamane-ye Ahmad Kasravi* (Los Angles: Ketab corporation, 2016), p. 50. This book is a newly edited and annotated collection of Kasravi's autobiographical texts, including *Zendegi-e man*, *Dah sal dar adlieh* and *Chera az adlieh birun amadm*.
4. Jalal Al-Ahmad, *Dar khedmat va Khianat-e Roshanfekran* (Tehran, 1977), p. 327.
5. Mohammad Tavakoli-Targhi, "*Tajaddod-e ekhtera'i, tamaddon-e ariati va enqelab-e ruhani*," *Iran Nameh*, vol. XX, nos. 1–2 (spring–summer 2002), pp. 195–235. Reference to Al-Ahamd is on p. 223 and to "disremembering" on p. 197.
6. This feature of Kasravi's thought was occasionally noted in pre-revolutionary Iran. See, for instance, the article by Asil in *Negin*, no. 130 (spring 1976), pp. 30–36.

7. Ervand Abrahamian, "Kasravi: The Integrative Nationalist of Iran," *Middle Eastern Studies*, vol. 9, no. 3 (October 1973): pp. 271–295.

8. Hamid Dabashi, *Theology of Discontent: The Ideological Foundations of the Islamic Revolution in Iran* (New York: New York University Press, 1993), pp. 45–46. According to Al-Ahmad, he himself and the great majority of the 1940s communist generation had turned against religion after reading Kasravi during the 1930s. Al-Ahmad, *Dar khedmat va Khianat-e Roshanfekran*, p. 327. For a similar personal testimony of Kasravi's role, as a bridge to Marxism, see Fereydun Farrokh, "*Tasvir-e Kasravi dar azhan-e javanan,*" *Iran Nameh*, vol. XX, nos. 1–2 (spring–summer 2002): pp. 277–284. See also the memoirs of Enyatollah Reza, who says, during the early 1940s, he was both a Marxist member of the Tudeh Party and a follower of Kasravi. Reza later became a political refugee in the Soviet Union, where he wrote his doctoral dissertation in philosophy on Kasravi. See Enayatollah Reza, *Nagofte-ha* (Tehran, 2012), pp. 30, 84–87.

9. Mehrzad Boroujerdi, *Iranian Intellectuals and the West: The Tormented Triumph of Nativism* (Syracuse, NY: Syracuse University Press, 1996), p. 62. In the early 1990s, Asghar Fathi had written a chapter on Kasravi in Asghar Fathi ed. *Iranian Refugees and Exiles since Khomeini* (Costa Mesa, CA: Mazda Publishers, 1991).

10. Tavakoli-Targhi, "*Tajaddod-e ekhtera'i, tamaddon-e ariati va enqelab-e ruhani.*"

11. Ibid., p. 197.

12. Reza Afshari, "The Historians of the Constitutional Movement and the Making of Iran's Populist Tradition," *The International Journal of Middle East Studies*, vol. 25, no. 3 (1993): pp. 477–494.

13. For a perceptive discussion of Kasravi's historiography as nationalist "morality tale," with special attention to Azerbaijan, see Farzin Vejdani, *Making History in Iran: Education, Nationalism and Print Culture* (Stanford, CA: Stanford University Press, 2015): pp. 127–137.

14. Arthur Mitzman, *Michelet, Historian: Rebirth and Romanticism in Nineteenth-century France* (New Haven and London: Yale University Press, 1990), chapters 8, 9, and on socialism, p. 254.

15. Oscar A. Haac, *Jules Michelet* (Boston, 1982), pp. 74–75, 118–120.

16. Ibid., pp. 139–144.

17. See Alireza Manafzadeh, "*Jaigah-e Kasravi dar tarikhnegari va tarikh-shenasi*" in *Negah-e no*, vol. 96 (winter 1391): pp. 44–52, p. 47. A more extensive study of Kasravi is Manafzadeh, *Ahmad Kasravi, l'homme qui voulait sortir l'iran de l'obscurantisme* (Paris: L'Harmattan, 2004), p. 93.

18. Kasravi, *Payman*, p. 368. For his part, Taqizadeh also strongly denounced Kasravi's history of constitutional revolution. See Hasan Taqizadeh, *Khatabe-ye aqa-ye Seyyed Hasan Taqizadeh* (Tehran, 1959), pp. 47–48, 57.

19. Quoted in Homa Katouzian, *"Kasravi va adabiyat"* in *Iran Nameh* vol. XX, nos. 1–2 (Spring & Summer 2002): pp. 171–194, p. 176.

20. Kasravi, *Peyman*, p. 415.

21. A good comparative study of Asian intellectual responses to nineteenth-century European imperialism is found in Pankaj Mishra, *From the Ruins of Empire: The Intellectuals Who Remade Asia* (New York: Farrar, Straus and Giroux, 2012). A classical conservative critique of Western European modernity is Nicola Berdyaev, *The Russian Idea* (New York: Macmillan Company, 1948).

22. Afshin Marashi, "Imagining Hafez: Rabindranath Tagore in Iran, 1932," in *Journal of Persianate Studies*, vol. 3 no. 1 (2010): pp. 46–77.

23. Kasravi, quoted in Tavakoli-Targhi, *"Tajaddod-e ekhtera'i, tamaddon-e ariati va enqelab-e ruhani,"* pp. 218–219. Tavakoli-Targhi's perceptive study, however, does not probe further into possible Asian or European influences on Kasaravi's thought.

24. Muhammad Iqbal, *The Reconstruction of Religious Thought in Islam* (Stanford, CA: Stanford University Press, 2012), introduction and pp. xxi–xxv, pp. 114–115. For Spengler's characterization of Islam as "Magian" see Oswald Spengler, *The Decline of the West*, trans. Charles Francis Atkinson, (London: Allen and Unwin, 1959), vol. I, chapters vi and ix, and vol. II, chapters viii and ix. For a summary of Iqbal's idea see Chapter 1 in Farzin Vahdat, *Islamic Ethos and the Specter of Modernity* (New York: Anthem Press, 2015).

25. Ali Shariati was deeply influenced by Iqbal, whom he considered a "perfect human being." Ali Rahnema, *An Islamic Utopian: A Political Biography of Ali Shari'ati* (New York: I. B. Tauris, 1998), p. 65. See also Ali Shariati, *Ma va Eqbal* (Tehran, n.d.).

26. Kasravi, *Payman*, p. 508.

27. On Republican Turkey's cult of reason see Sukru Hanioglu, *Ataturk: An Intellectual Biography* (Princeton, NJ: Princeton University Press, 2011), chapter 7 on "nationalism and Kemalism." The ideology of Kemalism built on a powerful trend among late Ottoman Westenizers whose moto was: "civilization is European civilization"; ibid., p. 204.

28. I use the awkward but accurate English term "Europeanism" for *Orupa'i-gari*. Similarly, *"europeanisme"* has been used as the French equivalent of this term. See Manafzadeh, *Ahmad Kasravi*, p. 120. Kasravi' coining of this particular construction may have been influenced by his knowledge of the Turkish term *Avrupalilashmak*, meaning "Europeanization," and

used by his contemporary Ottoman and Turkish intellectuals. See Kemal H. Karapat, *The Politicization of Islam: Reconstructing Identity, State, Faith, and Community in the Late Ottoman State* (Oxford and New York: Oxford University Press, 2001), p. 375.

29. Ahmad Kasravi, *Zaban-e pak* (Tehran, 1999), p. 73. Similarly, Kasravi invented terms such as *Shi'i-gari* (Shi'ism) and *Baha'i-gari* (Bahaism). These neologisms did not catch on, while the problem of translating "ism" was solved by its direct appropriation as a suffix in modern Persian.

30. Ahmad Kasravi, *Dar piramun-e falsafeh* (Tehran, 1943), p. 83.

31. Tavakoli-Targhi, "*Tajaddod-e ekhtera'i, tamaddon-e ariati va enqelab-e ruhani*," p. 214.

32. Echoing Kazemzadeh, he wrote:

Europe is finished. Where greed is the foundation of life and humans must think solely of monetary gain, hundreds of thousands of youths must be sacrificed to a single weapons factory. That is why we consider Europe's followers among Easterners the most ignorant and confused people. Knowing Europe and its ways makes us certain that on Europe lacks reason and humanity. A similar future awaits the East if it follows Europe.

Kasravi, *Payman*, pp. 218–219.

33. Ahmad Kasravi, *Varjavand-e Bonyad* (Koln, Germany, 1980), pp. 20–21. Accepting Darwinism partially, Kasravi says evolutionary mutations prove God's hand at work. He also rejects the materialist view of humans as animals. "In addition to life (*jan*), which is physical and animal, humans also possess soul (*ravan*), which is goodness, exalted and eternal." Ibid., pp. 28, 31.

34. Quoted in Nizai Berkes, *The Development of Secularism in Turkey* (Montreal: McGill University Press, 1964), p. 287.

35. Kasravi, *Varjavand-e Bonyad*, p. 24.

36. Ibid., pp. 44, 47, 56–57, 118–119.

37. Kasravi, *Peyman*, p. 412. On Kasravi's defense of Reza Shah era nation-building see Asghar Fathi, "*Kasravi cheh miguyad*," *Iran Nameh*, vol. XX, nos. 1–2 (spring–summer 2012), pp. 261–275. Kasravi quoted on p. 269.

38. Kasravi, *Payman*, pp. 225–226. He also blames "the West" (*gharb*) for inducing self-doubt among Iranians.

To a people, nothing is worse than self-loathing. Such people will never see success. I repeat that such shameful behavior among Iranians is linked to the European policy of world domination. The awareness

Notes to Pages 120–121

and competence of Iranians during the Constitutional Revolution clashed with Western policies of world domination. Opposing it, the latter relied on their lackeys to spread shameful self-loathing in Iran.

Kasravi, Payman, pp. 410–411.

39. Turkish alphabet was Romanized in 1928, and in 1932 the Turkish Language Institute was set up to, among other things, "purify" Turkish of foreign words and replace them with authentic Turkish words. This Turkish Language project was closely linked to the Turkish History project, which placed Turks at the highest position in the historical hierarchy of civilizations, close to European nations. The 1932 congress officially called for studies on the relationship of Turkish to Indo-European languages, "the languages of the white races." Ilker Ayturk, "Turkish Linguistics against the West: The Origins of Linguistic Nationalism in Ataturk's Turkey," in *Middle Eastern Studies*, vol. 40, no. 6 (November 2004): pp. 1–25, pp. 1–2, 11. By 1936, the work of this institute culminated in the Sun Language Theory, according to which Turkish was the root of all languages of the world, having originated in Central Asia, "It was very likely that it was the language of the Sumerians and Hittites . . . Turkish was the language of the first and oldest culture. It was at the roots of Sanskrit, Greek and Latin, which make up the basis of modern linguistics. Initially endorsed by Ataturk, these views continued to be officially propagated, though gradually somewhat modified. Yilmaz Colak, "Language Policy and Official Ideology in Early Republican Turkey," in *Middle East Studies*, vol. 40, no. 6 (November 2004): pp. 67–91. p. 77

40. Hasan Shayegan, *Eqbal va tarikhnegari* (Tehran, 2004), p. 151.

41. Kasravi, *Payman*, pp. 144–145.

42. Kasravi admitted new languages could emerge when older ones mixed together. But he insisted that once a language was fully formed it had to be "protected" from mixings with other languages. He thus advocated "linguistic independence," based on the belief that open-ended interaction of languages endangered the unity of their speakers. See *Payman*, pp. 144–145.

43. Kasravi, *Sarneveshat-e Iran cheh khahad bud?* Quoted in Shahrokh Meskoob, *dasatan-e adabiyat va sargozasht-e ejtema'* (Tehran, 1994), note number 39 on p. 35. See also Kasravi's *Zaban-e pak* (Tehran, n.d.)

44. As well as political self-determination and independence, Gandhi's notion of "Sawaraj" meant mastery of the self or understanding "self-dom." This concept of Sawarai was rooted in Hindu texts and traditions, particularly in Bhagavad-Gita. See Ananya Vajpeyji, *Righteous Republic* (Cambridge, MA: Harvard University Press, 2012), chapter 1. According to Vajpeyji, Gandhi interpreted the

Hindu tradition outside of its Brahman commentaries, hence making an epistemic break, pp. 59–66.

45. Kasravi, *Varjavand-e Bonyad*, pp. 127–129, 132, 138–140.
46. Ibid., pp. 39, 42, 134–137. He believed crises like the Great Depression were endemic to Europe and the US:

Unemployment is due to the increase in machinery and the accelerating pace of their operation. This is an inevitable consequence. Obviously, when one worker can rely on machinery to do the job of one hundred, the other ninety-nine workers must go job-less.

Kasravi then argued that mechanization also led to over-production and the saturation of markets beyond consumer capacity. This happened because "ignorant and greedy individuals placed commerce above people's livelihood, constantly building machines and factories while using oppression and deceit to turn the entire world into their markets," *Payman*, p. 501. He insisted that the mere use of large machinery causes unemployment: "Unemployment is due to the increase in mechanization and its rapidity. It can be remedied only by using less machinery." Ibid., p. 503. Finally, according to him, larger and faster mechanized production should not replace labor that could be done by manufacture or small machines. Ibid., pp. 504–505.

47. Kasravi, *Payman*, pp. 548–549.
48. "Some talk of women's rights, demanding their participation in government. Such idiocies ruin the world. As if women were created for such tasks, or such duties could befit them! A Woman's value is acknowledged when she becomes a man's spouse, sharing his life and adorning his home. She would then become a mother to sons and daughters, enjoying her life raising them. What negates women's rights is the refusal of some men to marry."

Ibid., p. 239.

49. Kasravi, *Payman*, pp. 235–236. He believed God created men and women for different tasks; therefore, women should perform only women's tasks:

Some consider women deficient in reason. This is true only when they perform men's tasks ... Women are to raise children, make homes, sew, cook and perform similar tasks. Thus, God has given them more intelligence and perception so that they could better perform their own tasks. Men, however, can perform their tasks only by using thought and reason, hence being granted more reason by God.

Therefore, women lack nothing as long as occupied with their own tasks, yet they appear incapable and deficient in reason when put to men's tasks.

Kasravi, *Payman*, p. 237.

50. Kasravi, *Payman*, p. 186.

51. He approved of the "European" idea of educating girls. Iranians and other "Easterners," he believed, should educate girls along with boys. But boys and girls were to be educated differently. Like contemporary Muslim modernists, Kasravi noted that both urban and rural women worked as much as or even more than men. But this was acceptable as long as they performed "women's work," i.e. tasks to which they were "naturally" suited. Ibid., pp. 239–243 and *Varjavand-e Bonyad*, p. 146.

52. For a revisionist interpretation of the Reza Shah era unveiling campaign see Jasamin Rostam-Kolayi and Afshin Matin-asgari, "Unveiling ambiguities: revisiting 1930s Iran's *kashf-i hijab* campaign," in Stephanie Cronin, ed. *Anti-Veiling Campaign in the Muslim World* (London and New York: Routledge, 2014), pp. 121–148.

53. Arnold Toynbee in a 1947 *New York Times* article, quoted in William H. McNeill, *Arnold J. Toynbee: A life* (New York and Oxford: Oxford University Press, 1989), p. 223.

54. Ibid., p. 220. Toynbee's influential critics, such as British historian Hugh Trever-Roper and Dutch historian Pieter Geyl, had pointed out his prophetic posture. Ibid., pp. 224, 239, 256.

55. Kasravi, *Varjavand-e Bonyad*, pp. 70, 95–97.

56. Kasravi claims there is another world, but we can know nothing of it and therefore should not be concerned about it. This makes religion a secular pursuit, entirely focused on the affairs of this world. Those who do right in this world may earn a higher spiritual status in the next one, where there is no physical resurrection. Ibid., pp. 111–113. Zoroaster, Moses and Jesus, he insisted, preached the same basic message, but most of their followers were led astray by interpreting them differently. *Peyman*, pp. 256–258. Kasravi vehemently opposed Sufis, including "saintly" ones like al-Hallaj, for claiming direct connection to God. He also rejected much of the Bible's content, as well as the divinity of Jesus. Ibid., pp. 263, 264. During the 1930s, however, he still claimed to be preaching "True Islam," and not a new religion:

Not knowing Islam properly, Muslims unfortunately imagine I preach a new religion beyond Islam. However, founding a new religion beyond Islam means nothing but ignorance ... I consider religious divisions among people to be the cause of their misfortune, cursing those who put people on separate paths. How can I then come up with yet another path?

... I merely wish and preach that Muslims know Islam truly, discarding the added beliefs which cause divide them. Moreover, not only Easterners but the whole world must follow this God-knowing religion, along with Muslims.

Kasravi, *Peyman*, p. 267.

57. Abrahamian, "Kasravi: The Integrative Nationalist of Iran," pp. 280, 288–289. Kasravi sometimes expresses the same idea clearly: "What is religion (din)? Religion is the proper knowledge of the world, its workings and of the people in it, the knowledge of the truth of life, of the essence of humanity, and of how to live a rational life." *Varjavand-e Bonyad*, p. 69.

58. Karapat, *The Politicization of Islam*, pp. 379–381; quoted on p. 370.

59. Hanioglu, *Ataturk*, pp. 48–51, 54–57.

60. While strongly rejecting both Babi and Baha'i religions, Kasravi approvingly cites the Baha'i belief that "every age has its own particular needs; therefore, in every age, a manifestation of God's Cause arises to establish a religion according to the needs of the times." Ahmad Kasravi, *Baha'i-gari* (Tehran, 1944), pp. 65–66.

61. Ibid., pp. 121–122.

62. Ibid., pp. 14–17, 20, 84–97.

63. The Bab's scripture, *Bayan*, called for the burning of all books contradicting its new dispensation. Abbas Amanat, *Resurrection and Renewal: The Making of the Babi Movement in Iran, 1844–1850* (Ithaca and London: Cornell University Press, 1898), p. 409.

64. Fatemeh Sayyah, *"Keyfiyat-e roman"* (the Quality of the Novel), first published in the newspaper *Iran*, February 1934, and reproduced in Mohammad Golbon, *Naqd va siahat: Doktor Fatemeh Sayyah* (Tehran: Qatreh, 2004), pp. 333–342. Sayyah's doctoral dissertation, submitted to Moscow University, was on Anatole France. Ibid., pp. 66–67. The above collection of Sayyah's published writings in Persian is the only source on her life and works. Clearly the most outstanding woman intellectual of her generation, Sayyah is basically absent in intellectual histories and other studies of modern Iranian women, apparently due to her affiliation with the Tudeh Party in the 1940s.

65. Going beyond Islamic strictures, Kasravi rejected not only usury but even the borrowing of money. Kasravi, *Peyman*, pp. 151–153, 156, 168.

66. Ibid., pp. 182–185.

67. "Among Europe's strange traits is the abnormal and excessively high place accorded to trade and commerce. In fact, commerce becomes more important than the people's livelihood. Neglecting their duty to protect the people, governments instead support only merchants and capitalists,

going to war and shedding blood for their sake." *Peyman*, pp. 207–209, 400, quoted in pp. 404–405.

68. Kasravi, *Dar rah-e sisat* (Tehran, 1945), section 2. This text lacks page numbers, therefore references are to its numbered sections. As for political figures in recent Iranian history, Kasravi approved only of the ferocious warrior king Nader Shah and reformist Qajar prime minister Amir Kabir. According to him, Nader's wars with the Ottomans and bloody invasions of India and Central Asia were not acts of aggression but proof of "Iranian superiority" forcing other countries to accept friendly relations with Iran. Ibid., section 4.

69. Ibid., section 9.

70. Ibid., section 42.

71. Ibid., section 43. For Kasravi's views on the Tudeh Party, as well as the Soviet Union and its intervention in Iranian Azerbaijan see Manafzadeh, *Ahmad Kasravi*, pp. 130–140.

72. Ruhollah Khomeini, *Kashf al-asrar* (Los Angeles: Ketab Corporation, 2009). Ali-Asghar Hakamizadeh, *Asrar-e hezar saleh* (Tehran, 1943).

73. *Secrets Exposed* has not received the scholarly attention it deserves. It was not discussed in Said Amir Arjomand's *The Turban for the Crown: The Islamic Revolution in Iran* (New York: Oxford University Press, 1988) and *Shadow of God and the Hidden Imam* (Chicago and London: University of Chicago Press, 1984) or in his "Ideological Revolution in Shi'ism" in Arjomand, ed. *Authority and Political culture in Shiism* (Albany: State University of New York, 1988), pp. 178–209. Nor did it appear in these works' references. Shaul Bakhash, *The Reign of the Ayatollahs: Iran and the Islamic Revolution* (New York: Basic books, 1984), p. 24, and Shahrough Akhavai, *Religion and Politics in Contemporary Iran* (Albany: State University of New York, 1980), p. 163 mention it in passing. Bakhash and Akhavi note an intellectual rupture between *Secrets Exposed* and Khomeini's *Hokumat-e Eslami* (Islamic Government) (Najaf and Tehran, 1977).

74. Yann Richard, "Shari'at Sangalaji: A Reformist Theologian of the Rida Shah Era," in Said Amir Arjomand, ed. *Authority and Political Culture in Shi'ism* (Albany: State University of New York Press, 1988), pp. 159–177.

75. Hakamizadeh, *Asrar-e hezar saleh*, pp. 47–49.

76. "Some of our writers have taken it upon themselves to attack Islam and the clergy ... [But] writing against the clergy helps destroy the country and its independence. Readers therefore are asked to carefully study this book's discussion of the clergy and government, impartially *judging it according to reason*, in order for matters to be clarified." Khomeini, *Kashf al-asrar*, p. 2, emphasis added.

77. Ibid., p. 3. Khomeini does mention Shari'at-Sangelaji by name, yet attacks him vociferously. See, for example, pp. 77, 333.

78. Ibid., pp. 112–120.

79. Ibid., pp. 3–4 and 5–6.

80. Here, Khomeini recounts, as his own personal observation, an anti-clerical anecdote, according to which Iran's first generation of *chauffeurs* refused to allow "mullahs" to ride in automobiles. Ibid., p. 9.

81. Ibid., pp. 11–23.

82. For example, in a clear yet unnamed reference, Kasravi is accused of following "the Magian, non-believing (*moshrek*) fire-worshipping Zoroaster," p. 59. On growing official and unofficial appreciation of neo-Zoroastrianism in the Reza Shah era see Monica M. Ringer, *Pious Citizens: Reforming Zoroastrianism in India and Iran* (Syracuse, NY: Syracuse University Press, 2001).

83. Khomeini, *Kashf al-asrar*, pp. 32–37.

84. Khomeini's own education and teaching curriculum included philosophy and *Erfan* (mysticism) topics that were marginalized, if not rejected, by mainstream Shi'i clerical hierarchy. See Mohammad-Taqi Haj-Bushehr, "*Mo'alem va morad-e Ruhollah Musavi Khomeini*" in *Cheshm andaz*, no. 13 (spring 1994): pp. 32–41.

85. Khomeini, *Kashf al-asrar*, p. 269.

86. Ibid., pp. 272–273. Throughout *Kashf al-asrar*, Khomeini uses the term "*tudeh*," (the mass/mases), apparently borrowed from Kasravi.

87. Khomeini, *Kashf al-asrar*, pp. 53–54.

88. On the transformation of Khomeini's themes and vocabulary see Ervand Abrahamian, *Khomeinism: Essays on the Islamic Republic* (Berkeley, CA: University of California Press, 1993).

89. A reference to European colonialism (*este'mar*) appears in *Kashf al-asrar*, p. 330, where Khomeini argues the clergy are Iran's only defense against foreign domination. See also *Kashf al-asrar*, pp. 216, 107–108. In passing, he expresses sympathy for "old women" and "poor children," as well as a "mass of workers whose blood is being sucked by a bunch of cruel users." pp. 242–243.

90. Vanessa Martin, *Islam and Modernism: The Iranian Revolution of 1906* (London: I. B. Tauris, 1989), p. 24.

91. Khomeini, *Kashf al-asrar*, pp. 186–187. Bakhash notes this passage and its important implications in *The Reign of Ayatollahs*, p. 23.

92. Amir Arjomand, "Ideological Revolution in Shi'ism." See Mohsen Kadivar, *Nazariyeha-ye dowlat dar fiqh-e Shi'eh* (Tehran, 1376).

93. Khomeini, *Kashf al-asrar*, p. 290.

94. Khomeini, *Kashf al-asrar*, pp. 184–185. The same formula for a government ultimately controlled by jurists is repeated on pp. 222, 233.

95. Ibid., pp. 275–276.
96. Ibid., pp. 232, 74. Similar pronouncements are found on p. 18 and pp. 55–56.
97. Fakhreddin Shadman, *Taskhir-e tamaddon-e farangi* (Teharn: Gam-e no, 2003).
98. See Christoph Schumann, "The 'Failure' of Radical Nationalism and the 'Silence' of Liberal Thought in the Arab World," in *Comparative Studies of South Asia, Africa and the Middle East*, vol. 28, no. 3 (2008): pp. 404–415. England, the purported birth place of liberalism, was only a tiny part of the highly illiberal trans-oceanic British Empire. On the illiberal character of the British Empire see, for instance, Jack P. Greene, ed., *Exclusionary Empire: English Liberty Overseas, 1600–1900* (New York: Cambridge University Press, 2010).
99. Choi Chatterjee, "Imperial Incarcerations: Ekaterina Breshko-Breshkovskaia, Vinayak Savarkar, and the Original Sins of Modernity," in *Slavic Review*, vol. 74, no. 4 (winter 2015): pp. 849–872; quoted on p. 870.
100. Abbas Milani, *The Persian Sphinx* (Washington DC: Mage, 2000), p. x. Milani's *Tajaddod va tajaddod-setizi dar Iran* (Tehran, 1997), follows the same line of argument, for example in the chapter that insists Fakhreddin Shadman believed in constitutionalism, "the rule of law," and a "democratic government" (*hokomat-e azadi*), p. 209. See also the entry on "Forughi" in Abbas Milani, *Eminent Persians: The Men and Women Who Made Modern Iran, 1941–1979* (Syracuse, NY: Syracuse University Press, 2008), vol. 1, pp. 152–157. Another portrayal of Forughi as a liberal is Ali-Asghar Haqdar, *Mohammad-Ali Forughi va sakhtarha-ye novin-e madani* (Tehran, 2005). For the actual political ideas of leading Reza Shah era intellectual statesmen see Ali-Asghar Hikmat, *Si Khatereh az asr-e farkhonde-ye Pahlavi* (Tehran, 1975). Ali Akbar Siasi, *Yek zendegi-e siasi* (Tehran, 2014). Isa Sadiq, *Yadegar-e omr* (Tehran, 1966).
101. Ramin Jahanbeglu, "Iranian Intellectuals and Cosmopolitan Citizenship" in Lucian Stone, ed. *Iranian Identity and Cosmopolitanism: Spheres of Belonging* (London and New York: Bloomsbury, 2014), pp. 17–33; quoted on p. 24.
102. Forughi considered Montesquieu "one of the first individuals who have looked at history philosophically." Mohammad-Ali Forughi, *Seyr-e hekmat dar Orupa* (Tehran, 2000), vol. 1, p. 161. However, even Montesquieu could be considered a subversive thinker in early twentieth-century Iran. Forughi's father, Mohammad-Hosein, had begun the translation of Montesquieu's *Spirit of the Laws*, whose complete Persian translation appeared in the early twentieth century

but was vehemently denounced by some clerics as anti-Islamic. See Reza Bigdelu, *Bastangara'i dar tarikh-e mo'aser-e Iran* (Tehran, 2001), p. 75.

103. Forughi, *Seyr-e hekmat dar Orupa*, vol. 2, pp. 186, 123.
104. Milani, *Tajaddod va tajaddod-setizi dar Iran*, pp. 195–196.
105. Boroujerdi, *Iranian Intellectuals and the West: The Tormented Triumph of Nativism*, p. 62.
106. Quoted in Milani, *Tajaddod va tajaddo-setizi in Iran*, p. 211.
107. This is noted in Ali Gheissari, *Iranian Intellectuals in the 20th Century* (Austin, TX: University of Texas Press, 1998), pp. 87–88.
108. Boroujerdi, *Iranian Intellectuals and the West*, p. 62.
109. Shadman, *Taskhir-e tamaddon-e farangi*, p. 31.
110. Ibid., p. 46.
111. Ibid., p. 38.
112. Ibid., p. 39.
113. Ibid., p. 45.
114. Ibid., p. 43.
115. Holly Shissler's "Afterword" to Ahmet Midhat, *Felatun Bey and Rakim Efendi*, trans. Meliheh Levi and Monica M. Ringer (New York: Syracuse University Press, 2016).
116. A "materialist" Young Ottoman in his youth, Midhat later became a defender of Sultan Abdulhamid's conservative modernization, opposing "decadent" materialists, atheists and socialists. Nizai Berkes, *The Development of Secularism in Turkey* (Montreal: McGill University Press, 1964), pp. 281–285; Midhat quoted on p. 285. See also Shissler, "Afterword," pp. 157–159.
117. "Both the *alaturka* and the emancipated *alaftanga* man or women, were living in a moral vacuum. Hence, their behavior lacked rationality and they engaged in all sorts of eccentric, dishonest, degenerate, or other antisocial behavior." Berkes, *The Development of Secularism in Turkey*, pp. 303–304.
118. Ibid., p. 48.
119. Shadman, *Taskhir-e tamaddon-e farangi*, p. 53.
120. Ibid., p. 75.
121. Ibid., p. 106.
122. Ibid., p. 86.
123. Fatemeh Sayyah quoted in Golbon, *Naqd va siahat*, pp. 341–342.
124. On the similarities and differences of Toynbee's and Spengler's notions of the rise and fall of civilizations see William H. McNeill, *Arnold J. Toynbee: A life* (New York and Oxford: Oxford University Press, 1989), pp. 98–103.
125. Shadman, *Taskhir-e tamaddon-e farangi*, p. 61.

126. Jalal Al-Ahmad, *Gharbazdegi* (Tehran, 1962), footnote to p. 36.
127. Recently Shadman has received attention in a revisionist trend seeking to rehabilitate pre-revolutionary "establishment" intellectuals. Thus, Abbas Milani's introduction to the 2002 edition of *Taskhir-e tammadon-e farangi* upholds the relevance of Shadman's prognosis of European culture, claiming Al-Ahmad's criticism of Shadman betrays his own "shallowness" and *fokoli*-mannerism. Yet, Milani fails to show why Al-Ahmad's specific objection is incorrect. See p. 17.

The Mid-century Moment of Socialist Hegemony

1. George Allen's "forward" to George Lenczowski, *Russia and the West in Iran, 1918–1948* (Ithaca, NY: Cornell University Press, 1949), p. vii.
2. Ervand Abrahamian, *Iran between Two Revolutions* (Princeton, NJ: Princeton University Press, 1982), p. 345.
3. Homa Katouzian quoted in Negin Nabavi, *Intellectuals and the State in Iran: Politics, Discourse and the Dilemma of Authenticity* (Gainesville, FL: University of Florida Press, 2003), p. 5.
4. British Foreign Office (May 5, 1931) document, quoted in Abbas Milani, *Eminent Persians: The Men and Women Who Made Modern Iran, 1941–1979* (Syracuse, NY: Syracuse University Press, 2008), vol. 1, p. 154.
5. See Fakhreddin Azimi, *Iran: The Crisis of Democracy* (London: I. B. Tauris, 1989), p. 39. For a nuanced evaluation of Forughi's "liberal" credentials see ibid., pp. 36–39.
6. Anonymous, *Gozashteh cheragh-e rah-e ayandeh ast* (Tehran, n.d.), vol. 1, p. 118. Contemporary press severely criticized Forughi for such views. See ibid., pp. 119–120.
7. Many sources have attributed this sentence to Forughi. See, for example, Ali-Akbar Sisai, *Yek Zendegi-ye siasi: Khaterat-e doctor Ali-Akbar Siasi* (Tehran, 2014), p. 139.
8. On bread riots and political unrest, see Baqer Aqeli, *Ruzshomar-e tarikh-e Iran: Az mashruteh ta enqelab-e Eslami* (Tehran, 1990), vol. 1, pp. 233–234, 245, 250, 255.
9. Lenczowski's *Russia and the West in Iran* set the tone for Cold War studies of the Tudeh Party outside of Iran, while official Iranian historiography avoided the subject or repeated obligatory condemnations of the party's "betrayal." Similarly harsh judgments, however, were held by Iran's more independent-minded historians. See, for example, Fereydun Adamiyat, "*Ashoftegi dar fekr-e tarikhi*" in *Mellat-e bidar*, vol. 4, no. 2 (February 1985): pp. 14–24. According to Adamiyat, the Tudeh was "a party that forever turned its back on the

nation, always served foreign interests, betrayed Iran's national movement, and was the most untruthful of all Iranian political parties." Ibid., p. 22.

10. R. M. Burrel, ed., *Iran Political Diaries (1881–1965)*, vol. 12 (1943–1945). Archives Edition, 1997: Military attaché's intelligence summary no. 15 for the period April 7–13, 1943, quoted on p. 3.

11. Abrahamian, *Iran between Revolutions*, p. 284.

12. Azimi concurs that the British recognized the Tudeh as the only party with a popular program and hence recommended reforms to Iran's upper classes, who adamantly refused to carry them out. Nevertheless, the Tudeh Party remains marginal in Azimi's otherwise admirable study. See Azimi, *Iran: The Crisis of Democracy*, pp. 81–84.

13. Mahnaz Matin and Nasser Mohajer, *"Peykar-e zan-e Irani baray-e dastyabi beh haq-e ra'y, 1320–1325," Iran Nameh*, vol. 30, no. 3 (Fall 2015): pp. 184–228, pp. 187–190. See also Maryam Farmanfarma'ian, *Khaterat-e Maryma Firuz* (Tehran, 2003), pp. 40–54. Hamid Ahmadi, *Ma ham dar in Khaneh haqi darim: The Memoir of Najmai Alavi* (Tehran, 2004), pp. 60–70.

14. The Tudeh Party's 1944 program, quoted in Matin and Mohajer, *"Peykar zan-e Irani,"* pp. 190–191.

15. Camron Michael Amin, *Gender, State Policy, and Popular Culture, 1865–1946* (Gainesville, FL: University Press of Florida, 2002), p. 226. According to Amin, the Women's Party was established in 1944; p. 234.

16. Sayyah quoted in Matin and Mohajer, *"Peykar-e zan-e Irani,"* pp. 221–222. *Sokhan* is quoted in ibid., p. 212.

17. Matin and Mohajer, *"Peykar-e zan-e Irani,"* pp. 225–228. Amin, *The Making of the Modern Iranian Woman*, pp. 237–238.

18. Abrahamian, *Iran between Revolutions*, p. 300.

19. This was attested to years later by Taqizadeh, then a Senator and member of the political establishment. See Taqizadeh, *Seh Khatabeh* (Tehran, 1965), p. 117. The same point is noted in recent studies that are hostile to the Tudeh Party. Thus, according to Sadeq Zibakalam, "properly speaking, the Tudeh was the only political party in modern Iranian history." Zibakalam quoted in Mojtaba Maqsudi, ed. *Tahavolat-e sisai-ejtema'i-ye Iran 1320–57* (Tehran: Rozaneh, 2000), p. 48. On the deep impact of the left on the Iranian Revolution and Islamic Republic see Zibakalam, *Moqaddame-yi bar enqelab-e Eslami* (Tehran: Rozaneh, 1983).

20. Abrahamian, *Iran between Revolutions*, pp. 299–303.

21. Ibid., p. 285.

22. Ibid., p. 300.

23. Enyatollah Reza estimates that the Tudeh Party branch in Azerbaijan had suddenly grown to a membership of 30,000 to 50,000. The figure was bolstered by 10,000 new members coming across the border from the Soviet Union. Enayatollah Reza, *Khaterat-e doctor Enyatollah Reza* (Tehran, 2013), pp. 38–39. A British Foreign Office confidential report on "Activities and Development of the Tudeh Party," Persia, May 23, 1951, UK, National Archives, EP 1016/12, states that "by 1951 [T]he party is now more strongly organized than a year ago."

24. The US embassy in Tehran, August 31, 1953, estimates the Tudeh Party's national membership to be somewhere between 15,000 and 22,000. See UK National Archives, Foreign Office document 371/104573. A May 1951 Foreign Office report had estimated only 2,500. Abrahamian, *Iran between Revolutions*, pp. 303, 321.

25. Maziar Behrouz, *Rebels with a Cause: The Failure of the Left in Iran* (London: I. B. Tauris, 1999), pp. 18–19.

26. The Tudeh Party of Persia, "A Test Case for Communist Planning in the Middle East," UK National Archives, FO 975/69, pp. 12–15; quoted on p. 13.

27. Behrouz, *Rebels with a Cause*, p. 15. On the Tudeh's non-revolutionary character see also Azadeh Kian-Thiebaut, *Secularization of Iran: A Doomed Failure?* (Paris: PEETERS, 1998).

28. This is from Anatole France's 1923 introduction to *The Iron Heel* (Tehran, 1952), p. 9.

29. M. Hushiar (pseudonym), trans. *Seh maqaleh dar bare-ye enqelab-e mashrute-ye Iran* (Tehran, 1978), pp. 5–7. On p. 8, the translator's introduction is dated 1952. More official examples of Stalinist philosophy were pamphlets like *Marksizm va falsafeh* [Marxism and Philosophy] (Tehran, 1953), trans. Nozar (pseudonym).

30. Translator's intro to Gerorgi Plekhanov's *The Role of Individual in History* (Florence Italy: Mazdak, n.d.).

31. Marxist translations of the 1940s and 1950s were often hasty and not on par with the higher standards set by older, more experienced translators. Foroughi, for example, had coined a new compound Persian phrase for "determinism." He also used three different Persian words for "necessity," none of which had the religious and metaphysical connotations of *jabr*, which he equated with the French term *fatalisme*. See Mohammad-Ali Foroughi, *Seyr-e hekmat dar Orupa* (Tehran: Zavvar, 2000), vol. 1, the glossary, pp. 269–271, 277, 279.

32. Dariush Homayun, *Diruz va farda* (n.p., 1981), p. 54.

33. Croce quoted in Hans Roger and Eugen Weber, eds. *The European Right: A Historical Profile* (Berkeley and Los Angeles: University of California Press, 1974), p. 223.

34. These included Nima Yushij, Ahmad Shamlu, Siavosh Kasara'i, Sadeq Hedayat, Bozorg Alavi, Mahmud E'temadzadeh, Jalal Al-Ahmad, Sadeq Chubak, Ebrahim Golestan, Parviz Natel-Khanlari, Fatemeh Sayyah, Fereydun Tavallali, Ehsan Tabari and Karim Keshavarz. See Nureddin Nuri, *Nokhostin kongere-ye nevisandegan-e Iran* (Tehran: Ostureh, 2005), pp. 12–11. Hekmat's speech on pp. 25–67 and Tabari's on pp. 69–73.

35. He later proudly listed his service to the crown in *Thirty Remembrances of the Glorious Pahlavi Era*. Ali-Asghar Hekmat, *Si Khatereh az asr-e farkhonde-ye Pahlavi* (Tehran, 1975).

36. Nuri, *Nokhostin kongere*, pp. 51–52.

37. Congress resolution in ibid., p. 278.

38. A good brief discussion of the first Writers' Congress and the leftist drift in translation movement is in Hasan Abedini, *Sad sal dastan-nevisi dar Iran*, vol. 1 (Tehran: Tondar, 1987), pp. 117–124. For a sample of mostly leftist best-seller translations see Mohammad Qazi, *Sargozasht-e tarjomeha-ye man* (Tehran, 1995).

39. This definition of an "intellectual international" is by Valery Larbaud, cited in Pascale Casanova, *The World Republic of Letters*, M. B. DeBevoise, trans. (London and Cambridge, MA: Harvard University Press, 2004), p. 5. On the formation of an "international literary space," its historical evolution, internal tensions, and relation to various "national literary spaces," see Casanova.

40. Shahrokh Meskub, *Ketab-e Moretza Keyvan* (Tehran: Nader, 2003), pp. 23–24.

41. Meskub quoted in ibid., pp. 24, 26.

42. Afshin Matin-asgari, "Modern Iran's Ideological Renegades," in *Critique*, vol. 16, no. 3 (fall 2007), pp. 137–153. The reference to "neo-scholasticism" is on p. 150.

43. Cosroe Chaqueri, "Iraj Esknadri," in www.Iranicaonline.org.

44. Leonard Binder, *Iran: Political Development in a Changing Society* (Berkeley, CA: University of California Press, 1962), p. 204.

45. Examples of the latter are Maziar Behrooz, *Rebels with a Cause: The Failure of the Left in Iran* (London and New York: I. B. Tauris, 1999) and Abrahamian, *Iran between Revolutions*.

46. *Niru-ye sevvom dar moqabel-e do paygah-e ejetma'i-ye amperyalism* (Tehran, 1951), p. 87.

47. See Maleki's editorial in *Elm va zendegi*, vol. 1, no. 7 (September 1952), reproduced in Abdollah Borhan, ed. *Khalil Maleki, Nehzat-e Melli-ye Iran va edalat-e ejetma'i* (Tehran, 1999), p. 30.

48. Khalil Maleki, "*Mobareze ba bozorgtarin khatari ke nehzat-e melli ra tahdid mikond*" (Fighting the Greatest Threat to the National Movement), editorial of *Elm va zendegi*, second series, no. 3, June 1953

in Borhan, *Khalil Maleki*, pp. 79–94. See also *Nabard-e zandegi*, vol. 1, no. 4 (June 1955), in Borhan, *Khalil Maleki*, p. 112.

49. Another article in *Rahbar* insisted: "Most party members are Muslims, having particular affection and respect for [The Prophet] Mohammad's *shari'a*, never deviating from the path of this religion or accepting a creed opposed to it." See the 1942 issue of *Rahbar*, quoted in anonymous, *Gozasheteh*, vol. 1, p. 136. On Tudeh Party's denial of being communist see ibid., p. 137.

50. Significantly, it was the rejection of Marxism as ideology that led advocates of "Islamic Ideology," like Abdol-Karim Sorush, to critically reflect on the ideological features of the Islamic tradition itself. Afshin Matin-asgari, "Abdolkarim Sorush and the Secularization of Islamic Thought in Iran," in *Iranian Studies*, vol. 30, nos. 1–2 (winter–spring 1997): pp. 95–115.

51. H. E. Chehabi, *Iranian Politics and Religious Modernism* (Ithaca, NY: Cornell University Press, 1990), pp. 117–122. Taleqani and Bazargan quoted on p. 118. After Reza Shah's fall Tehran University became a legally independent entity administered by its faculty. The Shah increasingly applied pressure to curtail the university's independence, particularly to purge faculty affiliated with the Tudeh Party or the National Front. See Siasi, *Yek Zendegi-ye siasi*, pp. 145–149, 252–253, 3–4, 390.

52. Dabashi's study of the emergence of "Islamic Ideology" in 1940s to 1970s Iran includes both Bazargan and Taleqani among authors whose works helped bring about a "Marxist metamorphosis of Islam." Hamid Dabashi, *Theology of Discontent: The Ideological Foundations of the Islamic Revolution in Iran* (New York: New York University Press, 1993), p. 353. According to Dabashi, this kind of writings shows how "Marxist discourse had successfully and thoroughly established the Iranian political agenda from the 1940s through the 1970s." Ibid.

53. This was pointed out by Khomeini, who criticized Marxist and materialist-influenced Qur'anic exegeses, such as Taleqani's, for being one-sided and excessively worldly. He wrote:

Now that materialism has become so powerfully predominant in the world … a group of people have now come forward who maintain that the ultimate principle of all Islamic rule is to create social justice, that social classes are [to be] eliminated, and that there is nothing more to Islam …
Quoted in Dabashi, *Theology of Discontent*, p. 477.

54. "God-worshipping Socialists" is the more familiar English translation of the organization's name. For the reasons explained in the text, I will use this, rather than more recent translations, such as "Theist Socialists."

Mahmud Nekuruh, *Nehzat-e khoda-parastan-e sosyalist* (Tehran, 1999), pp. 47–54 and Ali Rahnema, *An Islamic Utopian: A Political Biography of Ali Shari'ati* (London: I. B. Tauris, 1998), pp. 24–29.

55. Rahnema, *An Islamic Utopian*, pp. 31–32.
56. Alexandre A. Bennigson and S. Enders Wimbush, *Muslim National Communism in the Soviet Union: A Revolutionary Strategy for the Colonial World* (Chicago, IL: University of Chicago Press, 1979). See also the section on "Muslim communists" in Adeeb Khalid, *The Politics of Muslim Cultural Reform: Jadidism in Central Asia* (Berkeley and Los Angeles: University of California press, 1998), pp. 278–301.
57. Farzin Vahdat, *Islamic Ethos and the Specter of Modernity*, Anthem Middle East Studies (London and New York: Anthem Press, 2016), p. 48.
58. Sukarno wrote: "To me, both the [US] Declaration of Independence and the Communist Manifesto contain undying truths, but the West doesn't permit a middle road." Ahmad Sukarno quoted in Cindy Adams, *Sukarno: An Autobiography* (New York: The Bobbs-Merrill Co., 1965), p. 294. Sukarno's claims of "God-sent inspiration" informed his five guiding principles of for Indonesian independence. These were nationalism, internationalism, democracy, social justice and belief in God. According to Sukarno, Indonesian "democracy" was made authentic as it corresponded to "democratic consultation Asian-style." Similarly, social justice was sanctioned by the indigenous authority of "our Goddess of Justice who stands for Social Equality." Ibid., pp. 197, 198. For Sukarno's ideas on the unity of Muslims and communist and nationalists, see also Herbert Feith and Lance Castle, eds. *Indonesian Political Thinking, 1945–1965* (Ithaca and London: Cornell University Press, 1970), pp. 357–361, 368–372.
59. Quoted in Nekuruh, *Nehzat-e khoda-parastan-e sosialist*, pp. 80–81.
60. Quoted from Nakhshab's article in the March 14, 1952 issue of *Mardom-e Iran*, reproduced in Nekuruh, *Nehzat-e khoda-parastan-e sosialist*, pp. 83–85.
61. Mohammad Nakhshab, *Majmo'e-yi az asar-e doktor Mohammad Nakhshab* (Tehran: Chapakhsh, 2002), pp. 207–208.
62. Ibid., p. 339.
63. Ibid., pp. 267–268.
64. As early as 1966, the Shah was referring to his revolution as "the Shah-People Revolution" (*enqelab-e shah va mardom*). See Mohammad Reza Pahlavi, *Enqelab-e Sefid* (Tehran, 1966), p. 3.
65. The Shah quoted in Oriana Fallaci, *Interview with History* (Boston, MA: Houghton Mifflin, 1976), John Shepley, trans., p. 277.

66. Fereydoun Hoveyda, *Fall of the Shah* (New York: Wyndham Books, 1980), Roger Liddell, trans., p. 19.
67. Ali M. Ansari, "The Myth of the White Revolution: Mohammad Reza Shah, 'Modernization' and the Consolidation of Power," in *Middle Eastern Studies*, vol. 37, no. 3 (July 2001), pp. 1–24; quoted on p. 2.
68. On the Pahlavi regime as a US "client state" see Mark J. Gasiorowski, *U.S. Foreign Policy and the Shah: Building a Client State in Iran* (Ithaca, NY: Cornell University Press, 1991).
69. Henderson paraphrased in Top Secret British Foreign Office report, "From Washington to Foreign Office"; no. 1085 (May 21, 1953), UK, National Archives, EP 1943/1.
70. Mark J. Gasiorowski, "The Qarani Affair and Iranian Politics," in *International Journal of Middle East Studies*, vol. 25, no. 4 (November 1993): pp. 625–644. On Kennedy imposing Amini's premiership see Mohammad Reza Pahlavi, *Answer to History* (New York: Stein And Day, 1980), pp. 22–23.
71. Pahlavi, *Answer to History*.
72. Ali Rahnama, *Behind the 1953 Coup in Iran: thugs, turncoats, soldiers, and spooks* (Cambridge: Cambridge University Press, 2015). Mark J. Gasiorowski and Malcolm Byrne, eds. *Mohammad Mosaddeq and the 1953 Coup in Iran* (Syracuse, NY: Syracuse University Press, 2004). Ervand Abrahamian, *The Coup: 1953, The CIA, and the Roots of Modern US-Iranian Relations* (New York and London: The New Press, 2013). See also Abrahamian's analysis of CIA documents declassified in 2017 see https://lobelog.com/new-revelations-of-the-us-in-iran/. Accessed July 4, 2017.
73. About a year after the coup (on December 1, 1954), an editorial in the daily *Kayhan*, wrote:

[E]verybody knows that this permanent martial law administration in Iran is the result of the disorder and chaos caused by the Tudeh … If, during the cooperation of the Tudeh Party with the Qavam government, the former had not frightened the people … nor encouraged chaos by supporting the occupation of Azerbaijan and the granting of an oil concession in the north of Iran to the Soviet Union, the people would not have turned away from them, and the country would have continued on its way to democracy and freedom …

Quoted in Nabavi, *Intellectuals and the State in Iran*, p. 12
74. Hedayat's correspondence show his initially positive attitude toward the Tudeh Party and the Democrats in Azerbaijan changed to utter disillusionment. Sadeq Hedayat, *Hashtad-o do nameh be Hasan Shahidnura'i* (Paris: *cesmandaz*, 2000), pp. 72 and 83–85.

75. The traumatic experience of defeat and repression is documented, for example, in Meskub, *Ketab-e Morteza Keyvan*. Published almost fifty years after the 1954 execution of Morteza Keyvan, a young idealistic Tudeh Party intellectual, this volume includes the testimony of about a dozen prominent writers, poets, translators and scholars lamenting his loss. See also Shahrokh Meskub, *Ruzha dar rah* (Edition Khavaran: Paris, 2000), vol. 1, pp. 1–79.

76. For an excellent study of these periodicals see Nabavi, *Intellectuals and the State in Iran*, chapter 2.

77. On San'atizadeh and Franklin Publishers, see Datus C. Smith Jr., "Franklin Book Program" and Cyrus Alinejad, "*San'atizadeh Kermani, Homayun*," both in www.Iranicaonline.org. On NIL see Abdol-Hosein Azarang, "*Tarikh-e nashr-e ketab dar Iran, 32*," in *Bokhara*, no. 108 (October–November 2015): pp. 113–117. On Amir Kabir, see Abdol-Hosein Azarang, "*Tarikh-e nashr ... 33*," in *Bokhara* (December 2015–January 2016), pp. 29–36. On Ja'fari's leftist background and promotion of leftist books see Iraj Afsahr's article in *Bokhara*, 18, no. 109 (December 2015–January 2016), pp. 81–85. See also Abdol-Hosein Azarang and Ali Dehbashi, *Tarikh-e shafahi-ye nashr dar Iran* (Tehran: Qoqnus, 2004).

78. Alam's reputation for drawing former Tudeh members to serve the regime was widely known. See, for example, Gholam Reza Afkhami, *The Life and Times of the Shah* (Berkeley and Los Angeles: University of California Press, 2009), p. 277. Abdul-Hosein Adharang, "Parviz Khanlari," in www.Iranicaonline.org.

79. Mohammad Reza Pahlavi, *Safarname-ye shahanshah be keshvar-e Amrika* (Tehran, 1950), pp. 80–82, p. 89.

80. The report of Henderson's August 25, 1953 meeting with the Shah is translated in *Ardashir Zahidi, Khatirat-i Ardashir Zahidi (The Memoirs of Ardeshir Zahedi)* (Bethesda MD: IBEX Publishers, 2006), p. 383.

81. A few sources have noted, in passing, the precedence of Azerbaijan's 1946 land reform. See Eric J. Hooglund, *Land and Revolution in Iran: 1960–1980* (Austin, TX: University of Texas Press, 1982), p. 43, and Ervand Abrahamian, *Iran between Two Revolutions* (Princeton, NJ: Princeton University Press, 1982), p. 408. For a brief list of Azerbaijan government's social reforms see Anonymous, "21 Azar" in *Donya* third series, vol. 3, no. 8 (November 1976): pp. 18–24, pp. 21–22. For a collection of documents, interviews and commentaries on the 1946 Azerbaijan government see Shahrokh Farzad, *Ferqe-ye demokrat-e Azarbaijan: Az takhlie-ye Tabriz ta marg-e Pishevari* (Tehran: Ohadi, 2000).

82. Arsanjai's remarks are cited in Ali Behzadi, *Shebhe khaterat* (Tehran: Zarrin, 1997), p. 23.
83. Matin and Mohajer, "*Peykar-e zan-e Irani,*" pp. 188–191.
84. Borhan, *Khalil Maleki*, pp. 235–243.
85. Naser Pakdaman's article was published in *Nemeh-e Parsi*, no. 1, May 1959. For specific references to a national literacy corps see p. 38.
86. Borhan, *Khalil Maleki*, pp. 214–215; quoted on p. 216.
87. Borhan, *Khalil Maleki*, p. 235.
88. Ibid., p. 3.
89. Ibid., pp. 5–6.
90. Ali Behzadi, *Shebhe khaterat*, p. 30.
91. The Shah often contrasted the "whiteness" of his revolution to a "dark" combination of internal and external enemies, dubbed "Red and Black Reaction." Red of course was the symbol of the Tudeh Party and communism, while "Black" symbolized Iran's "feudal" ruling classes and their obscurantist clerical allies. This terminology too was borrowed from the Marxist left, for example from Khalil Maleki, who had used it in his writings of the early 1950s. Maleki's editorial in the first issue of *Elm va zendegi* (February 1953), where warnings against the danger of "Red and Black dictatorship" appear several times. Borhan, *Khalil Maleki*, pp. 63, 64, 65.
92. Jalal Al-Ahmad, *Dar khedmat va khianat-e roshanfekran* (Tehran, 1977.), pp. 336–337. I use the simplified transliteration "Al-Ahmad," which is also closer to how the name is often pronounced in Persian.
93. Mohammad Reza Pahlavi, *Enqelab-e Sefid* (Tehran, 1965). For references to Iran's "feudal and capitalist ruling clique," "social conflict and injustices," and "the necessity of reducing class differences by the just distribution of national wealth" see, for example, pp. 16–18. The Shah's socialist pretentions were noted also by Iranian statesmen such as Alinaqi Alikhani, minister of the economy during the crucial early years of the Shah-People Revolution. He wrote: "In my opinion, had he not been a king, he would have been an engineer with socialist ideas, joining the Iran Party." Moreover, according to Alikhani, major economic development projects in the 1960s, such as land reform and industrialization, "had the socialist coloring the Shah very much liked to give his endeavors." Alinaqi Alikhani, *Kahterat-e doktor Alinaqi Alikhani (Tehran*, 1996), pp. 46, 48, see also ibid., p. 18.
94. Baheri, then minister of justice while teaching at Tehran University, says he saw this slogan at the university's entrance. Interview with Mohammad Baheri, Tape no. 8, p. 14. www.fas.harvrad.edu/.
95. Alam boasts he was responsible for "the killing of opponents," claiming ninety persons had died. He adds that the killing of thousands more

would have been justified. Mahdavi, *Goftoguha-ye man ba shah*, vol. 1, p. 95. Exact figures are not available, but hundreds of casualties seems more likely than thousands. See Maqsudi, ed. *Tahavolat-e sisai-ejtema'i-ye Iran*, chapter 15, p. 371.

96. Bazargan is quoted in Peyman Vahabzadeh, *A Guerrilla Odyssey: Modernization, Secularization, Democracy, and the Fadai Period of National Liberation in Iran, 1971–1979* (Syracuse, NY: Syracuse University Press, 2010), p. 1. CISNU resolution quoted in Afshin Matin-Asgari, *Iranian Student Opposition to the Shah* (Costa Mesa, CA: MAZDA Publishers, 2002), p. 62.

97. Nabavi, *Intellectuals and the State in Iran*, p. 91.

98. Quoted in ibid., p. 99.

99. "West-struck-ness" best conveys Fardid's original usage, as for example, in the following phrase: "The West *struck* me like a thunderbolt" (*Gharb mara zad mesl-e sa'egheh*). Quoted in Mohammad Mansur Hashemi, *Hoviyat-andishan va miras-e fekri-ye Ahmad Fardid* (Tehran, 2005), p. 29. Al-Ahmad also introduces his usage of *gharbzadegi* by comparing it to *vaba-zadegi*, that is, "being struck by cholera." Jalal Al-Ahmad, *Gharbzadegi* (Tehran, n.d.), p. 1.

100. Farhang Rajaee, *Islamism and Modernism: The Changing Discourse in Iran* (Austin, TX: The University of Texas Press, 2007), p. 103.

101. Ali Mirsepassi, *Political Islam, Iran, and the Enlightenment: Philosophies of Hope and Despair* (Cambridge: Cambridge University Press, 2011), particularly his discussion of *West-struck-ness,* pp. 120–124.

102. The preface to *West-struck-ness* mentions feedback on its manuscript by Mahmud Human, who had translated Ernst Junger's *Crossing the Line* from German, then letting Al-Ahmad to redact it into Persian prose.

103. In *Rushed Appraisal (Arzyabi-ye shetab-zadeh)*, a work whose title alludes to Al Ahmad's intellectual predicament, he wrote:

Waiting for the next hundred years, in other words waiting for history [or] having hope in history ... is the same as putting off what needs to be done today for the sake of tomorrow ... I have never wasted the present state of being (*alam-e vojud*) for those two states of non-being (*adam*), that is, tomorrow and yesterday.

Al-Ahmad, *Arzyabi-e shetab-zadeh* (Tehran, n.d.), p. 75. Even the inevitably awkward translation of this short passages conveys the rhetorical strength of Al-Ahmad's prose. Al-Ahmad imbues everyday words, such as "the present ... tomorrow and yesterday," with an existentialist flair, while making them also equivalents of centuries-old Persian-Arabic philosophical jargon (*alam-e vojud* and *'adam*). On the one hand a notable success, this kind of rhetoric involves an incongruent mélange of meanings from highly diverse linguistic, historical and cultural contexts, arbitrarily joined together.

104. "I noticed that by 'the plague' Camus means *machinisme*, this nemesis of beauty, poetry and heaven.'" Al-Ahmad, *Gharbzadegi*, p. 114.

105. Ibid., pp. 8–9.

106. Mehdi Bahar, *Mirath-khar-e este'mar* (Tehran, 1965) and Ali-Asghar Haj-Seyyed Javadi, *Arzyabi-ye arzeshha* (Tehran, 1977). The 1997 edition of the latter work was its ninth printing.

107. Mostafa Rahimi and Abol-Hasan Najafi, *Adabiat chist?* (Tehran, 1969). See also Rahimi, *Didgah-ha* (Tehran, 1973), particularly the essay "*Sharq va gharb dar tasallot va raha'i*" (The East and the West: In Dominance and Freedom), pp. 101–136.

108. "Apparently insular to becoming an object of study, enclosed within our Islamic wholeness, we eventually suffered deepening calamities. This was why, in confronting us, the West not only challenged our Islamic wholeness ... but rushed to tear up our internally decomposed homogeneity, which retained only an illusory wholeness, turning us first, like African natives, into raw material, before taking us to the laboratory."
Al-Ahmad, *Gharbzadegi*, pp. 10–11.

109. His hyperbolic excursion into the past begins a few pages into the text:

History shows we always looked to the West, having coined the term "Western" before Europeans were to call us Eastern ... Our initial attention to the West was perhaps an escape from Mother India ... Perhaps pressure from Oriental nomads caused the Westward fixation of our gaz. Hence, the Aryans came to drive the *Shahnameh*'s demons from Mazandaran to the Gulf ... Every time we built a home, just before the finishing touches, yet another hungry invading folk arrived from the East, not just to bring us down, but to wipe the slate clean to its very foundation ... That is why we had little experience with urban life, never attaining a proper urban "bourgeois" civilization.
Al-Ahmad, *Gharbzadegi*, pp. 11–15.

110. Ibid., p. 15.

111. Fanon finished *The Wretched of the Earth* just before his death in 1961. See Homi K. Bhabha's preface to Richard Philox trans. *The Wretched of the Earth* (New York: Grove Press, 2004), p. viii. Fanon's argument, concerning the creative political deployment of national culture, as opposed to returning to "indigenous" culture, is spelled out in ibid., chapter IV. "On National Culture."

112. Ibid., pp. 17–18.
113. Dariush Ashuri, *"Hoshyari-e tarikhi"* (Historical Awareness), first published in Tehran in 1967, reproduced in Dariush Ashuri, *Ma va moderniyat* (Tehran, 1995), pp. 13–42; quoted on pp. 17–18. See also pp. 22–23.
114. Ibid., p. 33.
115. Ibid., p. 38.
116. Ibid., p. 39. *Gharbzadegi*'s last paragraph resorts to Western authority to prove the bankruptcy of the West:

> the end of faith is a time of torments. The end of belief is the time of experimentation and the age of the atom. And now, my humble self, not as an easterner, but as a believing Muslim, living at dawn of Islam and expecting to see the final resurrection in his own lifetime, I see that Albert Camus, Ingmar Bergman, and many others are harbingers of resurrection. They all are the heartbroken with mankind's destiny... These fictional endings reflect humanity's actual terminus. They all promise the final hour, with the demon of the machine placing the hydrogen bomb at humanity's end point.
>
> Al-Ahmad, *Gharbzadegi*, p. 116.

117. Ashuri, *Ma va moderniyat*, p. 35.
118. Ibid., p. 39.
119. Ibid., p. 41.
120. Though cognizant of Al-Ahmad's nuances, Dabashi ultimately concludes "the major message that can be deduced from West-struckness is a kind of return to 'genuine, progressive' Islam (whatever that might be)." See Dabashi, *Theology of Discontent*, p. 88.
121. Nabavi *Intellectuals and the State in Iran*, p. 63.
122. Mirsepassi, *Political Islam, Iran, and the Enlightenment*, p. 33.
123. Farhang Jahanpour, "Reverse Orientalism: Iranian Reactions to the West" in Ali Ansrai, ed. *Perceptions of Iran: History, Myth and Nationalism from Medieval Persia to the Islamic Republic* (London and New York, I. B. Tauris, 2014), pp. 77–99; quoted on p. 88. Mehrzad Boroujerdi also links *On the Services and Betrayal of Intellectuals* deals with the idea of return to Shi'ism. Boroujerdi, *Iranian Intellectuals and the West: The Tormented Triumph of Nativism* (Syracuse, NY: Syracuse University Press, 1996), p. 72.
124. Al-Ahmad, *Safar be velayat-e Ezrail* (Tehran, 1995), p. 62.
125. Jalal Al-Ahmad, *Khasi dar Miqat* (Tehran, 1966), p. 135. The Persian term is *"badaviyat-e motorizeh."* He also projects his impression of Arabia's "violent" natural environment onto a surprising comment on the harsh nature of Arabian Islam and Abrahamic religions in general:

In this journey one feels badly deprived of beauty ... The rocks, desert
and sky are all strange ... Living in the desert, the need for prophet-hood
is felt in the air and the sand. Can it be that the violence of authority,
necessary in all religion, arises from this violent nature? ... You then
realize that Abraham was a smasher not only of idols but also of the arts
... Are not the Wahhabis then following in his path?

Ibid., p. 149.

126. Ibid., pp. 181–183.

127. Jalal Al-e Ahmad, *Safar-e Rus* (Tehran, 1990). Al-e Ahmad's visit took
place in summer 1964, several months after his return from Saudi
Arabia, where he had performed the Hajj, and less than a year before
his first visit to the US. See Al-Ahmad, *Khasi dar Miqat* and *Karname-ye se-saleh* (Tehran, 1979). Back from the USSR, he gave a talk on this
trip at VOX (Soviet Cultural Institute in Tehran), which was published
in VOX magazine *Payam-e no* (December 1964). See Al-Ahmad, *Safar-e Rus*, pp. 101–113. The full text of this travelogue, however, was not
published until 1990, perhaps accounting for the fact that its richness
and irony is missed by intellectual historians. Mehrzad Boroujerdi, for
example, overlooks the work's ambivalence, considering it a dismissal
of the Soviet Union. See Boroujerdi, *Iranian Intellectuals and the West*,
p. 75.

128. Jalal Al-Ahmad, *Safar-e Rus* (Tehran, 1999) and *Bazgasht az Shuravai*
(Tehran, 1954), his translation of Andre Gide's *Return from the USSR*.

129. Al-Ahmad "*Karname-ye do mahe-ye Harvard*" (Two-month Report
Card at Harvard) in *Jahan-e no*, vol. 1, nos. 2–3 (summer 1966), pp.
12–28; quoted on p. 25.

130. The interview with Al-Ahmad is in *Andishe va honar*, fifth series, no. 4
(September 1964), pp. 388–406; quoted on pp. 393–394 and p. 399,
where he uses the French term "*cosmopolite.*"

131. This list includes some of the country's most influential academics and
intellectuals, starting with his wife the writer and university professor
Simin Daneshvar, historian Fereydun Adamiyat, leftwing sociologist
Naser Pakdaman, French-educated Marxist Manuchehr Hezarkhani
and of course Al-Ahmad's foremost intellectual and political mentor
Khalil Maleki. His citations throughout the book include works by
Jean-Paul Sartre, Herbert Marcuse, Raymond Arron, Albert Memmi,
Aimé Césaire, Marshal McLuhan, Maxime Rodinson, Marshall
Hodgson, Jacques Berque, J. Bloch-Michel, Peter Avery, Maurice
Duverger, Franz Fanon, Seymour Martin Lipset, Arnold Hauser,
Martin Heidegger and Albert Camus. See Al-Ahmad's numerous

acknowledgments and references throughout *Dar khedmat va khianat-e roshanfekran.*

132. Ibid., pp. 24–25.
133. Ibid., p. 67.
134. Ibid., p. 27.
135. Ibid., pp. 30–31.
136. Ibid., p. 33.
137. Going farther, he ponders whether the necessity of absolute obedience (*ta'abod, bandegi*) to God, ostensibly more emphasized in Islam than other religions, might not have caused a particular weakening of the Islamic intellectual tradition. Ibid., pp. 34–35.
138. According to its introduction, *Dar khedmat va khianat-e roshanfekran* owed its initial "inspiration" to "the 1963 bloodshed in Tehran, to which the intellectuals reacted by washing off their hands indifferently," p. 15. The uncensored editions of the book included the full text of Khomeini's 1964 speech, accusing the Shah of betraying Iran and Islam through subservience to the US. Translation of that speech is in Ruhollah Khomeini, *Islam and Revolution: Writings and Declarations of Imam Khomeini* (Berkeley: Mizan Press, 1981), translated and annotated by Hamid Algar, pp. 181–188.
139. Al-Ahmad, *Dar khedmat va khiant-e roshanfekran*, p. 355. Khomeini is also mentioned on p. 406, where Al-Ahmad notes the Iranian press reported neither his presumed replacement of Ayatollah Boroujerdi nor his 1964 exile from Iran.
140. Ibid., pp. 48–49. In a footnote, he mocks Bazargan's attempts at justifying religion scientifically; p. 49.
141. He refers to Persian translations of Aimé Césaire, *A Discourse on Colonialism*, Franz Fanon, *The Wretched of the Earth*, and Albert Memmi, *The Colonizer and the Colonized*. Ibid., p. 85. Al-Ahmad recognized his own "nativism" fitted a global intellectual genre. This is shown, for instance, in his quoting a passage, from Jacques Berque, *Egypt: Imperialism and Revolution* (1967), which, he says, poses the very same question *On the Service and Betrayal of Intellectuals* has tried to answer:

The West that Egypt had accepted as its teacher ... has lost its self-confidence. How is it possible then to remain a student of this West? Certainly, one can point to another West, the one that talks of peace and socialism ... But is it enough to trade the bankrupt West with a real one? Does not the acceptance of a foreign culture, whether socialist, secular or revolutionary, inevitably amount to losing one's own identity? What replaces this loss? The most determined Marxist youth cannot ignore how deeply Islam, ethnicity and tradition shape the behavior of ordinary people. How logically reconcile is double-edged logic of being at once effective and traditional, individual and universal? pp. 288–89. But check original translation.

142. Al-Ahmad, *Dar Khedmat va khiant-e roshanfekran*, p. 89.
143. Ibid., pp. 157–165.
144. Ibid., p. 170.
145. Ibid., pp. 251–252. He goes on to say, however, that "as long as the constitution makes Shi'ism the country's official religion, and as long as graduates of modern schools and universities have not replaced them, the clergy's power to advance social movements cannot be overlooked," p. 253. He admits, however, that the clergy can be reactionary, even vis-à-vis the existing political regime, for example on such issues as "women's participation in social life, their enfranchisement and unveiling," p. 252. Still, he concludes:

> Whether we like it or not, the great 80% majority of the population, who lack access to modern schools and universities, are subject to two influences, to the clergy and its institutions, on the one side, and to the government and its institutions and means of communication, on the other.
>
> *Dar Khedmat va khiant-e roshanfekran*, p. 257

146. Ibid., pp. 259–276.
147. Ibid., pp. 278, 280.
148. Ibid., p. 305.
149. Ibid., pp. 316–317.
150. Ibid., p. 332.
151. Al-Ahmad, *Dar khedmat va khiant-e roshanfekran*, pp. 366–367.
152. Ibid., pp. 369–371.
153. Ibid., pp. 375–376.

Revolutionary Monarchy, Political Shi'ism, and Islamic Marxism

1. Dariush Ashuri, *Ma va moderniat: Ostore-ye falsafeh dar mian-e ma* (Tehran, 2004), p. 311.
2. Janet Afary and Kevin B. Anderson, *Foucault and the Iranian Revolution: Gender and the Seductions of Islamism* (Chicago, IL: The University of Chicago Press, 2005).
3. Mohammad Reza Pahlavi, *Bargozide-i az neveshte-ha va sokhanan-e Shahanshah Aryamehr* (Tehran, n.d.), p. 48.
4. Djamchid Behnam, *Cultural Policy in Iran* (Paris: Unesco, 1973), preface and p. 15. See also Changiz Pahlevan, "*Barnamerizi-ye farhangi dar*

Iran," in *Farhang va zendegi* 15 (summer 1974): pp. 53–73. According to Pahlevan, after 1967 Iran began developing a comprehensive national cultural policy in line with UNSECO's recommendations to its member countries, p. 54.

5. Nabavi correctly identifies "West-struck-ness" as an expression of contemporary intellectual sentiments. To this effect, she quotes the following 1961 editorial in *Andisheh va honar*: "For us, other countries have lost their attractions. The style of life that we approve for ourselves must take its inspiration from this very country. Packaged democracy, exported from the West, and freedom bearing the stamp of the East, regardless of their advantages – and we do regard them with respect – are not suitable for this people ... The legacy of human civilization if altered in color and flavor to suit this country, would be useful." Quoted in Negin Nabavi, *Intellectuals and the State in Iran: Politics, Discourse and the Dilemma of Authenticity* (Gainesville, FL: University of Florida Press, 2003), p. 58.

6. Behnam, *Cultural Policy in Iran*, pp. 16–17.

7. Ibid., pp. 42–43.

8. Behnam, ibid., pp. 19–20. Pahlevan, *"Barnamerizi-ye farhangi dar Iran"* pp. 53–54.

9. Leftist, nationalist, and authenticity-advocates writing in *Culture and Life* included Dariush Homayun, Ehsan Naraqi, Hushang Vaziri, Dariush Ashuri, Changiz Pahlevan, Manuchehr Hezarkhani, Mehrdad Bahar, Abdolhosein Zarinkub, Reza Davari, Ahmad Fardid, Aramesh Dustar, Nader Naderpur and Hamid Enayat.

10. For a list of such periodicals see Nabavi, *Intellectuals and the State in Iran*, p. 215. Nabvai's excellent study analyzes these periodicals for the period of the 1950s and 1960s.

11. *Jahan-e no* began publishing in 1946, as a "magazine of arts, social studies and literature," and continued into the 1960s under the editorship of Amin Alimard and then Reza Baraheni. Left-leaning but less political was *Negin*, edited by Mahmud Enayat and published from 1965 to 1980. See Ali Dehbashi, *"khaterati az doktor Mahmud Enayat"* in *Bokhara*, vol. 15, no. 92 (April–May 2013): pp. 232–238.

12. See, for example, *Jahan-e no* vol. 25, nos. 1–2 (spring 1969); vol. 22, nos. 8–10 and 11–12 (1965); and vol. 24, no. 3 (1967). An example of attention to contemporary world politics was a 1968 article in *Jahan-e no* coving the 1967–1968 French student uprisings, referencing commentary by Louis Althusser and Alain Touraine. See Baqer Parham, *"Negahi be jonbeshha-ye daneshjui dar vaz'iat-e konuni-ye jahan,"* republished in Baqer Parham, *Ba-ham negari va yekta-negari* (Tehran, 1998), pp. 25–59.

13. The High Council for Culture and the Arts published annual statistical studies of national book, newspaper and motion picture production and consumption. See *Gozaresh-e farhangi-ye Iran (Iran Cultural Report)* published by the High Council for Culture and the Arts (Tehran, 1971).

14. Deputy minister and head of Tehran University, Mohammad Baheri, prepared annual reports for the Shah on higher education. During the 1973 Ramsar Conference, for instance, Baheri's report on "the students' general behavior" noted that despite access to scholarships and financial aid, students were mostly "indifferent" to the county's progress. Baheri saw himself as a "leftist presence" in premier Alam's cabinet. Mohammad Baheri, Iran Oral History interview, tape, 7, p. 6. www.fas.harvrad.edu/. Alam too believed students were indifferent because they were barred from participation at the university level and also in the country's political affairs. Abdolreza Hushing Mahdavi, *Goftoguha-ye man ba shah: Khaterat-e mahramane-ye Amir Asdaollah Alam* (Tehran, 1993), vol. 2, pp. 496–497.

15. Afshin Matin-Asgari, *Iranian Student Opposition to the Shah* (Costa Mesa, CA: MAZDA Publishers, 2002).

16. Outstanding examples were Hamid Enayat and Amir-Hosein Aryanpur, the most distinguished and popular political scientist and sociologist at Tehran University, both former Tudeh Party members.

17. Leftist writers, translators and academics affiliated with the Institute included writers Jalal Al-Ahmad and Gholam-Hossein Sa'edi, translator Karim Keshavarz, historian Baqer Mo'meni, sociologists Hushang Keshavarz-Sadr and Ahmad Ashraf, and jurist Mostafa Rahimi, as well as soon-to-be guerrilla leaders Amir-Parviz Puyan and Mostafa Shoa'ian. See Safa'odin Tabraian, *"Mo'assese-ye motale'at va tahqiqat-e ejtema'i"* in *Tarikh-e Moaser Iran*, vol. 13, no. 51 (fall 2009): pp. 51–127. For Naraqi's account see Moretza Rasulipur, *"Sakhtar-e artesh va SAVAK va nakaramadi-ye rezhim-e Pahlavi az zaban-e doktor Ehsan Naraqi"* in *Tarikh-e Moaser Iran*, vol. 6, no. 24 (winter 2003): pp. 195–224.

18. Published between 1974 and 1977, these were *The Estrangement of the West (Ghorbat-e Gharb), One's Own Possession (ancheh khod dasht)* and *Naïve Longing (Tama'-e kham)*.

19. According to Naraqi, in a 1978 conversation, he reminded the Shah that during the past thirty years, the regime's key political and ideological posts were filled with ex-communists. The Shah reportedly agreed. Ehsan Naraqi, *From Palace to Prison: Inside the Iranian Revolution* (Chicago: Ivan R. Dee, 1994), Nilou Moaser trans., pp. 110–111.

20. Modern theatrical acting and directing was pioneered by Tudeh Party central committee member Abdol-Hosein Nushin, whose students

became leading stage and film actors and directors into the 1970s. Nushin's students, most of whom were left-leaning or Tudeh Party members in their youth, included Mohammad-Ali Ja'fari, Nosrat Karimi, Ezatollah Entezami, Akbar Meshkin, Mahin Deyhim, Turan Mehrzad, Hasan Khashe'i, Mostafa and Mahin Oskui, Sadeq and Abbas Shabaviz, Loreta Hairapetian, Iren Asemi, Hamid Qanbari, Sadeq Bahrami, and Hosein Kheyrkhah. See Nosrat Karimi, ed., *Yadname-ye Abdol-Hosein Nushin* (Tehran, 2008). Leftist sympathies among the most talented and popular theatre, film, radio and television writers, directors, actors, actresses, singers, musicians, song-writers, are noted in the memoir of Parviz Khatibi, himself a leftist and a leading figure in almost all of these fields. See Parviz Khatibi, *Khaterati az honarmandan* (Remembering Artists) (Los Angeles: Parviz Khatibi Cultural Foundation, 1994).

21. Former Queen Farah mentions having had communist friends while a student in Paris during the late 1950s. One of them, Vida Hajebi, served a long sentence, as a political prisoner, while her former friend was the Queen. See Farah Pahlavi, *An Enduring Love*, translated from the French, Patricia Clancy (New York: Miramax Books, 2004), pp. 66–67. For Hajebi's case see interviews with Pari Hajebi, Paris, November 11, 1989, and Hasan Qazi, Paris, 22 February, 22, 1990. Both cited in Matin-asgari, *Iranian Student Opposition to the Shah*, p. 261. On Amir Arjomand's leftist backgrounds, see Mozaffar Shahedi, *Hezb-e Rastakhiz: eshtebah-e bozorg* (Tehran: Mo'assese-ye motale'at va pazhuheshha-ye sisai, 2003), vol. 2, p. 199. Prominent leftists or former communists who worked and published at the Center for the Intellectual Cultivation of Children and Adolescents included scholar and linguist Mehrdad Bahar (1930–1994), translator Mohammad Qazi (1913–1997), poets Mehdi Akhavan-Sales, Siavosh Kasra'i (1926–1995) and Mohammad-Ali Sepanlu, essayist Daruish Ashuri, writer translator Mahmud E'temadzadeh (1904–2006) and writer Nader Ebrahimi (1936–2008). On the Center for the Intellectual Cultivation of Children and Adolescents, see "*Kanun-e Paravaresh Fekeri-ye Kudakan va nojavanan,*" in www.Iranicaonline.org and Keyvan Bazhen, *Samad Behrangi* (Tehran, 1383), p. 32.

22. Gholam Reza Afkhami, *The Life and Times of the Shah* (Berkeley and Los Angeles: University of California Press, 2009), pp. 401–403.

23. On Nikkhah's case see Matin-asgari, *Iranian Student Opposition to the Shah*, pp. 86–89. See also Bijan Jazani, "*Mohre-i bar safhe-ye shatranj*" written in 1970 but published in *Ketab-e Jomeh* vol. 1, no. 36 (June 1980): pp. 46–57. On Jafarian see Hamid Qazvini, "*baz-khani-ye parvande-ye*

Mahmud Jafarian" in *Fasl-nameh-e motalat-e tarikhi*, vol. 5, no. 19 (Winter 2008): pp. 185–223.

24. A randomly chosen issue of *Tamasha*, for example, featured translated pieces from Alvin Toffler's *Future Shock* and Andre Malraux's *Antimemoirs*, as well as articles on avant-garde cinema, theatre and music. *Tamasha*, no. 88 (December 9, 1970).

25. See the column "Bread, Water and Thought" in *Tamasha*, no. 161 (May 18, 1974); no. 184 (October 26, 1974); and no. 192 (November 23, 1974).

26. *Tamasha* no. 187 (November 16, 1974), pp. 16, 73. Nikkhah's interviews and writings can be found in Parviz Nikkhah, *Javedaneh* (Los Angeles: Ketab Corporation, 2014).

27. Parviz Nikkhah, *"Kam dar kam"* in *Tamasha* no. 184 (October 26, 1974), p. 9.

28. See his editorial, *"donya-ye chap"* [The World of the Left] in *Tamasha*, no. 187 (November 16, 1974), p. 5.

29. Mohammad Reza Pahlavi, *Answer to History* (New York: Stein and Day, 1980), pp. 13, 23.

30. According to Reza Qotbi: "On several occasions the general question of the regime's ideology was discussed. The Shah proposed that we should develop our dialectic against the communists' dialectic." Quoted in Afkhami, *The Life and Times of the Shah*, p. 455.

31. Nabavi, *Intellectuals and the State in Iran* concludes that "in the 1960s and 1970s, inspired by the current Third Worldist discourse, intellectuals took on the language of authentic culture. However, once the establishment also adopted this concept, there was a search for a counter-discourse, and this they found in their discussion of a good society once again inspired by the counterculture discourse prevalent in the West." Ibid., p. 142. Tehran's leading paper *Ayandegan* was another example of leftist intellectual presence. *Ayandegan* was a pro-regime daily, yet regularly featured leftist writers and themes. This was clearer in *Ayandegan*'s weekly literary supplement, published from 1974 to 1979 under the joint editorship of Hushang Vaziri and Shahrashub Amirshahi, both from leftist backgrounds. Anonymous, *"Hafete-name-ye Ayandegan Adabi,"* in *Andisheh Puya*, vol. 4, no. 33 (September 28, 2015): pp. 136–141.

32. Mohammad Madadpur, *"Nazari Ejmali be hekmat-e ma'navi-ye tarikh va falsafe-ye tarikh-e roshnagri"* in *Tarikh-e Moaser*, vol. 6, no. 24 (Winter 2003): pp. 115–160. Fardid quoted on p. 9.

33. Seyyed Hossein Nasr, *"Negahi digar be Hanri Korban,"* in *Iran Nameh* vol. IX, no. 4 (Autumn 1911): pp. 667–680; quoted on p. 669.

34. During the 1940s, Fardid was drawn to Tehran's modernist literary circle formed around the writer Sadeq Hedayat, to whom he remained exceptionally devoted. Fardid's description of his own youthful "West-stricken" condition is corroborated in passing comments by Hedayat, who rather harshly described him as "a weak and narrow-minded being, who believes a European porter understands more than learned Iranians; and who considers himself European. Apparently he knows this by intuition [*shohud*]." Hedayat had used "intuition." Sadeq Hedayat, *Hashtad-o do nameh be Hasan Shahidnura'i* (Paris: cesmandaz, 2000), p. 76.

35. Mohammad Mansur Hashemi, *Hoviat-andishan va mirath-e fekri-ye Ahmad Fardid* (Tehran: Kavir, 2005), pp. 51–60. The first English-language scholarly study of Fardid appeared when the present book was going to press and therefore is not discussed here. See Ali Mirsepassi, *Transnationalism in Iranian Political Thought: The Life and Times of Ahmad Fardid* (New York: Cambridge University Press, 2017). But see my forthcoming review of this book in *The American Historical Review* vol. 123, no. 2 (April 2018): pp. 668–69. Though a fine primary source-based study, Mirsepassi's book exaggerates Fardid's political and intellectual significance.

36. For a synopsis of Fardid's philosophy, in his own words, see the first two chapters of Madadpur. Fardid's ideas are briefly mentioned in Yann Richard, "*Clercs at intellectuels dans la Republique islamique d'Iran,*" in Gilles Kepel and Yann Richard, *Intellectuels et militants de l'islam contemorrain* (Paris: Editions du Seuil, 1990), pp. 29–70; pp. 49–51.

37. Fardid in *Culture and Life* (Winter 1972), pp. 33–34, 36.

38. Ibid., p. 39.

39. Fardid's ideas were featured in *Tamasha* and Rastakhiz Party organ *Talash*. See Hashemi, *Hoviat-andishan va mirath-e fekri-ye Ahmad Fardid*, pp. 43–44. Notes on pp. 49, 70–71.

40. Davari had a doctorate in philosophy from Tehran University, joined the post-revolutionary Council for Cultural Revolution and became head of the Iranian Academy of Science. See Mehrzad Boroujerdi, *Iranian Intellectuals and the West: The Tormented Triumph of Nativism* (Syracuse, NY: Syracuse University Press, 1996), p. 158.

41. Ashuri's 1974 article, "East and West," in *Farhang va Zendegi*, no. 15 (summer 1974): pp. 2–27, acknowledges Fardid as the source of terminology and concepts used to describe the modern world in terms of dichotomous contrast between Eastern and Western "worldviews." He concludes that the fashionable idea of retrieving Eastern values to

resist or temper Western influences is a futile dream of irreconcilable
worldviews, p. 27.

42. Ashuri, *Ma va moderniyat*, p. 309.

43. Widely recognized by contemporaries, Corbin's intellectual resonance
    diminished, or was "politely ignored," due to his controversial
    methodology and problematic politics. Nile Green, "Between
    Heidegger and the Hidden Imam: Reflections on Henry Corbin's
    Approaches to Mystical Islam," in *Method & Theory in the Study of
    Religion*, vol. 17, no. 3 (2005): pp. 219–226; quoted on p. 247.
    Nevertheless, Corbin's legacy lingers indirectly, for example on the
    margins of French anthropology, where Fariba Adelkhah constructed
    an understanding of Iranian modernity in terms of Corbin's notion of
    javanmardi, "an existential ethic" or "life style" defined by two essential
    traits: "the spirit of generosity" and "courage." Fariba Adelkhah, *Being
    Modern in Iran*, trans. from the French by Jonathan Derrick (London: C.
    Hurst & Co., 1998). Corbin is not credited in the text, but cited only in
    two footnotes to pages 4 and 33.

44. Corbin's 1920s academic training combined medieval philosophy with
    Orientalist and Islamic studies. His first graduate degree was in
    philosophy, focusing on traditional hermeneutic interpretations of
    Latin texts. He then studied Sanskrit, Arabic, Persian, Pahlavi and
    Turkish, receiving another graduate degree in languages. Corbin
    claimed his phenomenology assumed a spiritual link between the
    interpreter and the author. Since "each being can know and
    comprehend only its like. Each mode of comprehension corresponds to
    the interpreter's mode of being. I am too convinced of this not to confess
    that I cannot communicate the meaning of symbols to persons blind to
    them by nature if not deliberately." Henry Corbin, *Avicenna and the
    Visionary Recital*, Willard R. Trask trans. (New York: Pantheon, 1960),
    p. xii. According to Nasr, Corbin considered himself a Shi'i, but in an
    esoteric (*bateni*) sense. Seyyed Hossein Nasr and Ramin Jahanbeglu,
    Dar jostoju-ye amr-e qodsi (Tehran: Ney, 2006), p. 146.

45. Supposedly, Massignon gave Corbin a copy of twelfth-century mystic
    Suhravardi's *Book of Illumination Wisdom*, saying "take this book, I
    think it will suit you." Corbin then immersed himself in studies of Sufism
    and in 1939 published *Suhravadri of Aleppo: Founder of the
    Illuminationist Doctrine*. See Dariush Shayegan, *Hanri Korban: Afaq-e
    tafakkor-e ma'navi dar Islam-e Irani*, Baqer Parham trans. (Tehran,
    1994), pp. 22–23. See also Green, "Between Heidegger and the
    Hidden Imam," pp. 251–22.

46. Corbin's 1938 translation of Heidegger's *What Is Metaphysics*
    introduced French intellectuals, including Jean-Paul Sartre, to the

German master thinker. Ethan Kleinberg, *Generation Existential: Heidegger's Philosophy in France, 1927–1961* (Ithaca, NY: Cornell University Press, 2005).

47. Martin Heidegger, *Being and Time*, John Macquarrie & Edward Robinson trans. (New York: Harper, 1962), pp. 26–27, 44–45.

48. Nasr and Jahanbeglu, *Dar jostoju-ye amr-e qodsi*, pp. 152–154. Shayegan, *Hanri Korban*, pp. 66–7. See also, Kaveh Bayat, *"Piramun-e bateni-gari"* in *Jahan-e ketab*, vol. 10, no. 5 (September 2005): pp. 10–13.

49. "Technological frenzy," "spiritual decline of the earth," darkening of the world," "emasculation of the spirit" are themes of Heidegger's *What Is Metaphysics*. See Julian Young, *Heidegger, Philosophy, Nazism* (New York: Cambridge University Press, 1997), p. 33.

50. During the following twenty-five years, Corbin and his Iranian collaborators edited and published twenty-two volumes of rare Persian and Arabic manuscripts as part of the French Institute's *Iranshenasi* (Iranology) collection. Dariush Shayegan, *Hanri Korban*, p. 38.

51. According to Shayegan:

> Two worlds existed culturally and sociologically apart in Iran: the world of Shi'i thought and its religious schools in Qom and a modern Iran rapidly embarking on industrialization. Between these two worlds stood intellectual groupings with opposite ideological choices ... Mired in vulgar Marxism or the scarps of Western culture, a large segment of Iran's intellectual world was cut off from both its own heritage and the valuable products of Western culture. As if trapped in a vacuum, this large intellectual grouping was unable to move beyond ideological disputes. Corbin's work, however, was inspirational to the traditional circle of young intellectuals, articulating and expressing the great moments of Iranian thought in a clear language and casting old ideas in glorious new garb.
>
> Shayegan, *Hanri Korban*, p. 40.

The irony of this contention apparently escapes Shayegan who goes on explaining it further in Orientalist fashion:

> [Iranians] could not distance themselves sufficiently from their own philosophical tradition, hence remaining unable to place it in a systematic scientific perspective, something that came to Corbin naturally. Objectivity, distance, evaluation and analysis, are essential attributes of the Western analytical view and approach.
>
> Ibid., p. 41.

Shayegan's interpretation is contradicted by other commentators. According to Mohammad Mehdi Khalaji, for example, Corbin's "philosophical conservatism" made his thought incapable of "bridging between tradition and modernity." Mohammad Mehdi Khalaji, *"Korban va ravayati sisai az tarikh-e andishe-ye falsafi dar Iran" Iran Nameh*, vol. XX, no. 4 (Fall 2002): pp. 417–450; quoted on p. 420.

52. Shayegan, *Hanri Korban*, p. 40.

53. On Corbin in Eranos see Ibid., pp. 46–53. See also www.eranosfounda tion.org.

54. Theosophy started in 1875 when the New York Theosophical Society was founded by Colonel Henry Olcott who searched for "ancient wisdom" in the "primeval sources of all religions, the books of Hermes and the Vedas," an idea going back to Freemasons. Following similar ideas, Emerson and Thoreau had led the Transcendentalist Movement in the United States. The Theosophy movement began mixing in popular and pseudoscientific ideas when Helena Blavatski joined. Mark J. Sedgwick, *Against the Modern World: Traditionalism and the Secret Intellectual History of the Twentieth-century* (New York: Oxford University Press, 2004), pp. 40–44.

55. Sedgwick, *Against the Modern World*, p. 46. This is how Guenon defines his book's main theme:

> The civilization of the modern West appears in history as an anomaly: among all those which are known to us more or less completely, this civilization is the only one which has developed along purely material lines, and this monstrous development, whose beginnings coincide with the so-called Renaissance, has been accompanied, as indeed it was fated to be, by a corresponding intellectual regress ... This regress has reached such a point that the Westerners of to-day no longer know what pure intellect is.
>
> Rene Guenon, *The Crisis of the Modern World*
> (London: Luzac and Company, 1941), p. 23.

56. Eliade's idea of language representing ontological truths, as well as his core concepts such as the scared as metaphysical reality, the illusory character of history and time, the valorization of archaic religions, were all linked to Traditionalism. Sedgweick, *Against the Modern World*, pp. 111–113. Eliade was connected to the American Bollingen foundation of Paul Mellon, which sponsored the annual Eranos meetings (since 1933 in Ascona, Switzerland), led by Carl Jung. British religious studies scholar Martin Lings joined Traditionalism, while American sociologist Robert Merton and religion scholar Houston Smith were also close to it. Smith's widely read books, like *The Religions of Man* (1958), popularized the basic idea of a single transcendental Truth uniting all religions. Originally a Methodist, Smith prayed like a

Muslim and practiced Yoga. Sedgwick, *Against the Modern World*, pp. 119, 164–166.

57. Nasr and Jahanbeglu, *Dar jostoju-ye amr-e qodsi*, pp. 61–67.

58. Nasr names Guenon and Schuon as the "philosophers" who influenced his thought even more than Molla Sadra or Suhravardi. Nasr and Jahanbeglu, *Dar jostoju-ye amr-e qodsi*, pp. 86–92. The Alawiyya was established in the early twentieth-century by the Algerian Ahmed al-Alawi. Another Guenon associate was the Italian Julius Evola who tried to merge Traditionalism and fascism. His attempts had little success since neither Nazis nor Italian fascists were interested in Evola's arcane mysticism. Sedgwick, *Against the Modern World*, p. 108.

59. For a succinct account of the Nasr-Corbin Circle see Nasr, "*Negahi digar beh Hanry Korban.*"

60. Tabataba'i apparently shared Corbin's and Nasr's interest in studying Shi'i mysticism along with similar esoteric approaches in other religions. Thus he would teach the group Molla Sadra's philosophy, interpret the Qur'an and the Gospels and even give commentaries on the Upanishads. Nasr claims Tabataba'i was in agreement with his own espousal of "perennial philosophy" and "the esoteric unity of all religions." Nasr and Jahanbeglu, *Dar jostoju-ye amr-e qodsi*, pp. 126–127. However, Tabataba'i's *Aghaz-e Falsafeh* (Tehran, n.d.) and his *Shi'eh* (Tehran, 1960) show he followed Molla Sadra, trying to synthesize rationalist (Aristotelian or *masha'i*) philosophy, *erfan*, and Twelver Shi'ism (the so-called "three tiers"). Illumination, therefore, was one of his three focus areas, and not necessarily the most prominent.

61. Nasr claims Tabataba'i was very concerned with the sway of Marxism among intellectuals and thus worked on *Asul-e falsafeh va ravesh-e re'alism* (Qom, n.d.) with Motahhari's help. Nasr and Jahanbeglu, *Dar jostoju-ye amr-e qodsi*, pp. 1129–1131.

62. Nasr says he and Corbin held "roundtable" presentations for Tehran University faculty and students for almost two decades. During these sessions, Corbin would read a text in French, which Nasr would then translate, adding his own commentary. Corbin's French was very difficult to comprehend due to his peculiar vocabulary and also because he himself was almost deaf. Apparently in jest, Nasr claims he would translate Corbin's incomprehensible lectures into Farsi with the help of angles. Nasr and Jahanbeglu, *Dar jostoju-ye amr-e qodsi*, p. 141.

63. Shayegan, *Hanri Korban*, pp. 40–42. According to Nasr, "Iran's modernist circles had no interest in the discourse of Tabatab'i, who spoke as a Qom cleric. But the same traditionalist teachings were better accepted from a Frenchman such as Corbin." Nasr and Jahanbeglu, *Dar jostoju-ye amr-e qodsi*, p. 140.

64. "He cannot see Iran as anything but a world generating cultural unity and totality, a philosophical conception of Iran making his work unique among Orientalists. This new approach is an attempts at understanding Iran as a philosophical object, rather than a geographic or political realm. Thus, Corbin's understanding of Iran may be considered the most philosophical and idealist system of Iranology in the twentieth century." Khalaji, *"Korban va ravayati sisai az tarikh-e andishe-ye falsafi dar Iran."* Quoted on pp. 435–436.

65. Nasr and Jahanbeglu, *Dar jostoju-ye amr-e qodsi*, p. 144.

66. Ibid., pp. 165–166.

67. It was too late. Despite his close personal relations with Motahhari and other influential clerics, he had been too close to the court to be acceptable to Khomeini. Thus, he left the country for good in January 1979. Ibid., pp. 185–189.

68. Dariush Shayegan, *Asia dar barabar-e Gharb* (Tehran: Amirkabir, 1977), p. 9. Shayegan cites Guenon positively, but says his critique of the West is fanatical. p. 77.

69. Ibid., pp. 21–33, 238–239.

70. Here, Shayegan parts ways with the West's conservative detractors to heed the advice of its liberal and leftist critics, such as Hamid Enayat, who had written:

> The cultural war on "West-struck-ness," which in the last decade became the catchphrase of intellectuals and statesmen, has turned into an excuse for thwarting efforts to learn or teach about the West. But the meaning of "West-struck-ness" is never made clear ... As long as this is unclear, we must at least acknowledge that resisting the West's purportedly dangerous moral influence requires a proper understanding Western culture and civilization, otherwise we are fighting an unknown enemy.
>
> Hamid Enayat in *Farhang va Zendegi* no. 9 (September 1973): pp. 15–16. See also Enayat's 1969 interview, reprinted in *Bokhara*, vol. 15, no. 92 (2013): pp. 199–221.

71. The term "cultural mutation" appears in the French title of Shayegan's Persian book, which, in English, reads: *Asia Facing the West: Essays on the Socio-cultural Mutations of Traditional Societies.*

72. Shayegan, *Asia dar barabar-e Gharb*, p. 94. Years later, Shayegan explained his allusion to Asian cultures being swamplands fermenting intellectual monstrosities was taken from a passage in Arthur Gobineau's *Religions and Philosophies of Central Asia. Dariush Shayegan, Zir-e asemanha-ye jahan* (Tehran: Farzan, 1997), pp. 225–226.

This book is a Persian translation of *Sous les ceils du monde* (Paris: Edition du Felin, 1992).

73. Shayegan, *Asia dar barabar-e Gharb*, p. 293.
74. Ibid., p. 301.
75. *L'Impact planétaire de la pensée occidentale rend-il possible un dialogue réel entre les civilisations?* (Paris: Broché, 1979), translated into Persian as *Andishe-ye gharbi va goftogu-ye tamaddonha* (Tehran, 1990), p. 17 (*hefdah*).
76. See the table of contents and contributions by Henri Corbin, Ehsan Naragi and Dariush Shayegan. Ibid.
77. Ali Rahnema, *An Islamic Utopian: A Political Biography of Ali Shari'ati* (London: I. B. Tauris, 1998), p. 127.
78. Mojtaba Mahdavi, "Post-Islamic Trends in Postrevolutionary Iran" in *Comparative Studies of South Asia, Africa and the Middle East*, 31, no. 1 (2011): pp. 94–109.
79. Ruhollah Hoseinian, *Chahardah-sal reqabat-e ideolozhik-e shi'eh dar Iran* (Tehran, 2004), p. 762.
80. Ibid., pp. 766–767; Rahnema, *An Islamic Utopian*, chapter 11: "Mystical Murmurs."
81. Siavash Safari, "Reclaiming Islam and Modernity: A Neo-Shari'ati Revisiting of Ali Shari'ati's Intellectual Discourse in Post-Revolutionary Iran." Ph.D. dissertation submitted to University of Alberta (2013), p. 6, footnote 14.
82. Kasravi, *Shariati* (n.p., n.d.), for example, pp. 1–11.
83. Ali Shari'ati, *Tashayyo'-e Alavi va Tashayyo'-e Safavi* (Tehran, 1969). Rahnema, *An Islamic Utopian* pp. 9–10.
84. H. E. Chehabi, *Iranian Politics and Religious Modernism* (Ithaca, NY: Cornell University Press, 1990), p. 130.
85. Neither publication acknowledged Shakibinia's original articulation of these ideas. Rahnema, *An Islamic Utopian*, pp. 61–64. By 1953, Shariati joined or became closely affiliated with Nakhshab's League. In summer 1953, before the coup, Shariati is recorded to have given a speech sponsored by the League, on "The contradictions between Islam and the monarchy." Ibid., pp. 52–53.
86. Rahnema, *An Islamic Utopian*, pp. 57–58.
87. According to Rahnema, the presiding professor, Gilbert Lazar, had a low estimation of Shariat'i overall performance and his competence in French. Rahnema, *An Islamic Utopian*, pp. 117–118.
88. Massignon's own contribution did not impress scholars like Maxime Rodinson and Steven Humphreys. See Robert Irwin, *For Lust of Knowing: The Orientalists and Their Enemies* (London and New York: Penguin, 2006), p. 223 and its references.

89. Rahnema, *An Islamic Utopian*, pp. 120–128.
90. Shariati also was interested in Pierre-Joseph Proudhon's moralistic and anti-statist socialism, occasionally citing Proudhon against Marx. Rahnema, *An Islamic Utopian*, pp. 123–125.
91. Ali Rahnema's labeling of Shariati as an "Islamic utopian" is apt, as is his overall study of Shariati, which is solidly informed and both sympathetic and critical.
92. This is why figures like the medieval mystic Al-Hallaj were his heroes and role models. Rahnema, *An Islamic Utopian*, pp. 127–128. "Che Guevara becomes an armed and socially responsible reincarnation of Hallaj." Ibid., p. 159.
93. Rahnema, *An Islamic Utopian*, pp. 131–132.
94. Ibid., pp. 133–134, 141–143. On SAVAK's attitude to Shariati see pp. 21–220.
95. Rahnema, *An Islamic Utopian*, chapters 11–13. On Shariati's mystical experiences see ibid., pp. 177–186.
96. Rahnema, *An Islamic Utopian*, p. 274.
97. Anonymous, *Bahthi dar bare-ye marja'iat va ruhaniat* (Tehran: Enteshar, 1962), especially the chapters by Morteza Motahhari and Morteza Jazayeri.
98. Chehabi, *Iranian Politics and Religious Modernism*, pp. 174 and 204.
99. Hoseinian, *Chahardah-sal reqabat-e ideolozhik-e shi'eh dar Iran*, p. 752.
100. Ibid., pp. 753–754.
101. Rahnema, *An Islamic Utopian*, chapter 15, particularly pp. 216–19 for the "Cat and Mouse Game." See also Hoseinian, *Chahardah-sal reqabat-e ideolozhik-e shi'eh dar Iran*, pp. 771–775. SAVAK chief Parviz Thabeti says the same about SAVAK's relation with Shariati. See Erfan Qanei-fard, *Dar Damgah-e Hadethe* (Los Angeles: Ketab Corp., 2012), pp. 277–280. According to a 1969 report by the SAVAK's Khorasan branch:

    As repeatedly stated in previous reports, while useful to extremists and foreign agents, Dr. Shariati could be even more useful to the SAVAK and the country, provided he is managed properly. This is a very learned person, unacceptable to extremist clerics and accepted by leftists. The SAVAK of Khorasan believes imposing restrictions will cause Dr. Shariati to lose confidence in the country and the system, which, given his popularity, will have negative consequences. Managed with a proper plan and guidelines, however, his innovative ideas could be influential.
    Quoted in Hoseinian, *Chahardah-sal reqabat-e ideolozhik-e shi'eh dar Iran*, p. 771.

102. Rahnema, *An Islamic Utopian*, 240, 48–49, 266–276.

103. Ibid., pp. 26–270.

104. In November 1972, Ershad was closed and its directors and lecturers were arrested. The official reason given was clerical protests and *fatwas* against the ideas expressed there. Though this was true, a more important reason was that Ershad had turned into a recruiting ground for Mojahedin guerrillas. Hence the political cost of keeping it open outweighed its benefits to the regime. Prior to Ershad's closure, the Shah had sent a directive to the SAVAK saying most Islamic Marxists can be traced to Hosseinieh Ershad and therefore the activities of Ershad needed to be closely investigated. Following Ershad's 1972 closure and the arrest of its leading personnel, the Shah ordered: "You must severely punish all of these individuals, because they have gravely betrayed the country." Hoseinian, *Chahardah-sal reqabat-e ideolozhik-e shi'eh dar Iran*, pp. 758–759.

105. The Shah quoted in Mahdavi, *Goftoguha-ye man ba shah*, vol. 2, p. 734.

106. Mohammad Reza Pahlavi, *Bargozide-ye az neveshte-ha va sokhanan-e Shahanshah Aryamehr* (Tehran, n.d.), p. 13.

107. See Khomeini's October 13, 1971 speech in Ruhollah Khomeini, *Islam and Revolution: Writings and Declarations of Imam Khomeini* (Berkeley: Mizan Press, 1981), translated and annotated by Hamid Algar, pp. 200–208.

108. See Matin-asgari, *Iranian Student Opposition to the Shah*, chapter 8. In a famous 1971 speech, Khomeini asked Iran's clerics to "break their silence":

Would all of Iran's ulama be arrested ... executed or exiled, if they were to protest in unison? If all of Iran's more than hundred and fifty thousand clerics, all those mollas, marja's, hojat al-Islams and ayatollahs, were to break the seal of silence and protest ... would they all be annihilated?

Khomeini quoted in Hoseinian, *Chahardah-sal reqabat-e ideolozhik-e shi'eh dar Iran*, p. 581.

109. Charles Kurzman, *The Unthinkable Revolution in Iran* (Cambridge, MA: Harvard University Press, 2004).

110. See Maziar Behrooz, *Rebels with a Cause: The Failure of the Left in Iran* (London: I. B. Tauris, 1999) and Peyman Vahabzadeh, *A Guerrilla Odyssey: Modernization, Secularization, Democracy, and the Fadai Period of National Liberation in Iran, 1971–1979* (Syracuse, NY: Syracuse University Press, 2010). Ervand Abrahamian, *The Iranian Mojahedin* (New Haven, CT: Yale University Press, 1989).

111. The same argument was made by a few smaller groups, including the right-wing Muslim guerillas who in 1965 assassinated Prime Minster Hasan-Ali Mansur. Matin-asgari, *Iranian Student Opposition to the Shah,* pp. 77–82.

112. Already under attack by the postrevolutionary regime, the People's Fada'ian Organization received about 10 percent of the national vote in a 1980 election. Vahabzadeh, *A Guerrilla Odyssey,* p. 67. At that time, the People's Mojahedin Organization had at least an equal, and most likely, a larger following.

113. Fereydun Adamiyat, "*Ashoftegi dar feker-e tarikhi,*" *in* Mellat-e Bidar 4, no. 2 (January 1986): pp. 14–24, quoted on p. 22. The article was first published in 1982. Adamiyat's estimation of the 1970s guerrillas' positive accomplishment is endorsed by Maziar Behrooz, whose *Rebels with a Cause,* p. 94, concludes the guerrilla campaign of armed struggle had reached a "stalemate" with the regime.

114. It is notable also that the most ardent Marxist advocates of armed struggle, i.e. theorists like Amir-Parziz Puyan and Mas'ud Ahmadzadeh, came from Islamic backgrounds, whereas Bizhan Jazani, the leading advocate of subordinating guerrilla warfare to broader political strategies, had a Tudeh Party background. Behrooz, *Rebels with a Cause,* pp. 43–47.

115. For the Shah's comments on the guerrillas see Alam in Mahdavi, *Goftoguha-ye man ba shah,* vol. 2, p. 734. In April 1975, a few days after SAVAK murdered Bizhan Jazani and his eight comrades, Catherine Adl, daughter of one the Shah's closest friends, and her husband Bahman Hojjat-Kashani, son of a favorite general of the Shah's, attacked a gendarme post in Qazin, killing a colonel. Both were soon gunned down, she in a cave, he in a Tehran street confrontation. Afkhami, *The Life and Times of the Shah,* p. 399.

116. Jazani did not coin the term "Islamic Marxism," whose origin remains obscure. However, the term had acquired such wide currency that, according to Alam, even the Shah was using it as early as 1972. See Mahdavi, *Goftoguha-ye man ba shah,* vol.1, p. 400.

117. Bizhan Jazani, *Marksism-e Eslmai ya Isalm-e Marksisti* (Koln, 2001), p. 10.

118. Ibid., pp. 11–12.

119. Ibid., p. 26.

120. Ibid., pp. 27 and quoted on pp. 31–32.

121. Mahdavi, "Post-Islamic Trends in Postrevolutionary Iran," p. 18.

122. A title of his new writings was *Return to Which Self?* (*Bazgasht be kodam khishtan?*). This presumably being a corrective sequel to his earlier *Return to the Self* (*Bazgasht be khishtan*). See Ali Rahnema, *An*

Islamic Utopian: A Political Biography of Ali Shari'ati (London: I. B. Tauris, 1998), p. 347.

123. See Rahnema, *An Islamic Utopian*, pp. 339–349.

124. Ruhollah Hoseinian, *Chahardah-sal reqabat-e ideolozhik-e shi'eh dar Iran*, pp. 776–781. Said Hajarian, then a follower of Shariati, says that after the publication of his "Islam and Marxism" the Islamic Students Association of Tehran's Technical University broke with Shariati and removed all of his books from their campus library. Emaddein Baqi, *Baray-e Tarik: Goftogu ba Sa'id Hajjarian* (Tehran, 2000), p. 54.

125. Moretza Motahhari, *Name-ye tarikhi-ye ostad Motahhari be Emam Khomeini* (Tehran: Sadra, 1997), p. 16.

126. Ibid., p. 18.

127. Ibid., p. 20.

128. Ibid., p. 22.

129. Ibid.

130. Ibid., p. 26.

131. Ibid., pp. 29–30.

132. Motahhari ends the letter by expressing "amazement" at "the unprecedented freedoms recently allowed to political groups" in the country, a topic of this book's concluding discussion of the complex intellectual makeup of the pre-revolutionary crisis emerging in Iran during 1977–1978. Hoseinian, *Chahardah-sal reqabat-e ideolozhik-e shi'eh dar Iran*, pp. 790–793, and Rahnema, *An Islamic Utopian*, pp. 275, 336–337.

Conclusion: Aborted Resurrection: An Intellectual Arena Wide Open to Opposition

1. Ruhollah Khomeini, *Mostazafin, Mostakbarin* (Tehran: Amirkabir, 1983), pp. 11–13.

2. Perry Anderson, *The Antinomies of Antonio Gramsci* (London and New York: Verso, 2017), author's new preface, especially pp. 16–20. Studies of the "intellectual origins" of the French Revolution, for instance, include Michael Sonenscher, *Before the Deluge: Public Debt, Inequality, and the Intellectual Origins of the French Revolution* (Princeton, NJ: Princeton University Press, 2007); Robert Darnton, *The Forbidden Best-Sellers of Pre-Revolutionary France* (New York & London: Norton, 1995); Daniel Mornet, *Les origines intellectuelles de la Révolution française, 1715–1787* (Paris: A. Colin, 1934); Karl Marx, *The Eighteenth Brumaire of Louis Bonaparte* (Moscow: Progress Publishers, 1972). Alexis de Tocqueville, *The Old*

Notes to Pages 224–226

Regime and the French Revolution (New York: Doubleday & Anchor, 1955).

3. Ervand Abrahamian, *The Iranian Mojahedin* (New Haven, CT: Yale University Press, 1989) and *Khomeinism: Essays on the Islamic Republic* (Berkeley, CA: University of California Press, 1993). Abrahamian's longer-term perspective, in *A History of Modern Iran* (New York: Cambridge University Press, 2012), relates the strength and longevity of the Islamic Republic to its massive expansion of the monarchist state apparatus, and particularly its welfare aspects.

4. See Charles Kurzman, *The Unthinkable Revolution in Iran* (Cambridge, MA: Harvard University Press, 2004). Behrooz Ghamari-Tabrizi, *Foucault in Iran: Islamic Revolution after the Enlightenment* (Minneapolis, MN: University of Minneapolis, 2016).

5. Upset by a *New York Times* article saying that Iranian intellectuals wanted fundamental social reforms, the Shah was referring to a group of intellectuals gathered at the Shiraz (Aspen) Conference. Abdolreza Hushing Mahdavi, *Goftoguha-ye man ba shah: Khatertat-e mahramane-ye Amir Asdaollah Alam* (Tehran, 1993), vol. 1, p. 715.

6. The Shah's most elaborate description of this project appeared in his 1976 book *Toward the Great Civilization*. However, as early as 1971, he had declared Iran's passage to the era of "Great Civilization" would begin by the early 1980s, coinciding with the completion of the sixth five-year development plan (1979–1984). See his February 1971 speech in Mohammad Reza Pahlavi, *Bargozide-i az neveshte-ha va sokhanan-e Shahanshah Aryamehr* (Tehran, n.d.), pp. 36, 40.

7. Alma's reference to Parvizi is quoted in Mozaffar Shahedi, *Hezb-e Rastakhiz: eshtebah-e bozorg* (*Tehran: Mo'assese-ye motale'at va pazhuheshha-ye sisai*, 2003), vol. 1, p. 101.

8. On Hoveyda as an intellectual, see Abbas Milani, *The Persian Sphinx: Amir Abbas Hoveyda and the Riddle of the Iranian Revolution* (Washington, D.C.: Mage Publishers, 2000). See also Afsin Matin-asgari, "The Transparent Sphinx: Political Biography and the Question of Intellectual Responsibility." in *Critique*, no. 10 (fall 2001): pp. 87–108. For contemporary satirical depictions of Hoveyda see Farideh Towfiq, *Ruzname-ye Towfiq va kaka Towfiq* (Tehran, 2005).

9. Azimi, *Iran: The Crisis of Democracy* (London: I. B. Tauris, 1989) and Marvin Zonis, *Majestic Failure: The Fall of the Shah* (Chicago, IL: The University of Chicago Press, 1991).

10. The Shah's autocratic mindset precluded the acknowledgment of intellectual contributions similar or complementary to his own. Therefore, even purported scholarly attempts at the elaboration of his ideas were inevitably bland and apologetic. See, for example, the

collection of articles in Jane W. Jacqz, ed. *Iran: Past, Present and Future: Aspen Institute/Persepolis Symposium* (New York: Aspen Institute for Humanistic Studies, 1976). Catering to the peak of the Shah's political and intellectual arrogance, this volume lacked even the mildly critical perspective of 1960s scholarly studies collected in Ehsan Yar-shater, ed. *Iran Faces the Seventies* (New York: Palgrave, 1971). On the intellectual poverty of official texts celebrating Pahlavi-era accomplishments see Kaveh Bayat, "The Pahlavi School of Historiography on the Pahlavi Era" in Touraj Atabaki ed. *Iran in the 20th Century: Historiography and Political Culture* (London and New York: I. B. Tauris, 2009), pp. 113–120.

11. According to Nasr, the Shah was a strong believer in the wholesale appropriation of modern technology, whereas the Queen was somewhat more attentive to native Iranian culture. "I had often talked with both the Shah and the Queen, and also with the Shah alone, about the necessity of incorporating modern concepts into our domestic culture." Seyyed Hossein Nasr and Ramin Jahanbeglu, *Dar jostoju-ye amr-e qodsi* (Tehran, 2006), pp. 173–174.

12. Ghoalm Reza Afkhami, *The Life and Times of the Shah* (Berkeley and Los Angeles: University of California Press, 2009), pp. 55–56.

13. Mohammad Reza Pahlavi, *Bargozide-yi az neveshte-ha va sokhanan-e Shahanshah Aryamehr*, p. 48.

14. Afkhami, *The Life and Times of the Shah*, p. 57.

15. For a pertinent comment see Gary Sick, quoted in Afkhami, *The Life and Times of the Shah*, p. 305.

16. *Mission for my Country* quoted in Ervand Abrahamian, *Iran between Two Revolutions* (Princeton, NJ: Princeton University Press, 1982), p. 440.

17. Mozaffar Shahedi, *Hezb-e Rastakhiz eshtebah-e bozorg* (Tehran, 2003), vol. 1, p. 99.

18. Hoveyda quoted on p. 212 in Hamid Qazvini, "*baz-khani-ye parvande-ye Mahmud Ja'farian*" in *Fasl-nameh-e motalat-e tarikhi*, vol. 5, no. 19 (Winter 2008): pp. 185–223.

19. Leonard Binder, *Iran: Political Development in a Changing Society* (Berkeley and Los Angeles: University of California Press, 1962), p. 204.

20. Martin F. Herz, *A View from Tehran: A Diplomatist Look at the Shah's Regime in June* 1964 (Institute for the Study of Diplomacy, Georgetown University, Washington, DC, 1979), pp. 6–7; quoted in Homa Katouzian, *The Persians: Ancient, Medieval and Modern Iran* (New Haven and London: Yale University Press, 2009), pp. 265–266.

21. Abdolreza Hushing Mahdavi, *Goftoguha-ye man ba shah: Khaterat-e mahramane-ye Amir Asdaollah Alam* (Tehran, 1993), vol. 1, p. 121.

22. Ibid., p. 171.
23. Mahdavi, *Goftoguha-ye man ba shah*, vol. 2, p. 497.
24. "The Philosophical Foundations of Resurrection" [*mabani-ye falsafi-ye Rastakhiz*] was the title of the Resurrection Party's monthly organ, launched in 1978. See *Mabani-ye falsafi-ye Rastakhiz*, Vol. 1, no. 1 (February 1978).
25. Quoted in Ali Ansari, *Modern Iran: The Pahlavis and After* (London: Pearson, 2007), p. 206.
26. Oriana Fallaci, *Interview with History* (Boston, MA: Houghton Mifflin, 1976), quoted on pp. 268, 273, 277.
27. Shahedi, *Hezb-e Rastakhiz: eshtebah-e bozorg*, vol. 1, pp. 127–129. Alam was not alone in opposing the Resurrection Party. Ardeshir Zahedi, Mozaffar Baghai, Ja'far Sharif-emami, and Ebrahim Khajenuri were not supportive of the idea either. See ibid., pp. 197–200. Alam died in 1977, a dejected man ignored by his master (*arbab*), who returned his confidential letters of warning unread or torn up. Mahdavi, *Goftoguha-ye man ba shah*, vol. 2, pp. 858–859. On the humiliation the Resurrection Party imposed on the Iranian intellectual community see, for example, Shahrokh Meskub, *Ruzaha dar rah* (Paris: Edition Khavaran, 2000), pp. 20–22.
28. Robert Graham, *Iran: The Illusion of Power* (New York: St. Martin's Press, 1978), pp. 42–43; Dariush Homayun, *Diruz va Farda* (n.p., n.d), pp. 28–29. Abrahamian, *Iran between Two Revolutions*, pp. 496–498.
29. Farah Pahlavi, *An Enduring Love*, translated from the French, Patricia Clancy (New York: Miramax Books, 2004), pp. 258–259.
30. On the Shah's illness, including his chief French physician's detailed account, see Farah Pahlavi, *An Enduring Love*, pp. 241–248, 251–257, 263–266. The Shah's mention of his mortality, in the speech that launched the Resurgence Party, is noted in Marvin Zonis, *Majestic Failure: The Fall of the Shah* (Chicago, IL: The University of Chicago Press, 1991), pp. 154–157. In his 1976 speech, the Shah had said:

Obviously, until now, I alone have fashioned the seventeen points of this [Shah-People] Revolution, everything being done according to orders handed down by a commander. But I am not eternal, and so to ensure the country a secure future, we need organizations capable not only of preserving the fruits of Iran's revolution, and of these years' accomplishments, but to broaden and deepen their implementation.
Shahedi, *Hezb-e Rastakhiz: eshtebah-e bozorg*, vol. 2, p. 145.

31. The idea of the Resurrection Party was jointly conceived, he wrote, by ex-Marxists, looking to communist-style one-party models, and "young political scientists with Ph.D.s from American universities," influenced

by Modernization theorist Samuel Huntington's idea of one-party systems providing an "organic link between the state and society." Abrahamian, *Iran between Two Revolutions*, p. 441.

32. Afkhami, *The Life and Times of the Shah,* pp. 433–434.

33. The full text of the Shah's speech, declaring the launch of the Resurrection Party, is in *Kayhan Airmail Edition*, March 8, 1975. The Resurrection Party's constitution quoted in Shahedi, *Hezb-e Rasrakhiz: eshtebah-e bozorg*, vol. 1, p. 213.

34. Afkhami, *The Life and Times of the Shah*, p. 434. See also Shahedi, *Hezb-e Rastakhiz: eshtebah-e bozorg*, vol. 1, pp. 144–145.

35. Shahedi, *Hezb-e Rasrakhiz: eshtebah-e bozorg*, vol. 1, pp. 214–215

36. Hamid Shokat, *Negahi az darun be jonbesh-e chap-e Iran: Goftogu ba Kurosh Lasha'i* (Tehran: Akhtaran, 1992), pp. 266–269. *Baqer Aqeli, Sharh-e hal-e rejal-e siasi va nezami-ye mo'aser-e Iran*, vol. 1 (Tehran, 2000), pp. 270–271.

37. Enayatolah Reza, *Nagofte-ha* (Tehran, 2012), pp. 17, 84–87; and Ali Amui, *Dord-e zamaneh*, cited in Shahedi, *Hezb-e Rastakhiz: eshtebah-e bozorg*, vol. 1, pp. 178–179.

38. See Naser Mohajer's interview in www.akhbar-rooz.com March 20, 2017. Mohajer notes Bizhan Jazani's reference to *"rastakhiz-e siahkal"* cited in *19 Bahman-e Teorik*, no. 4 (1976): pp. 44–45. Another example is in Jazani, *Tarikh-e si sale-ye Iran* (Tehran, n.d.), p. 5.

39. Ali Ansari, *Modern Iran: The Pahlavis and After* (London: Pearson, 2007), pp. 235–236.

40. Ansari, *Modern Iran*, p. 206.

41. Dariush Shayegan, *Asia Facing the West* (Tehran, 1977), p. 94. Years later, Shayegan explained his likening of Asian cultures to "swamplands" fermenting intellectual monstrosities came from a passage in Arthur Gobineau's *Religions and Philosophies of Central Asia*. Dariush Shayegan, *Zir-e asemanha-ye jahan* (Tehran), pp. 225–226.

42. Shahedi, *Hezb-e Rastakhiz: eshtebah-e bozorg*, vol. 2, p. 150. This was the continuation of a project launched in 1973 whereby a group of about 500–600 academics were recruited in "the Task force for Investigating Iranian Issues in light of the Shah-People Revolution." Led by the ex-communist Hushang Nahavandi, this group continued its work until 1978. See ibid., pp. 471–473. See also *Mabani-ye falsafi-ye Rastakhiz*.

43. Hushang Nahavandi in transcripts of Harvard Oral History interviews, tape 25, pp. 6–11. Shapur Zandnia, for example, wrote theoretical tracts applying the Islamic concept of "divine unity" (*towhid*), to argue human society needed "unity of political command," exemplified best in the

Shah's style of rule via the Resurrection Party. Shahedi, *Hezb-e Rastakhiz: eshtebah-e bozorg,* vol. 1, notes to pp. 184–188.

44. Naraqi quoted in Shahedi, *Hezb-e Rastakhiz: eshtebah-e bozorg,* vol. 1., p. 170.

45. Baheri quoted in Shokat, *Negahi az darun be jonbesh-e chap-e Iran,* p. 273. According to Baheri, "His majesty's order had emphasized that the philosophy of revolution must be based on the dialectic." Harvard Oral History Interview with Baheri, Transcripts of Tape 25, p. 6.

46. Shahedi, *Hezb-e Rastakhiz: eshtebah-e bozorg,* vol. 1, p. 474.

47. In spring 1977, the shah acknowledged the shortcomings of Resurrection party, saying:

    The problem is to find solutions. Do you want to rejoin all those parties foreign-controlled parties again? ... Which beautiful unblemished Western model can you show us to embrace? Where can it be found? Let me know what it is.
                    Shahedi, *Hezb-e Rastakhiz: eshtebah-e bozorg,* vol. 2, p. 345.

48. Even Bizhan Jazani's faction of the guerrillas were implicitly in line with this position. See Bizhhan Jazani, *Nabard ba diktatori* (n.d., n.p.).

49. Fereydoun Hoveyda, *The Fall of the Shah,* Roger Riddell trans. (New York: Wyndham books, 1980), p. 19.

50. The Shah quoted in Mahmud Tolo'i, *Sad ruz-e Akhar* (Tehran, 1999), p. 404. Hushang Nahavandi claims the text of this speech was composed by Nasr and Qotbi. See his *Akharin Ruzha: Payan-e saltanat va dargozasht-e Shah* (Los Angeles: Ketab Corporation, 2005), p. 266.

Bibliography

Archives

Iran. National Documents Institute (*Sazman-e asnad-e melli*), Tehran. Great Britain. Foreign Office, London. Cited as FO.

Persian Periodicals

Andishe va honar
Andishe-ye Puya
Bokhara
Cesmandaz (Paris)
Donya (3rd series)
Elm va zendegi
Farhang va zendegi
Faslname-ye motale'at-e tarikhi
Iranshahr
Iranshenasi
Iran Nameh
Jahan-e ketab
Jahan-e no
Kaveh
Kayhan (airmail edition)
Ketab-e Jom'eh
Mardom
Mellat-e bidar
Name-ye Parsi
Negah-e no
Negin
Salname-ye Pars
Tamasha
Tarikh-e mo'aser-e Iran
Yadegar

Persian Sources

Abedini, Hasan. *Sad sal dastan-nevisi dar Iran,* 2 volumes (Tehran: Tondar, 1987).

Adamiyat, Fereydun. *Andisheha-ye Mirza Aqa Khan Kermani* (Tehran: Payam, 1967).

"*Ashoftegi dar fekr-e tarikhi,*" in *Mellat-e bidar,* vol. 4 no. 2 (February 1985): pp. 14–24.

Ideolozhi-ye nehzat-e mashrutiyat-e Iran (Tehran: Payam, 1974).

Feker-e azadi va moqaddame-ye nehzat-e mashrutiat-e Iran (Tehran: Payam, 1961).

Adharang, Abdol-Hosein. "Parviz Khanlari," in www.Iranicaonline.org. Accessed October 2017.

Afshar, Iraj. *Bokhara,* vol. 18, no. 109 (December 2015–January 2016): pp. 81–85.

ed. *Nameha-ye Qazvini beh Taqizadeh* (Tehran, 1973), pp. 174–176.

Zendegi-e tufani: khaterat-e seyyed Hasan Taqizadeh (Tehran, 1993).

Ahmadi, Hamid, ed. *Ma ham dar in Khaneh haqqi darim: The Memoir of Najmai Alavi* (Tehran: Akhtaran, 2004).

Tarikhche-ye ferqe-ye jomhuri-ye enqelabi-ye Iran va Goruh-e Arani (Tehran: Akhtaran, 2000).

Ajudani, Lotfollah. *Roshanfekran-e Iran dar asr-e mashrutiat* (Tehran: Akhtaran, 2008).

Ajudani, Mashallah. *Mashrute-ye Irani* (Tehran: Akhtaran, 2004).

Al-Ahmad, Jalal. *Dar khedmat va Khianat-e Roshanfekran* (Tehran: Ravaq, 1977).

Gharbazdegi (Tehran: Ravaq, 1962).

Khasi dar Miqat (Tehran, 1966).

Alikhani, Alinaqi. *Kahterat-e doktor Alinaqi Alikhani* (Tehran: Abi, 1996).

Amini, Mohammad, ed. *Zendegi va zamane-ye Ahmad Kasravi* (Los Angles: Ketab Corporation, 2016). Includes Kasravi's autobiographical writings *Zendegi-e man, Dah sal dar adlieh* and *Chera az adlieh birun amadm.*

Aqeli, Baqer. *Ruzshomar-e tarikh-e Iran: Az mashrute ta enqelab-e eslami,* 2 volumes (Tehran: Goftar, 1990).

Sharh-e hal-e rejal-e siasi va nezami-ye mo'aser-e Iran, vol. 1 (Tehran, 2000).

Arani, Taqi. *Defa'iyat-e doktor Arani* (n.p., n.d.).

Ariyanpur, Yahya. *Az Saba ta Nima,* 2 volumes (Tehran, 2002).

Ashuri, Dariush. *Ma va moderniat: Ostore-ye falsafeh dar mian-e ma* (Tehran, 2004).

"*Sharq va Gharb,*" in *Farhang va Zendegi,* no. 15 (Summer 1974): pp. 2–27.

Asil. *Negin,* no. 130 (Spring 1976): pp. 30–36.

Azarang, Abdol-Hosein. "*Tarikh-e nashr-e ketab dar Iran, 32*," in *Bokhara*, no. 108 (October–November 2015): pp. 113–117.

"*tarikh nashr ketab dar Iran, 33*," in *Bokhara* (December 2015–January 2016): pp. 29–36.

Azarang, Abdol-Hosein and Ali Dehbashi, *Tarikh-e shafahi-ye nashr dar Iran* (Tehran: Qoqnus, 2004).

Bahar, Mohammad-Taqi. *Tarikh-e mokhtasar-e ahzab-e sisai-ye Iran* (Tehran: Amir Kabir, 1978).

Bahthi dar bare-ye marja'iat va ruhaniyat (Tehran: Enteshar, 1962).

Bakhtiar, Manuchehr. *Nehzat-e mashrute va naqsh-e taqizadeh* (Toronto: Pegah Publications, 2015).

Baqi, Emad al-Din. *Baray-e Tarik: Goftogu ba Sa'id Hajjarian* (Tehran, 2000).

Bayat, Kaveh. "*Andishe-ye siasi-ye Davar va ta'sis-e dowlat-e modern dar Iran*," *Goft-o-gu*, no. 2 (1993): pp. 116–133.

Panturkism va Iran (Tehran: Shirazeh, 2008).

"*Piramun-e bateni-gari*," in *Jahan-e ketab*, vol. 10, no. 5 (September 2005): pp. 10–13.

Bayat, Kaveh and Iraj Afshar, eds. *Khaterat-e mohajerat: Az dowlat-e moqavemat-e Kermanshah ta komite-ye melliyun-e Berlan* (Tehran: Shirazeh, 1999).

Bayat, Kaveh and Reza Azari-Shahrezai, *Amal-e Iranian: Az konfrans-e solh-e Paris ta qarardad-e 1919 Iran va Engelis* (Tehran: Shirazeh, 2013).

Bazhen, Keyvan. *Samad Behrangi* (Tehran: Roznegar, 2003).

Behnam, Jamshid. *Berlaniha* (Tehran: Farzan, 2000).

Cultural Policy in Iran (Paris: *Unesco*, 1973).

"*Taqizadeh va mas'ale-ye tajddod*" in *Iran Nameh*, vol. xxi, nos. 1–2 (spring–summer 2003): pp. 77–89.

Behzadi, Ali. *Shebhe khaterat* (Tehran: Zarrin, 1997).

Bigdlu, Reza. *Bastangarai dar tarikh-e mo'aser-e Iran* (Tehran: Markaz, 2001).

"21 Azar" in *Donya*, third series, vol. 3 (November 1976).

Borhan, Abdollah, ed. *Khalil Maleki, nehzat-e melli-e Iran va edalat-e ejetma'i* (Tehran, 1999).

Dehbashi, Ali. "*khaterati az doktor Mahmud Enayat*" in *Bokhara*, vol. 15, no. 92 (April–May 2013): pp. 232–238.

Enayat, Hamid. 1969 interview reprinted in *Bokhara*, vol. 15, no. 92 (2013): pp. 199–221.

Entekhabi, Nader. *Nasionlaism va tajaddod dar Iran va Torkieh* (Tehran: Negare-ye aftab, 2011).

Ettehadieh, Mansureh. *Peydayesh va tahavvol-e ahzab-e sisasi-ye mashrutiat* (Tehran: Siamak, 2002).

Fardid, Ahmad. Interviewed in *Farhang va zendegi* (Winter 1972), pp. 33–34, 36.

Farrokh, Fereydun. "*Tasvir-e Kasravi dar azhan-e javanan*," in *Iran Nameh* vol. XX, nos. 1–2 (Spring & Summer 2022): pp. 277–284.

Farzad, Shahrokh. *Ferqe-ye demokrat-e Azarabaijan: az takhlie-ye Tabriz ta marg-e Pishevari* (Tehran: Ohadi, 2000).

Fathi, Asghar. "*Kasravi che miguyad*," *Iran Nameh*, vol. XX, nos. 1–2 (Spring & Summer 2012): pp. 261–275.

Forughi, Mohammad-Ali. *Seyr-e hekmat dar Orupa*, 2 volumes (Tehran: Zavvar, 2000).

Ghani, Qasem. "*Eslah-e nezhad*," in *Yadegar*, no. 8 (March–April 1945): pp. 8–26.

Golbon, Mohammad. *Naqd va siahat: Doktor Fatemeh Sayyah* (Tehran: Qatreh, 2004).

Gozaresh-e farhangi-ye Iran [Iran Cultural Report], published by the High Council for Culture and the Arts (Tehran, 1971).

"*Hafteh-name-ye Ayandegan Adabi*," in *Andishe-ye Puya*, 4 (September 28, 2015): pp. 136–141.

Haj-Bushehr, Mohammad-Taqi. "*Mo'alem va morad-e Ruhollah Musavi Khomeini*," in *Cesmandaz*, no. 13 (spring 1994): pp. 32–41.

Hakamizadeh, Ali-Asghar. *Asrar-e hezar saleh* (Tehran, 1943).

Haqdar, Ali-Asghar. *Mohammad-Ali Forughi va sakhtarha-ye novin-e madani* (Tehran: Kavir, 2005).

Hashemi, Mohammad Mansur. *Hoviyat-andishan va mirath-e fekri-ye Ahmad Fardid* (Tehran, 2005).

Hedayat, Sadeq. *Hashtad-o do nameh be Hasan Shahidnura'i* (Paris: cesmandaz, 2000).

Hekmat, Ali-Asghar. *Si Khatereh az asr-e farkhonde-ye Pahlavi* (Tehran, 1975).

Homayun, Dariush. *Diruz va farda* (n.p.: 1981).

Hoseinian, Ruhollah. *Chahardah-sal reqabat-e ideolozhik-e shi'eh dar Iran* (Tehran, 2004).

Hushiar, M. trans. *Seh maqaleh dar bare-ye enqelab-e mashrute-ye Iran* (Tehran, 1978).

Itscherenska, Isle. "*Taqizadeh dar Alman-e Qeysari*," in *Iran Nameh*, vol. xxi, nos. 1–2 (spring-summer 2003).

JAMA, *Gozashteh cheragh-e rah-e ayandeh ast*, 2 volumes (Tehran: JAMA, n.d.).

Jazani, Bizhan. *Marksism-e Eslmai ya Esalm-e Marksisti* (Koln, 2001).
    "*Mohre-i bar safhe-ye shatranj*," in *Ketab-e Jomeh*, vol. 1, no. 36 (June 1980): pp. 46–57.
    Tarikh-e si sale-ye Iran (Tehran, n.d.).

Kadivar, Mohsen. *Nazariyeha-ye dowlat dar fiqh-e Shi'eh* (Tehran, 1997).

Kalirad, Ali. *Az jame'-ye Irani ta mihan-e Turki* (Tehran: Shirazeh, 2014).

Karimi, Nosrat, ed. *Yadname-ye Abdol-Hosein Nushin* (Tehran, 2008).

Kasravi, Ahmad. *Baha'i-gari* (Tehran, 1944).

   Dar piramun-e falsafeh (Tehran, 1943).

   Dar rah-e sisat (Tehran, 1945).

   Shi'igari (Tehran, n.d.).

   Tarikhche-ye shir va khorshid (Tehran, n.d.)

   Tarikh-e mashrute-ye Iran (Tehran, 1940).

   Varjavand-e Bonyad (Koln, 1980).

   Zaban-e pak (Tehran, 1999).

Katouzian, Homa. *"Seyyed Hasan Taqiadeh: seh zendegi dar yek 'omr,"* Iran *Nameh* vol. XXI, nos. 1–2 (spring–summer 2003): pp. 7–48; and the preface to this issue.

Kazemzadeh Iranshahr, Hosein. *Tadavi-e ruhi baray-e afrad va jame'eh* (Tehran: Eqbal, 1978).

Kermani, Mohammad Nazem al-Islam. *Tarikh-e bidari-ye Iranian* (Tehran, 1910).

Keshavarz, Amir-Hushang. *Do maqale az Hosein Kazemzadeh Iranshahr* (n.p.: 1991).

Khaksar, Abbas. *Ta'amoli dar enqelab-e mashrute-ye Iran* (Tehran: Negah, 2015).

Khalaji, Mohammad Mehdi. *"Korban va ravayati sisai az tarikh-e andishe-ye falsafi dar Iran,"* Iran Nameh, vol. XX. no. 4 (fall 2002): pp. 417–450.

   "Naqd-e daruni-ye ruhaniat: gozaresh-e resale-i dar sekularizm," in *Iran Nameh*, vol. XXI, no. 4 (winter 2004): pp. 489–512.

Khatibi, Parviz. *Khaterati az honarmandan* [Remembering Artists] (Los Angeles: Parviz Khatibi Cultural Foundation, 1994).

Khomeini, Ruhollah. *Hokumat-e Eslami* (Najaf and Tehran, 1977).

   Kashf al-asrar (Los Angeles: Ketab Corporation, 2009).

   Mostazafin, Mostakbarin (Tehran: Amirkabir, 1983).

Khosro-Shahi, Seyyed Hadi. *Nehzat-e Aziadistan va Sheykh Mohammad Khiabai* (Tehran: Markaz-e asnad-e enqelab-e eslami, 2010).

Mabani-ye falsafi-ye Rastakhiz (February 1978).

Madadpur, Mohammad. *"Nazari Ejmali be hekmat-e ma'navi-ye tarikh va falsafe-ye tarikh-e roshnagri,"* in *Tarikh-e Mo'aser*, vol. 6, no. 24 (winter 2003): pp. 115–160.

Mahdavi, Abdolreza Hushing. *Goftoguha-ye man ba shah: Khaterat-e mahramane-ye Amir Asdaollah Alam*, 2 volumes (Tehran, Tarh-e no, 1993).

Maki, Hosein, ed. *Doktor Mosaddeq va notqha-ye tarikhi-ye o* (Tehran: 1985).

Manafzadeh, Alireza. *"Jaygah-e Kasravi dar tarikhnegari va tarikh-shenasi,"* in *Negah-e no*, 96 (winter 2002): pp. 44–52.

Matin, Mahnaz and Nasser Mohajer, *"Peykar-e zan-e Irani baray-e dastyabi beh haq-e ra'y, 1320–1325,"* Iran Nameh, vol. 30, no. 3 (fall 2015): pp. 184–228.

Meskub, Shahrokh. *Dastan-e adabiyat va sargozasht-e ejtema'* (Tehran: Farzan, 1994).

  Ketab-e Moretza Keyvan (Tehran: Nader, 2003).

  Ruzha dar rah (Paris: Edition Khavaran, 2000).

Minovi, Mojtaba. *Naqd-e hal* (Tehran, 1980).

Mojtaba Maqsudi, ed. *Tahavolat-e sisai-ejtema'i-ye Iran 1320–57* (Tehran: Rozaneh, 2000).

Momeni, Baqer. *Donya-ye Arani* (Tehran: Akhtaran, 2005).

Moshfeq-Kazemi, Morteza. *Ruzgar va andisheha* (Tehran, 1971).

Motahhari, Moretza. *Elal-e garayesh be maddigari* (Tehran, 1999).

  Name-ye tarikhi-ye ostad Motahhari be Emam Khomeini (Tehran: Sadra, 1997).

Nabavi-Tabrizi, Seyyed Meqdad. *Tarkih-e Maktum* (Tehran: Shirazeh, 2014).

Nahavandi, Hushang. *Akharin Ruzha: Payan-e saltanat va dargozasht-e Shah* (Los Angeles: Ketab Corporation, 2005).

Nakhshab, Mohammad. *Majmo'e-i az asar-e doktor Mohammad Nakhshab* (Tehran: Chapakhsh, 2002).

Nasr, Seyyed Hossein. *"Negahi digar beh Hanri Korban,"* in *Iran Nameh*, vol. IX, no. 4 (autumn 1911): pp. 667–680.

Nasr, Seyyed Hossein and Ramin Jahanbeglu. *Dar jostoju-ye amr-e qodsi* (Tehran: Ney, 2006).

Nekuruh, Mahmud. *Nehzat-e khoda-parastan-e sosialist* (Tehran: Chapakhsh, 1999).

Nikkhah, Parviz. *Javedaneh* (Los Angeles: Ketab Corporation 2014).

Niruy-ye sevvom dar moqabel-e do paygah-e ejetma'i-ye amperialism (Tehran, 1951).

Nozar, trans. *Marksizm va falsafeh* (Tehran, 1953).

Nozar, Mohammd-baqer. *"Naqsh-e komite-ye melliyun-e hendi dar sheklgiri-ye komite-ye melliyun-e Irani dar Berlin,"* in *Faslnameh motale'at-e tarikhi*, vol. 6, no. 23 (winter 2009): pp. 47–59.

Nuri, Nuraldin. *Nokhostin kongre-ye nevisandegan-e Iran* (Tehran: Ostureh, 2005).

Pahlavi, Mohammad Reza. *Bargozide-yi az neveshteha va sokhanan-e Shahanshah Aryamehr* (Tehran, n.d.).

Besu-ye Tamaddon-e Bozorg (Tehran, 1976).

Enqelab-e Sefid (Tehran, 1965).

Safarname-ye shahanshah be keshvar-e Amrika (Tehran, 1950).

Pahlevan, Changiz. *"Barnamerizi-ye farhangi dar Iran,"* in *Farhang va zendegi*, 15 (Summer 1974): pp. 53–73.

Pakdaman, Nasser. *Nameh-e Parsi*, no. 1, May 1959.

Parham, Baqer. *Ba-ham negari va yekta-negari* (Tehran: Agah, 1998).

Parham Baqer et al. *Andishe-ye gharbi va goftogu-ye tamaddonha* (Tehran: Farzan, 1990).

Pashne-ye ahanin (Tehran, 1952).

Parsinejad, Iraj. *"Yaddashtha-ye yek Irani-ye motemadden-e ba-ma'Raf'at,"* in *Bokhara*, no. 108 (October–November 2015): pp. 463–93.

Plekhanov, Georgy. *Naqsh-e shakhsiat dar tarikh* (Florence Italy: Mazdak, n.d.).

Qanei-fard, Erfan. *Dar Damgah-e Hadeseh* (Los Angeles: Ketab Corporation, 2012).

Qazi, Mohammad. *Sargozasht-e tarjomeha-ye man* (Tehran, 1995).

Qazvini, Hamid. *"baz-khani-ye parvandeh-e Mahmud Ja'farian,"* in *Fasl-nameh-e motalat-e tarikhi*, vol. 5, no. 19 (winter 2008): pp. 185–223.

Ra'isnia, Rahim. *Akharin sangar-e azadi: Majmo'e-ye maqalat-e Mir-Jafar Pishevari dar ruzname-ye Haqiqat, organ-e ettehadie-ye omomi-ye kargaran-e Iran: 1300–1301* (Tehran: Shirazeh, 1998).

Rasulipur, Moretza. *"Sakhtar-e artesh va SAVAK va nakaramadi-ye rezhim-e Pahlavi az zaban-e doktor Ehsan Naraqi,"* in *Tarikh-e Mo'aser-e Iran*, vol. 6, no. 24 (winter 2003): pp. 195–224.

Rasulzadeh, Mohammad-Amin. *Gozaresh-ha'i az enqelab-e mashrutiyat-e Iran* (Tehran: Shirazeh, 2016), Rahim Ra'isnia, trans.

Reza, Enayatollah. *Khaterat-e doktor Enyatollah Reza* (Tehran, 2013).

Nagofteh-ha (Tehran, 2012).

Sadiq, Isa. *Yadegar-e omr* (Tehran: Amir Kabir, 1966).

Salname-ye Pars (Tehran: The Organization of Iranian Ministries, 1927–1928).

Sasani, Khan-Malek. *Yadbudha-ye sefarat-e Estanbul* (Tehran: Ferdowsi, 1966).

Sepanlu, Mohammad-Ali. *Bahar* (Tehran, 1995).

Shadman, Fakhreddin. *Taskhir-e tamaddon-e farangi* (Tehran: Gam-e no, 2003).

Shahedi, Mozaffar. *Hezb-e Rastakhiz: eshtebah-e bozorg*, 2 volumes (Tehran: Mo'assese-ye motale'at va pazhuheshha-ye sisai, 2003).

Shahrokh Haghighi, *Gozar az mo derniteh? Nicheh, Fuko, liotar, derida* (Tehran: Agah, 2001).

Shakeri, Khosrow. *Pishine-ha-ye eqtesadi-ejetma'i-ye jonbesh-e mashrutiat va enkeshaf-e sosial demokrasi* (Tehran: Akhtaran, 1995).

Taqi Arani dar Ayene-ye tarikh (Tehran: Akhtaran, 2008).

Shayegan, Dariush. *Asia dar barabar-e gharb* (Tehran: Amir Kabir, 1977).

Hanri Korban: Afaq-e tafakkor-e ma'navi dar Islam-e Irani, Baqer Parham trans. (Tehran: Farzan, 1994).

Zir-e asemanha-ye jahan (Tehran: Farzan, 1997).

Shari'ati, Ali. *Ma va Eqbal* (Tehran, n.d.).

Tashayyo'-e Alavi va Tashayyo'-e Safavi (Tehran, 1969).

Shayegan, Hasan. *Eqbal va tarikhnegari* (Tehran, 2004).

Shirazi, Mirza Saleh. *Gozaresh-e safar-e Mirza Saleh-e Shirazi* (Tehran: Rah-e no, 1983).

Sho'aian, Mostafa. *Negahi be ravabet-e Shuravi and jonbesh-e enqelabi-ye jangal* (Florence: Mazdak Publishers, 1976).

Shokat, Hamid. *Negahi az darun beh jonbesh-e chap-e Iran: Goftogu ba Kurosh Lashai* (Tehran: Akhtaran, 1992).

Siasi, Ali-Akbar. *Yek zendegi-ye siasi* (Tehran: Thaleth, 2014).

Tabataba'i, Mohammad-Hosein. *Aghaz-e Falsafeh* (Qom: n.d.).

Asul-e falsafeh va ravesh-e re'alism (Qom: n.d.).

Shi'e (Tehran, 1960).

Tabraian, Safa'odin. "Mo'assese-ye motale'at va tahqiqat-e ejtema'i," in *Tarikh-e Mo'aser-e Iran*, vol. 13, no. 51 (fall: 2009): pp. 51–127.

Taqizadeh, Hasan. *Khatabe-ye aqa-ye seyyed Hassan Taqizadeh* (Tehran, 1959).

Seh Khatabeh (Tehran 1965).

Tolo'i, Mahmoud. *Sad ruz-e Akhar* (Tehran: Elm, 1999).

Towfiq, Farideh. *Ruzname-ye Towfiq va kaka Towfiq* (Tehran: Abi, 2005).

Yazdani, Sohrab. *Sur-e Esrafil: Name-ye azadi* (Tehran: Ney, 2007).

Zahidi, Ardashir. *Khatirat-i Ardashir Zahidi* (Bethesda MD: IBEX Publishers, 2006).

Zarinebaf, Fariba. "Az estanbul ta Tabriz," in *Iran Nameh*, vol. XXIII, nos. 3–4 (fall–winter 2007): pp. 305–332.

Zarrinkub, Abdol-Hosein. *Na sharqi, na Gharbi, ensani* (Tehran: Amir Kabir, 1974).

Zaryab, Abbas and Iraj Afshar, *Nameha-ye Taqizadeh* (Tehran, 1975).

Zibakalam, Sadeq. *Moqaddame-yi bar enqelab-e Eslami* (Tehran: Rozaneh, 1983).

English and French Sources

Abrahamian, Ervand. *The Coup: 1953, The CIA, and the Roots of Modern US-Iranian Relations* (New York and London: The New Press, 2013).

Iran between Two Revolutions (Princeton, NJ: Princeton University Press, 1982).

The Iranian Mojahedin (New Haven, CT: Yale University Press, 1989).

"Kasravi: The Integrative Nationalist of Iran," in *Middle Eastern Studies*, vol. 9, no. 3 (October 1973): pp. 271–295.

Khomeinism: Essays on the Islamic Republic (Berkeley, CA: University of California Press, 1993).

Adelkhah, Fariba. *Being Modern in Iran*, Jonathan Derrick trans. (London: C. Hurst & Co., 1998).

Afary, Janet. *The Iranian Constitutional Revolution, 1906–1911: Grassroots Democracy, Social Democracy and the Origins of Feminism* (New York: Columbia University Press, 1996).

Afary, Janet and Kevin B. Anderson. *Foucault and the Iranian Revolution: Gender and the seduction of Islamism* (Chicago: The University of Press, 2005).

Afkhami, Ghoalm Reza. *The Life and Times of the Shah* (Berkeley and Los Angeles: University of California Press, 2009).

Afshari, Reza. "The Historians of the Constitutional Movement and the Making of Iran's Populist Tradition," in *The International Journal of Middle East Studies*, vol. 25, no. 3 (1993): pp. 477–494.

Akhavi, Shahrough. *Religion and Politics in Contemporary Iran: Clergy-State Relations in the Pahlavi Period* (Albany: State University of New York Press, 1980).

Aksin, Sina. *Turkey: From Empire to Revolutionary Republic* (New York: New York University Press, 2007).

Algar, Hamid. *Religion and State in Iran, 1785–1906: The Role of the Ulema in the Qajar Period* (Berkeley, CA: University of California Press, 1969).

Alinejad, Cyrus *"San'atizadeh Kermani, Homayun,"* in www.Iranicaonline .org. Accessed September 2017.

Amanat, Abbas. *Apocalyptic Islam and Iranian Shi'ism* (London and New York: I. B. Tauris, 2009).

"Constitutional Revolution: I. Intellectual Background," p. 170. www .Iraniaonline.org. Accessed July 2017.

"Memory and Amnesia in the Historiography of the Constitutional Revolution" in Touraj Atabaki, ed. *Iran in the 20th Century: Historiography and Political Culture* (London and New York: I. B. Tauris, 2009), pp. 23–54.

Resurrection and Renewal: The Making of the Babi Movement in Iran, 1844–1850 (Ithaca and London: Cornell University Press, 1898).

Amanat, Abbas and Farzin Vejdani, eds. *Facing Others: Iranian Identity Boundaries and Modern Political Cultures* (London and New York: Routledge, 2012).

Amin, Camron Michael. *Gender, State Policy, and Popular Culture, 1865–1946* (Gainesville, FL: The University Press of Florida, 2002).

Amir Arjomand, Said. "*A la recherche de la conscience collective*: Durkheim's Ideological Impact in Turkey and Iran" in *The American Sociologist*, vol. 17, no. 2 (May 1982): pp. 94–102.

"Ideological Revolution in Shi'ism" in Said Amir Arjomand edited, *Authority and Political Culture in Shi'ism* (Albany: State University of New York Press, 1988), pp. 178–209.

The Turban for the Crown: The Islamic Revolution in Iran (London and New York: Oxford University Press, 1988).

Shadow of God and the Hidden Imam (Chicago and London: The University of Chicago Press, 1984).

Anderson, Perry. *The Antinomies of Antonio Gramsci* (London and New York: Verso, 2017).

Ansari, Ali M. *Modern Iran: The Pahlavis and After* (London: Pearson, 2007).

"The Myth of the White Revolution: Mohammad Reza Shah, 'Modernization' and the Consolidation of Power," in *Middle Eastern Studies*, vol. 37, no. 3 (July 2001): pp. 1–24.

The Politics of Nationalism in Modern Iran (Cambridge: Cambridge University Press, 2012).

Arvidsson, Stefan. *Aryan Idols: Indo-European Mythology as Ideology and Science*, Sonia Wichmann, trans. (Chicago, IL: The University of Chicago Press, 2006).

Atabaki, Touraj. "Constitutionalism in Iran and Its Asian Interdependencies," in *Comparative Studies of South Asia, Africa and the Middle East*, vol. 28, no. 1 (2008): pp. 142–153.

ed. *Iran in the 20th Century: Historiography and Political Culture* (London and New York: I. B. Tauris, 2009).

ed. *Iran and the First World War: Battleground of the Great Powers* (London and New York: I. B. Tauris, 2006).

Atabaki, Touraj and Eric J. Zurcehr, *Men of Order: Authoritarian Modernization under Ataturk and Reza Shah* (London and New York: I. B. Tauris, 2004).

Axworthy, Michael. *A History of Iran: Empire of the Mind* (New York: Basic Books, 2008).

Ayalon, Ami. *Language of Change in the Arab Middle East: The Evolution of Modern Arabic political Discourse* (New York: Oxford University Press, 1987).

Aydin, Cemil. *The Politics of Anti-Westernism in Asia: Visions of World Order in Pan-Islamic and Pan-Asian Thought* (New York: Columbia University Press, 2007).

Ayturk, Ilker. "Turkish Linguistics against the West: The Origins of Linguistic Nationalism in Ataturk's Turkey," in *Middle Eastern Studies*, vol. 40, no. 6 (November 2004): pp. 1–25.

Azimi, Fakhreddin. *Iran: The Crisis of Democracy* (London and New York: I. B. Tauris, 1989).

Bakhash, Shaul. *The Reign of the Ayatollahs: Iran and the Islamic Revolution* (New York: Basic books, 1984).

Barkey, Karen. *Empire of Difference: The Ottomans in Comparative Perspective* (New York: Cambridge University Press, 2008).

Bast, Oliver. "Disintegrating the 'Discourse of Disintegration': Some Reflections on the Historiography of the Late Qajar Period and Iranian *Cultural Memory*" in Touraj Atabaki, ed. *Iran in the 20th Century: Historiography and Political Culture* (London and New York: I. B. Tauris, 2009), pp. 55–68.

   "Duping the British and Outwitting the Russians? Iran's foreign policy, the 'Bolshevik threat' and the genesis of the Soviet-Iranian Treaty of 1921," in Stephanie Cronin, ed. *Iranian Russian Encounters: Empires and Revolutions since 1800* (London and New York: Routledge, 2013), pp. 261–297.

Bayat, Kaveh. "The Pahlavi School of Historiography on the Pahlavi Era," in Touraj Atabaki, ed. *Iran in the 20th Century: Historiography and Political Culture* (London and New York: I. B. Tauris, 2009), pp. 113–120.

Bayat, Mangol. *Mysticism and Dissent: Socioreligious Thought in Qajar Iran* (Syracuse, NY: Syracuse University Press, 1982).

Behrooz, Maziar. *Rebels with a Cause: The Failure of the Left in Iran* (London and New York: I. B. Tauris, 1999).

Bendersky, Joseph W. *Carl Schmitt: Theorist of the Reich* (Princeton, NJ: Princeton University Press, 1983).

Bendix, Reinhard. *Max Weber: An Intellectual Portrait* (New York: Anchor Books, 1962).

Bennigson, Alexandre A. and S. Enders Wimbush. *Muslim National Communism in the Soviet Union: A Revolutionary Strategy for the Colonial World* (Chicago, IL: The University of Chicago Press, 1979).

Berberian, Houri. "Nest of Revolution: The Caucasus, Iran, and Armenians" in Rudi Matthee and Elena Andreeva, eds. *Russians in Iran: Diplomacy and Power in Iran in the Qajar Era and Beyond* (London and New York: I. B. Tauris, 2018), pp. 95–121.

Berdyaev, Nicolas. *The Russian Idea* (Boston: Beacon Press, 1962).

Berman, Marshall. *All that Is Solid Melts into the Air: The Experience of Modernity* (New York: Simon and Shuster, 1982).

Berman, Nina. *German Literature on the Middle East* (Ann Arbor: The University of Michigan Press, 2011).

Berkes, Nizai. *The Development of Secularism in Turkey* (Montreal: McGill University Press, 1964).

Berlin, Isaiah. *Russian Thinkers* (New York: The Viking Press, 1978).

Binder, Leonard. *Iran: Political Development in a Changing Society* (Berkeley and Los Angeles: University of California Press, 1962).

Bird, Christiane. *Neither East, Nor West: One Woman's Journey through the Islamic Republic of Iran* (New York: Pocket Books, 2001).

Bisaha, Nancy. *Creating East and West: Renaissance Humanists and the Ottoman Turks* (Philadelphia: University of Pennsylvania Press, 2004).

Boroujerdi, Mehrzad. *Iranian Intellectuals and the West: The Tormented Triumph of Nativism* (Syracuse, NY: Syracuse University Press, 1996).

Browne, Edward Granville. *The Persian Revolution of 1906–1909* (Washington, DC: Mage, 2006).

Bulliet, Richard W. *The Case for Islamo-Christian Civilization* (New York: Columbia University Press, 2004).

Burbank Jane and Frederik Copper, *Empires in World History: Power and the Politics of Difference* (Princeton, NJ: Princeton University Press, 2010).

Cammett, John M. *Antonio Gramsci and the Origins of Italian Communism* (Stanford, CA: Stanford University Press, 1967).

Carhart, Michael C. *The Science of Culture in Enlightenment Germany* (Cambridge, MA and London: Harvard University press, 2007).

Casanova, Pascale. *A World Republic of Letters*, M. B. DeBevoise, trans. (Cambridge, MA: Harvard University Press, 2004).

Chakrabarty, Dipesh. "The Muddle of Modernity," in *American Historical Review*, vol. 116, no. 3 (June 2011): pp. 663–675.

   Provincializing Europe: Postcolonial Thought and Historical Difference (Princeton, NJ: Princeton University Press, 2000).

Chatterjee, Choi. "Imperial Incarcerations: Ekaterina Breshko-Breshkovskaia, Vinayak Savarkar, and the Original Sins of Modernity," in *Slavic Review*, vol. 74, no. 4 (winter 2015): pp. 849–872.

Chaqueri, Cosroe (Khosrow Shakeri). "Iraj Esknadri," in www.Iranicaonline .org. Accessed 2015.

   The Soviet Socialist Republic of Iran, 1920–1921 (Pittsburgh and London: University of Pittsburgh Press, 1995).

Chehabi, Houchang E. *Iranian Politics and Religious Modernism* (Ithaca, NY: Cornell University Press, 1990).

Chehabi, Houchang E. and Vanessa Martin, eds. *Iran's Constitutional Revolution: Popular Politics, Cultural Transformations, and Transnational Connections* (London and New York: I. B. Tauris, 2010).

Clark, James D. *Provincial Concerns: A History of the Iranian Province of Azerbaijan, 1848–1906* (Costa Mesa, CA: Mazda, 2006).

Colak, Yilmaz. "Language Policy and Official Ideology in Early Republican Turkey," in *Middle East Studies*, vol. 40, no. 6 (November 2004): pp. 67–91.

Corbin, Henry. *Avicenna and the Visionary Recital*, Willard R. Trask, trans. (New York: Pantheon, 1960).

Crone, Patricia. *God's Rule: Government in Islam* (New York: Columbia University Press, 2004).

  Roman, Provincial and Islamic Law: The origins of the Islamic Patronate (New York: Cambridge University Pres, 1987).

Cronin, Stephanie. *Soldiers, Shahs and Subalterns in Iran: Opposition, Protest and Revolt, 1921–1941* (New York: Palgrave Macmillan, 2010).

Dabashi, Hamid. *A People Interrupted* (New York: New Press, 2007).

  Shi'ism: A Religion of Protest (Cambridge, MA: Harvard University Pres, 2011).

  The World of Persian Literary Humanism (Cambridge, MA: Harvard University Press, 2012).

  "The Poetics of Politics: Commitment in Modern Persian Literature," in *Iranian Studies*, vol. 18, nos. 2–4 (1985): pp. 147–188.

  Theology of Discontent: The Ideological Foundations of the Islamic Revolution in Iran (New York: New York University Press, 1993).

Dale, Stephan Frederic. *The Orange Tree of Marrakesh: Ibn Khaldun and the Science of Man* (Cambridge, MA: Harvard University Press, 2015).

Dehkhoda, Ali-Akbar. *Charand-o-Parand: Revolutionary Satire from Iran, 1907–1909*, Janet Afary and John R. Perry, trans. and intro. (New Haven and London: Yale University Press, 2016).

Dignas, Beate and Engelbert Winter, *Rome and Persia in Late Antiquity: Neighbours and Rivals* (New York: Cambridge University Press, 2007).

Elias, Norbert. *The Civilizing Process*, Edmond Jeffcott, trans. (New York: Urizen Books, 1978).

Enayat, Hamid. *Modern Islamic Political Thought* (Austin, TX: University of Texas Press, 1982).

Engels, Friedrich. "On the History of Early Christianity," in Lewis S. Feuer, ed. *Marx & Engels: Basic Writings in on Politics & Philosophy* (New York: Anchor Books, 1959), pp. 168–194.

  The Peasant War in Germany (Moscow: Foreign Languages Publishing House, 1934).

Fallaci, Oriana. *Interview with History*, John Shepley, trans. (Boston, MA: Houghton Mifflin, 1976).

Faroqhi, Suraiya. *The Ottoman Empire and the World Around It* (London and New York: I. B. Tauris, 2004).

Farrenkopf, John. *Prophet of Decline: Spengler on World History and Politics* (Baton Rouge, LA: Louisiana State University Press, 2001).

Farzaneh, Mateo. *The Iranian Constitutional Revolution and the Clerical Leadership of Khurasani* (Syracuse, NY: Syracuse University Press, 2015).

Fathi, Asghar, ed. *Iranian Refugees and Exiles since Khomeini* (Costa Mesa, CA: Mazda Publishers, 1991).

Feith, Herbert and Lance Castle, eds. *Indonesian Political Thinking, 1945–1965* (Ithaca and London: Cornell University Press, 1970).

Garthwaite, Gene R. "Khan and Kings: The Dialectics of Power in Bakhtiyari History," in Michael E. Bonine and Nikki R. Keddie, eds. *Continuity and Change in Modern Iran* (New York: State University of New York Press, 1988), pp. 129–142.

Khans and Shahs: A Documentary Analysis of the Bakhtiyari in Iran (New York: Cambridge University Press, 1983).

Gasiorowski, Mark J. "The Qarani Affair and Iranian Politics," in *International Journal of Middle East Studies*, vol. 25, no. 4 (November 1993): pp. 625–644.

U.S. Foreign Policy and the Shah: Building a Client State in Iran (Ithaca, NY: Cornell University Press, 1991).

Gasiorowski, Mark J. and Malcolm Byrne, eds. Mohammad Mosaddeq and the 1953 Coup in Iran (Syracuse, NY: Syracuse University Press, 2004).

Geary, Patrick. *Before France and Germany: The Creation and Transformation of the Merovingian World* (New York: Oxford University Press, 1988).

Gellner, Ernst. *Post-modernism, Reason and Religion* (New York: Routledge, 1982).

Gershoni, Israel and Amy Singer. "Introduction: Intellectual History in Middle Eastern Studies," in *Comparative Studies of South Asia, Africa and the Middle East*, vol. 28, no. 3 (2008), pp. 383–389.

Gheissari, Ali. *Iranian Intellectuals in the 20th Century* (Austin, TX: University of Texas Press, 1998).

"Iran's Dialectic of the Enlightenment: Constitutional Experience, Transregional Connections, and Conflicting Narratives of Modernity," in Ali M. Ansari, ed. *Iran's Constitutional Revolution of 1906: Narratives of the Enlightenment* (London: Ginko Library, 2016), pp. 15–47.

Gluck, Carol. "The End of Elsewhere: Writing Modernity Now," in *American Historical Review* (June 2011): pp. 676–687.

Gnoli, Gherardo. *The Idea of Iran: An Essay on Its Origin* (Rome: E. J. Brill, 1989).

Goodman, Dana. *The Republic of Letters: A Cultural History of the French Enlightenment* (Ithaca, NY: Cornell University Press, 1994).

Graham, Robert. *Iran: The Illusion of Power* (New York: St. Martin's Press, 1978).

Gramsci, Antonio. *The Modern Prince and Other Writings* (New York: International Publishers, 1978).

Green, Nile. "Between Heidegger and the Hidden Imam: Reflections on Henry Corbin's Approaches to Mystical Islam," in *Method & Theory in the Study of Religion*, vol. 17, no. 3 (2005): pp. 219–226.

The Love of Strangers: What Six Muslim Students Learned in Jane Austin's London (Princeton and Oxford: Princeton University Press, 2016).

Greene, Jack P., ed. *Exclusionary Empire: English Liberty Overseas, 1600–1900* (New York: Cambridge University press, 2010).

"State Formation, Resistance, and the Creation of Revolutionary Traditions in the Early Modern Era," in Michael A. Morrison and Melinda Zook, eds. *Revolutionary Currents: Nation Building in the Transatlantic World* (New York: Rowman and Littlefield, 2004).

Griffin, Roger. *Modernism and Fascism: The sense of Beginning under Hitler and Mussolini* (New York: Palgrave, 2007).

Guenon, Rene. *The Crisis of the Modern World* (London: Luzac and Company, 1941).

Gurney, John. "E. G. Browne and the Iranian Community in Istanbul," in Thierry Zarcone and Fariba Zarinebafe, eds. *Les Iraniens d'Istanbul* (Istanbul and Tehran, 1993), pp. 149–175.

Haac, Oscar A. *Jules Michelet* (Boston: Twayne Publishers, 1982).

Hanioglu, Sukru M. *A Brief History of the Late Ottoman Empire* (Princeton, NJ: Princeton University Press, 2010).

Ataturk: An Intellectual Biography (Princeton, NJ: Princeton University Press, 2011).

Hanna, Mikhail. *Politics and Revelation: Mawardi and After* (Edinburgh: Edinburgh University Press, 1995).

Heidegger, Martin. *Being and Time*, John Macquarrie & Edward Robinson trans. (New York: Harper 1962).

Hegland, Mary Elaine. *Days of Revolution: Political Unrest in an Iranian Village* (Stanford, CA: Stanford University Press, 2014).

Herman, Arthur. *The Idea of Decline in Western History* (New York: The Free Press, 1997).

Hodgson, Marshall G.S. *The Venture of Islam* (Chicago, IL: The University of Chicago Press, 1974).

Hooglund, Eric J. *Land and Revolution in Iran: 1960–1980* (Austin, TX: University of Texas Press, 1982).

Hoveyda, Fereydoun. *Fall of the Shah*, Roger Liddell, trans. (New York: Wyndham Books, 1980).

Hunt, Lynn. *Writing History in the Global Era* (New York and London: W. W. Norton & Company 2014).

L'Impact planétaire de la pensée occidentale rend-il possible un dialogue réel entre les civilisations? (Paris: Broché, 1979).

Irving, Clive. *Crossroad of Civilization; 3000 years of Persian History* (London: Weidenfeld and Nicolson, 1979).

Irwin, Robert. *For Lust of Knowing: The Orientalists and Their Enemies* (London and New York: Penguin, 2006).

Iqbal, Muhammad. *The Reconstruction of Religious Thought in Islam* (Stanford, CA: Stanford University Press, 2012).

Jacqz, Jane W., ed. *Iran: Past, Present and Future: Aspen Institute/Persepolis Symposium* (New York: Aspen Institute for Humanistic Studies, 1976).

Jahanbeglu, Ramin. "Iranian Intellectuals and Cosmopolitan Citizenship," in Lucian Stone, ed. *Iranian Identity and Cosmopolitanism: Spheres of Belonging* (London and New York: Bloomsbury, 2014), pp. 17–33.

Jameson, Frederick. *Postmodernism, Or, The Cultural Logic of Late Capitalism* (Durham, NC: Duke University Press, 1991).

Kagan, Kimberly, ed. *The Imperial Moment* (Cambridge, MA and London: Harvard University Press, 2010).

Kaiwar, Vasant and Sucheta Mazumdar, eds. *Antinomies of Modernity: Essays on Race, Orient, Nation* (Durham and London: Duke University Press, 2003).

Karapat, Kemal H. *The Politicization of Islam: Reconstructing Identity, State, Faith, and Community in the Late Ottoman State* (Oxford and New York: Oxford University Press, 2001).

Karimi-Hakkak, Ahmad. *Recasting Persian Poetry: Scenarios of Poetic Modernity in Iran* (Salt Lake City, UT: University of Utah Press, 1995).

Kashani-Sabet, Firoozeh. "Fragile Frontiers: The Diminishing Domains of Qajar Iran," in *International Journal of Middle East Studies*, vol. 29 (1997): pp. 205–234.

  Frontier Fictions: Shaping the Iranian Nation, 1804–1946 (Princeton, NJ: Princeton University Press, 1999).

Katouzian, Homa. *Iranian History and Politics: The Dialectic of State and Society* (London and New York: Routledge Curzon, 2003).

  The Persians: Ancient, Medieval and Modern Iran (New Haven and London: Yale University Press, 2009).

  "Private Parts and Public Discourses in Modern Iran," in *Comparative Studies of South Asia*, vol. 28, no. 2 (2008): pp. 283–290.

  State and Society in Iran: The Eclipse of the Qajars and the Emergence of the Pahlavis (London and New York: I. B. Tauris, 2006).

Keddie, Nikki R. *An Islamic Response to Imperialism: Political and Religious Writings of Sayyid Jamal ad-Din "al-Afghani"* (Berkeley and Los Angeles: University of California Press, 1983).

  Iran: Religion, Politics and Society (London: Routledge, 1983).

  Modern Iran: Roots and Results of Revolution (New Haven, CT: Yale University Press, 2003).

"Religion and Irreligion in Early Iranian Nationalism," in *Comparative Studies in Society and History*, vol. 4 (1962): pp. 266–295.

Religion and Rebellion in Iran: The Tobacco Protest of 1891–92 (London: Frank Cass, 1966).

Keddie, Nikki R. and Mark J. Gasiorowski, eds. *Neither East, Nor West: Iran, the Soviet Union, and the United States* (New Haven, CT: Yale University Press, 1990).

Khalid, Adeeb. *The Politics of Muslim Cultural Reform: Jadidism in Central Asia* (Berkeley and Los Angeles: University of California Press, 1998).

Khazeni, Arash. *Tribes and Empire on the Margins of Nineteenth-century Iran* (Seattle: University of Washington Press, 2009).

Khomeini, Ruhollah. *Islam and Revolution: Writings and Declarations of Imam Khomeini*, Hamid Algar, trans. (Berkeley: Mizan Press, 1981).

Kia, Mehrdad. "Pan-Islamism in Late Nineteenth-century Iran," in *Middle Eastern Studies*, vol. 32, no. 1 (January 1996): pp. 30–52.

Kian-Thiebaut, Azadeh. *Secularization of Iran: A Doomed Failure?* (Paris: PEETERS, 1998).

Kleinberg, Ethan. *Generation Existential: Heidegger's Philosophy in France, 1927–1961* (Ithaca, NY: Cornell University Press, 2005).

Kontje, Todd Curtis. *German Orientalisms* (Ann Arbor, MI: The University of Michigan Press, 2004).

Kurzman, Charles. "*Mashrutiyat, Mesrutiyet*, and Beyond: Intellectuals and the Constitutional Revolutions of 1905–12," in Houchang Chehabi and Vanessa Martin, eds. *Iran's Constitutional Revolution: Popular Politics, Cultural Transformations, and Transnational Connections* (London and New York: I. B. Tauris, 2010): pp. 277–290.

The Unthinkable Revolution in Iran (Cambridge, MA: Harvard University Press, 2004).

Lambton, Ann K. S. "The Persian Constitutional Revolution of 1905–06," in P. J. Vatikiotis, ed. *Revolutions in the Middle East* (London: 1972).

"The Persian Ulema and Constitutional Reform," in T. Fahd, ed. *Le Shi'ism imamate* (Paris: 1970), pp. 245–269.

Qajar Persia: Eleven Studies (Austin, TX: University of Texas Press, 1987).

"Quis Custodiet Custodes: Some Reflections on the Persian Theory of Government," in *Studia Islamica*, vol. 5 (1956): pp. 125–148.

Lenczowski, George. *Russia and the West in Iran, 1918–1948* (Ithaca, NY: Cornell University Press, 1949).

Mahdavi, Mojtaba. "Post-Islamic Trends in Postrevolutionary Iran," in *Comparative Studies of South Asia, Africa and the Middle East*, vol. 31, no.1 (2011): pp. 94–109.

Majd, Mohammad Gholi. *The Great Famine and Genocide in Persia, 1917–1919* (Lanham, MD: University Press of America, 2003).

    Persia in World War I and Its Conquest by Great Britain (Lanham, MD: University Press of America, 2003).

Manafzadeh, Alireza. *Ahmad Kasravi, l'homme qui voulait sortir l'iran de l'obscurantisme* (Paris: L'Harmattan, 2004).

Manela, Erez. *The Wilsonian Moment: Self-determination and the International Origins of Anticolonial Nationalism* (Oxford and New York: Oxford University Press, 2007).

Mannheim, Karl. *Ideology and Utopia* (New York, 1936).

Marashi, Afshin. "Imagining Hafiz: Rabindranath Tagore in Iran, 1932," in *Journal of Persianate Studies*, vol. 3, no. 1 (June 2010): pp. 46–77.

    Nationalizing Iran: Culture, Power and the State (Seattle and London: The University of Washington Press, 2008).

    "Paradigms of Iranian Nationalism: History, Theory and Historiography," in Kamran Scot Aghaie and Afshin Marashi, eds. *Rethinking Iranian Nationalism and Modernity* (Austin, TX: University of Texas Press, 2014), pp. 3–24.

    "Print Culture and Its Publics: A social History of Bookstores in Tehran, 1900–1950," in *International Journal of Middle East Studies*, vol. 47 (2015): pp. 89–108.

Marchand, Suzanne. *German Orientalism in the Age of Empire: Religion, Race and Scholarship* (New York: Cambridge University Press, 2009).

Mardin, Serif. *Religion and Social Change in Modern Turkey: The Case of Bedizzaman Said Nursi* (New York: State University of New York, 1989).

Martin, Vanessa. *Islam and Modernism: The Iranian Revolution of 1906* (London and New York: I. B. Tauris, 1989).

Marx, Karl. "Toward the Critique of Hegel's Philosophy of Right," in Lewis S. Feuer, ed. *Marx & Engels: Basic Writings in on Politics & Philosophy* (New York: Anchor Books, 1959), pp. 262–263.

    The Qajar Pact: Bargaining, Protest and the State in Nineteenth-century Persia (London and New York: I. B. Tauris, 2005).

Matin-asgrai, Afshin. "Abdolkarim Sorush and the Secularization of Islamic Thought in Iran," *Iranian Studies*, vol. nos. 1–2 (winter–spring 1997): pp. 95–115.

    "The Academic Debate on Iranian Identity," in Abbas Amanat and Farzin Vejdani, eds. *Facing Others: Iranian Identity Boundaries and Modern Political Cultures* (London and New York: Routledge, 2012), pp. 171–190.

    "The Impact of Imperial Russia and the Soviet Union on Qajar and Pahlavi Iran: Notes toward a Revisionist Historiography," in Stephanie Cronin, ed. *Iranian-Russian Encounters: Empires and Revolutions since 1800* (London and New York: Routledge, 2012), pp. 11–46.

Afshin Matin-asgari, Iranian Student Opposition to the Shah (Costa Mesa, CA: MAZDA Publishers, 2002).

"Iranian Modernity in Global Perspective: Nationalist, Marxist and Authenticity Discourses," in Sucheta Mazumdar, Vasant Kaiwar and Thierry Labiaca, eds. *From Orientalism to Postcolonialism: Asia, Europe and the Lineage of Difference* (London and New York: Routledge, 2009), pp. 129–153.

"Iranian Postmodernity: The Rhetoric of Irrationality?," in *Critique*, vol. 13, no. 1 (spring 2004): pp. 113–123.

"Modern Iran's Ideological Renegades," in *Critique*, 16, no. 3 (fall 2007): pp. 137–153.

"The Transparent Sphinx: Political Biography and the Question of Intellectual Responsibility," in *Critique*, no. 10 (fall 2001): pp. 87–108.

Matin, Kamran. *Recasting Iranian Modernity* (London and New York: Routledge, 2013).

Matthee, Rudi. "The Imaginary Realm: Europe's Enlightenment Image of Early Modern Iran," in *Comparative Studies of South Asia, Africa and the Middle East*, vol. 30, no. 3 (2010).

Persia in Crisis: Safavid Decline and the Fall of Isfahan (London and New York: I. B. Tauris, 2012).

"Was Safavid Iran an Empire" in *Journal of the Economic and Social History of the Orient*, vol. 53, no. 1/2 (2010): pp. 233–265.

Matthee, Rudi and Elena Andreeva, eds. *Russians in Iran: Diplomacy and Power in Iran in the Qajar Era and beyond* (London and New York: I. B. Tauris, 2018).

McMeekin, Sean. *The Ottoman Endgame: War Revolution and the Making of the Modern Middle East, 1908–1923* (New York: Penguin Press, 2015).

McNeill, William H. *Arnold Toynbee: A life* (New York and Oxford: Oxford University Press, 1989).

Midhat, Ahmet. *Felatun Bey and Rakim Efendi*, trans. Meliheh Levi and Monica M. Ringer (New York: Syracuse University Press, 2016).

Milani, Abbas. *Eminent Persians: The Men and Women Who Made Modern Iran, 1941–1979*, 2 volumes (Syracuse, NY: Syracuse University Press, 2008).

"*Majalle-ye Kaveh va mas'ale-ye tajaddod*," in *Iranshenasi*, vol. ii, no. 3 (autumn 1990): pp. 504–519.

The Persian Sphinx (Washington, DC: Mage Publishers, 2000).

Tajaddod va tajaddod-setizi dar Iran (Tehran: Akhtaran, 1997).

Mingolo, Walter D. *The Darker Side of the Renaissance: Literacy, Territoriality and Colonization* (Ann Arbor: University of Michigan, 1994).

Mirsepassi, Ali. *Intellectual Discourse and the Politics of Modernization: Negotiating Modernity in Iran* (Cambridge, MA: Cambridge University Press, 2000).

   Political Islam, Iran and the Enlightenment (New York: Cambridge University Press, 2011).

   Transnationalism in Iranian Political Thought: The Life and Times of Ahmad Fardid (New York: Cambridge University Press, 2017).

Mishra, Pankaj. *From the Ruins of Empire: The Intellectuals Who Remade Asia* (New York: Farrar, Straus and Giroux, 2012).

Mitzman, Arthur. *Michelet, Historian: Rebirth and Romanticism in Nineteenth-century France* (New Haven and London: Yale University Press, 1990).

Moazami, Behrooz. *State, Religion, and Revolution in Iran, 1796 to the Present* (New York: Palgrave Macmillan, 2013).

Muthu, Sankar. *Enlightenment against Empire* (Princeton, NJ: Princeton University Press, 2003).

Nabavi, Negin. *Intellectuals and the State in Iran: Politics, Discourse and the Dilemma of Authenticity* (Gainesville, FL: University of Florida Press, 2003).

Naraqi, Ehsan. *From Palace to Prison: Inside the Iranian Revolution*, Nilou Moaser, trans. (Chicago: Ivan R. Dee, 1994).

Ohlig, Karl-Heinz. *Early Islam: A Critical Reconstruction Based on Contemporary Sources* (New York: Prometheus Books, 2013).

Pahlavi, Farah. *An Enduring Love*, Patricia Clancy trans. (New York: Miramax Books, 2004).

Pahlavi, Mohammad Reza. *Answer to History* (New York: Stein and Day, 1980).

Paxton, Robert O. *The Anatomy of Fascism* (New York: Alfred A. Knopf, 2004).

Pomper, Philip. *The Russian Revolutionary Intelligentsia* (New York: Crowell, 1970).

Pistor-Hatam, Anja. "Progress and Civilization in Nineteenth-century Japan: The Far Eastern State as a Model for Modernization," in *Iranian Studies*, vol. 29 (1996): pp. 111–127.

Pourshariati, Parvaneh. *Decline and Fall of the Sasanian Empire: The Sasanian-Parthian Confederacy and the Arab Conquest of Iran* (London and New York: I. B. Tauris, 2008).

Rahnema, Ali. *Behind the 1953 Coup in Iran: Thugs, Turncoats, Soldiers, and Spooks* (New York: Cambridge University Press, 2015).

   An Islamic Utopian: A Political Biography of Ali Shari'ati (London and New York: I. B. Tauris, 1998).

Superstition as Ideology in Iranian Politics: From Majlesi to Ahmadinejad (New York: Cambridge University Pres, 2011).

Reynolds, Michael A. *Shattering Empires: The Clash and Collapse of the Ottoman and Russian Empires, 1908–1918* (New York: Cambridge University Press, 2011).

Richard, Yann. "*Clercs at intellectuels dans la Republique islamique d'Iran,*" in Gilles Kepel and Yann Richard, eds. *Intellectuels et militants de l'islam contemorrain* (Paris: Editions du Seuil, 1990), pp. 29–70.

"Shari'at Sangalaji: A Reformist Theologian of the Rida Shah Era," in Said Amir Arjomand, ed. *Authority and Political Culture in Shi'ism* (Albany: State University of New York Press, 1988), pp. 159–177.

Ridgeon, Lloyd. "Ahamd Kasravi's Criticism of Edward Granville Browne," in *Iran*, vol. 42 (2004): pp. 219–233.

Ringer, Fritz. *Max Weber: An Intellectual Biography* (Chicago and London: The University of Chicago Press, 2004).

Ringer, Monica M. *Pious Citizens: Reforming Zoroastrianism in India and Iran* (Syracuse, NY: Syracuse University Press, 2011).

Rockmore, Tom. *Heidegger and French Philosophy: Humanism, Antihumanism and Being* (London and New York: Routledge, 1995).

Roger, Hans and Eugen Weber, eds. *The European Right: A Historical Profile* (Berkeley and Los Angeles: University of California Press, 1974).

Rostam-Kolayi, Jasamin and Afshin Matin-asgari, "Unveiling Ambiguities: Revisiting 1930s Iran's *kashf-i hijab* Campaign," in Stephanie Cronin, ed. *Anti-Veiling Campaign in the Muslim World* (London and New York: Routledge, 2014), pp. 121–148.

Safari, Siavash. "Reclaiming Islam and Modernity: A Neo-Shari'ati Revisiting of Ali Shari'ati's Intellectual Discourse in Post-Revolutionary Iran." Ph.D. dissertation submitted to University of Alberta (2013).

Said, Edward. *Orientalism* (New York: Vantage Books, 1979).

Sanjabi, Maryam B. "Rereading the Enlightenment: Akhundzada and His Voltaire," in *Iranian Studies*, vol. 28, nos. 1–2 (1995): pp. 39–60.

Schayegh, Cyrus. *Who Is Knowledgeable Is Strong: Science, Class, and the Formation of Modern Iranian Society, 1900–1950* (Berkeley and Los Angeles: University of California Press, 2009).

Scheidel, Walter, ed. *Rome and China: Comparative Perspectives on Ancient World Empires* (Oxford and New York: Oxford University Press, 2009).

Schmitt, Carl. *The Concept of the Political*, George Schwab, trans. (New Brunswick, NJ: Rutgers University Press, 1976).

Schumann, Christoph. "The 'Failure' of Radical Nationalism and the "'Silence' of Liberal Thought in the Arab World," in *Comparative Studies of South Asia, Africa and the Middle East*, vol. 28, no. 3 (2008): pp. 404–415.

Schwab, Raymond. *Oriental Renaissance: Europe's Rediscovery of India and the East, 1680–1880*, Gene Patterson-Black and Victor Reinking, trans. (New York: Columbia University Press, 1984).

Sedgwick, Mark J. *Against the Modern World: Traditionalism and the Secret Intellectual History of the Twentieth-century* (New York: Oxford University Press, 2004).

Shissler, Holland Ada. *Between Two Empires: Ahmed Agaoglu and the New Turkey* (London and New York: I. B. Tauris, 2003).

Shuster, W. Morgan. *The Strangling Persia* (New York: The Century Company, 1912).

Smart, Ninian. *Worldviews: Crosscultural Explorations of Human Beliefs* (New York: Charles Scribner's Sons, 1983).

Smith Jr., Datus C. "Franklin Book Program," in www.Iranicaonline.org. Accessed June 2016.

Sohrabi, Nader. "Global Waves, Local Actors: What the Young Turks Knew about Other Revolutions and Why It Mattered," in *Comparative Studies in Society and History*, vol. 44, no. 1 (January 2002): pp. 45–79.

"Historicizing Revolution: Constitutional Revolutions in the Ottoman Empire, Iran, and Russia, 1905–1908," in *American Journal of Sociology*, vol. 100, no. 6 (May 1995): pp. 1383–1447.

Revolution and Constitutionalism in the Ottoman Empire and Iran (New York: Cambridge University Press, 2011).

Sternhell, Zeev. *Neither Right nor Left: Fascist Ideology in France* (Berkeley and Los Angeles: University of California Press, 1986).

Subrahmanyam, Sanjay. "Connected Histories: Notes toward a Reconfiguration of Early Modern Eurasia," in *Modern Asian Studies*, vol. 3, no. 3 (July 1997): pp. 735–776.

Tapper, Richard. *Frontier Nomads of Iran: A Political and Social History of the Shahsevan* (New York: Cambridge University Press, 1997).

Tavakoli-Targhi, Mohammad. "Historiography and Crafting Iranian National Identity," in Touraj Atabaki, ed. *Iran in the 20th Century: Historiography and Political Culture* (London and New York: I. B. Tauris, 2009), pp. 5–22.

Refashioning Iran: Orientalism, Occidentalism and Historiography (New York: Palgrave, 2001).

"*Tajaddod-e ekhtera'i, tamaddon-e ariati va enqelab-e ruhani,*" in *Iran Nameh*, vol. XX, nos. 1–2 (spring–summer 2012): pp. 195–235.

Toynbee, Arnold J. and G.R. Urban, *Toynbee on Toynbee* (New York: Oxford University Press, 1974).

Vahdat, Farzin. *God and Juggernaut: Iran's Intellectual Encounter with Modernity* (2002).

  Islamic Ethos and the Specter of Modernity (New York: Anthem Press, 2015).

Vajpeyi, Ananya. *Righteous Republic* (Cambridge, MA: Harvard University Press, 2012).

Vali, Abbas. *Pre-capitalist Iran: A Theoretical History* (New York: New York University Press, 1993).

Vaziri, Mustafa. *Iran as Imagined Nation* (New York: Paragon House, 1993).

Vejdani, Farzin. *Making History in Iran: Education, Nationalism and Print Culture* (Stanford, CA: Stanford University Press, 2015).

  "Purveyors of the Past: Iranian Historians and National Historiography, 1900–1940." Ph.D. diss., Yale University, 2009.

Ward, Robert E. and Dankwart A. Rostow, eds. *Political Modernization in Japan and Turkey* (Princeton, NJ: Princeton University Press, 1964).

Wasserstein, David. *The Rise and Fall of the Party-kings: Politics and Society in Islamic Spain 1002–1086* (Princeton, NJ: Princeton University Press, 1985).

Wasserstrom, Steven M. *Religion after Religion: Gershom Scholem and Mircea Elaide, and Henry Corbin at Eranos* (Princeton, NJ: Princeton University Press, 1999).

Wokoeck, Ursula. *German Orientalism: The Study of the Middle East and Islam from 1899 to 1945* (London and New York: Routledge, 2009).

Yar-shater, Ehsan, ed. *Iran Faces the Seventies* (New York: Palgrave, 1971).

Yavari, Neguin. *Advice for the Sultan: Prophetic Vices and Secular Politics in Medieval Islam* (London: Hurst & Company, 2014).

Young, Julian. *Heidegger, Philosophy, Nazism* (New York: Cambridge University Press: 1997).

Zarcone, Thierry. "*Ali Akbar Dihkhuda et le journal Surush d'Istanbul* (Juin-November 1909)," in Zarcone and Fariba Zarinebafe, eds. *Les Iraniens d'Istanbul* (Istanbul and Tehran, 1993), pp. 243–251.

Zarinebaf, Fariba. "From Istanbul to Tabriz: Modernity and Constitutionalism in the Ottoman Empire and Iran," in *Comparative Studies of South Asia, Africa and the Middle East*, vol. 28, no. 1 (2008): pp. 154–169.

  "The Iranian (Azeri) Merchant Community in the Ottoman Empire and the Constitutional Revolution," in Thierry Zarcone and Fariba Zarinebafe, eds. *Les Iraniens d'Istanbul* (Istanbul and Tehran, 1993), pp. 203–212.

Ziba-Ebrahimi, Reza. *The Emergence of Iranian Nationalism: Race and the Politics of Dislocation* (New York: Columbia University Press, 2016).
"Self-Orientalization and Dislocation: The Uses and Abuses of the "Aryan" Discourse in Iran," in *Iranian Studies*, no. 24 (June 2011): pp. 445–472.
Zonis, Marvin. *Majestic Failure: The Fall of the Shah* (Chicago, IL: The University of Chicago Press, 1991).
Zubaida, Sami. *Law and Power in the Islamic World* (New York: I. B. Tauris, 2005).

Index